Also by

Zoml

Origins of the
Discovering Atlantis
Estranged from Atlantis
Atlantis Rising (coming soon)
Return to Atlantis (coming soon)

HELLO BEAUTIFUL.

Library of Congress Cataloguing-in-Publication Data Booth, Jean.

Summary: Divorced woman meets her perfect man online and discovers he's nothing more than a romance scammer.

ISBN-13: 979-8-9893415-7-3

Cover design by: Jean Booth
Printed in the United States of America

Donnie,
Without you, this book wouldn't be possible.

Disclaimer

This story is a true accounting of a romance scam. There are conversations of an intimate nature that are sexually explicit. Some things are mentioned in this book that may be triggering for some audiences such as child abandonment, child abuse, rape, and neglect. This book may be triggering for people who have experienced a romance scam.

The intent is not to trigger nor scar, but to let those who have experienced this horrific act of betrayal know that you are not alone. It is also being shared so that those who have not experienced a romance scam can better understand the nuances, manipulation, and tactics that scammers in today's society utilize. And unfortunately, there are more out there that are even more advanced with their tactics due to the advancement of AI. Names have been changed to protect the innocent.

The Author's Note at the end of this book will have links for assistance and reporting if you, or someone you know, feel they have been a victim of a romance scam.

Profile Creation

"I'm so sick of being alone," I complain to Bex, as I pace around my kitchen, looking for something to stress-eat. "But the caliber of men out there is ew."

I close the cupboards, appetite nonexistent, and realize I'm just frustrated and trying to eat my emotions, like I used to do. I'm forty-three, starting my life over completely, and am annoyed, stressed, and in an almost desperate need of human companionship. Human touch, even if it was just a hug or a handshake from the opposite sex, was something I've been craving since before I got divorced. What I didn't want were cookies. I really, really didn't want cookies. Especially not homemade chocolate chip ones, straight out of the oven.

Sigh.

"Anything is better than what you left. You know that, Annie," she replies in her no-nonsense way, voice echoing from the speaker on my phone, tucked into my bra, per usual. I hate earbuds, but also don't like the phone on my face, so bra it was. I can hear her clicking away on her keyboard in the background, like every other day we talked. We talk almost all day like this, both working together, but in separate jobs on separate sides of the country. It had actually become a habit when I physically worked with her, before the move. We used to be in the same division, but in different departments on different floors, and we often needed the other as a sounding board.

"Shawn was supposed to be the rebound, yah know," I start as I get out ingredients for a wrap, since there isn't a cookie to be had in this place. Damn healthy Annie and her healthy shopping choices. "We met like normal people. He thought I was hot, and now." I sigh. "I hate this ghosting shit. Why can't people be grown-ups and just say, 'hey, I'm not interested, but wish you well'? It's so annoying."

"Yeah, but that's how it is now. You knew that when you left," she replies, not unkindly, just practical. "Could be worse. You could still be with *him*."

I sigh again, knowing she's right and hating it. "So, what do I do now? I want to see if I can even manage to get laid, but I don't necessarily want a one-night stand. I've been with one guy for twenty-four years. I don't even know if I can kiss another man without feeling like I'm betraying my ex-husband." I barrel on, answering her without letting her speak. It's a bad habit of mine. "Which is stupid, I know. We've talked about this. I just want the opportunity to see if I can. Why is it impossible to have something in the middle?"

"What about one of those apps?"

"Yeah," I hedge, taking a bite of my club wrap. "My sister suggested those, and I have a couple downloaded to my phone, but I've been hesitant to actually use them. I'm not crazy about the idea of them."

To be honest, I'm massively insecure about my body and know I'll have to post at least one picture of myself on an app. My ex had reminded me so many times that I needed to lose weight—that if I just lost weight, everything in my life would be better. As if the number on the scale really *was* magic. And after Shawn ghosted me, I'm really having a difficult time finding my confidence again.

"Oh, crap," Bex's voice exclaims from my bra. "I'm late to a meeting. Talk to you later."

"'Kay, byeee," I say as I swipe the phone off and head back to my own job, my joke of a lunch break forgotten. I never really saw the point in taking lunches, especially when I'm able to work from home. I usually make a sandwich, or grab something equally as quick, and eat while I work. My breaks are often less than fifteen minutes long—there's too much to get done every day to actually stop, anyway.

Less than five hours later, I'm sitting on my couch, relaxing as I watch the devil drama I love, when I decide to go for it. Loading up an app I've at least heard about before, I start entering in my information. Pictures. I have to upload pictures. Not just one, but at least four. And I already know I don't have any on my phone because I absolutely hate pictures of me.

"Ugh," I complain to my cats, Spot and Furry as I peel myself from their cuddled forms. "I really hate pictures. Of course, I'm going to be judged by the way I look before anyone even tries to get to know me."

Putting a couple different outfits on, I take a few selfies that I don't think make me look too terrible and post them to the hook-up world. Once I'm done, I close out of the app and start playing one of the games I like on my phone, feed the cats, and then go to bed, deliberately forgetting about the step I just took to put myself into the dating pool.

Saturday is filled with cleaning and dragging my neighbor to the store, so we're forced to socialize for a couple hours. Without me, she'd be perfectly content in her rental, alone with her dog. And without her, I'd have minimal in-person contact with any other human. After we're done with the shopping, I make the two-hour drive to northern Maryland to play Dungeons and Dragons with my new friend group. The group just recently let me join and I was so excited, even though sometimes, I feel like the fifth wheel. The two couples had known each other for years and had silent conversations like I used to have when I hung out with my friends in Nevada.

I'd only just started playing with them a couple weeks ago, but it was the night I looked forward to most every week, and it did not disappoint.

We are deep in the castle, our characters surrounded by decay and dust, with nowhere to go but through the dungeon to another door that led farther down still. My character leads the way, unwilling to debate with the cleric and the idiot dwarf another moment. She promptly falls through the floor, landing in a heap onto an undead monster.

Chaos and battle ensue for the next three hours. We laugh, create an epic adventure, and bond in a way that isn't possible outside of D&D. I'm with my people and secretly hate when game night is over. It means I have to go back to the tiny, lonely little existence I chose for myself.

It isn't that I don't like my life. I actually really enjoy it. For the first time in years, I have possibility. I can see a future that isn't four walls, a couch, and a husband that just exists alongside me. For the first time in my adult life, I don't have to worry about anyone but myself. It's liberating just as much as it's terrifying. Being by myself means I don't have the safety net of a spouse or a second income if something happens, but it means that everything I do in my life is solely because *I* want to do it. It's a mix of emotions caused by a decision that was long overdue.

While it's lonely, it isn't any worse than being with my ex. Yes, I had another person in my house with me, sharing space, but we were little more than roommates. I was just as lonely there as I am here. I know that if I can make friends in my area that are either single, or able to do more things with me than my D&D group, or start dating, I won't feel so isolated, but that takes time. So, I try to remember that I like myself, I like the solitude of my space, and I like spending time with my cats. It helps to remember the things I enjoy about my new life, so I focus on those as I head home.

I drive through the dark, snowy, winding Maryland roads back to my little rental on the river, mindful of deer or other wildlife that could pop out. The trees were bare, and even though it was the first weekend of January, the Christmas lights still illuminated the neighborhoods. It's a beautiful, peaceful drive, one that I don't mind, but know lots of people who do. This state isn't very big; I drive from the southern point to the northern and back every Saturday. I couldn't have done that in Nevada, where I moved from. It's a much larger state than people think.

Getting home, I crash after feeding the cats. I'm not sure what I'm going to do tomorrow, but I never look forward to Sundays. They're the hardest days for me, yet I don't know why. They've become the days that really remind me that I left a life of comfortable routine - for what I have now. My old life wasn't bad; it just wasn't what I wanted. And my ex wasn't interested in changing anything about it. He had everything he wanted. A loving, devoted wife who catered to all his needs—not because she had to, but because she actually wanted to. He did whatever he wanted, whenever he wanted, and eventually stopped caring about what I thought, wanted, or needed. He took me for granted and continually made me feel bad about myself. I deserve better, but it took me longer than I cared to admit to realize it and actually do something about it.

Day 1

"Holy shit," I exclaim, as I open the app the next morning, shocked to see that fifty-seven guys stated they liked my profile in one day. A handful even sent messages. I didn't expect that—hell, I'd have been pleasantly surprised if five people wanted to talk to me. My first thought as I started leafing through my messages is, *I guess if I lose my job, I could always open an OnlyFans account.* I laugh at the absurdity of the thought.

Michael, a government contractor in northern Virginia, seems intense and is mostly looking for a hook-up. I'm not entirely opposed, so I reply to his message.

Michael

Hey beautiful, how are you?

Hey. How's your weekend going?

Slick, Annie. Absolutely a ten on the cool meter. Good lord, this is more difficult than I expected it to be. I mentally facepalm and just continue with sending out the generic "how are you" messages.

Kai

Good afternoon, beautiful woman. I hope I am not too forward, but you are quite stunning.

I snort; glad he can't see or hear me laugh in his face. I know I'm somewhat pretty, but quite stunning is stretching things. I'm massively overweight from the years of living on steroids. I have nice features, but there aren't that many people who like bigger women, are there?

Thanks, you seem really nice, from your profile. What kind of law do you practice?

Please, could we talk on the phone, the app is very impersonal. I understand if you don't want to.?

I think about it for a minute, but this is what I'm looking for—connection. And talking to him would mean he's at least a real person, which is something I was worried about when trying out the apps. I've heard horror stories of people being catfished or scammed, and I didn't want to be another statistic. The examples of catfishing and scams that I've found online were really quite obvious that the person wasn't real though, so I felt fairly confident that I'd be able to recognize a scam when I saw one. I give him my number and my phone immediately buzzes.

I talk to him for a few minutes and he sounds even more nervous than I am. We make tentative plans to try to get together in a few days, after the winter storm that everyone seems terrified of, passes, but I'm not optimistic about it. After hanging up with him, I call Bex.

"Oh. My. God. I signed up for that stupid app," I say without preamble as the phone connects and I hear her hello. "And a ridiculous number of dudes liked me, and I gave one of them my number, and he called. And he's just too sweet and precious to be real."

"Really," she asks, laughter in her voice—she's used to my word vomit by now. "What happened?"

"Okay, so he asked for my number right off the bat, and I thought, what the hell. This is why I'm doing this, right? He immediately calls me and probably thanked me no less than fifteen times for taking the time to talk to him. It was so weird and so cute." I laugh as I think about how sweet Kai was. "He's a lawyer that works sixty to eighty hours a week, so it'll never work, but he's sweet. I'll totally meet up with him if this storm doesn't bury us like it's predicted to."

"Oh, Annie, you're going to eat him alive." Bex says through her laughter. "You've got way too strong a personality for someone that gentle. He's not going to know what to do with you."

"I know." I lament, as I laugh a little, throwing my hands over my face, having thought the same thing while talking to him. "Maybe he'll ghost me, so I don't have to break his gentle little heart? Or, maybe he's just super nice and polite because that's his culture, and secretly, he's a BDSM freak, and I'll be the one fearing for my virtue?"

We both laugh at that thought, knowing the truth was that I'm a strong, independent woman who doesn't really need a man for anything in her life. But I want one and need him to match my strength of will at the very least.

"I can't believe how many guys reached out. I sent messages to four others, and I'm going through the ones that liked me but didn't send messages. Some of these profiles are really weird."

"Be careful," Bex says, her mom tone coming into play. "I'm glad you're doing this, but please be careful and safe."

I roll my eyes.

"I know," I reply. "I am. I won't meet anyone outside of a public place, and I'll make sure that you know everything about them, if and when a meeting happens. Oh, this guy looks sweet. He said he'd travel if money wasn't an option, doesn't smoke, and," I giggle, evilly, "his ideal fake sick day is sex all day."

"Sounds like your kinda guy. Go for it," she replies, her voice starting to sound distracted. I can hear her husband in the background and remember that today is their day to do puzzles and games.

"Okay, I'm going to play on this for a little while. I'll talk to you tomorrow and tell you all about it. Enjoy time with your man. Love you, boo."

"Love you, too. Be careful."

I get distracted with responding to messages but keep going back to one profile over and over. His name is Daniel. He's young—eight years younger than me. The age gap makes me wonder why he'd even like my profile. *Is he looking to replace his mom?* I think. I don't want that again. I spent twenty years being a grown man's mother, I wasn't going to let history repeat itself.

He has a really nice smile and kind but sad eyes. The first picture, his profile pic, looks like a recent one, while the rest looked older. I'm not exactly leaping for joy at the younger pictures—he seems like he used to be a player, but I keep going back to his profile pic. I'm drawn to the gentleness I can see, and something about it calls to me.

Michael starts sending dirty texts, distracting me from Daniel's profile. He talks about tying me up and spanking. It's both a turn on and makes me laugh with the absurdity. I was only looking for a little fling, so I reply, testing out my skills as a dirty-texter. They're nonexistent, but it's fun to try them out.

Michael

What's your fantasy?

Being splayed out, feasted on and worshiped by my partner. My pleasure his goal as he takes me to heights I've never been. There's bondage, biting, and spanking involved, but at the end of it, I'm so overwhelmed with pleasure, I'm spent and shaking.

What about him? You can't really be satisfied without reciprocating, can you?

Dude. You asked what my fantasy was. That was it. I'm normally very reciprocal and giving. My fantasy is having someone worship me.

But it would bring you pleasure to have your partner's needs met, wouldn't it?

Well, yeah.

He keeps pushing, insisting I play his game—that my fantasy should include making sure his every need is met, and I tune him out, only halfheartedly replying to his messages. I'm not really interested in anything at all with this dude, but maybe, with him, I could see if I could actually be with another man. If I could have sex for the sake of sex. It isn't what I want but it's a step into what I think I might need right now.

I keep going back to Daniel's profile. He claims to be a gentleman who has his shit together and wants to have someone in his life who's got hers together and doesn't play games. His fake sick day continually makes me smile, and all I can think about is, *it's what I've wanted for years and only rarely gotten. If he's interested, and nice, this could work.*

I marked that I liked him back and sent him a message.

Daniel

Hey. How are you doing?

Hello sweetness, I'm doing very well.

How are you doing?

I'm finishing up dinner and watching a show. What are you up to?

Nice that's good. I'm just relaxing myself. It's nice to meet you. What are you up to, you doing anything exciting?

OMG, this guy is ridiculous. I wonder if he's just nervous, like me. This is the weirdest experience of my life. I never would've thought I'd do this. I literally just told him what I was doing. Maybe he's in multiple conversations, too. Also, how do I make the most boring person in existence sound exciting? I'm watching a show, going to feed the cats, read some smut, and sleep. Not exciting, but it's my life.

I'm not really doing anything exciting tonight. Honestly, I'm not the most exciting person out there, but I do like to have fun. Currently just getting ready for bed. You?

Well, that's fun enough for me, I'm not up to much myself. Just had dinner and am lying down here, relaxing. Tell me more about you, where do you live, marital status, what do you do, and how long have you been on here?

Sounds nice. I recently moved to MD and am renting until things settle down. It's my second day on a dating app. I'm recently divorced, but very adjusted to it. I was having health issues in Nevada and my ex didn't want to move, so after 20 years, we divorced. It's a longer story than that, and the leaving process took about two years, but I'm happy. I do government work. What about you?

Oh wow, I'm so sorry to hear that. It must've been really tough for you moving here all by yourself. Can I ask why you got divorced after being married for that long and also why you moved here? I live in Hyattsville, am single, was married for 8 years but she passed 2 years ago. I have a four-year-old daughter. I'm a paratrooper. I've been on the app for a couple of weeks, but rarely use it. I haven't spoken to more than three people since I've been on.

I'm really getting sick of the "why are you divorced," conversation already, especially since I can't cut/paste the response to everyone who asks on the app. This is like the sixth time I've needed to explain the divorce, and while I know that it's necessary—no one else is reading my texts with other people, nor do I want them to—I was just really over it. And while I told him a little just a minute ago, there are always follow-ups. People want to know the gritty details. My ex was selfish. He didn't care that I was sick, nor that where we were living was making me sick. He just wanted his happy, perfect life. But I can't say that because it makes me sound bitter. And I'm not. His choice to not come with me was probably the best thing that could've happened to me.

I wasn't doing well in Nevada, it's too dry and I was having problems breathing. I have asthma and it was getting to the point where I had to make a change or things weren't going to end well for me. MD was where I found a job, so that's why I moved here. I don't know anyone, and it's been really hard. I've cried. A lot. But I feel so much better, and I know this was the best decision for me. I've started working out again and finally feel human.

I'm sorry about your wife. That has to be so hard. I hope you have a good support system. Your job sounds amazingly cool and terrifying.

My brother's sister-in-law lives out here, and I've started meeting up with her and her husband's friends to play Dungeons and Dragons. It's really nice to have the connection and to have made some friends. Helps me feel more grounded. Have you ever played?

Oh wow, that's totally understandable if it's about your health and it should be your priority. And it's all good, it was hard but I've moved on now, thanks. Good to hear that you've been able to make friends and get to know people. Do I play what, D&D?

Yes

Not really, maybe once but that's a while ago. What are you looking for on here?

How to answer that question without seeming like an absolute slut…*Maybe I should've signed up for the swipe app instead of this one.* And it's not like I don't want a relationship—that'd be nice. But right now, I really just want to get to know someone enough to feel comfortable getting naked around them. I really just want to feel desired and have a hot, steamy night of passion with someone I trust enough to not lie to me about STIs. Is that really too much to ask for?

I'd like to meet someone I could eventually date long term. In the short term, I want to find someone I click with.

I read over my response after carefully crafting it. I didn't lie. It's what I want, and the "clicking" is up to his interpretation.

Nice, same here. I'm looking to find friendship that'll ultimately lead to a commitment, something serious and long term. No games or hook up, I'm too old for all that.

Yeah, I've never liked games.

Good to hear. What do you desire in a man?

Honesty, loyalty, kindness, a good communicator, someone that tries. I want to feel wanted. What about you, but with a woman?

Nice that's good, we all want the good stuff. Well, I want a woman that's kind, has a good sense of humor, knows what she wants and has her life together, no drama. And I want to be loved unconditionally. I feel with that, every other things comes in handy.

I love to laugh. And while parts of my life are in limbo, I do have it together and absolutely hate drama. I know people that live in a drama-filled life and I find it exhausting.

Damn. This guy seems great, like he might be everything I want in a future partner. I'm not sure I'm ready for him now, but I'm not going to disregard him, either. He may actually have his crap together —that'd be rare, indeed. Do I really want to get involved with a dad, though? A few of the other guys have kids, but his is so young. And do I want something serious and long-term?

Maybe we'll start talking and find out this is nothing more than a passing attraction. We'll meet, he'll see me in person, and run. Or I will.

Ugh, I've got to stop thinking like that. I've got a lot more to offer than my looks, and according to this app, I'm the only one who's insecure about my squishiness.

It's only day one. Lots of things can change during the next few days.

Day 2

Mondays used to be my least favorite days of the work week. There's chaos from the end of the previous week and usually more meetings than there's time in the day to deal with. My new job has been a little bit of an exception to my work experience, in that I don't completely hate Mondays, nor are they insanely busy. I also started this job working mostly remotely, and I feel like that's making it more difficult to build any sort of rapport or relationships with my coworkers.

I think that because I started right before the holidays, and so many people plan vacations in November and December, I was a little bit forgotten. Now that January has rolled around, things seemed to be starting to pick up, and I am working on a plan for how to schedule everything that needed to get done. We've had a couple of staff meetings, and they haven't gone very positively for me—my coworkers have said some passive-aggressive things to me that I've studiously haven't paid attention to.

They mostly ignore me and make me feel like I'm not wanted or needed; so that's tough, but I finally have some direction on things that I need to get done. Things that will take a lot of time to complete and where I can showcase my ability to do this job as well, or better than, the people who talk at me. Grant Management isn't my dream job, but I'm good at it and feel like I can make a little bit of a difference in people's lives. Plus, it pays the bills.

I have a year-long probationary period, where I can be let go for any reason, or none at all. I hate the probationary period, but just like working for any government agency, the job security is worth it, if you can make it. And I already have over two months under my belt. I can make it. Nothing we do here is any different from what I'm used to. Except for the lack of communication and support between my coworkers. Being ostracized is a new experience for me.

Only one coworker has reached out to try to befriend me, but she's new too, and we were bonding over the stress of being newbies. Whenever we have staff discussions, the team bands around her, trying to encourage her and support her, and they completely disregard me. It isn't something I'm used to, but I'm not here to make friends. Besides, I know that with a little time, they'll come to see I'm valuable.

The day flies by, and I ignore the pings on my phone from the dating app. They're mostly just guys asking the same introductory questions. How are you? How long have you been divorced? What do you want out of this app? They're questions I need to just have ready in my notes app so that I don't have to keep retyping the answers in. Or just have the answers to all of them queued up in one paragraph and hope they find something new to ask me.

I've only been on this app for less than a week, and I'm already starting to hate it. I'm not a dating app kinda girl, apparently. It's annoying more than interesting or fun. I feel like a piece of meat, but without the ogling. It's like these guys saw my photos and I'm an object that they don't have to take a risk on I'm amorphous, fake, not a blood-and-flesh person who would actually want anything real.

It doesn't quite make me feel gross, just off. It isn't a feeling I can really pinpoint into something specific. It just makes me feel off-put. I didn't think I'd be on this app for too much longer. Either I'll meet someone worth talking to, or I won't.

And I was trying to be okay with that.

Jeff

Hello gorgeous woman, I hope you're not too cold after that storm last night. Can I get your number, so we can chat outside of the app?

Sure.

Hey, this is Jeff, from the app. I hope I'm not bothering you.

Not at all.

I'm just chilling in my room. It's snowing again.

Ew, yay. I'm just working.

Oh, do you want me to let you go?

Nah. I usually do better when I multitask.

My aunt is moving in with my dad. My mom and sister passed. Aunts and uncles are in other states. I have kids, but they're older and sometimes see me.

Okay...Info dumping is usually my thing. It's weird to be on the receiving end of it, though. I laugh. I guess this is better than the incessant questions that guys keep asking. At least his info dumping is unique and shows that he's nervous.

I shrug my shoulders, just going with it and not judging. This is what I wanted to do—date. I want to be able to meet new people and see what and who is out there. I'm just on the fence if I like it or not yet.

I have no idea what to say to this man, so I opt for something safe, something I at least know a little bit about. He's more intense than I expected and volunteered way more information than I thought people would to a complete stranger. I guess that's the whole point in getting on this app though—to try to find someone to spend some time with, get to know people, and to have some fun. I had my reservations with Jeff, though. He was older than me, and some of the things he said in the app were self-deprecating, which I hate. I hope he was just trying not to sound like a cocky ass and not that he really needed someone to boost and stroke his ego.

I so do not want to do that again. I did that with my ex—Peter always needed to know he was great and that I only had eyes for him. He needed me to be around him whenever he was home and thought quality time was us sitting on the couch, watching TV, while I played on my phone. I don't want a repeat of that relationship.

Jeff and I do have a lot in common though. We're both divorced, like similar music, have tattoos, and seem to talk to each other relatively easily.

The only person who hasn't texted yet is the only person I'm really interested in texting with. So, I do something I told myself I wouldn't do; I message him.

Daniel

I hope you have a nice, safe, and warm day. I'm snowed in, lol!

I close the app and go back to working, mostly watching trainings, forgetting about it and the texts buzzing on my phone. Daniel responds a few hours later.

Thanks, you're really sweet. I hope you stay warm as well and have a great day. And it's good to hear that you have your life together, drama is very exhausting and I don't want to have any parts of it.
I'm not on here often, and you seem like a very sweet lady. Would you like to text?

I laugh, groaning a little at the "lady," although I can't give myself a good reason as to why that term makes me feel old. I text him my number, thinking he'll be like the three other guys I'd given it to, and he'll text me right away.

He doesn't.

He must be busy at work. He's military, and I have no idea what he does on base all day, but I'm sure it's difficult to have his phone on him like civilians do.

His text comes in a few hours later.

Daniel

Hello beautiful

How are you doing?

It's Daniel , I hope you got my texts

I smile. He really is sweet, and I can almost read his nervous energy through his text.

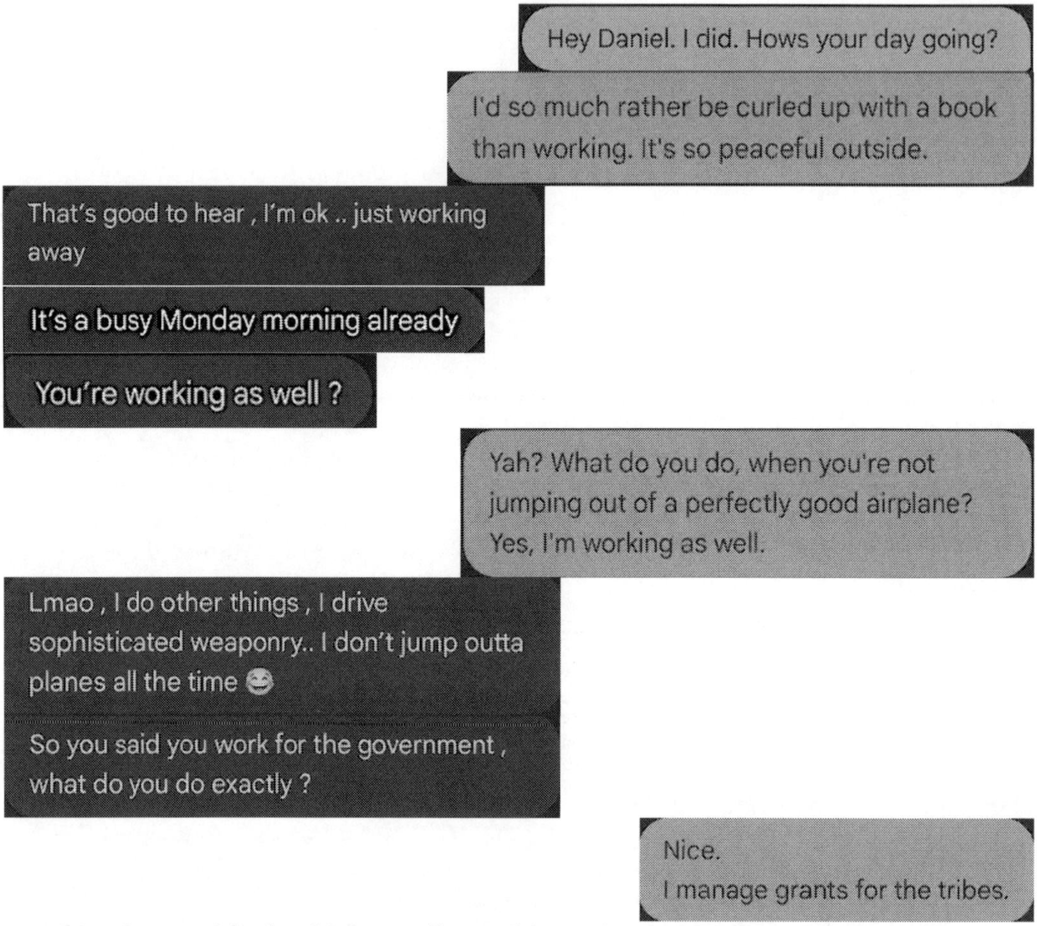

I get busy with checking emails, and he quits responding, which really works out. My phone pings about an hour later.

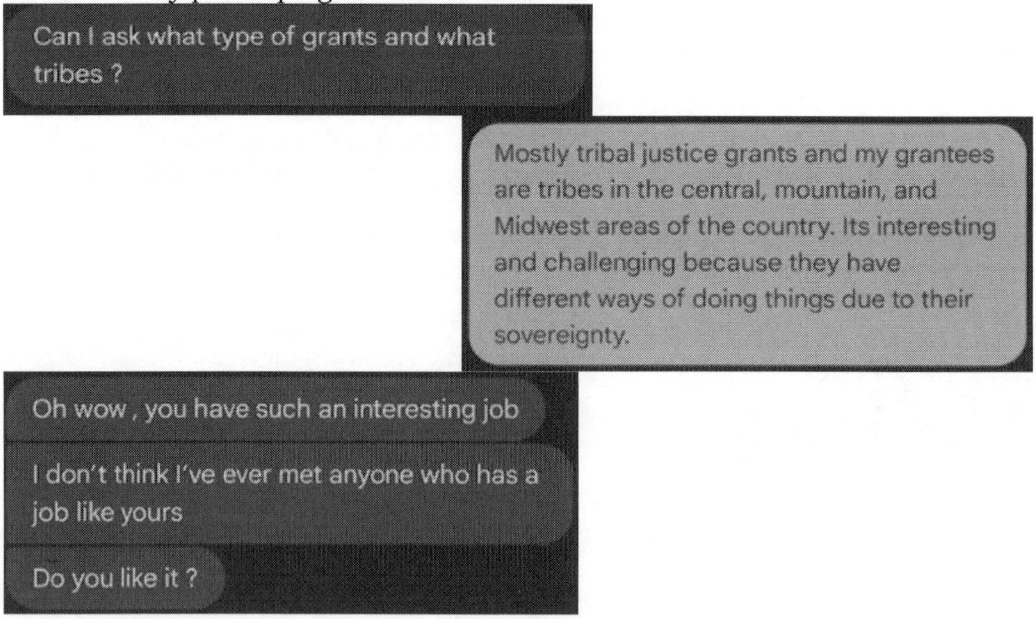

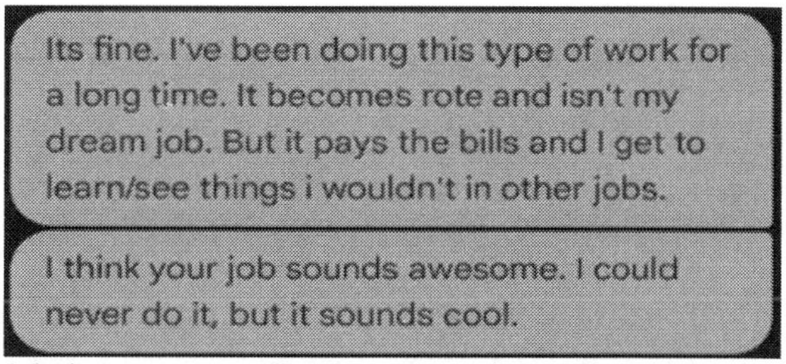

"So, how was your night filled with horny men?" Bex asks when she calls an hour later.

I laugh. "It's fine. Dudes are weird. There's this one guy, Michael, who's such a patriarchal prick I feel dirty just knowing his name, but he sounds like an absolute freak in the sack. I really want to see if he's all talk or just trying to sound like he's an alpha male, ya know?"

"Ew, yeah, you definitely don't want that," she replies, the disgust over the patriarchal term palpable over the phone.

"Kevin's really cute, and seems like he's interested in a friends-with-benefits thing, so that might work. Neither one has been married or has kids, so I'm sure there are loads of things wrong with them. Jeff has older kids, is very chill, and has been really nice but has zero self-confidence and it's a huge turn off."

"Okay, sounds like you're having fun," she replies. "Anyone else?"

"Daniel is a widowed paratrooper with a very young daughter, like four-years-old young." I hesitate because there's something about him that I'm drawn to that I can't explain. "He's been very nice and sounds like he's looking for his forever person. I'm scared that I might end up doing the same thing I did with Peter though, and become his mother."

"Oh, man. How old is he?"

"Thirty-five," I reply, blushing slightly at the age difference. I've never dated a younger man before. Not that I've dated a whole lot, but. I was getting lost in my thoughts.

"With him being so young, and having a kid that young, you might. Or you might become a babysitter," she confirms. "Legitimacy is my biggest worry. People are such good con artists these days. You really need to be careful. I'm also worried about your newly healing heart."

"Oh, that organ isn't involved in any of these. She's firmly locked down, and a different body part is ruling these decisions." I laugh.

"Just be careful," she warns in her mom tone, knowing I'm only half full of shit. "How's your day, other than the men?"

"SSDD. Same shit, different day," I begin, "It's really frustrating because I'm being told to follow the standard operating procedures, but I have to go find them. They don't give me anything to work off of. I think I'm doing things correctly, but I honestly have no idea. And every training I jump on is either old, or the trainer talks like everyone already knows everything. It's just frustrating. How was your weekend?" A cheeky, knowing grin enters my tone. She and her husband have such a loving relationship. It's what I want. Eventually.

"Henry left to hang out with his friends yesterday, so Jed and I had a really great day." She laughs, still shy enough, or respectful enough (I've never figured out which), to not say she got railed like a discount hooker, when we both know that's exactly what happened after her son, Henry, left.

We stay on the phone, working at our respective jobs, while occasionally talking about nonsense. It's something we started years ago when COVID hit, and we worked alone at home. We both like each other's company, and it makes us feel less alone. It's now become a comfort and a habit neither of us is willing to break.

Eventually, we hang up, and I return to working alone. A text comes in, in the afternoon, and I smile.

Daniel

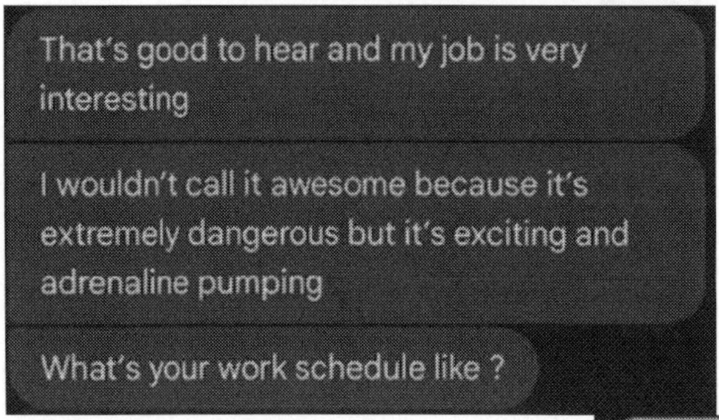

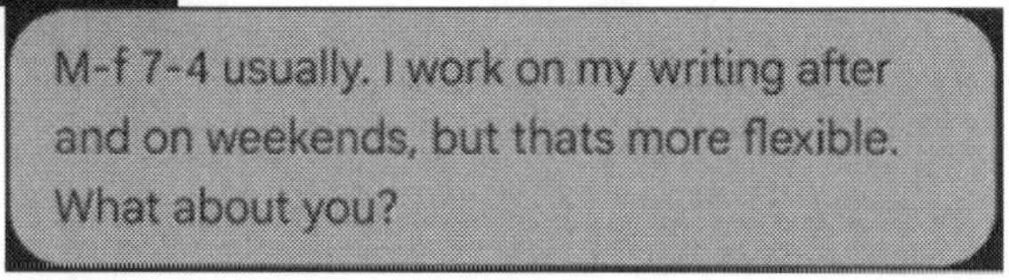

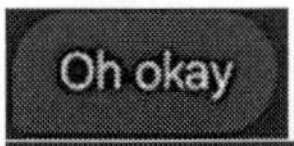

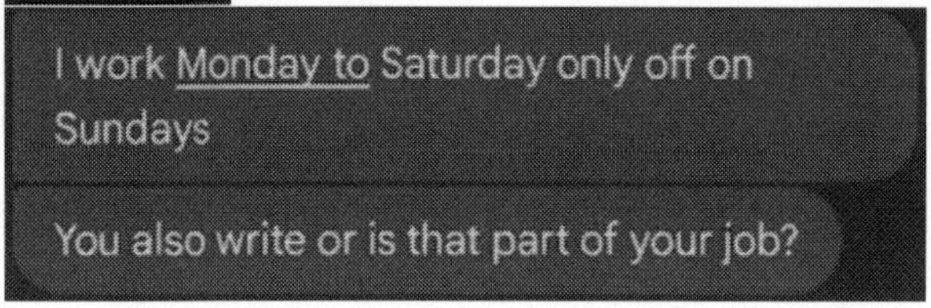

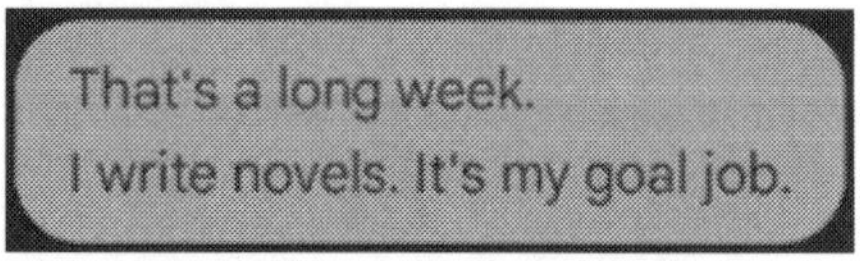

We stop talking for a while, not that his texts come in all that frequently, but it's nice to talk to him and see that he's genuinely interested in what I do and how I feel about it. I've never really looked at my job as interesting before, especially to someone who has such a dangerous profession, so it's nice to get a different perspective on it.

Work ends, and I load up my personal computer to start working on my marketing class, which I find so much more challenging than my actual job. It talks about data and market research, and I feel like my head is going to explode with information. I listen to trainings and walk through three lessons before I feel a headache coming on and go spend the rest of the evening sitting on the couch.

Daniel

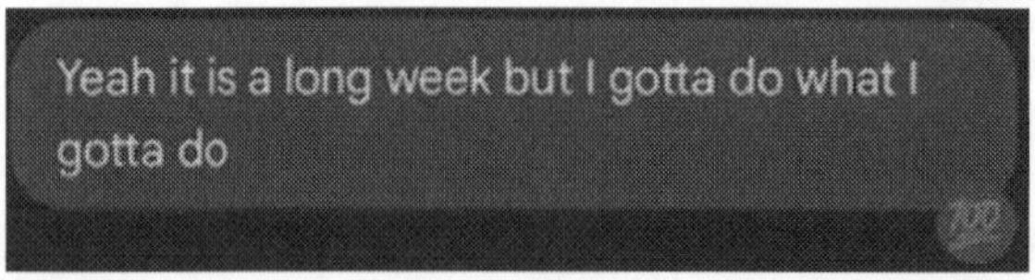

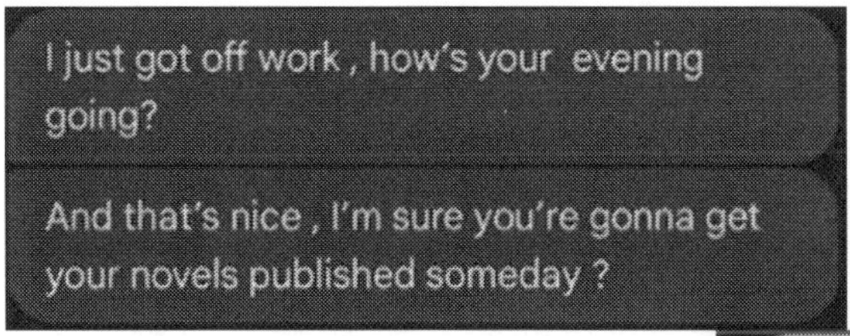

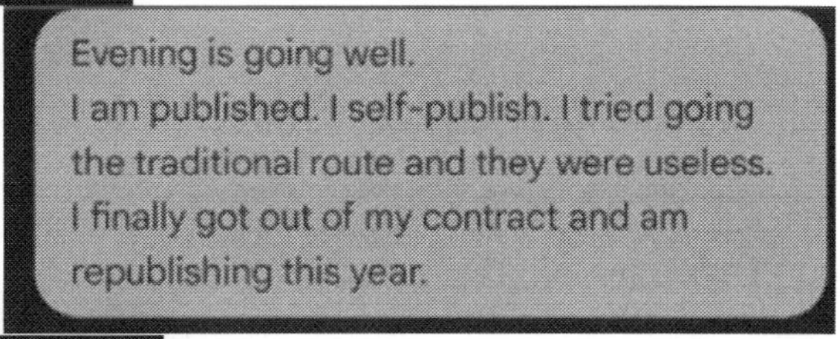

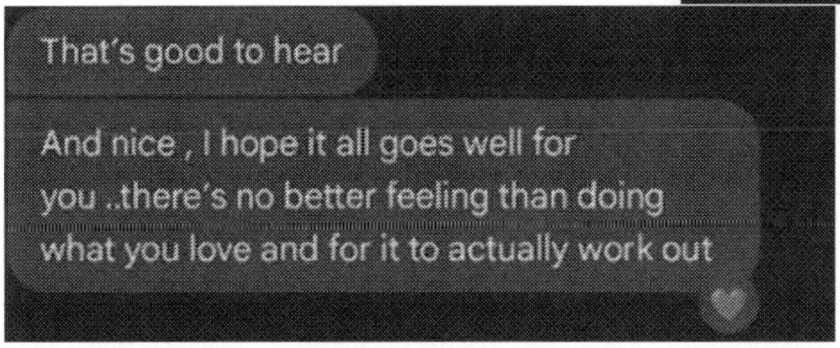

He's right and I feel validated. A smile curves my lips as the thought; *He actually gets it. He gets me*, crosses my mind. And without me realizing it, a tiny chink in the armor surrounding my heart breaks off. I go to bed, content and smiling for the first time in what feels like forever.

Day 3

Daniel

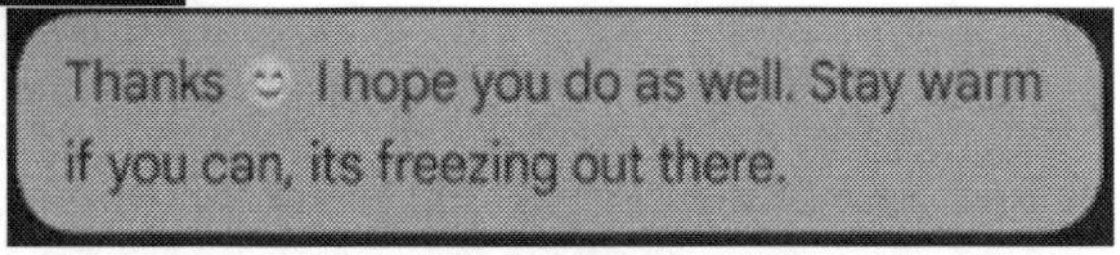

I smile, looking at my phone. *I could get used to this,* I think. *Being the first person someone thinks about when they wake up is really nice.*

I start working and zone out as the day drags on for what feels like an eternity of emails, spreadsheets, financial documents, and program reports that need to be reviewed. It's tedious, downloading document after document from the grant system we use just so I can ensure people complete the reports correctly and all the necessary information is included. It would be helpful to be able to click on the link and have it pop out in a different tab, but the extra steps aren't that annoying. At least, that's what I tell myself as I download and open my seventy-eighth document of the day.

I was freezing. The winter storm hit and left a cold front I can't seem to warm up from. I let the cats use the heating pad I got last week to help with cramps because I thought they might like a nice, warm spot to lay on. In between reviewing documents, I break up multiple cat fights over it.

I check my phone for my shopping app. The heated bed I ordered yesterday won't get here for another couple of days. Groaning, I resign myself to venturing out to the store in the storm to get another heating pad. I can't take another day of cat fights next to my keyboard.

I text Daniel as I leave. He's the first person I think of when wanting to talk about my day. I don't question it, just go with it as I drive. I wander around the store to see if there's anything else I might need to grab before I pick out another heating pad and head home. His reply comes after I settle into my chair to relax for the evening, the start of a crocheted blanket on my lap, waiting for me to continue working on it. A smile forms on my face as we talk.

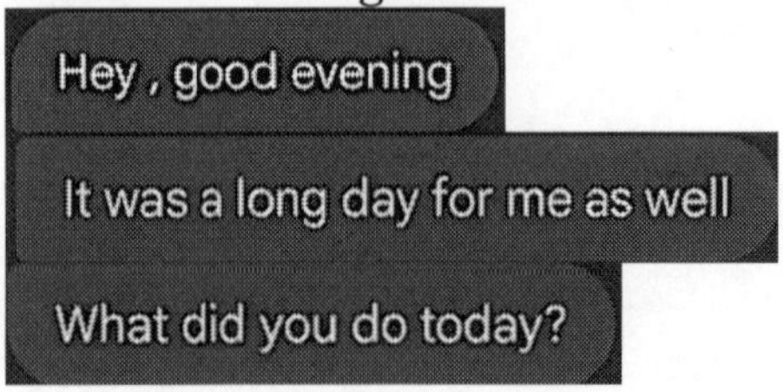

Just worked. Had to go to the store after to get my cat a heating pad so she can chill out while I work tomorrow. I hope it works. They've been fighting over the last one I got and her heated bed isn't here yet.

It was just a frustrating day at work.

Sorry to hear that

I'm sure you're feeling better now that you're off

And that's really thoughtful to hear about your cat , how many pets do you have ?

I have two cats. Furry will be 19 soon, and Spot will be 13 on Valentine's Day.

Speaking of the monsters, it is time to feed them. And with that, end this long, tedious day. I'm exhausted and the only reason I can attribute that to is that I'd been freezing most of the day. I'm not sure if Daniel will text back or not, but I'm too tired to care. I plug the phone into the charger in my room—the ringer on silent per usual—and go feed the cats. I don't look at it as I climb into bed and let sleep claim me.

Day 4

I smile at my phone when I wake up. He did text, but it was after ten when he did. *It seems like he works really late*, I think. *Between his long days and his daughter, how does he even have time to date?*

I have three other missed messages that I look at and ignore. Two are from Michael and are very sexual and moderately demeaning towards women. The third is Jeff being needy, making me very uncomfortable. I start to think that getting on that app wasn't the best idea. I text Daniel back as I get ready for work and start my day.

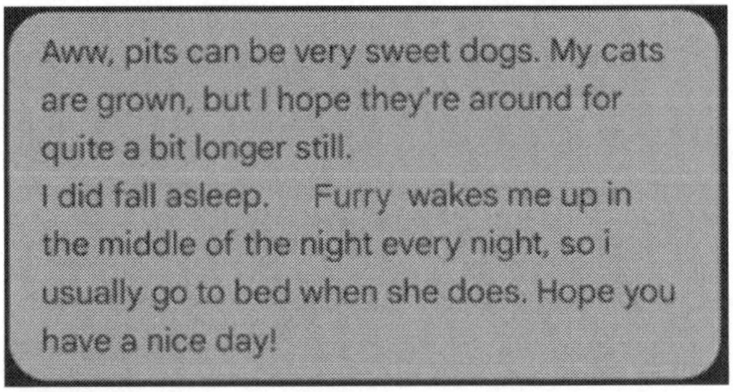

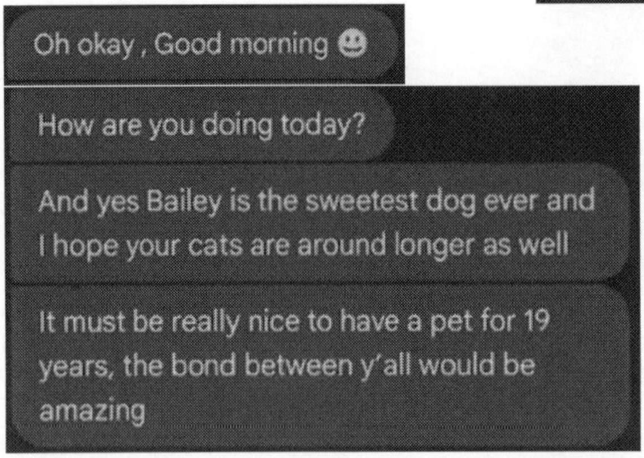

I cringe. Point against him. My cats aren't pets. They're my fur babies. He doesn't know that though, so I give him a little slack. But just a little.

> It is great. It's also devastating when they pass. Your whole world shifts. Furry's brother passed right before we moved, and it's been a difficult adjustment.
> Bailey is a cute name. Is she good with your daughter? It's nice that she gets to grow up with a pet friend.
> I'm good. Just working. You?

Sorry to hear that

And yes , she sure is adorable and they have a great loving relationship , Bailey and Trixie love each other , they always cuddle and fall asleep together lol 😆

I'm good as well , at work too

I hope works not too busy for you

> Its an ok day so far. I'm hoping to get some answers to a question I've been trying to approve for the past two and a half weeks today.

Oh okay , I hope you get them

Did you have breakfast yet?

I smile at our conversation. I can feel the nervous awkwardness between us, but I can also hear his sincerity and how much he loves his daughter. It's sweet, really. And it's an easy conversation. It hasn't felt like we're interviewing each other. We just click.

> Yes. I usually eat by 8

I laugh. It's almost 10:30 in the morning. Of course, I've had breakfast.

Oh okay

Tea or coffee ?

I enter my meeting and don't see his text until it's over.

I just got out of my meeting and got the answers I needed, so yay!

I do both, but prefer tea.

That's great , I'm happy for you

It's a slow morning for me , I'm just here rn

And it's coffee for me

Nice to have slow days occasionally

True

It's nice to text btw , way better than that app .. I'm never on there and barely get the notifications

Yah, this is definitely better. The app is weird. I wasn't sure i even wanted to get on it, but my sister encouraged me to get out there and said that'd be the best way to meet someone that's somewhat decent. Her words, lol

Do you get to spend a lot of time with your daughter, with how much you work?

lol right , I didn't want to either but I haven't dated in a while but my friends gave me the nudge and I'm trying to put myself back out there

And I try , not as much as I would really love but I always try to make the most of the time I've got

I melt a little, feeling the wall around my heart crumble even further. A man who tries to make the most of the time with his kid is sweet. And the fact that he recognizes his crazy work schedule is a point in his favor. My mind wanders a bit on what it'd be like to date him. Would he have time for me? I'd be one more thing blocking his time with Trixie. Would that be fair for her?

I stop those thoughts before I can obsess over and overanalyze them. He's grown. If he thinks he's able to date, that's his choice. I can't make decisions for him based on what I think or assume is best. I hate when people do that to me, and I refuse to do that to him.

The question I should be asking myself, is if I can handle being a step-mom to a kid that young. I know we haven't even talked about meeting in person yet, but neither of us have feelings yet and there's a kid involved. I went through too many boyfriends of my mother's when I was young. I'd never subject a child to the possibility of me as a step-mom if I wasn't sure I wanted it. If I could handle the idea of it. If I can't, I should stop this before it gets any further. Neither of us deserves to waste our time, if being a mom is something that I may not even want. I think about it while he texts. Could I be a mom to a four-year-old at this point in my life? I expected to date a guy with kids at this point in life, but not any so young. I think I could. I like kids.

It was never that I didn't want kids with my ex. It was more that he didn't, so we didn't. I love kids, and I've always wanted to be a mom. I guess that answers my question.

Can I ask you why you never wanted kids because you've been married for sometime and I knew you would've definitely thought about it at some point

I wanted them. My ex did not. And now that I'm in my 40s I don't want them. For me, I'm too old. It works for other people, and im happy for them. But the idea of pregnancy, childbirth, and the first two years of the baby stuff makes me queasy. I like kids, don't get me wrong. My window of procreation is just over.

I have 7 nieces and a nephew 5 that are under 10, and I LOVE being an auntie. I can go in, spoil them, have fun, and leave when they start getting cranky. When i visit, it feels like I'm a superhero. They're fun. Their little minds are so interesting.
My older nieces and I have great relationships. I run a D&D game with one, and the other is 21 and figuring out her life. We talk and do the insta thing and it's fun.

And he disappears again. I get that. We're both in the middle of our workdays, and his hours seem insane. I don't give it another thought as I go back to what I was doing and finish my day out.

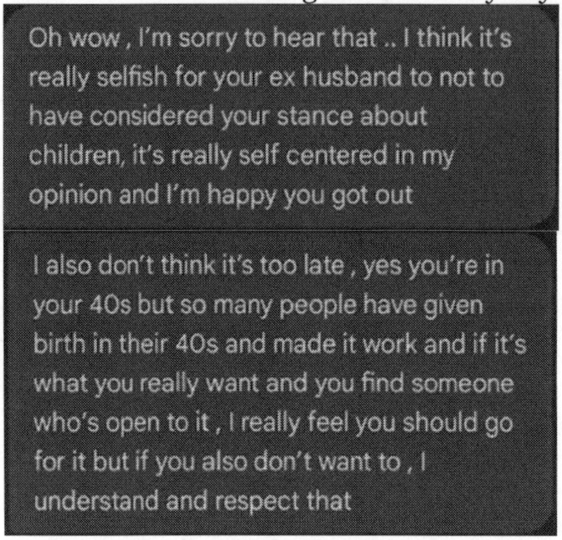

Um, I think. *No. I absolutely do not want children.* "Dude, if you're insinuating that I should start popping out babies with you, that block button is becoming my second BFF," I say to myself. I'd already blocked a couple of guys, including Jeff and Kevin, and another handful who were obvious scammers on the app. They wanted me to send gift cards to them and told me they loved me in less than five days. I get that I'm a loveable girl, but holy lord. That's insanity.

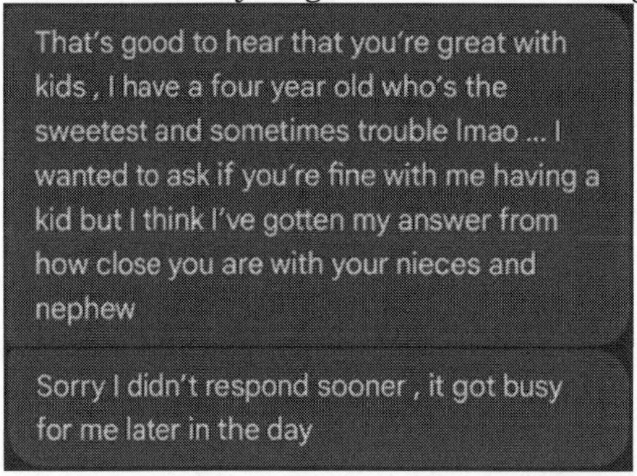

Aww, that's sweet. He didn't need to apologize. The dopey smile is practically permanently etched on my face as we talk.

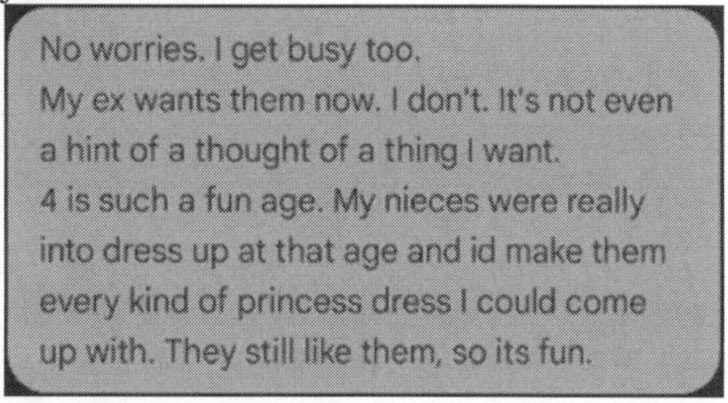

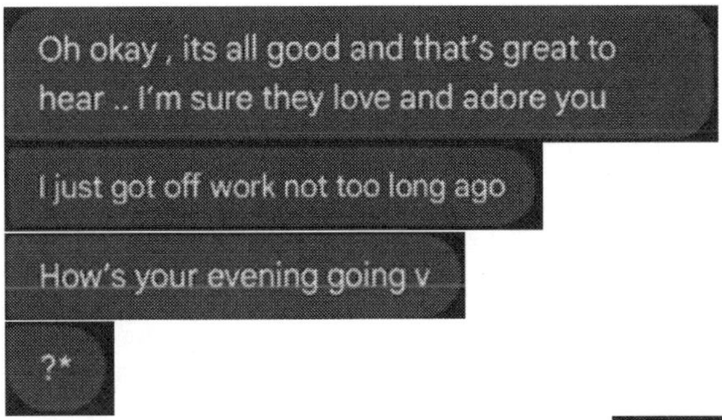

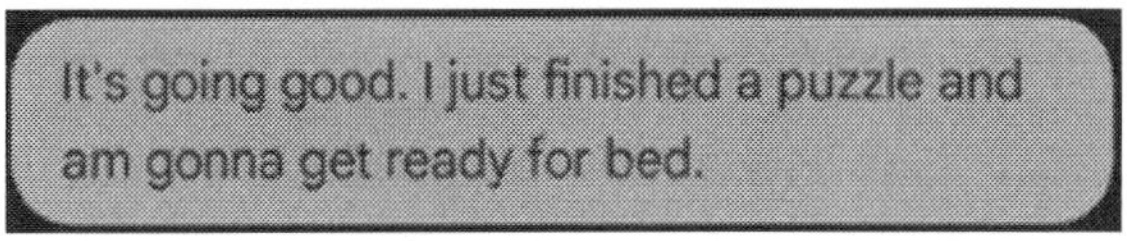

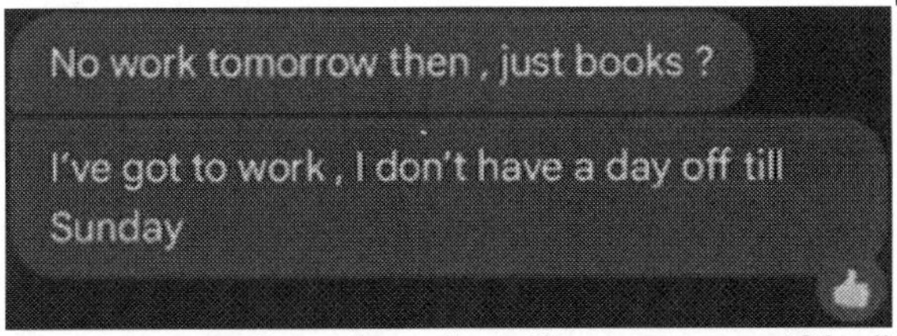

I remember that, but I'm not sure if he'll have the day off on base because of the death of the ex-president. It's kind of a big deal in DC, so I figure it'd be a big deal on base, too. I guess not.

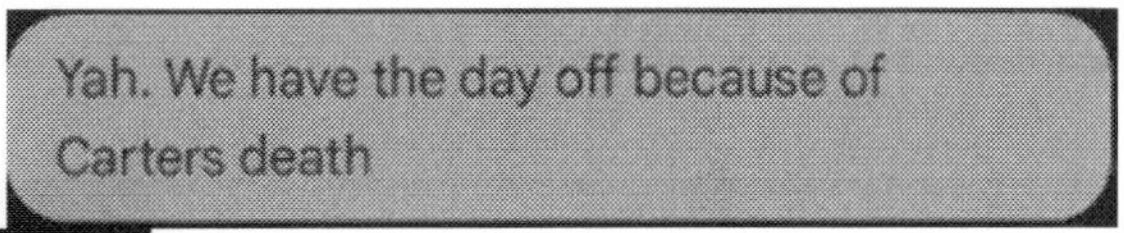

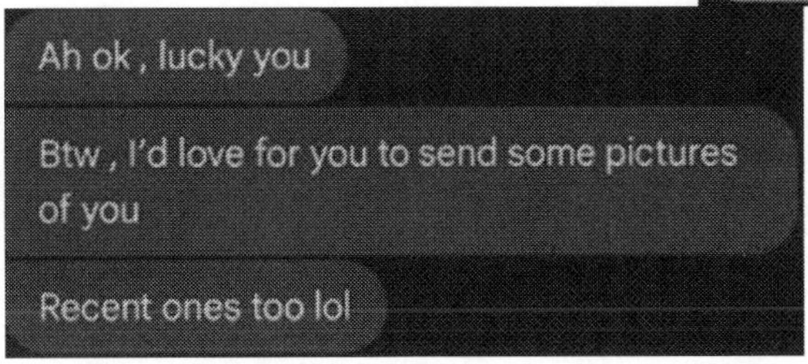

The pictures I posted are recent. I groan. I hate pictures of me. Why did I go on that app before I lost the weight I wanted to? I know being overweight doesn't make a person ugly. There are beautiful voluptuous women who have amazing, healthy relationships and lives. I just struggle with it because so much of mine is medication related. Society says women are all supposed to be practically skeletal, and I'm the fattest of all my siblings. By a lot. After listening to and watching your skinny sisters lament about their weight, it gives you a bit of a complex, even if you do like yourself.

They all tell me I'm beautiful, and I should only lose weight if I want to—not because I need to. And then, in the next breath, they talk about needing to lose twenty pounds or something else related to their weight. It's extremely frustrating. I have curves, and I love my curves. I just don't want as much squish on the curves.

I think about his pictures and decide to be cheeky as he has old photos on his profile. I'd love to see something current of him.

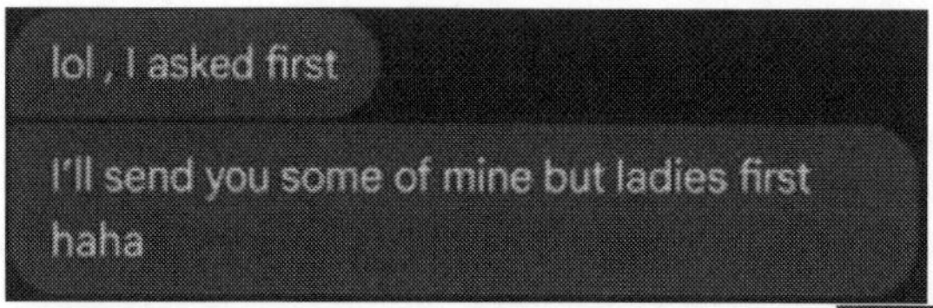

I have a stupid grin on my face as I get ready for bed and lay down. He's cute, and he sounded shy and a little uncertain, but he was trying to flirt. I don't feel so awkward talking to him as I do with other people. In fact, I barely give the other guys a thought throughout my day. It's just Daniel, which should scare me, but I'm finding the feeling to be really nice. I fall asleep thinking about him, wondering if he's real, and what dating him would look like.

Day 5

Daniel

Have a good day!

I'm in such a grumpy, foul mood after the night I had with the cats. Furry's to the point where she's got dementia and just screams every four hours. It doesn't matter if it's day or night, she just screams. And I'm exhausted. I jump into the shower, and she wanders the house, yelling her head off. I can't focus on anything, nor can I relax in the shower, like I want to. My bad mood just worsens as I listen to her yowls.

I get out, dry off, and get dressed. I put on a little bit of makeup, to hide the dark circles underneath my eyes from lack of sleep, knowing I'm going to take a selfie and not wanting to feel like I look like a complete troll. I sit against the edge of the bed, both cats laying behind me, finally quiet and ready for their morning nap. Furry is settling, thinking I'm going to hang out in the bedroom with them, and she's finally quiet for the first time in an hour. I look at the messages that came in while I was getting dressed.

Hi beautiful, how are you doing?

Have a good day as well

I'm a lil grumpy- cats aren't helping with the stuff I'm trying to do today.

What did they do lol

They just won't leave me alone. Furry keeps yelling, and Spot keeps trying to antagonize her.

I send the picture without looking too closely at it. My wet hair is drying naturally, the way I usually let it, and I look like I'm not wearing any makeup. My brown eyes glitter as I try—and fail—not to laugh while taking the photo. I am not a selfie person, but I try.

<sends pic>

Well you're home all day today and they probably just miss you lol

I'm home almost every day. I telecommute most of the time.

Oh okay

Pets can be too much sometimes lol

And you look really pretty 😍

Is that a picture of you right now ?

Yah. I just got out of the shower.

Thanks

You look really good

So how long have you been single ?

I've been single since the end of September and have not dated.

He disappears again; he must have gotten busy with work. I hop onto the computer and start back in on my author training. I'm incredibly frustrated with all the data language, so I load up Facebook and start asking questions in the group chat. For people who say they understand introverts, being told we need to ask questions in a group setting is not ideal. My anxiety is through the roof as I type in my questions and frustration. Maybe this wasn't a good idea.

I get responses from people who are either struggling like I am or have some of the same questions I have and have moved past them already. Everyone's crazy nice, and I finally figure out that I'm overthinking the task. That's me. I overthink, over-care, over-love, and over-trust. And then the anxiety comes to kick my ass. I am currently on the anxiety let-down, where my body is dealing with all the craziness the anxiety brought and trying to relax now that we're not filled with adrenaline, so I text my mom, hoping she's available so we can chill out and play a game together, and I can rest my overactive thoughts.

Michael

You should send me a pic of your tits, so I can see what I'm going to cum on later.

Hard pass. Why not start with, IDK, meeting each other, first? Want to have coffee or something tomorrow? We can see where things go from there?

Where are you thinking?

I have no idea; I just moved here. Is there a good Thai place near you?
Also, your profile lied. You are SO not shy, lol

I am, it's just easier to talk like this. Less pressure.

Wow, I think. *I'm really not interested in this. I'll give him until tomorrow to talk to me like a normal human, and if he can't, I'm blocking.*

My phone rings, and it's Jeff. I wasn't expecting a call. I thought he'd text like a normal person, but I guess this was okay. We talk for a while, and he's even more pessimistic over the phone than he is via text. He also barely lets me talk. He keeps talking about his friend's band and music he likes. When he does ask me a question, he just barrels on over my answer. I really don't think this is going to work, but I'm hoping that maybe he'll chill out a little with time.

Currently though, I'm not a fan.

It isn't until after I finish dinner and start working on the blanket I was now regretting starting, while watching the devil drama I love—that my phone buzzes. I smile as I see the text. I don't think I would ever tire of seeing a text that starts like that, especially from Daniel.

Daniel

Hi beautiful, how's your evening going?

Good. How s yours?

Busy , still here but getting off soon

What did you do today ?

Apart from writing your novel lol

Played a game with my step mom and watched a show while working on a blanket.

Sounds like a chill day

Does Your step mom lives close to you ?

In Ohio with my dad.
It was a nice day. Busy with the writing stuff though. Would've really liked to have finished this lesson, but such is life.

Oh okay

Well how long does it normally take for you to finish a novel ?

Btw , I took this earlier today .. I hope you like

<sends pic>

He's in a black hoodie with an obviously fake smile. I already knew he was tall from his dating profile—just over six feet, with brown hair and a lean, but muscular body. In this picture, his blue eyes almost look brown, and I laugh because like my ex, he has a large nose. *Apparently, I have a type.* I laugh to myself. I'm struck with how much I want to see him in person. I want to know if he'll look at me with as much enthusiasm as he says he does. I was already starting to like talking to him and looked forward to his texts. His picture looked so much like the one I liked off of his profile. I was excited. The other pictures made him look like a player, but this one just made him look sweet.

I couldn't come off as eager or too interested. I've been warned against that from younger girls who'd been dating like this their whole life. I'm already starting to hate this dating crap. I want to be excited. I want to show I'm interested. I want to feel that way in return. It'd be worth it if he met up with me and we hit it off as well as we do in texting.

Nice.
I'm taking a class to increase marketing and sales. It's supposed to take a minimum of 6 months to get through, but I'm hoping it'll let me quit my day job in the next year.

Usually it takes me about a month or two to write a book. Longer to edit.

Oh nice , well I hope it all works out for you

You had dinner yet ?

I did, about an hour ago.
Maybe we could do something tomorrow night?

I'm shaking. I haven't asked a guy out in over two decades. Sure, I'd asked other guys from that stupid app to meet up, but I didn't actually care if they did. I don't feel for them what I'm starting to feel for Daniel. My stomach is in knots, butterflies churning as I hit send. What the hell am I doing? My heart pounds in my chest as I wait for his answer.

Please say yes. Please say yes, I think as I wait.

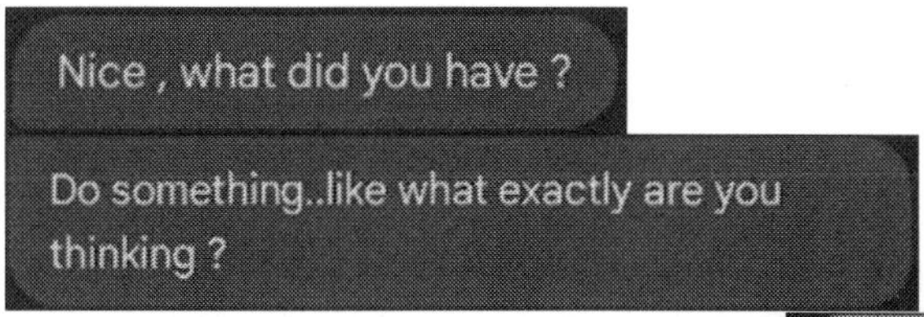

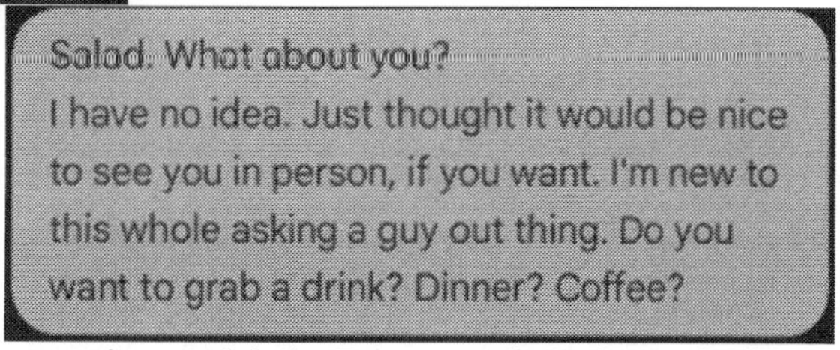

For the love of all that's holy—stop texting, I think. Be casual. He's probably just being nice and not really interested. Or he's catfishing. This dating app thing really isn't my thing. *Don't let on just how much you'd like to see him in person. Just be casual.*

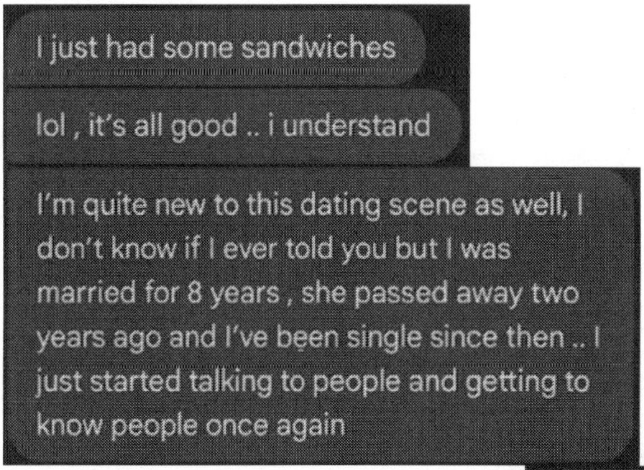

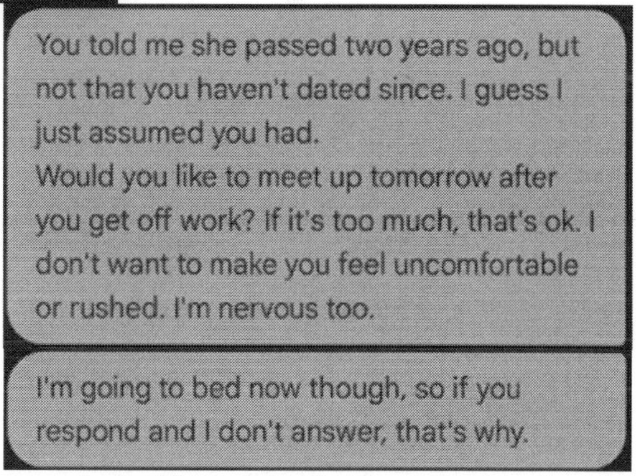

I lay down in bed, my mind racing and unable to handle the rejection I could feel coming. He is the first guy that I actually want to meet since my divorce. The first guy I genuinely feel a connection with, and I think he is attractive. I really want him to like me, and I think we have a connection, but I can feel from his texts after I asked, that he is trying to let me down gently.

Why get on a dating app, if you don't actually want to date? I toss and turn. Furry keys into my anxiety and didn't know what else to do except yell at me for the rest of the night.

Day 6

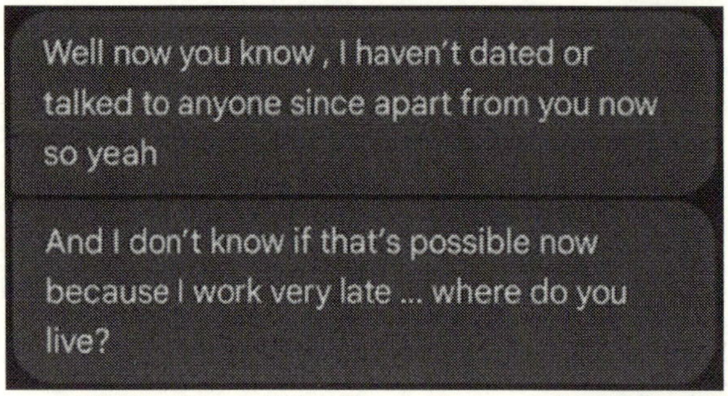

Well, there it is. I'm not surprised, but I'm still disappointed. I reply, thinking, *well, if he changes his mind, at least he'll know.*

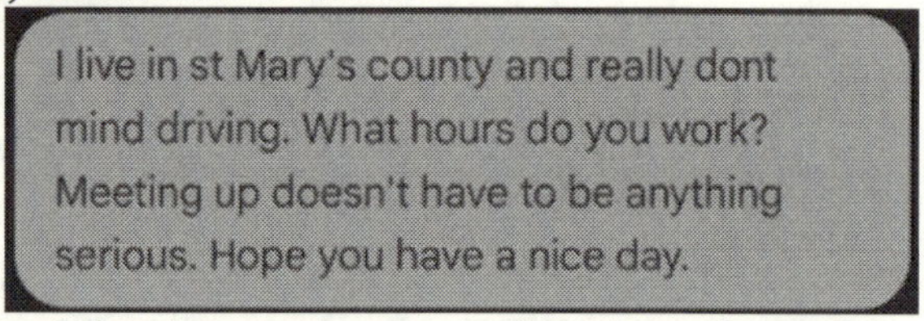

I don't hear from him for the rest of the day, and a part of me is so hurt, I want to block his number. Another part of me understands. This is new for me, and I'm terrified. He has to be feeling even worse because of his kid. Not only is dating taking time away from her, but it'll also bring someone new into her life. He really has to be careful with navigating things.

Day 7

I can't believe this was happening. I stare at my phone, wishing I was back home to hug my friend and curse her husband to the ends of the Earth. I just finished texting with her about her husband doing unspeakable things to their daughter. She just found out and left him. The rage I feel on her behalf almost scares me with its intensity. I talk with her, listen to the horror she's been dealing with this past week, and do my best to support her from across the country.

My heart absolutely breaks as I talk with her about her plans, and how her kids are feeling. During all of it, Daniel messages and I don't even think about being upset that he ghosted me yesterday. I was just oddly grateful to see his name pop up on my screen.

Daniel

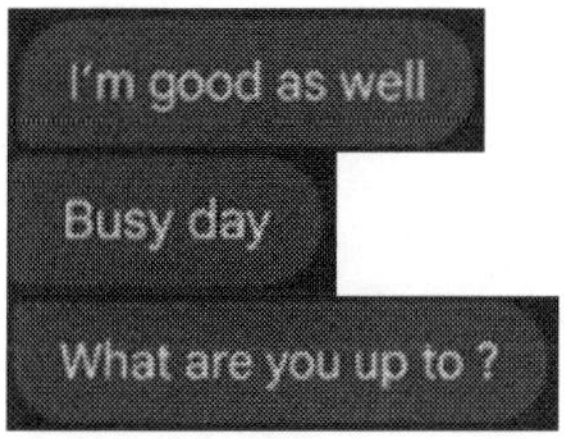

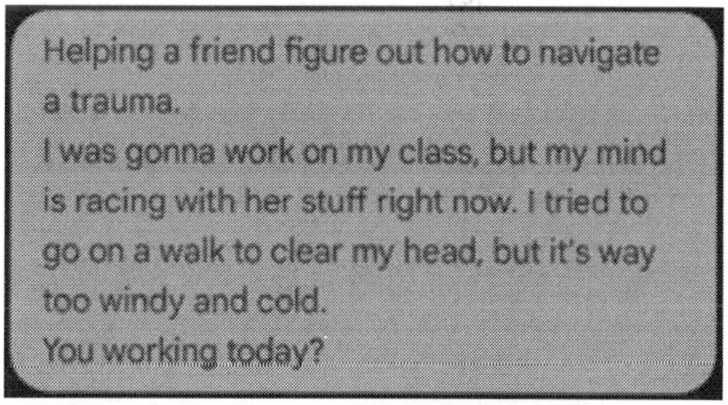

It snowed again last night and is nothing but sheets of ice and freezing weather. I know he normally only had Sundays off, but I wonder, with the weather, if the base shuts down like other places.

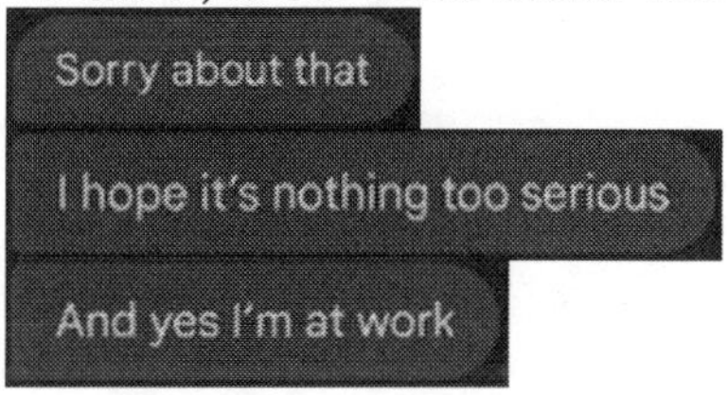

I only have Sundays off remember ?

It's bad, but i know she'll get through it. I remember. Wasn't sure if you got a snow day or not though.

I hope she does as well and I trust you'd be there for her

Snow day does not affect me lol, I gotta work all day , everyday ... it's not fun but it's what I gotta do

Blah. No fun. Hows work going today though?

He stops texting, and I shrug it off. He works so much; I'm starting to think that this won't work between us.

"It's weird, right?" I asked Spot as he comes to sit on me for snuggles. "What kind of job makes you work six days a week, twelve-hour shifts? That's insanity." I pet him, ignoring my phone buzzing on my desk. "Maybe things are different on base. It's just weird."

Michael

Hey sexy, what're you wearing and how soon can I take it off you?

I'm in leggings and a long shirt. Maybe we can meet tonight and you can see what's underneath?

I am so sick of his inuendo. Shit or get off the pot, dude.

You want to get together? Tonight?

Sure.

While I wait for his response, another text comes in.

Kevin

Hey, how are you doing?

I'm ok, how are you?

Kevin and I talk about the normal things that I've told everyone I've met on social media or the app. Why are you here? What are your expectations? How long have you been single? What do you like to do? I'm not even excited to have these conversations anymore. I want to meet people in person, go back to guys asking for your number to your face, not through the apps where no one even bothers to read your bio.

Through texting with Kevin, I know he's not what I'm looking for, but he's a nice enough guy. He's on his third DUI, which seems to be a theme for guys that live in this area and can't drive. So, if we get together, I'm going to have to pick him up or meet him somewhere close to his house.

"Why did I feel the need to get on that dating app?" I ask Bex as she picks up the phone.

"Because you're an awesome person who deserves to have someone good love her," she replies without hesitation. "What's going on?"

"The guys here are awful. Between being ghosted, the few obvious scammers I've run across, and the people with DUIs, I don't think decent, single men exist."

I open up my document on my computer, hoping our chat will help get me focused back on writing my romance. As I was currently against anything romantic, this book was proving to be difficult to dive back into.

"The good ones are out there. They're just going to be hard to find," she replies, a bit distracted. It is the weekend, and her hubs is home. "What happened to the military guy with the kid?"

"I asked him out, and he ghosted me yesterday," I answer. "He texted this morning like nothing happened. I like him, but..." I leave the sentence open, not knowing how to finish it. I really liked Daniel. More than I probably should at this point, but I don't know what to do about him. I'm getting discouraged with the whole dating scene and just really don't know if I want to continue.

"Maybe this was a mistake," I start. "Maybe leaving Peter was the wrong thing to do. I mean, I don't feel like it was but holy shit. I knew dating would be tough. I just didn't realize it would be this bad. I don't know what to do."

"Well, coming back here is not an option, no matter how much I want you back," she says. "And going back to a one-sided, loveless marriage is also not an option. You were lonely in that, too, remember? You'll find someone. It's just going to take time."

I groan.

"I know, it sucks," she replies. "You gonna be okay now?"

"Yeah, get back to your man, and be gross," I say. "Thanks for letting me vent."

"Anytime," she says as she hangs up.

I don't take it personally. She's more than happily married, and the weekends are her time for her family. I boot up my training and start reviewing it instead of working on the romance I pulled up. I'm just really not feeling romantic in any way. I figure figuratively banging my head against the wall, trying to get through this program, will be a better use of my time instead. Hours fly by as I work.

Daniel

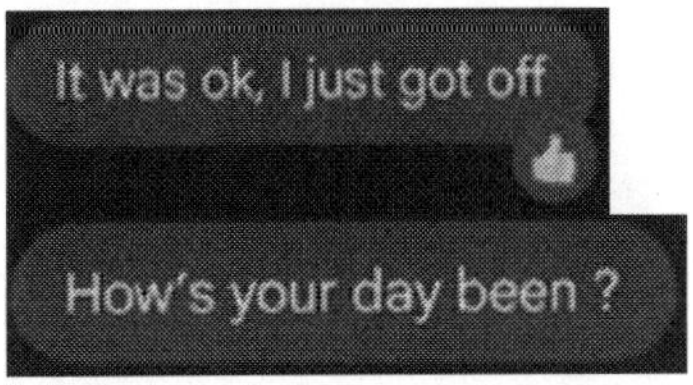

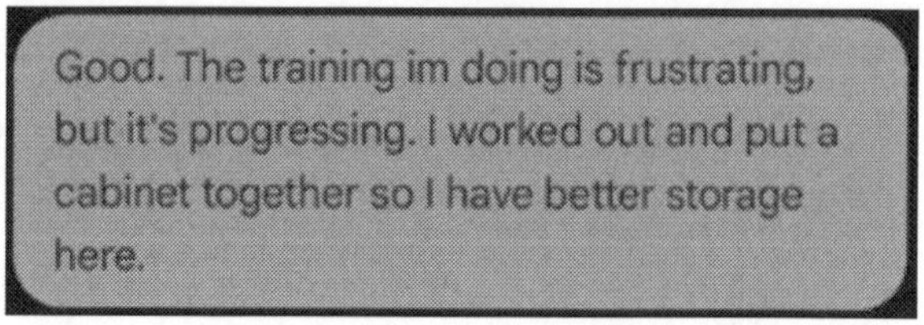

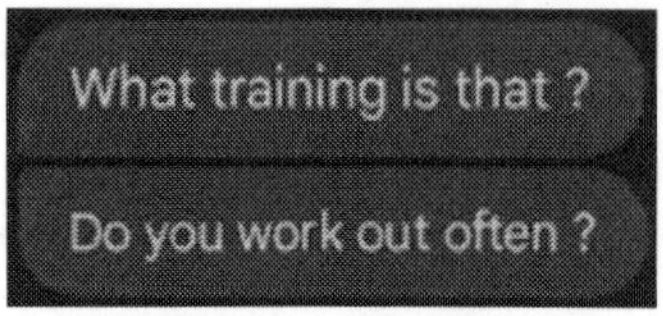

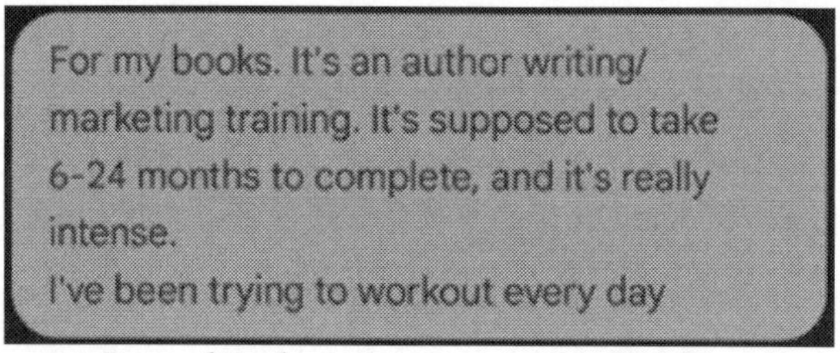

And he disappears. Which is fine because I need to leave to get to my D&D game. I love Saturdays.

Day 8

I wake up today with actual things to do, which I love because it's Sunday and I'm not the biggest fan of Sunday. A girlfriend of one of my D&D friends is selling their house and suggested I come look at it because they know I'm looking for a house. I'm still not certain what I want, or where I want to live exactly, but I want to see what's available. I drive to their house, and while it's adorable, I know it's not for me.

It just doesn't feel like home.

"I can't believe how much snow we got this year," Elise says to me when they're done showing me around the house.

"Really," I ask. "This is a lot for you guys?"

"We usually get a dusting or enough that the snow melts the next day. This has been a lot."

"Huh," I reply, as intelligent as possible. "That explains the snow days, then."

"How's dating going?" Josie, Elise's girlfriend, asks.

"Awful," I reply without hesitation. "I have no idea what's wrong with guys nowadays. I half think about batting for y'all's team, even though I'm so not interested. How did you guys meet?"

"A dating app, actually," Josie replies. "And it isn't any better for us, either, so don't feel so bad. There are a lot of bad ones out there. Like, a lot."

"I'd be happy with bad dates at this point," I lament. "I can't even find someone who wants to actually meet in person. I don't understand it!"

"Ahhh," she muses like an old, wise person. "You've entered the land of the pen pal."

"What's that?" I ask, laughing at her sage tone.

"It's where people will only text. It seems to be the norm for relationships lately, especially after COVID," Josie explains. "For some reason, even in 2025, people are still hesitant to want to do anything in person, even though we're all supposed to be getting back to normal. It's weird, I know."

"Yeah, it's really weird. How are you supposed to have a relationship with someone if you never see them?" I think about my pseudo-relationship with Daniel and wonder if he's in the pen pal club. I really hope not. I've liked getting to know him and really want to see him in person.

"So far, I've gotten ghosted, sexted and then ghosted, pen-pal-ed, and have deleted a various number of scammers. How are you supposed to find someone to actually date that's real and wants to see you in person?" I barrel on before either woman has a chance to respond. "I've gotten some weird scams, too. Have you ever heard of a sugar daddy scam?"

At their blank, confused expressions I continue. “Apparently, it’s this thing where a guy sends you something in the mail that’s from overseas or another country. But in order for it to clear customs, you have to pay a fee. Only, he sends you a check to cover those expenses. And the check is a lot of money, like over ten grand, so you really want to cash it. But as soon as you do, he gets access to all your banking stuff and drains you dry.”

“What?” Elise exclaims. “How?”

“I honestly have no idea. My neighbor told me when I told her what was happening. She apparently worked at a bank years ago and this happened to someone. I swear, it’s a minefield out there.”

“Well, you should have my dad research anyone you’re interested in. You know he works cybersecurity, and I’m sure he’d be happy to look into people for you,” Josie offers. “He looked into girls for me when I was dating.”

That’s a really good idea, I think. I’ll ask him about Daniel during game next week. I hate asking people for favors though.

We talk a little longer about nonsense, and I leave so that I can get home before the roads ice over.

I was watching a show, winding down for the evening when Daniel texts. I smile as I see his name pop up.

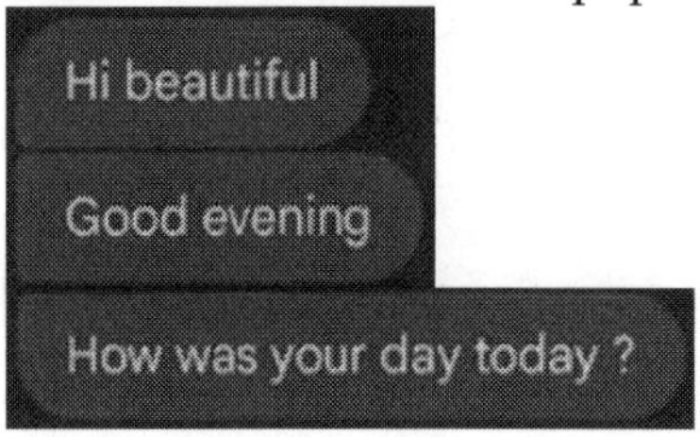

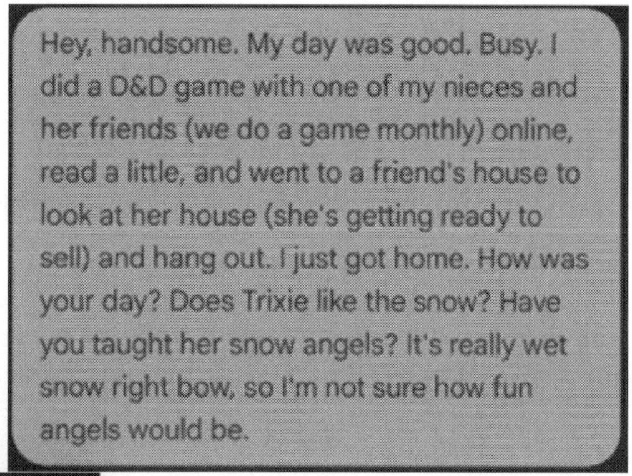

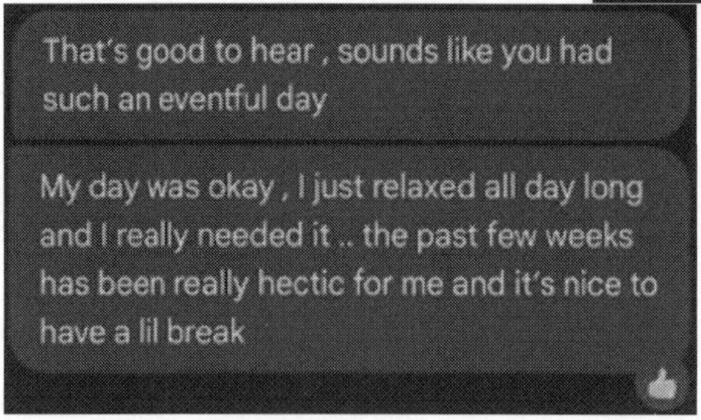

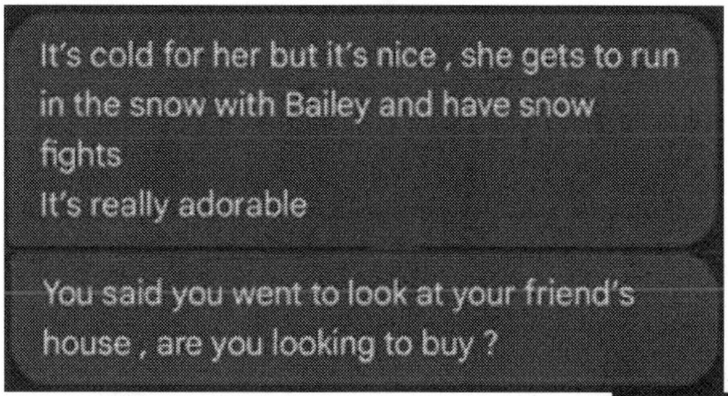

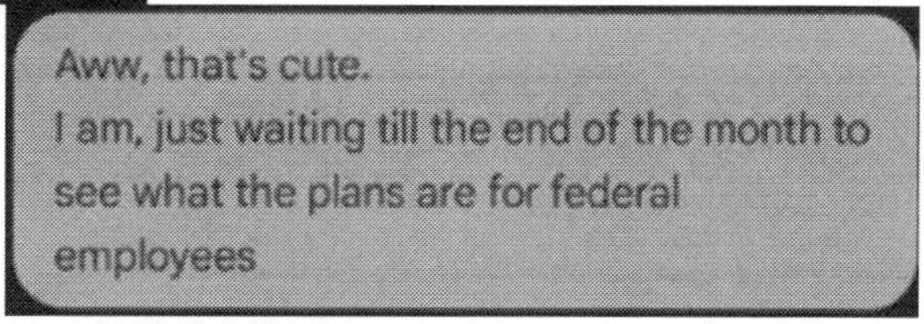

I feed the cats and fatigue hits, so I go to bed. He hasn't been responding very quickly, and it's been a good half-hour at this point. Maybe he's putting his daughter to sleep. I wonder, again, if this is a smart idea. He seems really busy and I'm still not completely sure about us or being a stepmom to such a young kid.

Day 9

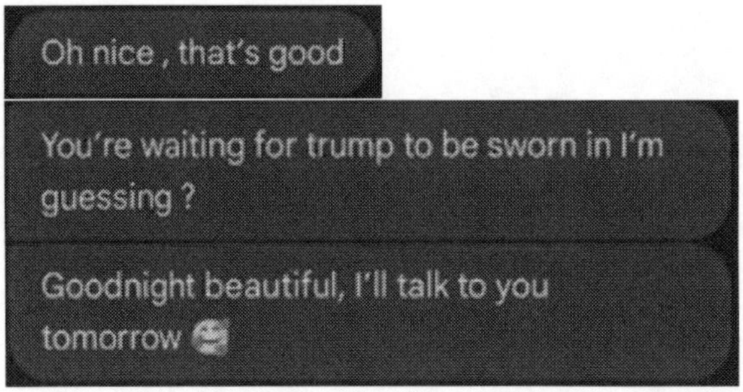

I wake up early, like I do every day, and take a short walk around my area. It's about a mile and makes me feel good because I can actually do it and breathe. It's been so long since I could do activities without feeling like I'm dying, that I relish my morning walks. I see that Daniel texted after I crashed last night, so I reply to him as I walk.

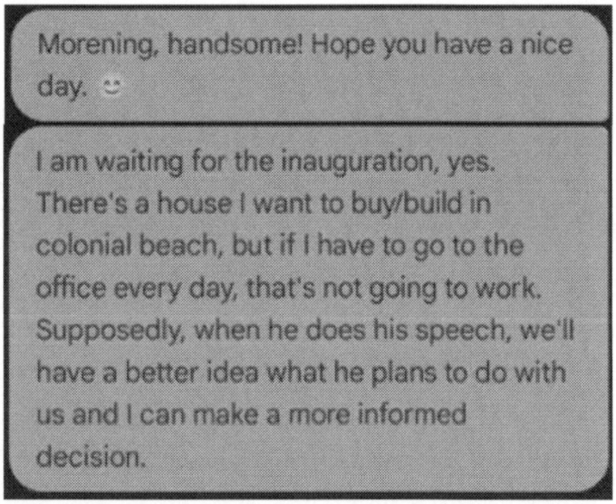

Once I'm done, I log into my work computer and start my workday. It's a lot of paperwork, reading, and scheduling meetings; but it's enough to keep me busy and distracted throughout the day.

I end my completely uneventful day, do some of my author work, have dinner, feed the cats, and go to bed.

Day 10

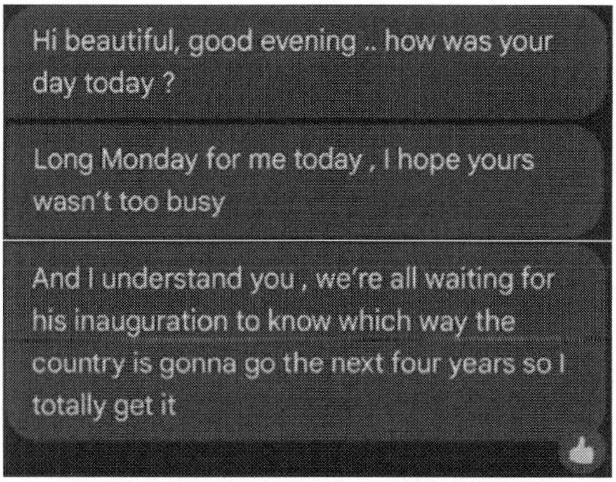

Daniel's texts are the first thing I see when I turn my alarm off, and I smile. He wasn't wrong on his profile; communication really isn't his forte, but he does try. I give him that. It's too cold to go for my walk, which bums me out, but the cats had a rough night, and I didn't sleep well. I'm hoping that today will be good and not terribly busy. I just don't have the energy for it.

My sister calls, and she's still upset that I left her and Nevada, so we don't have the best conversation. I know she doesn't truly understand how miserable I was there, or how bad my health had gotten, so I try not to take her jabs personally as I don't even think she realizes she's dishing them out. But they still hurt. I didn't leave her. I left for my health. I just wish I didn't have to continually explain that.

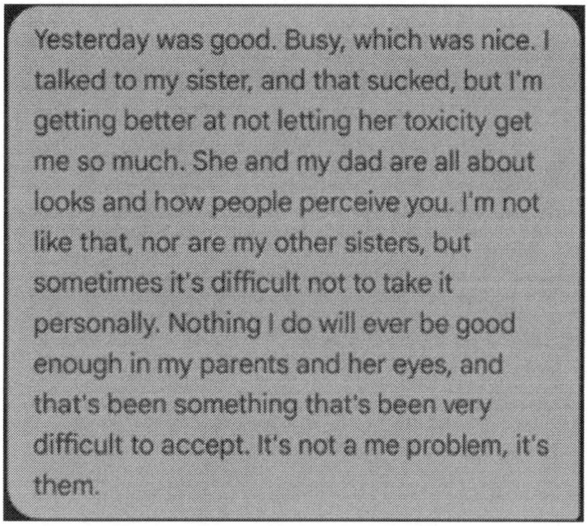

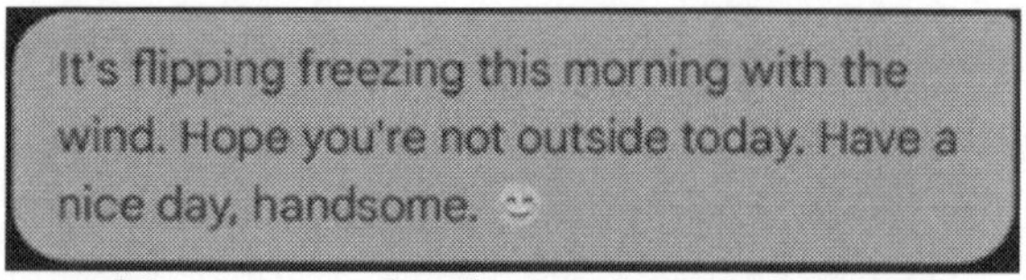

I finish my work day and start working on my books again. It's basically my routine until I can focus on the writing full time. That's the dream, the goal. I think I'll get there at some point, but until then, I work and then work. It's good that I live alone now. I don't have to worry about hurting anyone's feelings or not doing things with them, and I can eat whenever I want, not around their schedule.

The only thing I worry about is the cats. They demand a lot more of my attention than people think cats do. Which is great, it's just frustrating when I get into the zone either with work or my books.

I have a fairly uneventful day, filled with interruptions of cats alternating needing attention and sitting on my lap. I lose track of time most of the day and only realize time has passed when I'm hungry. My phone starts pinging just as I finish dinner. My heart does a tiny little flip as I hear Daniel's ringtone go off.

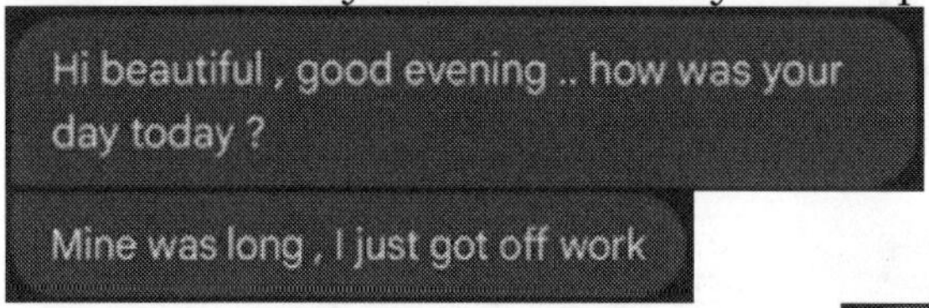

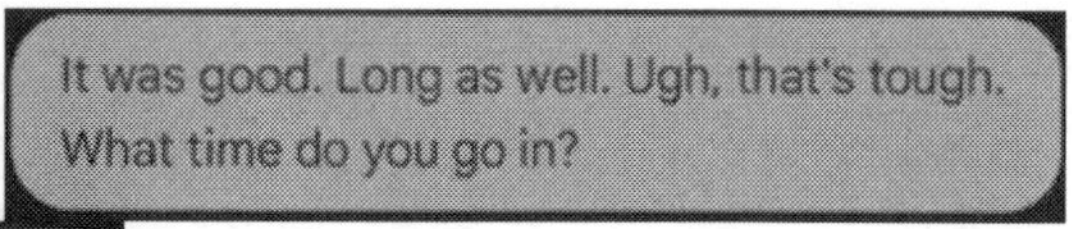

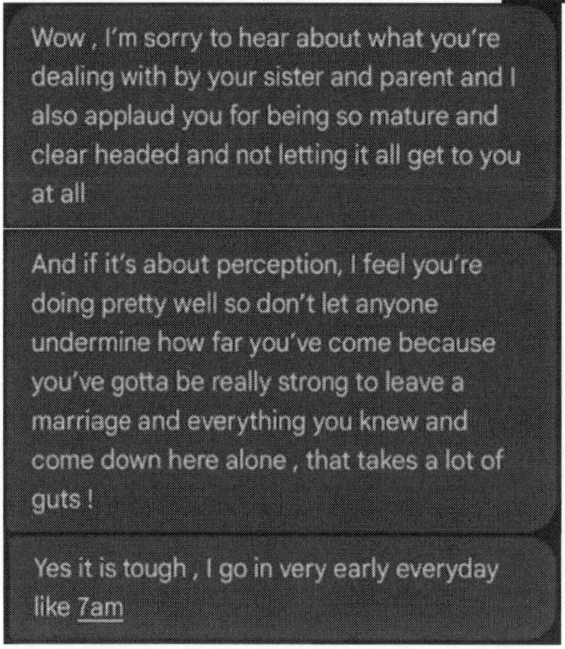

I don't understand how he can work so much, raise a young daughter, and still have time to date. I guess, from my experience with him so far, that the dating life suffers more than the rest of his life. Which is completely understandable and kinda what I expected. I just don't know if it's something we should continue or not.

But I really like talking to him. He's supportive and kind. I can't help the small smile that curves my lips.

What time do you go in ?

Thanks. There are days I'd give anything not to have to be strong. Then there are days when a friend calls to tall me that I've inspired her and give her courage to file for divorce and put her soon to be ex in jail for doing horrible things to their daughter. It's all about perspective. If what I did helps someone like that, I'd go through it 100 more times. Without question.

Ick. Those are long days for you. Is it hard for Trixie, or have you guys figured out a routine where she can spend time with you? I start at 7 and usually end by 4. On days I go to DC, I have to leave the house by 5. Those days suck. I'm not a morning person.

Oh wow , that's very horrible

I mean about your friend and her situation , it's good that you can help

Yes they are long days but it's what it is and I've gotta do what I gotta do

So you travel to DC , how often do you do that and what do you go there to do ?

I'm supposed to go in 4 days a pay period. I'm a tribal grant manager for DOJ. The rest of the time i work remotely. I like it. It's a nice blend of in person and not.
I feel like your work schedule has to be rough for any type of home life. Do you have help with her? Grandparents or other family?

Oh ok , gotcha

How long are you gonna be there for ?

And yes , my work schedule is very rough and I don't live close to family at all .. I moved to hyattsville with my former wife and all my family are back in Napa

But I've got a nanny that takes care of Trixie while I'm away

Hopefully, until retirement.
Thats tough. Good that you found a nanny that im assuming you like and who probably loves your little girl. I know it's hard not to love my nieces and nephew.
Have you thought about moving back?

I meant how long are you gonna be in DC for

And I don't think I'd ever see myself moving back , my relationship with my family is a bit estranged these days

Ill be there tomorrow and Thursday. I drive back and forth, I don't stay in DC. I dont mind the drive. I listen to books and usually enjoy the trips.

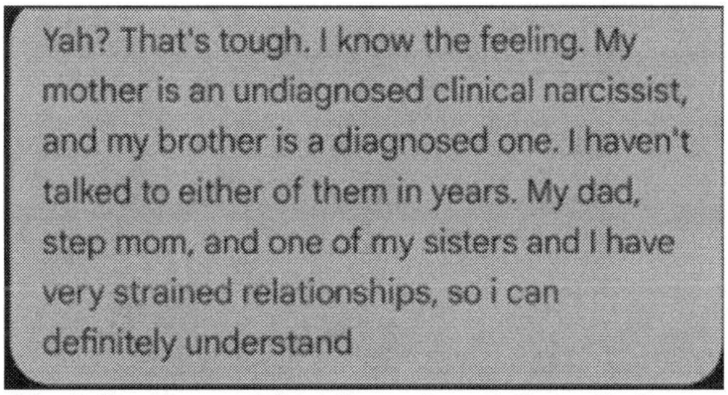

And he's gone again. He probably fell asleep. It's after nine, after all. I really enjoy our conversations, and I hope that one of these days he'll feel comfortable calling or meeting in person. I like him. More than I think I should.

Day 11

I drive into work today, and it's a ghost town, just like every other time I've gone into the office. The building is made for a smattering of workers, not for all of us to be there at once, so even with just a handful of people there, you can hear everyone's conversations. It's nice to be around other humans instead of my cats for once, but it's still lonely as we all ignore each other to get our work done.

The day flies by, and I'm home before dark. I continue to work from home, freezing because of the low temperatures this close to the Potomac, but enjoying the solitude of living in rural Maryland. Once my work day is complete, I doomscroll on social media for longer than I care to acknowledge, have dinner, and work on my books.

I only put in a couple of hours before staring at the computer screen gives me a headache and I log off, turning on the TV for some noise as I work on my diamond painting. I can't ever just sit still and watch a show. I have to be doing something, or I get bored.

My heart does a little flippy thing again as Daniel's ringtone goes off.

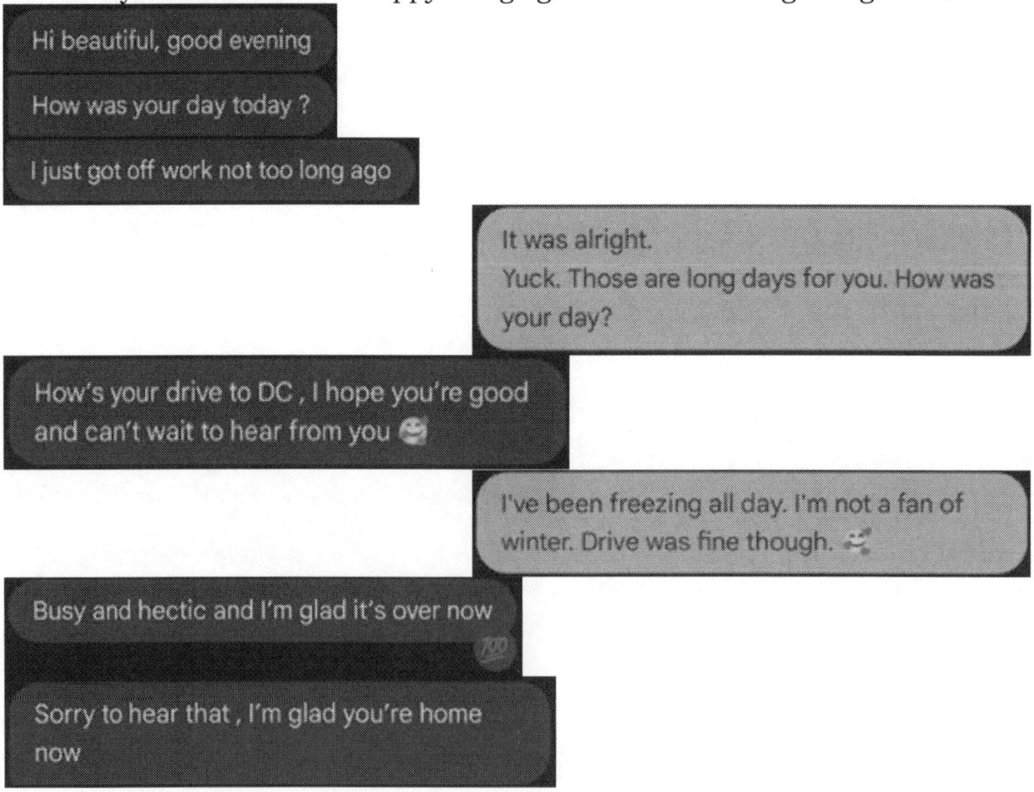

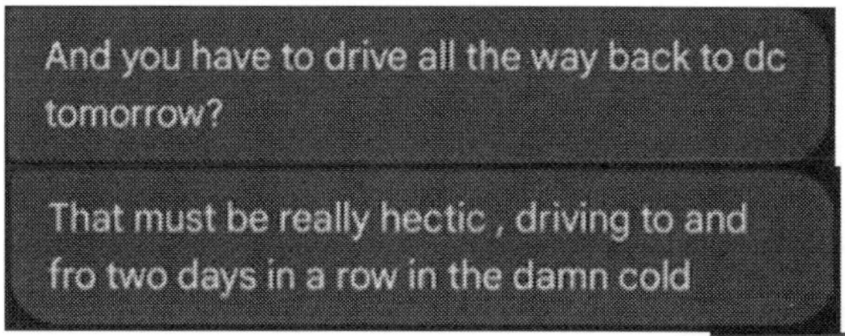

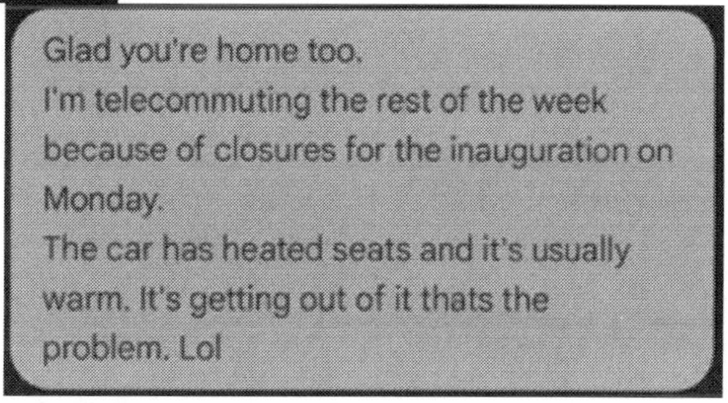

I fall asleep waiting for his response.

Day 12

lol , I understand

You must really enjoy the long rides lol

How's your evening going , you doing anything exciting?

Btw , you said you live in St Mary's county ?

I wake up and see that I missed Daniel's texts. I reply as I boot up my computer and get ready for my day. I actually slept last night, which has been rare lately. My oldest cat is showing signs of dementia, and I've been ignoring them as I'm not even close to ready to say good-bye to her. I can handle a few sleepless nights if it means she's around for a bit longer.

I don't mind the drives, but I'm also not excited to make them all the time. I'm not sure if that makes sense, but there it is.
I slept. That was my excitement last night, lol. Furry usually wakes me up once or twice to give her snacks, and last night it was just once and I was actually able to fall back to sleep - which has been rare lately.
I do live in St. Mary's county, why?

He doesn't respond, which doesn't shock me. He's at work, just as I am, and I have no idea how strict they are on base about having phones. He usually just texts in the evening, after he gets home anyway.

"Hey, girly chick, how are you doing?" I ask a few hours later when Bex calls.

"Can I get a tranquilizer and just sleep for the rest of my life?" she asks, tone exhausted.

"Hot flashes keeping you up again?"

"All flipping night," she replies. "Jed kept trying to snuggle, and all I wanted to do was stab him."

I laugh, understanding that feeling all too well. Hot flashes were no joke, and I knew hers were really bad.

"Well, you can always come here. Your room is all set for you," I reply, referencing the room she stayed in when she helped me move. She stayed with me for the first week I was on my own to help the transition not feel so drastic. She's truly my ride or die and one of the best people I know.

"I might actually take you up on that one of these days," she answers.

Our conversation slowly fades as we both get distracted with work. We still randomly talk to each other, but it's really just the comfort of having someone sort-of there that we did this. It makes us both feel less alone, even though we're actually physically alone—her in her office and me at home.

> Hey beautiful, good morning 😃 .. I hope today isn't too busy for you

"Oh my god, Bex. He's texting," I exclaim as my phone pings with another message from Daniel. "Daniel never texts me this early. I should probably let you go."

She laughs as I simply hang up on her. She's used to me by now and knows that's not abnormal behavior from me. I open up my texts and read.

> And yes I understand what you meant , I'm sure the drive can't be fun all the time but you've gotta do what you gotta do

> How do you feel when your cats have to wake you up twice every night .. I'd be very grumpy , I can't even lie lol

> My day is fine. How's yours going? I have to take the cats to the vet at 3, so that's the big adventure of the day. Lol
> I do get irritated and grumpy, and then I feel bad because she lost her brother, who she was attached to in September, and then we moved, and she'll be 18 on Sunday. So I try to put it into perspective, and usually, I'm ok with it. If I'm able to go back to sleep, it's no biggy. If I can't, I try to avoid people for the day. Lol

> Do you like Indian or thai food? I've been trying to find a good place for both and have not gotten lucky. I'm really missing the Indian place I used to go to in Nevada. It was the absolute best.

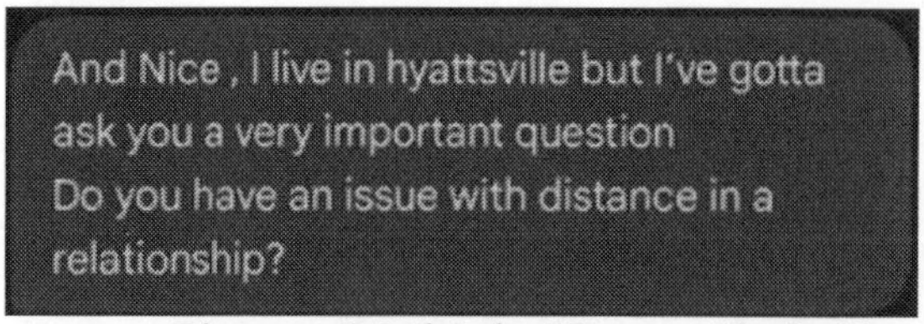

Distance? I think. Hyattsville is like an hour from me. I seriously don't understand people who think that anything more than ten minutes is too far. Uh, no. I don't have a problem with distance. It's a freaking hour.

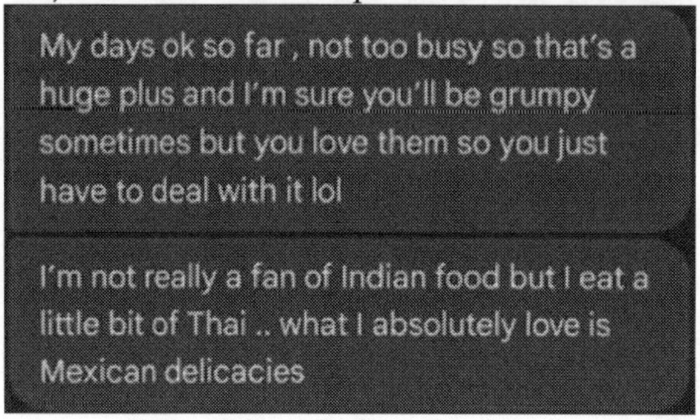

Dang. I love Indian food and was really hoping to be with someone who would enjoy that with me. I roll my eyes at the stereotypical love of Mexican, since he's Latin-American.

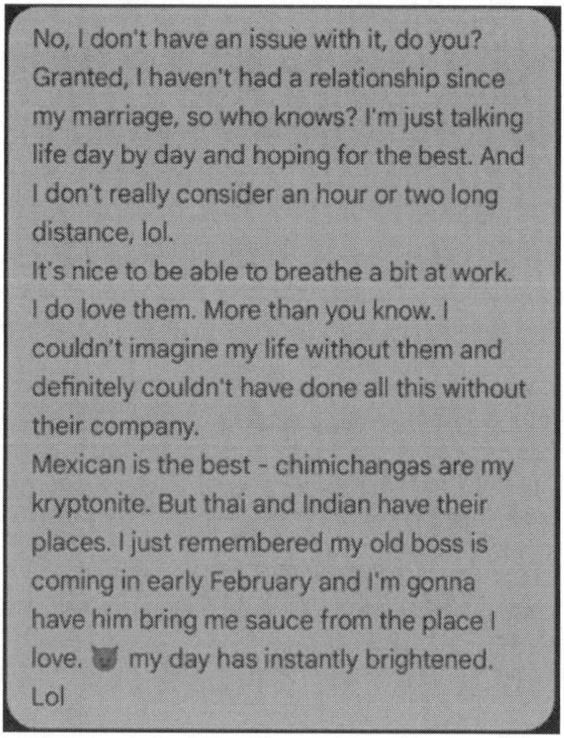

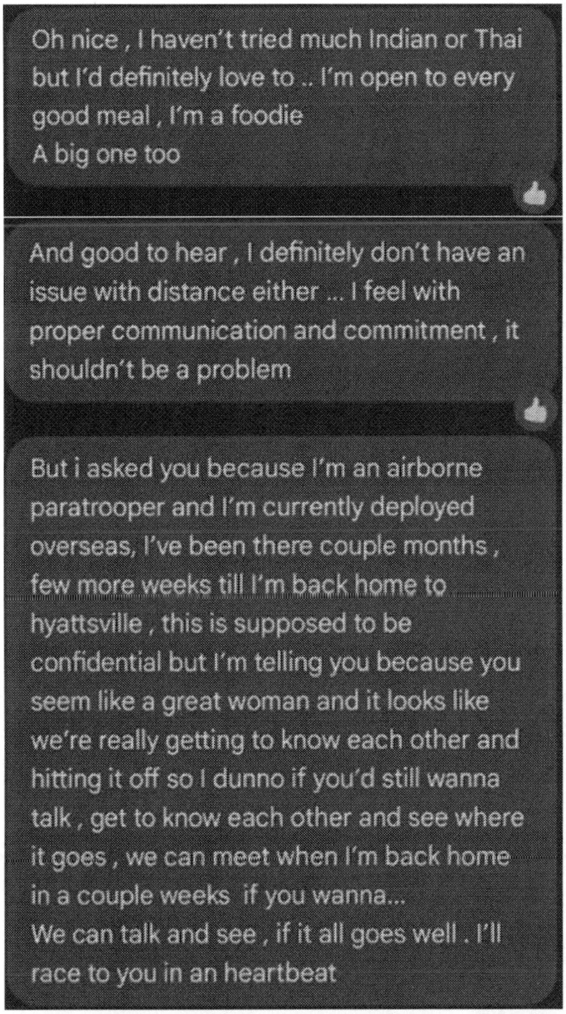

Ahhh, I think. That makes so much more sense and clears up my insecurity about why he ghosted me the other week when I asked him out. My heart does a little flip as I feel both impressed and scared for him. I know in an overarching capacity what being active duty means, but not having actually experienced it, I'm sure it's more intense than I can even imagine. I feel myself fall a little more for him, knowing how difficult it has to be to try to start a relationship with someone with that hanging over his head.

I distantly wonder why he'd even bother trying to start a relationship while deployed but shrug it off with the assumption that he's seen some shit and just wants human connection. He probably wants someone to come home to other than his kid. I already know I want to meet him and see if we're as connected in person as we seem to be just with texting. I already find myself thinking about him way more than I expected to. A part of me is scared about that, but another part of me hasn't felt this in so long., I want to enjoy it.

That makes so much more sense now, lol. I don't have any problem with it, and I will keep your secret. I enjoy talking with you too. I would love to meet you in person.

I like that you seem laid back and responsible. It's got to be hard being away from your kid for so long. Hopefully, you're able to face time her, and her nanny is helpful with your schedule.
I like what we have - it's not too intense or intimidating, and I *think* you get my humor. But the way we talk, it doesn't feel forced. It's just nice. And I'd like to see if there's anything more.

I'm looking at a townhouse in WV this weekend. It should be marginally closer to DC, but im not sure yet. Only one house I've looked at screamed home, but that's in Colonial Beach. And I was really intimidated by the commute. And it's 40k more than the place I'm looking at Saturday

I'm glad to hear you don't have a problem with it , I'm so relived because I've looking for ways to break it down to you over the past few days and I'm glad I did today ... we were just talking on the app and I never thought you'd be so cool and we'd have similar interests and so many things to talk about but I'm very glad to have met you and I wanna keep talking and see where this goes hopefully we're able to start something special together

And what makes so much sense lol

Your workload. It makes more sense now. No other job i could think of works like that, and it was bothering me a little because I couldn't make sense of it.

It makes sense now.

When do you come home? Where are you most looking forward to eating when you get here? I'm assuming you're most excited to see Trixie.

And he's gone again. Now that I know he's deployed, his disappearances make more sense, too. He probably only talks to me when he's got a minute. Knowing he's deployed also makes the disappearances scarier. Especially since I don't know where he's at or exactly how dangerous his job is. *Just another reason to keep him at arm's length*, I remind myself, knowing full well that I'm the last person who actually listens to my logic.

Hey beautiful, good evening

How's it going?

I smile, seeing his texts come through. It's late and even later wherever he's at.

Hey, handsome. How was your day?

Im just chillin before bed.

Busy but ok

Nice

Writing as usual ?

Not tonight. Had to take the cats to the vet for checkups, so they had a traumatic evening 🙄 and are snuggling.

I'm gonna work on the writing tomorrow, though.

lol understandable

Why do all pets hate going to the vet lol 😆

😆

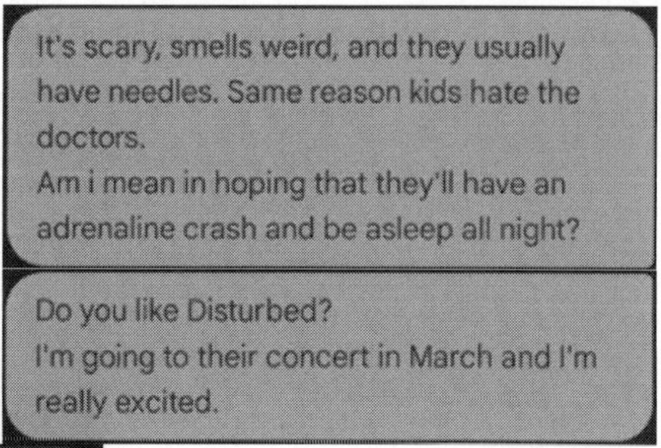

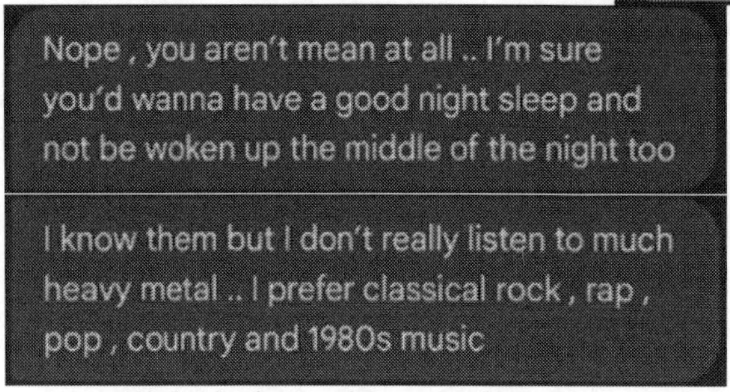

Ugh, he's an 80s music guy. I grew up with 80s music. It's terrible and nostalgic. I always wonder how many drugs people were on when they made 80s music, especially the music videos. Cocaine was a big thing then, and I feel that it really showed in the music that was created. I didn't say any of that to him, but the 80s isn't my favorite decade.

There are other reasons for that, I think, but I'm not ready to get into all that with him. Especially not through texting.

I fall asleep waiting for any further reply.

Day 13

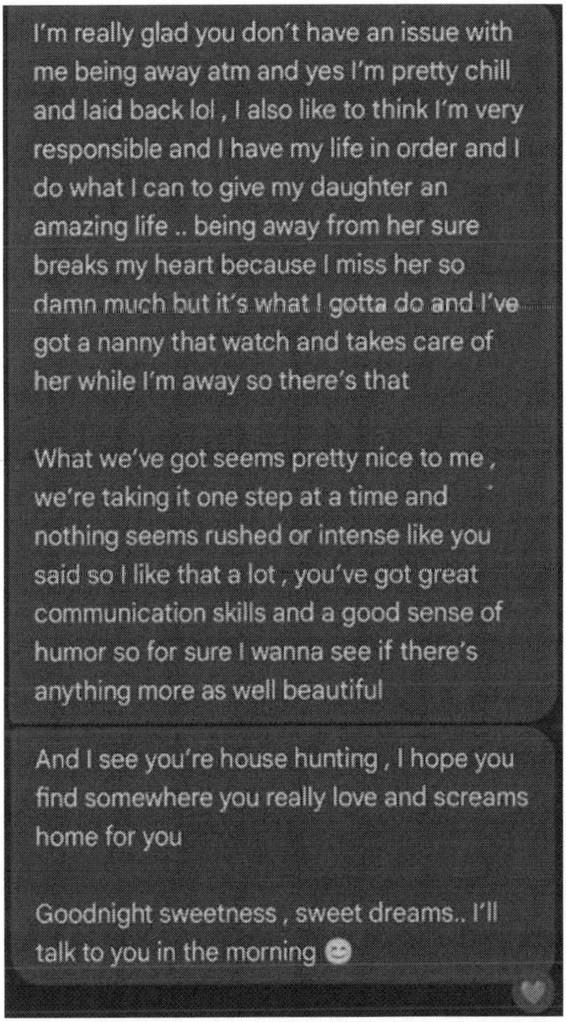

"Ugh, he is so freaking cute," I tell the cats as if they care about anything other than their breakfast. "He seems like such a good dad and loves his little girl like I love you two. I think I'm in trouble, guys."

I feed them and text Daniel back with a stupid grin on my face.

Holy cow, they slept through the night! I wasnt allowed to listen to Disturbed when I was in high school (when they were big), but I caught their rendition of sound of silence as an adult and have discovered how much I enjoy them. Not all of it, but quite a lot is really good. I'm also mildly obsessed with Ed sheeran. Love country, but not the twangy stuff. Rap depends on my mood and who it is. The rest, I'm totally into.

I don't know if it helps, but my ex is an electrician, and he travels all around northern Nevada for work and was gone a lot. Im used to being on my own and keeping myself entertained. He'd be gone all week, usually come home on the weekend, and then leave again. It was honestly the reason our marriage worked for so long. I think I was able to ignore how massively one-sided our relationship was and how broken it was for years.

There were things I learned about that, though. I'm totally OK with living on my own or having a partner that isn't always here physically. I'm relatively low maintenance but need to feel wanted and appreciated. I'm a giver, and it's extremely easy for people to take me for granted. So, even if someone isn't with me physically, texting or calling to let me know they think of me is important to me. Telling me im appreciated matters. And when we are together, I like touch. Holding hands, snuggles, sex, whatever. I may be rambling, but just trying to let you know that you being gone isn't a big deal to me.

Stop, I think as I start texting again. *You're oversharing and rambling. You're going to scare this guy off. Hold some of your crazy back! For the love of all that is holy, stop texting!* And my fingers keep going. If I could peel them away from the phone, I'd totally be facepalming right now. I'm never going to hear from him again.

> I want to find something, too. It's been very frustrating trying to find something out here. Everything in a decent area is insanely expensive, and the places that are in the price range I'm willing to buy in need more work than I can do on my own. It's worse in Virginia. And when I do find something that i like, either the realtor or my sister, Tracy tries to talk me out of it. Tracy thinks I should have a mini mansion, and I keep having to remind her that I'm alone and have zero desire to clean that much space. But everything I've talked to her about, she craps on, so it's hard to get excited about things.

Day 14

Morning, handsome. Are you ok?

I wake up mildly worried that I haven't heard from Daniel. He's texted every day since we first started talking, so not hearing from him is weird. Either I scared him off with my long, rambling texts, or something happened at work.

I spiral all day, the distractions of D&D, looking at the townhouse, and my writing didn't help. I catch myself checking for texts every hour until I fall into a fitful sleep.

Day 15

Hello beautiful, good evening.. how was your day today?

I'm sorry I haven't been able to respond to your texts .. it's been extremely busy 3 days for me , I miss talking to you and hope to hear from you soon 😊

I immediately look at my phone to see if he texted and feel relief and disappointment at seeing that I missed his texts. I kind of almost wish he hadn't told me he was deployed. Now I'm worried about him, and I've never even met him. Stupid feelings.

Hey. My day yesterday was long but good. I'm glad you're ok. Sorry it's been a rough couple of days. Hugs!

Hi , good morning 😃

Why was your day long , I thought you don't work weekends

And it's all good , it's been really tough and extremely hot , the temperature today is over 110 degrees right now

Oh, yuck. That's awful. We're getting another cold front, so of course, I'm freezing again. Lol
I don't work weekends, but I had D&D and then looked at that townhouse. I did a lot of driving yesterday - was on the road 6 hours. It was just long. It was a good day, though. You jump out of perfectly good helicopters this week? I have no idea how you do that. It's very impressive. I get freaked out on the top parts of ladders. Heights and I are not friends.

Do you actually get your day off today?

I send him a picture of me with wet hair just hanging out in my office. My shirt is a little low-cut, so I know he's getting some cleavage. It'll be interesting to see what he has to say about it.

Hair's wet cuz shower.

I don't hear from him all day, but I don't worry too much about it since I know it's supposed to be his day off and he's probably relaxing or sleeping. I go out to look at houses with my neighbor, knowing that I love the layout of this one home, but I'm not sure about the location. I want another opinion, and there was an open house with a different layout from the same builder.

"I really like this open concept," I tell my neighbor. "But I'm not sure about how they did the flooring, and it smells like cigarettes in here. I know they cleaned and tried to get rid of it, but that stench seeps into the walls, and you can almost never get rid of it."

"Really?" she asks. "I don't smell anything. This house is super cute, too."

"I'm allergic to cigarettes, so I'm super sensitive to it," I explain.

We thank the realtor for showing us the house and head on home.

Daniel texts me shortly after I walk in the door and sit down with the cats.

Hi beautiful, good evening and yes todays my off day so I slept in all day

I got some well needed rest

How was your day today ?

I see you had a long day yesterday and I sure hope it was worth it and I hope you liked the house you went to check out

Thanks for the picture , you look really gorgeous and I don't mean to be inappropriate or anything but you look very busty and I love it lmao 🤣

I'm glad you were able to sleep, that's what I figured you were doing. Feel better?
My day was good. I went to an open house with my neighbor today, and we both like it, but I'm not a big fan of the location. I'm ridiculously picky. I liked the townhouse too, and im actually leaning more towards that, which i find really weird.

Glad you liked it. I am busty.

Yeah , I feel a lil bit better

Good. I hope this week is quieter for you.

And that's good to hear , you should be picky because it's gonna be you're house that you're gonna be possibly spending the rest of your life so I'd advice you take time to really look and be certain it's what you want

And yes I can see that you are busty , I love it lol 😆

Can you send a full picture of you ?

I sure hope this week is quieter but I really doubt it , shit is bonkers down here hahaha

I will, tomorrow. The pics on my profile are current.

Okay then , I'll wait for a recent one lol and will send you one of mine as well

Wyd ?

You had dinner yet ?

Im in my jammies right now. My neighbor can be draining and im being a vegetable tonight

Im playing a game and watching castle. Just lounging on the couch.

Oh , you're with your neighbor right now ?

I had ledos pizza with my neighbor. No, she's back at her house.

Oh okay , it's nice .. it's good you have someone to talk to and hang out with

Do you like to cook ?!

And what's your favorite meal to make ?

I do like to cook. Not sure if have a favorite meal to make.

Do you?

That's surprising

I don't really understand that statement. Is it because I'm a woman, and we should just like cooking, or is there something else behind that statement? I know he's kind of food-obsessed, so I try not to read into it, but I can feel my hackles raise. I spent my entire life with people trying to ensure I lived up to the stereotypical woman, and I'm not that.

While I love cooking, baking, and feeding people, that's not my beginning and end of joy in life. It's more because I like to make people happy, and feeding them usually does that.

Why?

You don't have a favorite meal you enjoying making or a meal that you crave after a long day at work ?

There's a soup I like that I can never remember the name of. It's a Mexican soup with noodles and tomato sauce

And yes I cook , I believe I'm a good cook and I've been told so but I prefer to grill , I'm really great on the grill , steaks , fish , hotdogs, burgers .. I can make it all

I roll my eyes. Why do all guys think they're gods on the grill? Why is grilling more manly than cooking in a kitchen, and, therefore, more widely accepted that men grill? I love grilling and am quite good at it, not that anyone in my life has believed me without having to have me prove it.

Nice , I love me some good soup

I like grilling, too. That was a big issue with my ex.
I make a bunch of stuff. But I love baking. I used to go all out for Halloween and would make all the food myself. I spent days cooking and baking prior to the parties.

Oh nice , so what was the issue exactly ?

That he doesn't help with the cooking ?

Because he worked out of town a lot, he didn't grill as much as I did, so i grill better than him and when I cleaned the outside of the grill, it got scratched. He didn't talk to me for two days after that and accused me of using a scotch pad on it to destroy it. I didn't. I used soap and water with a rag. It was just insanely dirty.

I make the best air fried pork chops.

Really, that's very childish of him

So care who grills the best , as long as the food comes out great , I'm good lol 😆

And I'd definitely love to try those pork chops , I'd kill for some right now .. the food we eat here is shit , mre that has been packed and stored of months , sometimes years

Yah. It wasn't a great relationship. He is very selfish and wasn't supportive in anything i wanted to do for me.

Ugh, that's tough. When do you come home, or can't you say?

I'm sorry to hear that , how long were you married for ?

And why didn't you see all this signs before yall got married ?

What signs? I think. I was nineteen when I met him. We were completely different people. There weren't signs that we'd wind up being incompatible. We were young, starting life, trying to figure things out. We were together for over twenty years. No one is the same as they were twenty years ago.

It is tough but that's how it is down here and I've gotta find a way to deal with it even though it's not pleasing and I've been here for months , few more weeks to go till our objectives are completed and I get to come home

We were married for 20 years and together for 24. It wasn't all bad. He's a good guy with a lot of positive qualities. We just grew apart and aren't good for each other. He needs a wife that wants nothing more than to be his mom.

We were young when we started dating and got married. I was dealing with a lot of insecurities from childhood trauma and was taught to put my husband first and my needs didn't matter. I've since healed and realized I have worth. My ex didn't really like that I was making myself more of a priority than him and our relationship suffered.

I know I'm a good person and an amazing partner. And I want someone who will call me beautiful, even when i dont feel like it; and appreciate what I have to offer as a person and a partner.

Oh okay , I understand and totally get what you're saying

You said your divorce has been finalized, when exactly did it get finalized?

And do yall still talk at all ?

September 27.
We do. I send him pictures of the cats. I'm not interested in ever taking him back, if that's what you're worried about. I was done a long time ago. Just needed the courage to leave and change my entire life. Plus, I was waiting for the cat to pass because I didn't want to leave any of my cats, and he was his person.

Oh okay , it's all good .. I'm not worried , I'm just curious

But I'm glad to hear you're never going back , better for me hahaha

Leaving a long term relationship like that because my needs weren't being met and never would be, wasn't easy. It almost would've been easier if we hated each other. My sister, Tracy, still lives in NV and talks to him. She likes to make sure I get a nice guilt trip each time she talks to him. When I left, he said he'd wait for me to feel better and come back. Which just reinforced why I was leaving. I guess he's now realizing that I'm really not coming back and he's grieving.

Today is Furry's birthday. She's 18.

I told her she was an adult now, so she needed to find her own place. Then laughed and gave her baby food. My neighbor suggested it because Furry has become a very picky eater. She loves the turkey, chicken, and ham baby food. I have no idea what to do with the glass jars though.

And he disappears. *Hopefully, he's sleeping,* I think. *He works entirely too much.* I text him one last time before going to bed.

Goodnight

Day 16

I take a picture of me in a dress and send it to him, smiling the entire time. I've never liked pictures of me, but he seems to love seeing me and thinks I'm beautiful. It makes me bold and brings my confidence back up a little. The dress hugs my curves and shows off my arms, so my tattoos are visible. We've not talked about how he feels about tattooed women yet. My ex hated them, but I love them. Each one has a story or a reason I wanted it on my body. I hope Daniel doesn't have an issue with them.

I find myself checking my phone all day, to the point where I take the ringer off silent and actually allow it to ring for the first time in well over a decade. Not for the first time do I realize that I actually care about Daniel more than I expected to. He's on my mind throughout the day, and my heart skips a beat each time I see a text from him. I'm not really sure what to do or say about how I'm feeling. I love and hate feeling this way in equal measure.

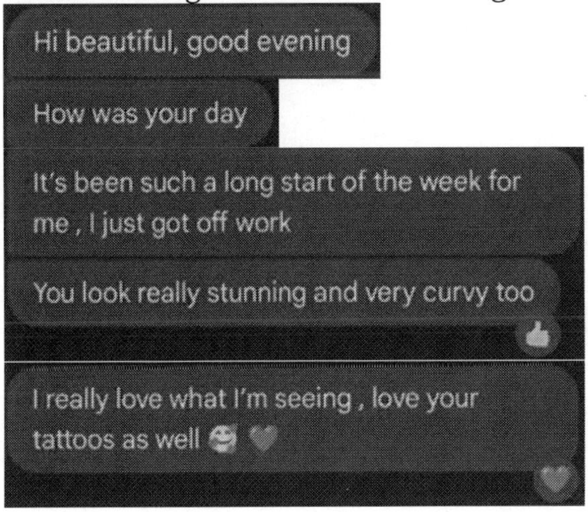

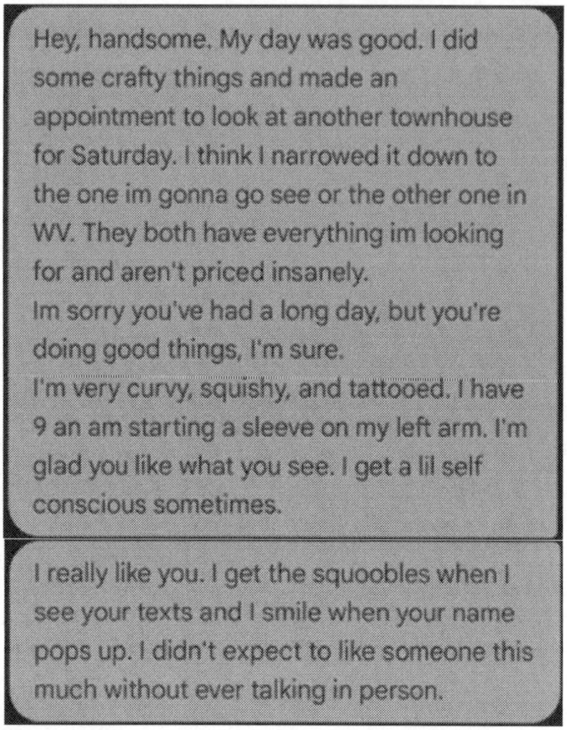

I blush at the admission; mildly afraid I'm going to scare him off. But I think he feels the same, or close to what I feel. *He has to*, I think, heart pounding in my chest. *I really, really like this guy*.

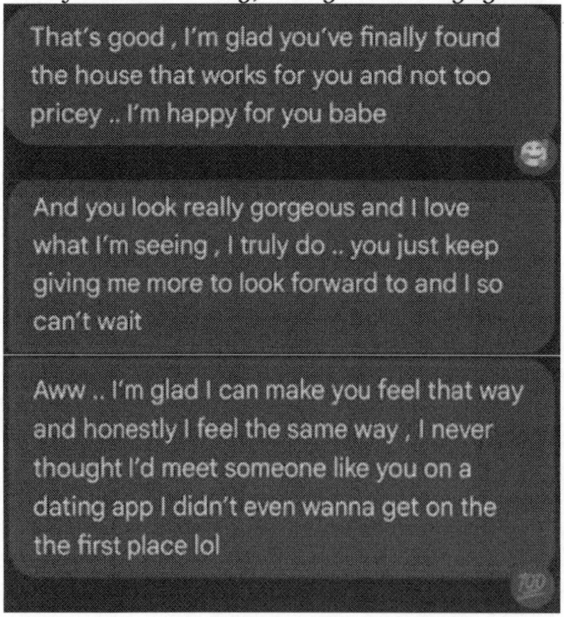

I laugh, thinking the same thing. I didn't really want to get on that app either, but it really worked out. He's been just about everything I've been looking for, and I realize that I want him here with me more than anything else in the world. Our conversations are easy and feel natural. I really want to be the person he comes home to, when his deployment is up, and I really want to see where this will go. I can see us working out and doing things together. I love how devoted he is to his daughter and how he talks to me.

It's so surreal but I'm glad I did , I truly am

I really can't wait to see you, too. I really want to kiss you.

I feel this is a beginning of something really special.. I just hope we can keep getting to know each other and keep improving

I hope so, too

I would love that and I'll kiss you so hard while grabbing those curvy cheeks and squeezing em lol

Omg. I love it.

Seeing that picture of you already got me making things up in my head lmao

Yah? Fork, you're cute.

A part of me really wants to know what you're thinking, but i have no idea when we can make that a reality and that's just not fair. Lol

And we are so making those thoughts reality.

Well I try lol and we will make it a reality , I'm sure of that 100 percent

Thank god.

Jean Booth

I kinda enjoy that we're far apart right now .. it really gives us a opportunity to take things one step at a time and not actually get to know each other and not rush into anything

So when I'm home , it's time for some action and trust me when I say you're gonna be up all night long !!!

Do you get all goofy when talking to me? Or do you remain quiet, so no one knows who you're texting?

Im completely down for that.

There's zero way I can hide my sappy grin when we text.
Im honestly glad things have worked out this way too. It wasn't what I was expecting. I think this is better.

Day 17

I'm exhausted. Furry has dementia, of that I'm almost certain, and of course I forgot to ask the vet when I was there. Denial is a beautiful thing. I have absolutely no idea how to deal with it. But she doesn't sleep much anymore, so no one is allowed to sleep if she can't. I've been up most of the night and decided to get some work done on my books before logging onto my actual workday.

Trump is being sworn into office today, so we're expecting a bunch of executive orders to come through. I'm not political in any capacity, but after hearing the rumors for a while, I'm nervous about what to expect for my job. Sure enough, we hear about a ton of orders, and I have no idea what they mean for our agency yet. The emails we keep getting are from people freaking out, scared that we're all going to lose our jobs. It's not making for a relaxing day at all.

Hi gorgeous

Good evening

How was your day today ?

I miss talking to you and I hope to hear from you soon

Hey, handsome. My day was ok. Trump signed an executive order canceling remote work for us, which doesn't affect me yet, but it's causing a lot of tension at work. How was your day?

Did you fall asleep during our chat last night, or get busy? You usually say goodnight so I figured you were busy with stuff and was trying not to distract with texts.

Furry woke up at around 230 last night, and i couldn't get back to sleep, so I've been up and freezing for a while. I need some snuggles.

Are you still working?

I just got off work right now

It's 12:39am over here

What's the time over there ?

Oh shit. That's late. It's 645 here.

Pm

Your poor internal clock is all messed up.

Are you going to bed?

What time did you start work today?

<two hours later>

Good night.

I've been off bout an hour ago , I needed to get something to eat and showered

It's been such a long , hot and dusty day

And yes , my internal clock is all fucked up lol ... i usually start my day 6am for the morning drills then start my shift after

Sorry to hear trumps executive order is already causing tension for you and it's just day one , the next 4 years is gonna be crazy lol

Ugh, that's terrible. I'd be so bitchy by the end of the day, lol.

I'm really impressed with you. You've got so much going on, and you're starting a relationship with me, and you're always so nice. I think you're amazing

I hope today is better for you.

Day 18

It's 2 am and I can't sleep. I wonder if Daniel is awake and available, so I start texting. He's been on my mind anyway.

> Do you like seeing a bunch (or long) texts from me, or is it annoying? I can't sleep tonight. Tomorrow is gonna be rough. Sometimes, I hesitate to text you because I don't want you to think im annoying. But I absolutely love picking up the phone and seeing texts from you, so i thought I'd ask how you felt before reading into things. In my mind, right now we only have texting and are trying to learn about each other. So infodumps aren't necessarily bad. They are in a story, and when we can actually "chat," i find that amazing. But i want to know you and think you feel the same? So, because of the limitations we have right now, I kinda think the infodumps are necessary

I finally fall asleep but know the next day is going to be rough because I have to work and I'll have only had less than five hours of sleep—and that's if the cats actually leave me be for the rest of the night. These sleepless nights were really starting to get to me.

> Hey, babe. I hope you're ok and are having a good day. I miss talking with you. Kisses.

Two hours fly by with me working in a semi-zombified state. My phone starts ringing.

"I'm exhausted," I answer as I see Bex's name on my screen.

"Oh, my god, right? I wish these damn hot flashes would stop already," she complains back. "I'm lucky if I even got five hours of sleep. Jed ordered me Starbucks, and I'll probably have him send another order at lunch."

"Oh, man, I miss Starbucks before work," I reply. "It's like twenty minutes away, and I need a coffee just to get the stupid coffee."

We laugh at each other before devolving into our normal pre-work conversation for her and my morning tea break. We talk about her family and the annoyances she's having at work until she asks about how things are over here.

"Everyone is super-stressed out about the executive orders over here. So far, they don't seem to be affecting our department, but rumors are flying everywhere. I've gotten a ton of emails and meeting invites to update us on what's going on and to try to keep people calm. It's cool that they're keeping us informed, but I feel almost more stressed out with all the information. I'm still brand-new here, and on probation. I'll be the first to be let go if something happens," I vent to Bex, knowing she's a safe person to talk to. "I wouldn't have left Peter if I knew I'd lose my job right away."

"Um, yes, you would have," she interjects. "You were dying here, and we all would've made you leave. You're doing so much better there. I can't remember the last conversation we've had when you didn't struggle to breathe. This was a good decision, and you're going to be okay."

"I know," I reply, resigned. I knew she was right. I didn't leave for the job. I left for my health, and it was the right decision, no matter how nervous I was to be living on a single income for the first time since I was eighteen. "It's just scary, and I'm not sure what's happening, you know? I miss the safety net of two incomes."

"Yeah, I understand that, but you'll make things work. You're smart and hardworking. No matter what, you'll be okay. You know that, right?"

And this is why she's my best friend. She's always believed in me and reminds me that I'm awesome, even when I forget it. Granted, I do the same for her, so it works out.

"How's your harem going?" she asks.

I laugh.

"I've stopped talking to most of the guys," I start. "Michael and Kevin both ghosted me when I told them I wanted to meet them, so they've been blocked. Jeff still calls, and I still don't really know what to do about him. He's so pessimistic that it makes me uncomfortable. I feel like if we tried to have a relationship I'd spend most of the time trying to build him up, and I just don't have the energy to do that all the time. I want someone who's got confidence in themselves and can find at least a little positivity in their life."

"Yeah, that's annoying," she agrees. "What about the military guy?" Her tone gets playful and teasing.

"I really freaking like him, Bex," I confess. "Like way more than I expected or think I should. He's so sweet. He calls me beautiful—"

"They've all called you beautiful," she interrupts. "And you are."

I laugh, not believing it. I'm cute or borderline pretty, not beautiful. But I don't argue.

"He's sweet and conversation with him is easy, like it is with us. I look forward to his texts, even though they don't come as frequently as I'd like. And I hate that he's deployed." I knew I told him I wouldn't share anything about our conversations, but best friends don't count. Bex knows everything about me and I about her. It's just a given. Best friends and spouses are the clause in any secret keeping.

"Have you talked to him on the phone or video, yet?" she asks.

"No," I begin, pausing as I hear a beep on my phone indicating that I have an incoming text. I open my message app and squeal. "He's texting me! He almost never texts this early. Do you want me to let you go?"

"No." She laughs. "I like hearing you happy, and I'm just doing evaluations anyway."

I text him back, mostly ignoring Bex and knowing she'll understand. She bails on me any time her husband calls or texts too, so I don't worry about being rude.

Hi beautiful, good morning to you .. I hope you have an amazing day today

I miss talking to you and I took a picture for you , I'll send it to you in a few

Can't wait to hear from you

I hope you do too.

There you are !

I smile, hearing the excitement in his text.

How's your day going?

How are you ?

Im way better now. Stupid grin and all.

Aww , that's so sweet

It's been a busy and such a hot day but I'm on a lil break right now so I can talk

Im talking with my bestie in NV and she's laughing because I got really excited to see your text

How's your day and what are you up to ?

Nice.

Day has been good.

I hope those executive orders aren't affecting your job too much

Aww that's so sweet , you told her about me ?

Of course i did. I like you.

We don't really know how much it will affect my department yet. Right now, it doesn't change anything. Yet.

Ok, since I've got you for a min, when's your birthday?

And of course I don't have a problem with your long texts , I really appreciate it
It shows me you care and you're invested in this and I love it so don't you ever stop , I wanna know all about you .. I really like you a lot and I see this growing into something absolutely special
Talking to you gives me more motivation to keep going and have me getting excited and having something to look forward to

Aww that's so sweet , I told some of my mates about you as well .. because they see me more on my phone and was curious to who I was talking to lol

Mates. I laugh at the European term; he must be overseas a lot to pick up that language. My smile doesn't leave my face as I read his text. I'm glad he reads my messages and actually likes my rambling.

I picture him sitting on a bench, typing away on his phone with the same stupid smile on his face as I have on mine, and it has my emotions all over the place. I haven't felt this giddy excitement in a very long time.

Well my birthday is August 10th babe

Im really glad. About all of that.

Jean Booth

What's yours ?

Nice. You're a leo

Yup , a lion 🦁

Haha

Mines July 16. I'm a crab. Lol

This is the best part of my day.

Wow , our birthdays are so close

Less than a month from each other

The dates are, years, not so much.

This is gonna be so niceeee

We have so much in common, it's surreal

It really is.

I believe us meeting each other isn't just a mere coincidence because everything feels so right with you

It's really crazy but it's good crazy 😄

And who cares about the years , I don't

Btw , I've been trying to ask you lol .. what's your full name ?

Omg, right! It's everything I've wanted. I told my friends I wanted what they have and I wouldn't settle for lwss again. And I feel like I'm finding that in you.

Annie Winters

Hello Beautiful

You?

Are you on any socials?

Aww , I'm glad I can be that for you babe .. there's so much more to come , let me home first

Nice , I'm Daniel Rodriguez Fanelli

Yes , I have Facebook and instagram but I'm rarely on there because of the nature of my job , I haven't used it in years

How about you ?

Ok, so, weird insecure me has to know - are you talking with anyone else? I can't believe I was the only one who was interested in you.

Im on all of them for the books. Even have my own website AWinters.com . I'm usually only on Instagram though

I cant wait for you to come home.

I was thinking about it last night - when you asked me if I was cool with long-distance, and I am. This is a challenge though, because we're getting to know each other long distance. We don't have the base that most people start with. I'm not saying it's bad or anything. It's just different. More of a challenge to see if we actually like each other for who we are, instead of what we look like

Honestly , I was talking to others on the app but I haven't been on it since we started texting and getting to know each other
I'm a one woman type of guy and I don't like to share or be shared and I also don't want the attention of whoever I'm talking to be divided so I wouldn't do that to whoever I'm talking to as well

I wasn't sure of that with you , I'm sure you've got tons of guys trying to talk and get with you lol

Oh nice , I'll check out your website when I have time babe 😀

Same.
I was honestly surprised at the number of dudes that liked my profile. I talked to a handful the first like 5 days and dropped em all.

No worries about looking at the site. I was just sharing. ☺

I love when you call me babe.

I also love your honesty. Relationships can't exist without trust and honesty.

Oh wow , so you're saying I'm the one person you're talking to right now ?

I must be really special Lmaoo 😂

And of course I'm gonna check the site out , I want to know all about you and it wouldn't cost me a thing to just surf through it so it's all good babe

Yep. You are! I can see us together and Im all in.

Well if there isn't trust and honesty .. there can't be a good foundation for an amazing relationship, it's very essential

Aww that's so sweet , you always manage make me smile and blush 😊

You're a really sweet woman

I'm really glad to have met you

That's awesome. I don't think my ex ever looked at it.
Im so glad we met. Like, insanely glad.

Well that's why he's gone and I'm here , he's old news and I'm gonna treat you like the queen that you are

You already do. 🤗🤗

And I know it's gonna be reciprocated, I can tell you're a good and kind woman who just wants to be loved correctly

I cant believe it's only been 16 days.

lol , this is just the beginning and just words

The action will come

Its so much. And I hope you know that you will be well taken care of when you get home.

Gutter question, because all I can think about is you and the promise of all night... do you like tacos? Because I love sausage. Like a lot. And I really want to hear what you sound like when I'm on my knees in front of you.

Do you think you'll be home before the end of March? Im going to a fantasy ball with my sisters and would like to bring you, if you're interested and here.

Also, I want my picture, sir. I don't have nearly enough of them.

Please be safe while you're there. I'll be thinking about you. I have (hopefully) my final background investigation in 20 minutes. Barf. Im sure it'll be fine, I'm just not a fan.
Kisses

<One and a half hours later>

That meeting is finally over. 1.5 hours left of my workday, so yay! I haven't stopped smiling since you messaged. You really are the highlight of my day.
The cats have been snoozing all morning, which is rare for them. Usually, they bug me at least once every 2 hours. I think they realized I'm happy and don't feel the need to make sure I know they love me. I have no idea how I'd have done all this without them.

Does Bailey like cats or does she try to eat them? My dad's pit isn't good with other animals and killed my uncle's dog this summer. What about Trixie? Do you talk to her often? Is she in pre-k? Do they still have that? My niece, Kate is 13 and about to start high school. My other sisters homeschool, so I'm not familiar with when they usually start doing the school thing anymore.

My cats are fine with other animals as long as they stay away from them or have low energy. Spot has experienced my neighbors dog a few times and other than poofing up and hissing, he hasn't done anything to her dog. But her dog is a spaz and really wants to chase Spot.

Speaking of, Spot sits down in front of me and meows. I can tell that he'd like to go outside, so I get up, put my jacket on, and go outside with him. I can't let him out on his own because of the bald eagles and the turkey vultures that live around here. They're large enough to be able to pick his fat butt up off the ground and fly away with him. I don't make it more than five minutes before I'm shivering and can't feel my fingers, so I make him go back inside with me. He grumbles and meows his displeasure the whole way inside, only stopping when I give him treats.

Holy shit its cold out. Spot wanted to go outside since the dog is at daycare and my fingers are shivering.

Government hiring freeze in effect. 53 people who were offered employment no longer have the offer in our organization. So far, 153 people have been impacted by his EOs and it's day 2. Ugh. I'm almost afraid to buy this townhouse. I'm going to, but dang.

<two hours later>

I miss my sewing machine. It's in storage, and a huge part of wanting my own place and not wanting to wait until the insanity dies down is that. I always forget how much i sew and how much i enjoy it until I have a "fancy" machine to work with. They're infuriating.
How's your day? Thanks for making mine so great.
Also, your perception and slight aggression against my ex was hella hot. "Well that's why he's gone and I'm here , he's old news and I'm gonna treat you like the queen that you are"
Favorite.

<two hours later>

I hope you're not still working and that you're sleeping. You have such long days. I'm not sure if you're allowed to call or if texting is all you can do, but you're welcome to call me. It'd be nice to hear your voice. If you can't, I completely understand and am looking forward to the next time you can chat.
What do you like to do for fun, when you're home, outside of eating? Are you bilingual?

<two hours later>

What do you need out of a partner? I know you've been single since your wife died - I'm so sorry that happened, and I'm here if you ever want to talk about her or feelings - and I was just wondering. You're obviously very strong, competent, and able to figure out your life. What would a good partnership look like to you?

I can't seem to stop thinking about Daniel. My fingers fly over the keyboard on my phone as I text, a little grin on my face at just the thought of him reading them. I have it bad for him. I want to talk to him all day and would even be happy to talk on the phone all day with him if it meant I could hear his voice. I hated talking on the phone. I was much happier with texts.

> My friends tease me that my ex set the bar so low that the next person I'm with could suffer their feet on the ground and still leap over it. And while they're not wrong, I've learned what I need over the years. I need someone who will love and accept me for who I am, quirks and all. I crave touch. Not just sex, but casual touch. I need someone who's smart and independent but still caring. I need to feel wanted, not needed. As a kid, you need your parents - you shouldn't need your partner like that. You should want them. I think they should be an improvement to your life - make you want to be better because of their love and support. Does that make sense? I had to teach my ex how to make appointments and how to use the computer before I left.

I head to bed, lying there, tossing and turning and unable to sleep. I leaf through the reels on Instagram for a while, trying to force myself to stop thinking about him for five freaking minutes. It only helps a little. I want to know everything about him. And he said he likes my long, random texts. I guess we'll find out if he was telling the truth or not. Two hours fly by on Insta, and I switch back over to my texts.

Random middle of the night musings because I can't freaking sleep. Again.
I think I'm a good partner, but I want to make sure I'm what you're looking for. I love taking care of people but hate being taken for granted. Touch is important - holding hands, hugs, booty grabs, couch cuddles, random grazes just because you can. One of my biggest love languages is gift giving, but I'm not great at receiving. I usually feel more guilty than grateful. I like feeding people. Kinda goes along with the gift giving because it's fulfilling a need, but less like I'm trying to buy your love. I'll do random things simply because it reminds me of you, or I want to make you smile. And I love sex. It's the deepest form of intimacy you can show a person and was the #1 issue with my ex. He never cared if I enjoyed it, and when he was done, we were done.

I need someone who will support me in my dreams - not financially, but how you've told me that I'll be a success with my writing - even if it's not something you're passionate about. I'll be your biggest cheerleader and supporter. I listen and will either help you find a solution or just sit in the dark with you until you're ready. I love to laugh and joke and think the punny, corny, dad-joke humor is hilarious. I want to experience life, not just couch surf it.

Day 19

> Gah. Be careful what you wish for... i obviously think about you a lot. Is it weird to miss you this much when we've never actually met?

I get a text from one of my besties letting me know that her mother-in-law finally passed. She had cancer and thankfully didn't suffer, but her husband wasn't dealing well with it. We talk in our group chat for a little bit, but there's not really anything I can do across the country except support her and be there for her. It was one of the things I hated about my move. Everyone I loved lived in another state, and I felt so impotent.

<three hours later>

> One of my besties lost her mother in law to cancer this morning. She went quickly, which is a blessing, but it's so sad. Her stepson and husband are numb right now, and I'm sure they'll be a mess later. A part of me wishes I could be there to help support them. They're some of my favorite people. It brings big, messy feelings to the surface.
> I hope you're ok. And I hope you know that there's someone out here that (obvi) thinks about you and wants you home safely. You said I give you motivation to keep going and have something to look forward to. I feel the same. Please be careful, and if you can, just let me know you're ok. I don't know how not to worry about you, and I know it's crazy and intense, but there it is. Kisses.

<two hours later>

> Hey babe, just thinking about you. Hope you're ok. 🥰 😘

<five hours later>

I head to bed, worry for Daniel causing anxiety to surface. I've never really had anxiety before, so this isn't something I know how to deal with well. I take a sleeping pill, knowing that even with it, I'm such a light sleeper that I'll wake up if my phone pings for a text. I close my eyes, hoping he'll text and let me know he's ok.

Day 20

Good morning, babe.

I hope you're ok. I miss you. I'm used to you texting at least once every day and am worried about you. Mostly, I worry about you being safe in a place i know isn't. A small part of me worries that I've scared you off, but I think we're on the same page, so that's silly, right?
These executive orders are stressing me out, and I'm barely sleeping. Which isn't helping anything. anyway, I'm thinking about you.

Hi babe , good morning.. how have you been?
The past few days have been very hectic and crazy for us with the new president getting sworn in , we've had a lot to do and objectives to carry out and I haven't had anytime to be on my phone ... I see you've left me a ton of texts and I appreciate it and I'll go through it one by one , I miss you as well and was thinking about you while I was gone and can't wait to hear from you

The amount of relief I feel at hearing Daniel's text tone has my body slumping in my office chair and every cell in my back finally relaxing for the first time in days. I'm hit with the knowledge that I'm in love with him. I wasn't looking for this and wasn't sure I wanted it this soon after my divorce, but I could no longer deny it to myself. I was massively, completely, irrevocably in love with a man I'd only ever texted. I'd been terrified about his safety—more so than even I realized until hearing that tone and reading his text.

This knowledge scared me almost as much as his disappearance over the past couple of days. So many thoughts rushed through my head, and I pushed them all away, so I could focus on what I was certain was limited time to talk to him.

Im so glad you're ok.

No worries about me, just be safe.

I'm ok , better now that I've heard from you

How have you been , it's seems like you've had so much going on from your texts lol

Me too

it's been a rough week.
But it's so good to hear from you.

It really surprised me how much I care about you and just how much it means to me when you can just say a quick hi. I know you're busy and your job is dangerous and I promise I'm not super needy and high maintenance, but I was more worried about you than anything else.

Like, I know I more than like you, but I wasn't expecting this. Especially not this soon and with just texts.

I'm glad to hear from you as well , it's been a very rough week for me as well , we had to go on raids days ago and weren't allowed to have our devices with us so that's why I couldn't text but I missed you so damn much and I knew you would be worried and would've left me a ton of texts and I'm glad I wasn't wrong

I rushed to my phone as soon as we got back today

You weren't wrong.

Do you have a few minutes now?

Are you allowed to call?

I'd give almost anything to hear his voice, to talk to him and to be able to tell him how I feel without texting it. I want to hear him. Hell, if I'm being honest with myself, I want to climb up him like a koala up a tree and never let go.

Of course you aren't needy , we simply like each other and that's what happens when two people are Into each other and have something real together

Aww babe , what do you mean exactly when you say you more than like me ?

Am I gonna scare you off if i do? Because, this scares the shit out of me. I didn't expect it and wasn't looking for it. But those three little words are there...

It feels both too soon and like we've always been here.

I think about you every day. I want you in my life. I want to be an integral part of yours. Every time I cook, I wonder if you'd like it, if you were here, would you be cooking with me? Would you want me to be part of Trixies life? Would she like me?

Of course I'm not scared , why would I be ... I just told you that while I was away , I was thinking about you all through and rushed to get my phone as soon as I got back

I feel the same way , how you feel .. I swear to you , it's absolutely mutual

I'm in love with you

There. I said the words. I am either going to scare him off, which I don't think will happen, or he'll say them back, which I really hope he will. I'm shaking, the nervous butterflies in my stomach fluttering as I wait for his response.

And I don't care if it's too soon , it feels just right and feels like it's simply meant to be baby

I wish you were here, so much.

I promised you a picture before I left so here ya go 😆

The picture he sends is of him in shadow, sitting against what looks like his bed, a travel cot. I can see the dirt and a truck behind him, but what strikes me is how unbelievably young he looks. I know I look young for my age, but without his beard, he looks like he's about twenty-three. I cringe a little because of our age difference. I've never dated someone so much younger than me. I remind myself that he's thirty-five, and he wasn't *that* young.

I did like the fuzzy hair though. I always have on guys. I like how it feels when I run my hand over the stubble, both prickly and soft. It made me smile.

You shaved your hair! I like it. 😍

I love the fuzzy hair.

lol , I'm glad you do baby .. I had to shave my hair while being down here

Ugh 😩

I prefer my hair full , this makes me look way younger and I lost my beard too

Can't wait to grow em back

I definitely prefer the hair and beard, but youre still super hot.

And I feel absolutely the same way , my heart always get that tingly happy feeling whenever I get to talk to you so I totally believe I'm in love with you as well and I can't wait to have you in my arms and kiss every inch of you 🥰❤️

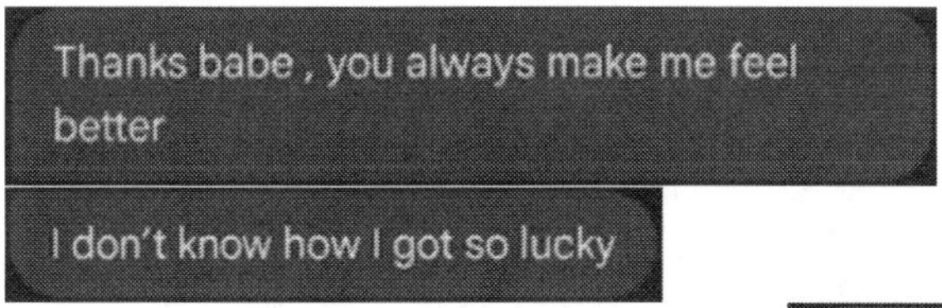

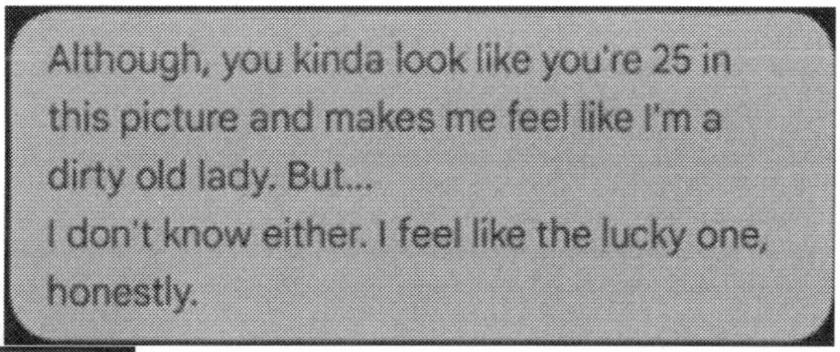

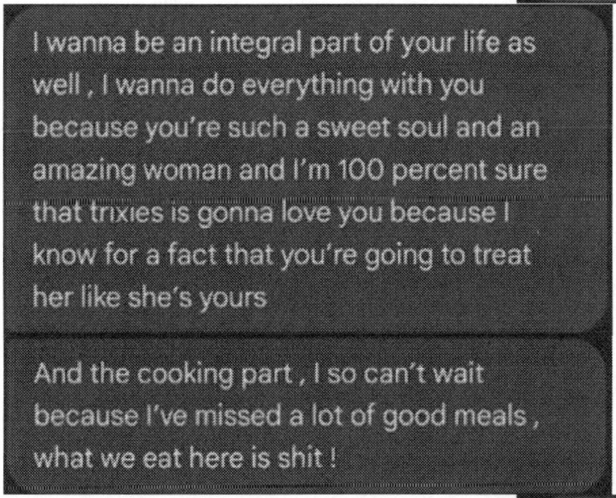

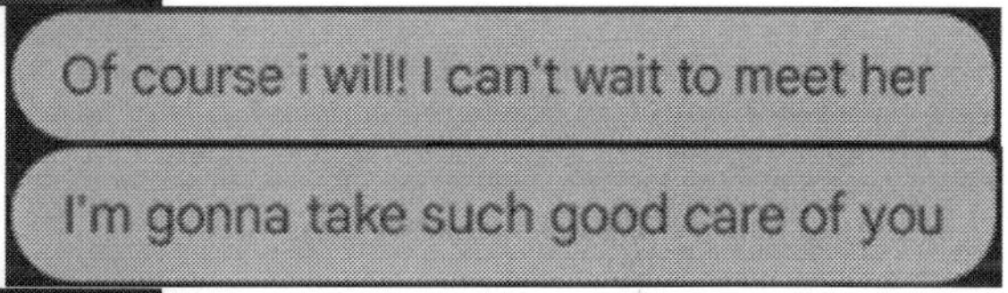

I laugh and groan at the same time. I think he's adorable, but I don't want him thinking I'm old. Forty-three isn't that old – I'm only eight years older than him. And with everything he's experienced in life, age really doesn't make a difference. I can feel myself melt as I read his words. He loves me.

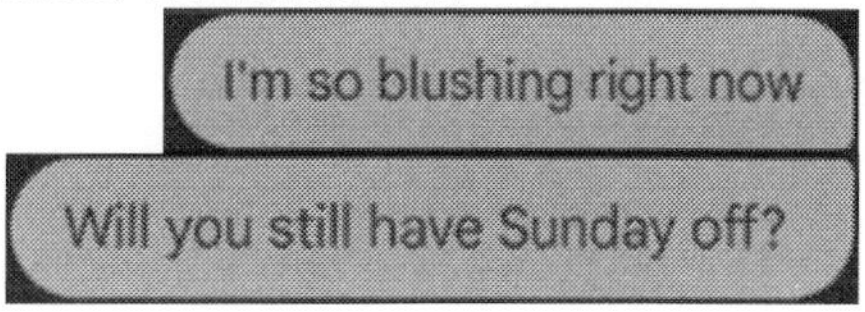

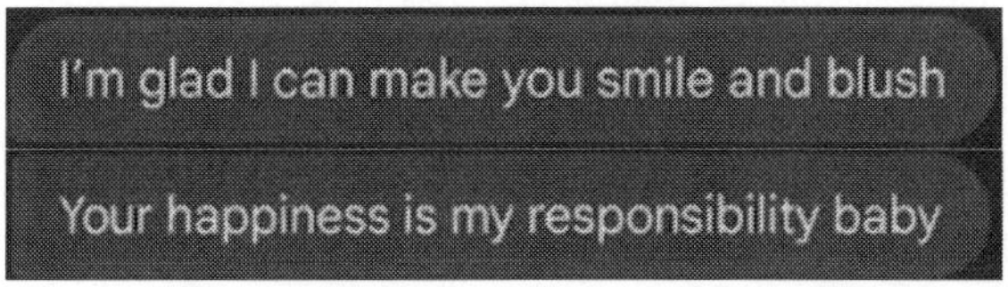

Jean Booth

And yes , I'm off Sundays

What have you been up to apart from writing of course lol

I see the executive orders have been affecting you , I hope it's not too much stress...

Smile, blush, feel like I'm loved and make my heart flutter. ❤️ you're it.
Im working on a blanket. I haven't crocheted in years, so thought I'd give it a try

I've been stressed out of my mind. I have no idea whats happening or if I should even try to get this townhouse, no matter how much I like it.

My parents are zero help. They just keep telling me I have a place with them and that everything's gonna be great.

If i hadn't met you, I'd probably just move back to Nevada and get my old job back. But that's not happening. Ever. I'm just trying to let go of as much as I can. It helps when you're around. Honestly, you're what I worry most about. I just want you safe and home. And while you're there, I want you in a bubble so you can't get hurt.
How much longer do you have with the military?

What's your absolute favorite meal? When you get home, I'll make it for you. Be safe. Love you.

I'm glad I can make you feel that way honey
and I didn't know you crochet too
You just do a lot of things , write , crochet,
you're so damn creative and I love it

Well it depends on what you wanna do
babe , I don't think you going back is a great
idea because you left in the first place for a
reason so you shouldn't even look back at
the past and all you should be focused on is
the future , our future

Your parents live in Nevada ?

And do they want you to come back and
move in with them ?

And about the townhouse , tell me more
about it .. do you have pictures and what's
the pricing like , do you really wanna get it
or would you simply wait till I'm back ?

I really do appreciate you worrying about
me but I'm fine , I can take care of myself ..
I'm trained and really one of the best at
what I do so put your mind at ease my love
I'm not gonna be here forever , I just have a
few more weeks to go and I'll be home to
you

They live in Ohio but are huge trum and my
ex supporters. Pricing is great. It's brand
new and cute. Ill send you a link.

I'm not into politics. At. All. My feeling is that it doesn't really matter who's elected into any seat. They're not looking out for the working family; they're trying to line their pockets and the pockets of their friends. To me, it doesn't matter what anyone followed or what political party they were involved in. It's all crap.

I'm not currently thrilled with our president though, and my feelings are solely based on how his orders are actively impacting my life and my career. Other than that, I have zero opinion on politics outside of hating it in general. My parents are very political, and it's very important to them. I listen and ask questions about things to stay informed, but I will never be as passionate about politics as they are.

I think they also hope that I'll come to my senses and go running back to Peter. They believe in marriage vows—I do as well—but I also believe in people being compatible. I need to be healthy, and I can't do that in Nevada, and he won't move. I refuse to have a long-distance marriage. I need someone that will be with me physically. It doesn't have to be every day, but I do need a partner who will support me and want to be with me in person. Peter isn't that guy. And my parents have been having a difficult with my decision to divorce. I hope they'll understand in time.

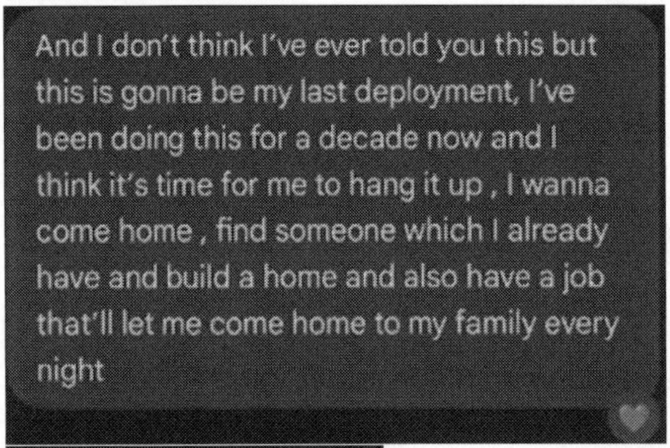

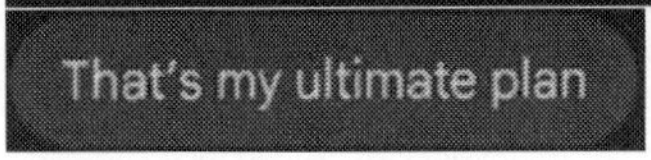

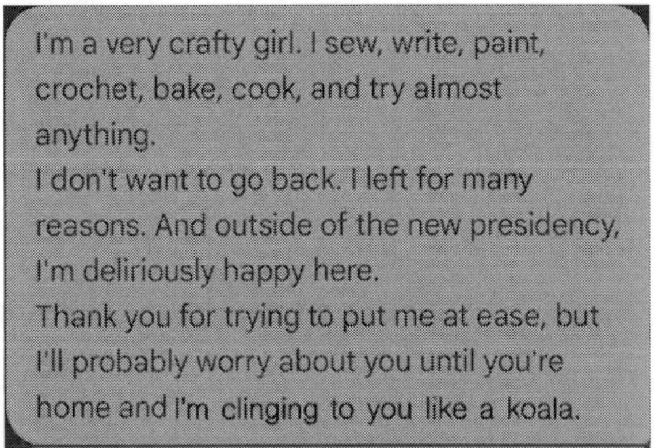

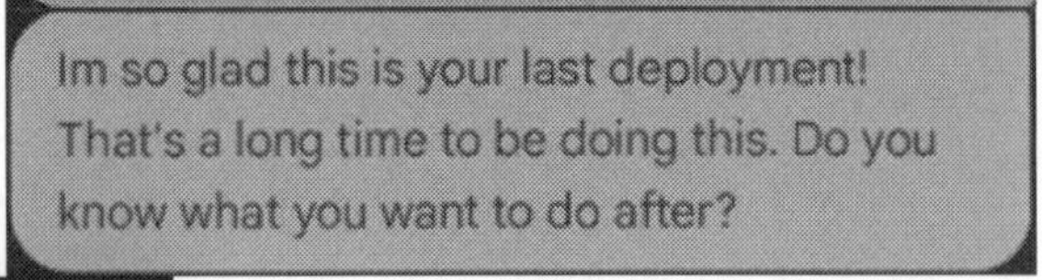

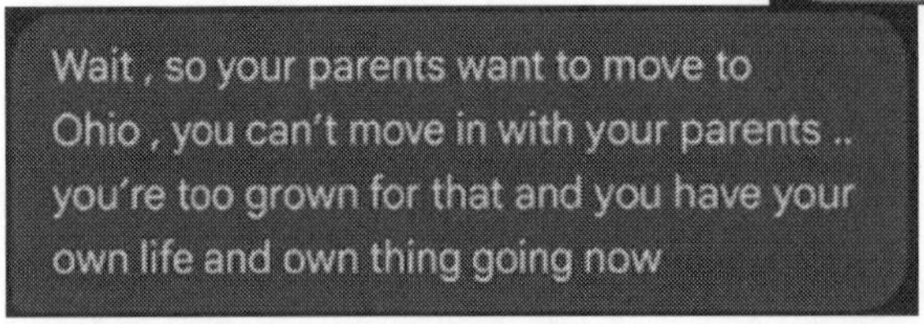

And good to hear it's a brand new house , please share the link so I can see it for myself

Right!! That's what I'm saying!!

I never really saw myself in a townhouse, but places out here are nuts for like hovels. I like to garden, and it's gonna be difficult in a townhouse.

And i don't want to be house poor because I want to travel and do things and take Trixie to Disney. And that can't happen if I'm working to just pay a mortgage

And what do you mean, do I really want to get it, or would I wait for you to get back?

Well I don't think the new president is going to affect you that much , he's just over the top because he just got it , I'm sure everything is gonna ease down pretty soon

Ugh, I hope so.

You're happy here and I'm coming home soon and we can build something special together here so leaving right now is a no no lol .. I want to have you in my arms all day long and make out with you in every corner of the house , bend you over the kitchen table and make love to you

I want that too.

And my advice for you is to take your time and keep looking, I'm sure you can find something better than a townhouse with a garden and that has everything you need, take your time .. it's not like you're being chased away from where you are right now

I asked you to wait till I'm home to make a final decision because I've got my own house , all paid for , 4 bedroom, 4 baths with a big ass garden and it's just trixie and I , you will love it here and I wouldn't mind you moving in with me my love

I know, but it's not my space, and it's very frustrating. I can't decorate how I want, or do the things I'm used to doing because everything is in storage. It's a petty issue, but it still irritates me

That's why I said you should wait a bit and let me be home if you can

Ok. I'll wait.

You should my love , I'd absolutely love you around me 24/7 making all the nice delicacy while I go crazy on the grill

Are you still crocheting, you aren't working today ?

I'm working

Talking to you is better though. And my bestie, Bex , is on the phone working with me. We do this all the time.

She calls on her way to work and we "work together" until one of us has a meeting or something.

Btw , I really love and enjoy how you always mention trixie and how you're already adding her to your plans and life .. it really warms my heart and I'm more than thankful to have met you on that app

I feel so lucky

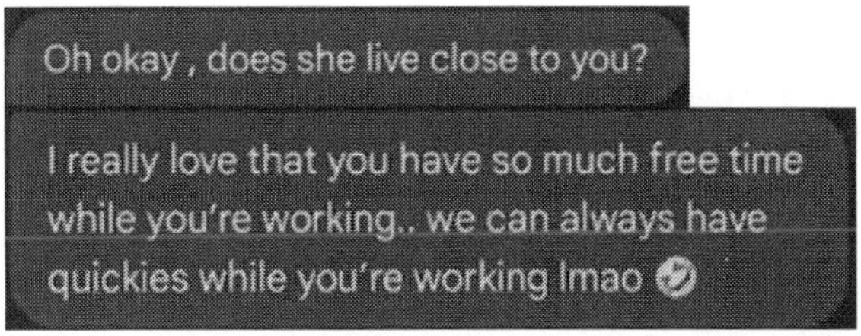

I snort and laugh, having to pause my texting to read what he wrote to Bex, who laughs with me.

"I'm really happy you seem to have found a guy that treats you well," she says. "I hope he comes home soon, and you can find out if he's this great in person. I really hope he is. You deserve to be happy."

"Thanks," I reply as I text him back. "I honestly can't wait until he's home, too. You probably won't hear from me for a few days when that happens, but I'm sure you understand." I laugh, knowing she got the inuendo and laugh harder at her

"Ew, I didn't need to know that."

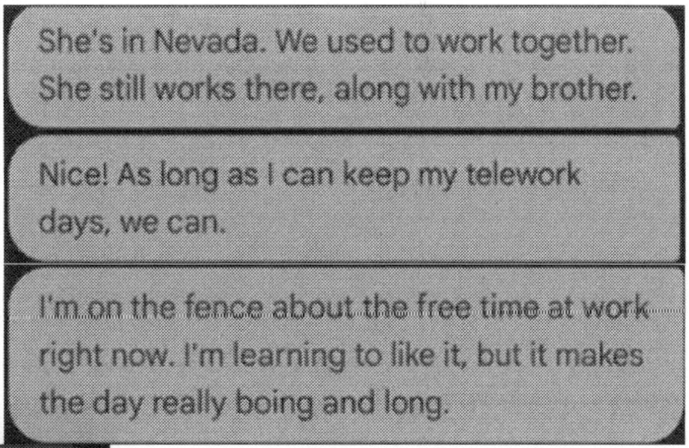

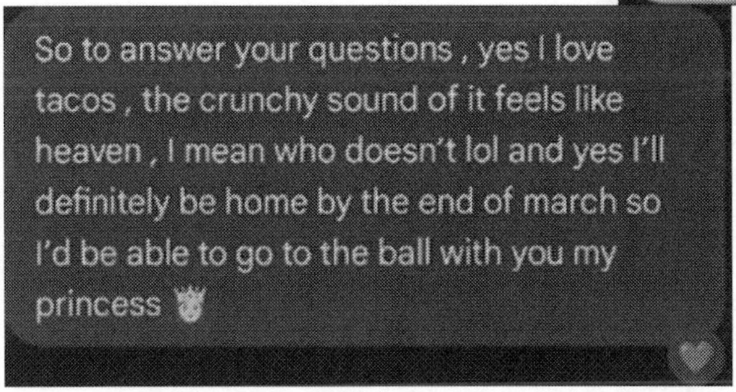

Well, crap. Did he not get the inuendo from that? I was trying not to be vulgar when I asked, but perhaps I shouldn't have been so coy.

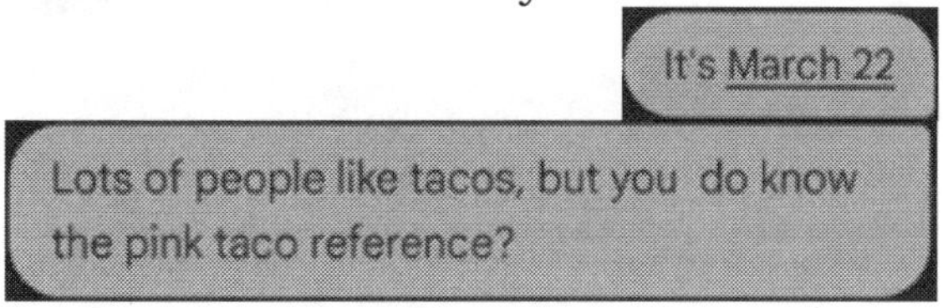

Yup I sure do , I just wanna bury my face in yours all day long , make you gasp for breath and make your toes curl

Screaming my name

I've been thinking and imagining things I'll do to you and trust me .. I've got a lot !

Holy shit. I think i just came a lil. My vibes had a workout the past couple of weeks.

Just wait until I'm home , you're gonna cum a whole lot

I just hope you can keep up

I'm really packing down here

Omg. We have to wait a whole two months, still?!?
I've yet to find someone who can keep up with me, so be careful what you wish for.

And I've got all the testosterone all built up haha , you're gonna need a chiropractor because that back of yours getting bent all day and you're really curvy too

Oh my god, this is amazing. We're actually going to sext. I feel my cheeks grow hot with a blush as I type. I can write sex scenes in books with zero problem, but sexting with a guy—even one I'm in love with—makes me blush and giggle.

Well you've met your match I'll tell you that

That's what I'm wishing for and so much more

Bring it on me baby

I am, and have great, big breasts and cannot wait to taste you. To have you in my mouth, watching you groan while I suck you off.

I can't wait, I noticed your breasts the first time you sent me a picture

You should see my breasts wrapped around your dick.

Was Trixies mom your last?
Peter was mine, and it wasn't great.

And just so we've had this conversation, I got tested, just in case, before I left NV. I'm clean.

And I'd love that so much and yes she was my last , I haven't been with anyone in 2 years now .. her passing really devastated and traumatized me .. I'm just glad I'm all better now and meeting you is helping me bring out that part of me again

All good babe , I'm very clean myself .. you've got to take tons of tests before you can get deployed and it's the same when you're coming back home so I'm certain

I'm sorry.
I'm glad you're doing better too.

Sorry to throw ice water on the conversation.

I love me some boob job while you suck me off .. damn , you've got me all hard and excited while at work 😄

It's all good my love

Yah, I'm wet too

I'm really comfortable with you so I can talk to you about anything and everything

Same. I've actually never really done dirty texts.

I send him a picture of me in a tiny top and skirt while on my knees. I'm struggling so much to not laugh from embarrassment.

That's me on my knees for you. Trying really hard not to giggle while I yook it.

Omg

I want every part of you and am so happy we met on that stupid app.
I feel like the lucky one. You're smart, funny, nice, hot, strong, caring, devoted. You're the whole package.

You're such a naughty girl

I love it

You gonna spank me?

Hell yeah , spank you till your ass pink

And make you beg for how much of a bad girl you've been

Just imagine me there, with my lips wrapped around your cock, licking and sucking.

Im suuuuch a bad girl.

I'll grab your ass as I deep throat you.

Fuck. I'm so turned on right now.

I'm more turned on my love

And I'll tell you to keep going while I rub your clit and whisper in your ears how I'm gonna fuck the shit out of you

Then I'm gonna turn you over on your chest pushing your head into the pillows

While I start slow and steady increasing the pace and hitting all the sides

My ass in the air, pussy soaked and ready for you

Yup babe , all mine

All yours

We're gonna keep the neighbors wondering WTH is going on Lmaoo

What are you doing today that allows us to actually talk?

I have to change the subject or things are going to get really out of hand. I am actually craving him, and I don't want to put him in an even more uncomfortable situation while he's working. This is going to be a long couple of weeks while we wait to see each other. Especially if we have conversations like this again. For someone who's been abstinent for two years, he really knows how to make a girl blush.

And I'm not really busy , I just got back from a raid so I'm just on the watch tower seated and talking to you

Oh, they'll know. And they'll be so jealous. Nice. Don't let me distract you too much.

I might go take care of things at lunch. And change my panties.

Do you have a buddy there? Is this making things awkward? I've thought about you between my thighs every day this week lol , they already know about you babe

Do they tease you about me?

I told you that I've told a few of my buddies about you because I use my phone more and they were wondering who I was talking to so I told them I found someone and she's amazing and makes me happy and showed them a picture of you as well

My friends are glad that I'm happy and want me to be careful. Bex knows she's gonna have to come out here if you break my heart. She's my ride or die.

And they were happy for me but yes they tease me all the time and they hope things doesn't change when I get home or maybe you're just bored and looking for someone to just talk to but I told off that that's not the case and we've got something real here

It's the same way with my buddies here lol and Bex has nothing to be worried about , I'll never break your heart , I'd rather break your back

Bored, I think to myself. What kind of person would put themselves through this crap because of boredom? Maybe there are people out there who can pretend to fall in love and pretend to care, but I'm not one of them. Never have been and most likely never will be. I have a seriously difficult time believing that happens to them.

But who knows? In the age that we live in, anything is possible.

And holy crap. How does one go about breaking backs with sex? I know that's what he's talking about, but wow. He could've used a very different way to explain that.

Im not bored.
Well, I'm bored at work. I'm not talking to you because I'm bored. I love you. I think you're great and that we really have something.
Lol, I'd rather neither gets broken, but holy dang.

<hour later>

What's your nanny like?

I hope things just keep getting better once you're home.

Are you ok that I don't want kids of my own?

<hour later>

If you can, will you send me a pic of you not in shadow? I'd like to have more things to oogle.
Be safe out there.

You make my whole day better. I've only told my neighbor that we're talking and that i can't wait to meet you, and she is totally freaked. I think she thinks you're Dahmer or something. she's overly paranoid about everything, so I'm glad she's looking out, but I don't think she has anything to worry about.

<three hours later>

And i can not stop thinking about you. It's like an obsession. I want to know everything and just be with you. Not sexually, although, that's a given, but just talking to you, sharing the same space. It's intense. I've never felt this way before. Not even with my ex.

<five hours later>

Hey baby, I hope you're sleeping and not doing your kick-ass thing. Although, thinking of you on a mission, all intense, sweaty, leading a team and kicking ass, is rather hot. And terrifying. But really hot. There might be something wrong with me. I miss you and am thinking about you. Shocking, I know, but I am. Anyway, I'm headed to bed and wanted to say good night. Stay safe. I love you.

Day 21

I'm still on a happy high from the previous day. Not only did I find someone who checks off all the boxes I want for my next person, but he loves me back and the sexting is crazy fun. I want him home so we can explore everything between us properly.

Instead, I say hello, letting him know I'm thinking of him, and head on out to my D&D game with my friends. The drive is fun, and I listen to music instead of my book today. I was feeling happy songs that I could sing along to.

"Good morning," I say, happiness in my tone this morning as I hand out the coffee I picked up for everyone.

"Oh, bless you," James says, handing Kathy her cup. She says something barely coherent in thanks. Neither of them are morning people, but we started a game with a couple that lives across the pond, and it was late there.

"So, Josie said I should talk to you about the people I'm interested in dating," I start to James. "She said you can look into them and let me know if they're decent people or not."

At his nod, I continue, "What information do you need from me for this?"

"The more information you can provide, the better. At a minimum, I'll need the same type of information you'd provide for a simple background check. The biggest red flag you can have is if they can't video chat for any reason. Make sure you can see them or preferably meet them in person before getting too involved."

I don't tell him that I'm already involved, and this is just a check for peace of mind. But, I do make a mental list of things that might be helpful to ask Daniel the next time he and I are talking so I can share them with James. I also make a note to take screenshots of the dating app profile and send those.

We have our D&D game, and it's filled with twists and turns, excitement and world building. I love game day, but a part of me can't help but continually glance at my phone, hoping Daniel will text. He didn't.

I text him as I leave my friend's house.

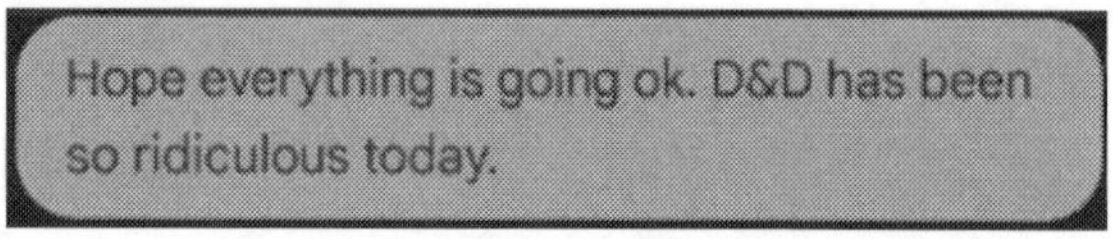

<six hours later>

Can we video chat tomorrow? I'd really like to see you.
I miss talking to you, and I'm hoping you're asleep, not on a raid. I've been trying to talk myself out of being worried all flipping day. It's only kinda working. Love you and can't wait to talk to you tomorrow

I don't hear from him all day, and the worry has anxiety speeding through my veins like nothing I've ever experienced before. I'm not a fan of this feeling and want it gone. I decide to call him tomorrow, and that'll alleviate some of my insecurities. I hope.

Day 22

I can't sleep. I keep thinking about Daniel and worrying about him in combat. I text him to try and release some of my worries.

I can't sleep. All I want is to be lying naked in bed with you, head on your chest, my palm covering your heart. You have an arm wrapped around me, idly tracing my body. Our legs are intertwined, and your other hand is holding mine over your heart. I tilt my head up and smile, content and blissed out. You take the hand that was holding mine to tilt my chin so you can kiss me. It's the most gentle, loving kiss that says more than all the lovemaking we just finished. Your thumb wipes away a tear from my cheek. You know it's because I'm so unbelievably happy. That we're finally where we're supposed to be.

I want this more than I've ever wanted anything. It scares me with the intensity, but it feels so right. And I know you're strong, I trust you to take care of you. But I can't help but be terrified for you. That all I'll get with you are these texts that have meant more to me than you'll ever know. And it isn't enough. I want to be yours.

I finally fall asleep, dreaming about being in his arms.

<four hours later>

Baby, are you ok?

<two hours later>

Hi babe

Good morning

How are you doing today?

The relief I feel at seeing his text is stupid in its intensity.

Morning.

So much better now. How are you?

That's good to hear , I'm glad

I'm ok , off today but had shit to yesterday and all morning

How have you been and what have you been up to all weekend?

The tone of his text feels off. I'm not sure if I'm projecting or if it's him, but he feels less like himself and either tired or grumpy or something. It just feels off.

Did D&D yesterday, looked at that townhouse, just to see, and worried about you. You seem off. What's wrong?

What d&d?

I'm ok , just tired

Dungeons and dragons

Can you sleep?

And it's all good babe , I'll be fine .. thanks honey

Oh ok lol

I've been trying but can't seem to close my eyes

I'm alright , feel better now that I get to talk to you

I have a standing game with friends on Saturday. It's fun.
That was me all night. Finally fell asleep at 530am and was up at 730

iPhone or Samsung?

I took a shower around 330 and my hair was still wet when I fell asleep, so its a hot mess today.

Oh okay , that's good

iPhone for me

Any plans for today ?

I'm hoping to video chat with my boyfriend...

Oh okay , well I'd absolutely love to faceTime or Skype sometime soon but we are not allowed to make or receive any form of calls because it can be traced and used to pinpoint our exact location by the insurgents and that's gonna be catastrophic if our location is all out in the open
It's all for our safety babe , I hope you understand my love

I haven't even been able to talk to Trixie directly just through the nanny and it breaks my fucking heart

I'm devastated. All I want to do today is talk to him, see his face. All the military shows and movies show that soldiers get to talk to their loved ones. I hate that he can't. His reasoning makes sense, but I can't help but think about the conversation I had yesterday, and a tiny kernel of doubt settles itself into my psyche.

Oh. Ok. I understand.

Im sorry you're so cut off.

I can only imagine how hard that is with Trixie.

Yeah it's fucked up and it's so damn hard but it's what I've gotta endure for the next few weeks

I know all the perseverance is gonna pay off at the end and that's what keeps me going

Do you have a specific day you're coming home, or just March?

And I really don't have plans , there's not much to do here other than rest and chill with the guys

How about you?

I really just wanted to talk to you.

And yes , I don't have a specific date yet but I'll be home before march ending , that I know for sure
All we were told is a few more weeks left and that shouldn't be more than 6-7 weeks

Ugh, six or seven weeks! That's an eternity! I don't let on how disappointed I am with that news, and I hope I'm able to hide the massive disappointment from my texts, but I'm not sure that I do.

Even if it's just texting. I don't get enough of you and don't want to squander any time we get

I know babe , I wanna talk to you as well , see your face , your voice , your boobs as so much more

But I appreciate that we get to text even though it's not much

Im yours, you know that, right?

Jean Booth

All mine ?

You sure about that ?

Yes

There's nobody else ?!!

Nope.

You're it for me. We've been talking for 3 weeks and I'm not even gonna try to fight how much i want you in my life. It's a lot, really fast, and seems surreal, but it is what it is.

You're in my thoughts all the time, and I finally relax when I see your texts. I can't explain it, but I know it's true.

I told you that the other day. Did you not believe me?

I love to hear it from you , I feel absolutely the same way

I really do and I totally believe you , I just need some reassurance lol

Lol, ok. I think we both do.

I checked the dating app today and I found out your profile is gone lol

Yah, i took it down a while ago, maybe a week?

Well you know I'm all yours no one else's and I got rid of mine as well , I don't need it

You're all I need

Good to hear.

I reread our texts sometimes, when I'm really missing you.

It makes me feel better.

Aww that's so sweet

I do as well

And I wanted to ask , you said you're the eldest of 5 kids and you don't talk to some and your mom , can I ask why's that ?

Mom and brother are clinical narcissists.

They're very toxic and difficult to be around.

It's been much better since I stopped talking to them. I'm still friendly if we run into each other, which i don't see happening anymore, but i can't have them in my life.

You said your fsmily was strained. What's going on there?

I hope i don't wake you up/bother you with my 800 texts while I worry about you.

Did i lose you? Did you fall asleep?

And he's gone. I hate that he disappears. It's so frustrating, and I keep trying to remind myself that he's in the middle of an active deployment. I'm so far down on the priority list, it's not funny. He needs sleep if he can get it. I refuse to think that his location has been compromised, and he's fighting. I worry enough about that on days I know he has to work.

I try to get busy with my own work to distract myself from missing him. I hate this. I've done long-distance with my ex, but this is so different. I could call Peter any time I wanted, and he wasn't in a war zone, so I didn't really worry about him. This sucks. And I have six or seven more weeks to learn to deal with it.

I'm still here

Would you rather not talk right now?

Jean Booth

Wow , I'm sorry to hear that

Does your parents live together in Ohio ?

Its fine. It was years ago.
My dad and step mom are in Ohio. My mom lives in Nevada.

Naah , I'm good .. just got a lil occupied but I can still talk , it just might not be as fast

Ok. With what?

Oh ok

Gotcha

And we're having a lil debrief , nothing too serious

Oh ok

I have just one younger brother and he lives with my parents down in Napa , CA
We've got a complicated relationship, we barely talk

Growing up just made me realize that we're so different and have really opposite mentalities

It's been really hard to talk to them since the election, and there are days where I wonder why I even bother.
When i left Peter, my dad told me that he deserved better than me. That shit hurt.

It's not like we don't talk at all , we do but it's rare and it's quick , hello , hi and it's done with

They neglected me when I lost my former wife and didn't give a shit and that's will never settle with me

Ever !

That's awful. I'm so sorry. No one should go through that alone. Can I ask about her?

Oh wow , that must be really hurtful , why would he say that to you

Not gonna lie, I'm not a big fan of your family because of that.

And of course you can and yes it was awful , they didn't like that I moved down here with her

My dad LOVES my ex. They're very similar and hes like the son my dad always wanted.

What was her name? What did she do? How did she die? How does Trixie cope with it? Does she remember her mom? Do you keep in touch with any of her family?

I'm going to be honest, I'm good for the most part, but there are parts of me that are still wounded. You've actually helped a lot with your "good morning, beautiful" texts. In 24 years, no one has ever said that to me. I struggle to feel important.

<3 hours later>

Busy day?

<hour later>

Hi babe

How's it going?

Got busy for a bit

It's going. How about you?

Obviously, lol

So much for a day off.

lol yeah

I'm ok, just here

Like I told you the other day , it's always something lol

Yep. I'm not exactly thrilled about it, but trying my best.

It's getting a smidge easier. At least this time I didn't think you were in a fire fight. My imagination can run away into dangerous territory sometimes.

My landlords (hosts?) I don't know what to call them, came by and there's something wrong with the HVAC unit. I had to turn the heat off and run the fan for a few hours. Not really thrilled about this.

Yeah, I know it's not the best but it's what we gotta deal with for now babe and we gotta make the most of the free time I get

lol , I understand how your imagination gets and it does be like that sometimes but we deal with it

Oh wow , I hope it's not too cold for you

I know. It's fine. I'm in a mood today, don't mind me. I'm trying to remind myself that none of this is in either of our control and things will be better when you're home.
I was just really looking forward to talking (texting) with you and plans change. It's ok.

Yeah , I can tell .. you asked me earlier if I can talk or do I need to sleep so I kinda felt that you were in a mood

It was ok, but the sun is starting to set and i still have like 2 more hours for the fan to run and im starting to shiver. I'm probably going to finish buying your ball ticket and then snuggle cats on the couch.

And yes , we've just got 8 weeks at most so things is definitely gonna get better

I got a weird vibe from you. Bex said I was projecting. Sorry.

lol weird vibe

And do you tell Bex everything

No, but almost everything.

You gotta keep some things to yourself babe , we can't have a third party and third opinion on our relationship, we've gotta be able to deal with things and be matured enough to handle it ourselves , that's the only way this will work

I snort. *Who's the one who had a successful twenty-year marriage before she left to prioritize herself,* I think.

No shit we don't need other people in our relationship. But Bex is my best friend. Get used to her knowing things. She's the one who's kept me sane the past few months. There's no way I won't tell her about the guy I like and try to find out if I'm being a lunatic or have valid annoyances.

She's my best friend. My ride or die. She's been there for me when no one else was. And I've done the same to her.

I know , I'm not disputing that but still

She's not the one you're dating lol

I know. And every once in a while, I need a reminder that I can't be expecting to be the center of the universe like I want to be. <pouts>

You can't tell me everything about her and it should be the same for me

I'm just saying...

lol well , you can be my center of universe 😉

I keep a lot of our relationship private. I can't right now. Right now, work is the center of your universe. And thats OK. It should be.

lol , well you're not me and I'm telling you what's the center of mine so don't fight it , just accept

And good , I'd really appreciate that

I needed that reminder because I was bitching that you were ignoring me and hated me. Totally untrue things, I know. But hormones are tricky bastards.

I'm a very private person and I love the feeling of it's just me and my woman

You n me against the world, huh?

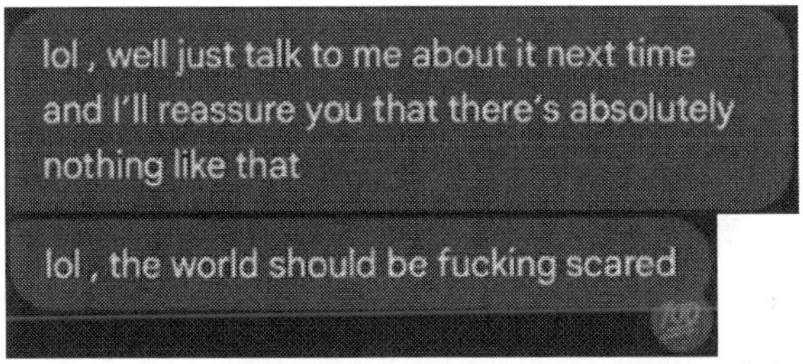

"I can't talk to you about it," I exclaim to my phone. "You're not around! Girls need their girlfriends to vent and to keep them grounded. It's a completely different relationship, and if your wife didn't show you that, you'll learn with me. Good lord. You can't be my only form of communication."

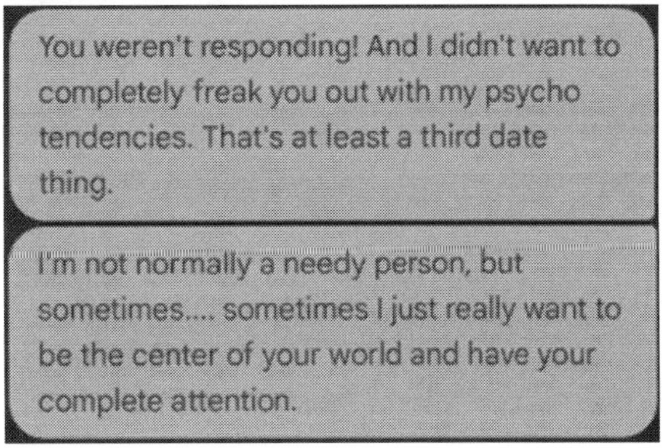

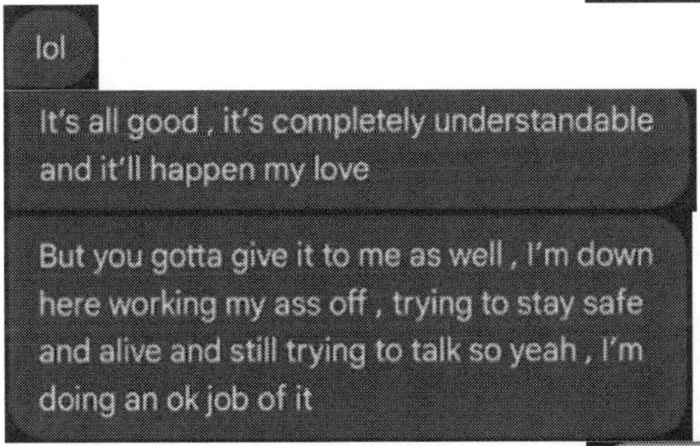

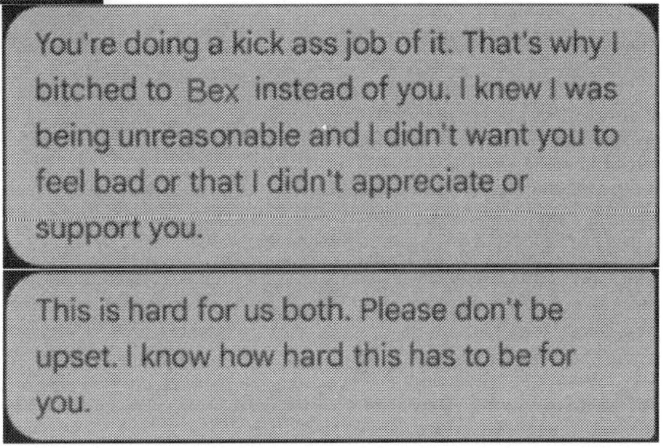

We're trying to build a foundation for a relationship through texting while we're both stressed. Granted, yours is way more valid and intense than mine. But neither of us is at our best. And you lose tone, inflection, and facial cues through texting. The fact that we're doing so well should say something about us.

I look forward to every second I get with you. And I was being needy and selfish, wanting you all to myself today. It was unreasonable. I know that.

I feel like you're mad at me and I'm really not ok with that.

I'm not mad at you

Why would I be

I dunno. You seem defensive. I think i need more than 2 hours of sleep a night.

I was just saying that we are both trying and we should be thankful for the progress we've made mostly through text and that it's only going to get better from there

If it's so good now , imagine how it would be when we're actually together

You were not saying we were both trying. You were explaining how you have it so much harder than I do, asshole. The thought runs through my head as I text back.

lol

I know you want to fuck me

That's common knowledge

So, so much.
But so do you.

Of course

So what made you respond to my message on that app , I'm curious lol

I have to go back and look at his profile. I pull up the screenshots, so I can answer him honestly. I look through his pictures again. The only one I really like is the first one on his profile. He's standing in front of a curtain and seems like he's sweet, if not a little haunted. The rest of the pictures remind me of guys I knew in my twenties who were nothing but alpha a-hole players. If those had been his only pictures, I never would've replied. I didn't like those guys and remembered being hopeful that he'd outgrown the person he was in earlier pictures, that he'd grown up.

I liked what you had to say about being a gentleman and what your favorite "sick" day was.

What was up with the white shirt pic, and the beer pick?

Pic, ugh

I like dichotomy in my man. Gentleman in public, freak in the sheets.

I also thought your first pic looked like you were sweet.

I will admit, I have your photo up on my phone as I go to bed. The first one you sent me, with the hoodie. I almost sent you a pic of my O face last night.

What drew you to me?

Aww , that's so sweet

And the only reason I got any sleep last night was because I pictured us laying together.
I've got it pretty bad for you.

Jean Booth

Well you were really gorgeous, looked really young for your age and from your profile , you looked like someone who has her shit together

And I saw your boobs from the pictures on your profile and it was huge lol

I look very young for my age. I stopped getting carded for rated- r movies when I was your age.

Glad to know you're a boob man.

What are you doing?

Will you tell me about your ex?

<hour later>

Also, i know you're very private, but I would like to know more about you. You're really good at evading questions. Like the white shirt and beer pics.
And i took care of my mood.

I'm just laid down in bed and I'm a boob and booty person , I love both but I prefer boobs more

And I'm not evading anything , what do you wanna know

The stories behind those photos.

You've been asking about my former wife , her name was Maddie , we were married for 8 years , dated since high school and she passed through a car accident

What photos , the ones on my profile ?

I'm so sorry. That's awful.
Yes.

Good to hear you're in a better mood , what did you decide to have for dinner

It's all good but thanks

Did you guys want more kids? What brought you out here?

There's nothing special with the pictures , the one with the beer is a very old picture of me , I was just having a good time and I decided to take the pic and I was out with friends for a sip and paint party in the pic I was in white .. it was a really fun day now that I'm thinking about it lol

And yes we did , at least we planned to have more kids .. I wanted to have a boy lol and I moved out here for her , she's from around here

Do you like to paint?
Are you close to any of her family?

Are you ok with not having any more kids, or is that something you still want with someone?

Yea , I love to paint .. it's fun even though I'm not so good at it lol but I love to bring my artistic side to life

What kinds of things do you paint?

We talk but we aren't that close , they've kept their distance and I've honestly keep mine .. it's good that way for both

Why? They don't want to be part of Trixie's life?

I'm good with not having more kids and also if more comes , I'm fine with it but it's not a priority

I love painting nature and abstractly

Nice.
I paint landscapes too

I don't know, I'm sure they're pretty devastated and probably just wanna move on and find peace , I don't blame them honestly and I try to visit every once in a while and I'll when I get back home

That's super sad that Trixie's grandparents don't want to be part of her life. I can't even imagine that. The accident must have been horrific. I wonder if Daniel was involved in it. I want to ask so many more questions, but I refrain because that's a terrible thing to have to be reminded of. We'll talk about it when I can hold him and make sure he's okay after dredging up such painful memories.

Oh really , I didn't know you paint as well lol

If we wind up together, kids are out of the picture. I just want to make that clear. I think being in Trixie's life would be amazing, but that would be it for me.

That's nice that you try. And I guess i can understand that. But I still think it's sad.

What time is it there?

Of course I understand and I'm fine we that , we have trixie and we have to take absolute care of her and trust me , she's a lot of work lol

It's sad but it's what it is .. I just try to do the best I can and let the rest lie .. I still got my own life to live and lots of shit to take care of

It's 11:49pm

Do you want me to let you go so you can sleep? You have to be up at 6, right?

I wish we could snuggle.

If you haven't noticed, I've really wanted your arms around me.

I'm still up babe lol , I wish we could snuggle as well

I wanna motorboat those titties lmfaooo

I can.

I can also lick my own nipple.

You can lick your nipple ?!!

Yes, sir.

That must be some type of super power lmao

I have big boobs.

I can see they're really huge lol

Maybe someday you'll show me 😝😛😛😛

Maybe I will...

Can you send me a Pic?

And I'll never get tired of this. This gentle conversation, with teasing. This is what i look forward to every day. Just you n me. No worries, just us. When we can actually talk, it makes my day.

That's good babe , nobody is perfect, I most certainly I'm not , there's always room for improvement and we must always work on ourselves

I laugh. "We must, must we?" I giggle to my phone. Sometimes some of the things he says are just ridiculous.

Well I'd be waiting .. it'll surely make my whole week when you send it

It's very late out here , I'll send you a pic in the morning

Ok.

I'm glad you enjoy it , I do as well

Talking to you is the highlight of my day

Im not sending a picture of me licking my boob. You'll have to see that in person.

Mine too.

But fuck... it'll make your whole week?

If i send you something like that, you can't share it.

Of course not of you licking your boobs lmaooo

But yes it'll make my whole week and why would I share something like that babe !!

It's for my eyes and eyes alone

I take two pictures before I can lose my nerve. I've never done this before, and if I thought about it rationally, I wouldn't do it now. But I love him. I send the two pictures before I even look at them or can second guess myself. My cheeks are flaming with embarrassment and nerves. I cannot believe I just did that.

Omfg

You're so fucking crazy

I love you !!!

Im sorry, I'm blushing so much.
I love you too.

Are you turned on?

Is the sky blue?

Of course I'm fucking turned on

This shit is hot as fuck

Glad you like it. Can you imagine us when you get home?

I'm a lady, and your personal freak.

It's gonna be a freak off when I'm back home

I can't even imagine how crazy it's gonna be

I'm so fucking pumped

Do you know what you want to do when you get home? Besides me?

I'm counting the days.

I seriously can't wait.

Same here babe

Do like what exactly ?

Well, you'll be done with the military, right? Or are you gonna do something with it that doesn't take you away?

What can you tell me that you do? Cuz I picture black hawk down shit, with you leading a platoon and some craziness. I think that my overactive imagination causes more of my worry for you than is necessary

My dad was Air Force, but he doeant talk about it. And this is all new to me. All I have to go on are movies and video games. And I honestly believe them with a grain of salt.

Yes babe , I'll be done with the military and I'll have to find another job but I'm not too bothered about that right now and honestly not even thinking of it , what I'm gonna do at first is take a long and well deserved break from all the chaos and take my time to get to know you , spend time with you and trixie then I'll figure something out later

It shouldn't be much of a problem because I have an associates degree so I'd definitely find something to do

And my finances are pretty great too so I'm not worried at all

I love both pictures honey , I've been looking at it since , it's really hot

I love how you're so vulnerable you are with me , it's the purest form of love

I am. I love you.

And from what I know and have seen of you, I think you're pretty perfect. For me.

I love you too babe

And I think you are for me , I've told you before that this ain't a mere coincidence, this is meant to be

How'd we get this lucky?

That's why I told you to hold off from the townhouse because I know you're gonna really love my place when you see it

Timing

When the time is right , everything is just in place

Babe, you could live in a tent, down by the river, and I'd love it because you're there. I'd just question that lifestyle for Trixie.

And you don't have a problem with me being 8 years older?

You keep disappearing.

We've spoken about this before babe

I don't care about that at all

Well it's 1:25am and lights out so yeah , I might be closing my eyes for a couple seconds lol 😂

Why would it change when we're so good

Did your thoughts change

Lol, ok. I thought so. You should sleep. You have to be up at six.
No. They won't.

Insecurities can be a bitch sometimes.

I'll get over it.

They better don't

You should , you don't need it at all especially when I don't make you feel that way

I told you. I'm all in. Were good.

I know. You make me feel like a queen. And I love it.

I'm glad you do

Do you watch football

The eagles just kicked Washington's ass to the Super Bowl lol 😂 🤣🤣

Go to bed, baby.
Kinda. I'm not invested in it, but its fun.

Nice.

Nice. We're you watching on your phone?

Yeah , watching the highlights

I hope I don't waste all my internet lol 😂

Do you like football? 😆

I love sports

Of course, football , basketball, baseball , soccer .. I love it all

You're such a dude.

Did you ever play any?

Well I'm your dude

Yeah in high school, lacrosse

And I was pretty good at it

My senior year in high school had a girls flag football team and I was a linebacker. It was awesome.

Thats hella cool

That's really cool

Yeah, it was fun

I knew all that curves came from somewhere Havana

Hahaha *

I much prefer playing to watching.

Yah, I'm very strong, yet squishy

And freezing my ass off.

You're well balanced

And the heater hasn't been fixed ?!!

It supposedly keeps going off and the thermostat says it's 68 in here, but i think it's lies.

I haven't stopped shivering since 3.

That's crazy

What did the landlord or whatever say

You shouldn't have to stay cold all night long

I mean, I could also put pants on. Part of it's my fault.
And the landlord came out and unthawed the HVAC with a bunch of water. It's 35 degrees right now, so I'm sure all the water they poured on it will just help it freeze more. And theyre supposed to bring a temp heater by in case it stops working. They have a call into the repairman, but who knows. I'll warm up when I go to bed.
Furry and Spot snuggle and will keep me warm. And I have a ton of blankets. I'm just cold right now. It'll be fine.

Day 23

> Morning babe. I hope you have a good day. I finally slept!

I get up, feeling better mentally than I have in a few days, but cramping like someone is trying to rip my insides out. I guess I know why I've been a little extra lately. Stupid period. Stupid hormones.

> Had confirmation as to why I was a lunatic yesterday. Sorry about that. I'd kinda like to rip my insides out today, so I probably won't text much. I hate shark week. Please be safe. Love you.

<2.5 hours later>

> I put your picture as my phone screen background and smile every time I turn my phone on. You're so cute. you make me very happy.

> Guys are here looking at the HVAC. Spot is supervising. Lol

I send him a picture of the cat looking out the window at the HVAC guys. Spot is very interested in what they're doing.

<Two hours later>

> Thinking about you and feeling all sorts of mushy. I'm so grateful for you.

Hope your day doesn't suck and that you're being safe. I'm really ready for this day to be over, although I have to go into the office tomorrow, and that means I'll be up at 4. I'm tired and feel lousy and would very much like a hug. However, with how I'm feeling, a hug will probably just make me weep. Being crazy is hard. Like, I love being a girl - I can do amazing things with my body, but every once in a while, I hate it and feel extremely insecure.

<five hours later>

What kind of car do you drive? Favorite color? Holiday? Do you smoke/chew/vape? Do you miss me like i miss you? You're on my mind, baby. I hope you're ok.

It's my nightly stare at Daniel's picture and think all the things time. I think about how much you've come to mean to me in such a short time. I hope you're being as safe as you can and send whatever positive, loving thoughts I can to you. I wonder about what you're doing. And I daydream about seeing you in person for the first time. My favorite fantasy is running to you, grabbing (gently) your face between my palms and kissing you. You'd drop your bag and wrap me in your arms, fist my hair to deepen the kiss and position me just how you want me. I'd eventually wrap my arms around you, drop my head against your chest, and hope you don't notice how much I'm crying as I whisper, "You're here, you're home. You're really here." As I cling to you.

Eventually, I close my eyes, and the spell is broken. I whisper that I love you and go to bed.
Wherever you are, whatever you're doing, know that you're in my thoughts and always in my heart.

Day 24

I practically fall out of bed when my alarm goes off, I'm so exhausted. I feed the cats, text Daniel, get ready for work, and start my two-hour commute.

> Morning, my love. Office days suck - it's way too early for waking up. Ugh.
> I hope you have a good day.

It's as quiet as a tomb when I get to work, and I can't help but think about how stupid it is that we have to go into the office at all. All of our work can be done remotely, and it's a waste of space and money to have office space for us.

> I love you.

Hello love

Good morning

Why are you at work so early

> This is what time i go in when I have to be in the office. How are you?

> Are you able to relax at all today?

> Between the metro and my drive to the station, I have to leave before 5 so I can make it to work at 7. I'm really not a morning person and 4am is the devil.

> Do you still like getting my 800 texts? Lol
> I miss you.

Oh okay

It's been a busy start of the week for me

No time to relax

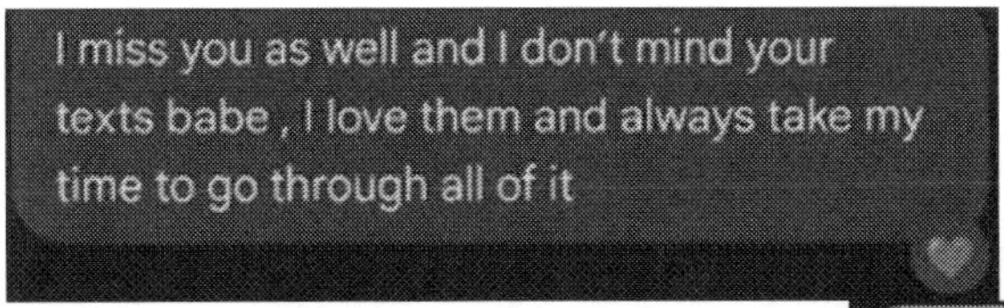

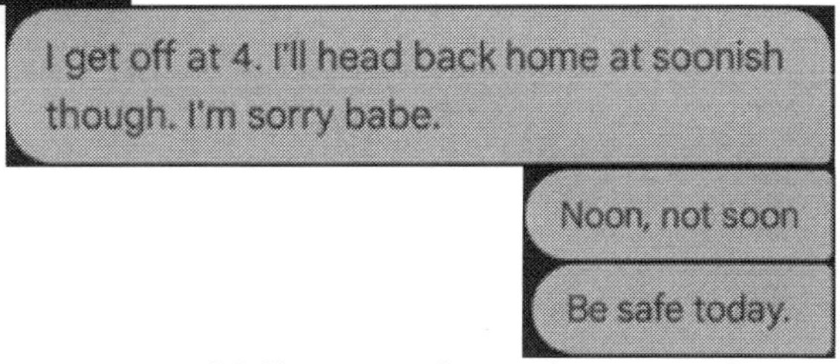

I go through my emails and have a ton of follow-ups from the executive orders that have been released, along with a lawsuit from the federal employees who are with the union. From everything I'm reading, this year is going to be a mess and unbelievably stressful, even more than it already has. Which really sucks, because I've already been at my max stress threshold for the past couple of weeks.

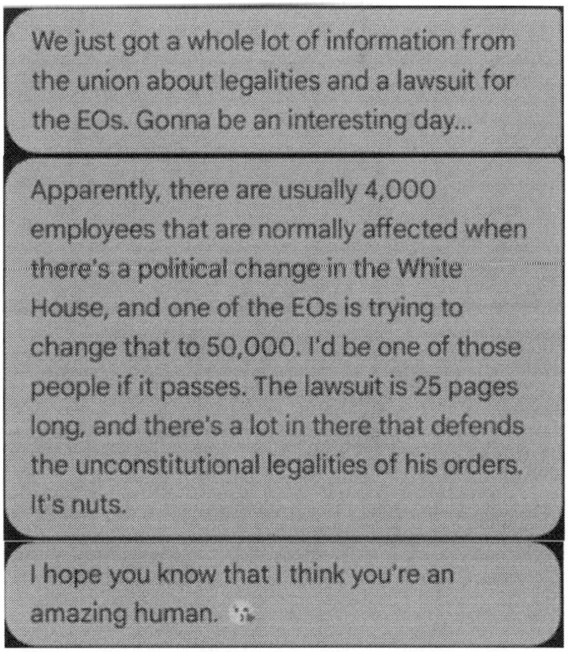

I've been home for less than an hour and keep hearing things from the base that's a few miles away. Helicopters keep flying by, making me think about Daniel, and noises that sound like cannons or a sonic boom keep rattling the house. It's the first time since I moved here that this much activity has happened from the base. It's slightly unnerving.

> There's a lot of weird stuff going on down here today. I left the office and have been in my rental all afternoon. There have been weird noises that sound like thunder or cannons and like 5 helicopters flying around. It's not usually this chaotic around here.
>
> Everyone is freaking out at work because Trump put a hold on funding effective tonight at 5. The grantees aren't going to get paid, and we have zero guidance. I've had so many emails and calls from freaked out agencies, and all I can tell them is, you know what we know. I'm not sure if you've realized this or not, but im a bit of a control freak. I don't do well without the information and at least an idea of a plan. I'm working on that. So having to constantly tell people, I have no idea, is annoying.

> And then it got me thinking about you (when don't I) and how chill you are like all of the time. How tf do you do that?!?! I'm in awe of you and have been trying to channel that part of me. I don't think it exists. Lol
>
> Hope you're doing ok. Love you.

I get a text from James, letting me know that he can't find anything on Daniel. He says that the pictures are most likely from a guy who's about twenty-three years old, not in his late thirties.

People think I'm in my late twenties, early thirties all the time, I think. *That doesn't prove anything.*

James suggests that I try to find out the name of Daniel's high school or college that he attended. He also advises that I get Daniel's address.

Well, he's special ops, and he's told me he doesn't do social media, I think. *Just because James can't find anything doesn't mean he's a scammer. It could just mean that he's really good at being private.*

The small kernel of doubt that started when Daniel told me he couldn't video chat grows.

Kinda crazy how you just came into my world out of nowhere. In no time at all, you became one of the most important things in my life. But I guess that's what makes this all so incredible. It proves there's always a reason to be hopeful for the future because you never know what wonderful things are yet to come.
Thank you for being you.

This week sucks as bad as last week. Hope you're doing good.

<six hours later>

I fell in love with you,
Not for grand gestures or sweeping words,
But because you brought back my smile,
You showed me what true love feels like.

In your presence, I found safety,
A place where I could rest,
Cared for in ways I had forgotten.
You are my peace,
A quiet haven in a noisy world,
And for that, I am forever grateful.

I sometimes wonder, how can this be real? Am I going to wake up one day to find this was all a dream?

Day 25

Things must be rally intense. Stay safe, baby. Love you.

Hi babe , good morning 😃

How are you doing?

I hope you have a good day today

And things aren't necessarily intense just busy and hot

Wait they want 50,000 people to lose their jobs .. I'm reading your texts

Oh, thank God, you're okay, I think as I see his texts. It only mildly relaxes me. Things happening at work have me completely in knots. I'm worried about losing my job and having to support myself completely alone. I could've done it with my savings and my income, but I have no idea what's happening with my job right now.

Yah. It's fucked right now.

We got an email from the AAG last night basically saying, "Resign or follow Trump." Got the same email from HR today.

My boss is having a meeting with us this morning, so we'll see what she has to say. No matter what happens, I know I'll be fine. I freaked out about it last night for a bit, but I'm really ok. I don't really need to work for the next two years, and I can use that time to build my business, which is what I want anyway. So maybe all of this is a blessing in disguise?

Hope you have a good day.

I take a walk to help with the stress. It was something my boss encouraged, and I've been going on almost daily walks anyway. I might just have to start adding to them. I'm grateful that I can actually walk here. I couldn't have done that in Nevada. I grab the mail when I get home, and the necklace I ordered with the little paratrooper is there. I put it on and take a picture for Daniel. I like that I can have a symbol of him to hold close to my heart.

Im really trying to like pictures of me, but it's hard. And I'm not a fan of looking at my face when I text you. Lol
I hope you like it though. I went for a walk and was doing a cool down when the mail came. I wanted to share.
I'm really ready for this week to be over. Normally, I like my job, but the past two weeks have been challenging. I hope your week gets better. Been thinking about you all day.

I think i might put some purple into my hair tonight.

I hope you're being safe, and I'm trying not to worry.
Sometimes, I feel like this isn't real, that it's right out of a story. I like romances. And most are whirlwind things that are completely unbelievable. Girl meets guy, they have to do some random thing together, and by the end of the week (or 2), they're in love and it's happily ever after. I never expected to live it.

I miss you. So freaking much. I got the necklace as a way to have you close. Is that weird? And also to show off that I'm yours. I keep telling myself you're safe, to let you be, to stop worrying. It's not working.

Day 26

Morning babe. Hope you're doing ok.

There was an accident late last night, and it's all anyone can talk about. A military helicopter crashed into a commercial plane, and both went down into the Potomac. It's scary, and the only thing being reported on is the ice skaters that were on the plane. There's nothing about the military personnel nor why this happened. It seemed like some planned thing to take the heat off the impact of the executive orders. Either that, or I was starting to look into conspiracy theories myself.

I couldn't stop thinking about Daniel and if he might have known any of those soldiers involved. It also reinforced how dangerous his job was, which only made my stress and anxiety worse. If this continued, I'd wind up having a heart attack before my forty-fourth birthday.

There was an accident last night. I'm m not sure how much info you get from outside of where you are, and I hope im not breaking the news to you. They're saying a Blackhawk helicopter hit a passenger jet and both went down into the Potomac. The articles are mostly focused on the plane and the fact that there were famous ice skaters on it. I'm being entirely selfish and thinking of the soldiers and completely freaking out about you and everything you go through.

I want to hold you, offer what little protection and comfort I can. I hate this. All of it. Senseless deaths, war, this debilitating fear, lack of any control, political machinations - it's nauseating and heartbreaking. Please, please be ok.

<*five hours later*>

Earlier today, I was thinking, what is all of this trying to teach me? I think every challenge in life holds a lesson that we need to learn about ourselves. The only thing that came to mind is tinkerbell. With faith, trust, and pixie dust, you can fly. I have the pixie dust in spades (glitter is my favorite color), but the faith and trust - those have alluded me my whole life. So, I'm trying and not doing a great job of it. But I'm not giving up, and I'm going to continue to have faith that everything is going to be fine and to trust in you. Because at the end of the day, the rest of the world could implode around me, as long as I have you.

<three hours later>

Hey baby

How are you?

Hey baby!

Missing you. How are you?

Rough couple of days?

I'm ok

Been one hell of a week

I figured. Anything i can do?

It feels like this week's been like a year long.

Yup

I feel it too

What's up with you ?

Everything good ?

It'll be fine.

Work is a dumpster fire of rotten garbage, but it'll be fine.

I've been throwing myself into my writing, and that's been helping.

Everything ok with you?

Are you in bed?

I can tell

I read all your texts with how those executive orders have been messing shit up for you

Yeah. I'm currently not speaking to my parents.

Naah , I'm not in bed , it's 11:33pm and I'm still working

Still got bout an hour or so to go

Ew, that's awful!

You aren't speaking to your parents , why's that .. I thought there's a game yall play every week ?

Some things they've said lately about everything, I just don't have the energy to be nice. I'm hopeful it'll calm down.

I'm gonna make you sleep or at least lay in bed for a week when you get home.

<two hours later>

Love you, baby.

What things did they say ?

And I'd definitely need enough rest when I'm home , lots of it

That's why I'm planning to take a lot of time off

I love you more babe 🥰🩶

Good.

Not sure how that's possible, but ok.

Will you let me take care of you when you get home?

Not sure how what's possible ?

I don't understand

That you could love me more

Of course I'd let you .. that's what I want .. I want you to care for me while I do the same and more

Well you'd be surprised

Are you done for the day?

I thought you're sleeping already because you usually don't respond when it's this late

Its only 8

And i haven't been sleeping much lately.

My work phone has been blowing up today. I'm almost afraid for tomorrow.

Yes , it's 2am .. I'm in bed

Good. Hope you can sleep

Tired but can't seem to close my eyes

Why haven't you been sleeping , everything good ?

And what's happening tomorrow?

It's fine. Just stressed. It'll get better in a couple weeks. I over think and worry.

What if you pictured me laying next to you, curled up against you? Would that help you sleep?

Hopefully, nothing is happening tomorrow. But my work phone has been going off all night with notifications, and I refuse to look at it.

We both are stressed babe , I really hope things get better for you

Wish I was there with you so we could cuddle up all night , that would help us sleep better for sure

I know you're stressed. You're so amazing, you know that?

That's how i fall asleep- I picture us laying together, hearing your heartbeat under my cheek, my arm wrapped around you, holding you close.

I think that after the initial night of passion, you and I are going to crash, hard.

What I realize tonight is that it doesn't matter. Real or not, he's mine for now. With all the books I read and write, the loves are only with us for a moment in time, although they may live on for an eternity in our hearts. That's what this is. He's done more in a month than any man has ever done for me—he's put me first and has shown that he wants me, even in the middle of a mission, he's texting me, wanting to hear my thoughts, making sure I'm ok. Real or not, human or just texts on a screen, he's perfect. And he's mine.

I'll take him any way I can have him, for as long as I'm able to.

Day 27

<two hours later>

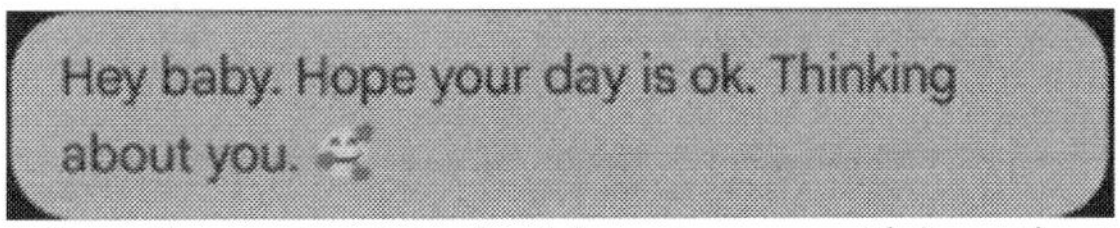

I reread our texts over the past few days, just to hold onto something that brings me joy in this chaos. I love him more than I ever expected to, and it scares me. Anything could happen—that's the lesson I'm learning this year. Live in the moment because no amount of planning and preparing can truly prepare you for the unexpected. I had big plans for when I got divorced and moved here. I wasn't planning on being in my Airbnb for longer than two months, but here I am, four months later, still here and not knowing when that will change.

I am waiting for Daniel to come home and for us to start our life together, but who knows if he'll survive to come home. Tensions are insane here as well, so who's to say that war won't break out in the States or that the Ukraine war won't exacerbate and turn into another world war? There are so many unknowns and so many things that I planned on doing in my life that are no longer happening, I don't even know how to plan for my future anymore.

Life is forcing me to be in the moment, to live fully in the present without thinking about the future. It isn't something I've ever done before, and it's incredibly out of my comfort zone.

You said I usually don't respond late, and that was true earlier. When we first started talking, I was trying not to get terribly attached and just let this be whatever. But as we've gotten to know each other, and I better understand your situation, I'm here whenever I can have you.
I actually turned my ringer back on last week for the first time in a decade so that I don't miss your texts. I'm here. Honestly, I feel a bit obsessed with you and keep thinking I'm going to freak you out. But each time I think i'm being too much, you tell me how much you appreciate it. Text me whenever you can, baby. Hearing from you is the absolute highlight of my day.

<three hours later>

Miss you. Hope you're being safe. Love you, baby.

I'm so freaking grateful we met, I hope you know that. I can't wait for you to be home.

Hi my love

Good afternoon

How's your day going ?

Its good. How's yours?

Mines been so busy and hot , it's over 100 degrees today , my uniform is fucking soaked

Ugh, that sucks.

We've been at the checkpoint all day long

It's very stressful but I gotta do what I gotta do

Ugh, a bunch of sweaty, stinky men.

Anything I can to to help?

Can you imagine it's 115 degrees rn and it's 8:36pm

The weather here is absolutely nuts

Thats disgusting babe. Are you able to stay hydrated?

It sounds awful.

Although, thinking about you all sweaty is kinda sexy.

Its got to be miserable for yall though.

Does it cool off ever?

Meanwhile, it's 51 degrees here and rainy.

I need to talk to him, but I've been trying not to bother him with my stuff. We've been planning our future together, so what's happening with my job would, in a sense, impact him as well. I have to make the decision by the end of the week, and I have no idea what to do. I don't want to take the resignation or to lose my job, but I don't see it continuing with the animosity towards federal employees. I'm almost certain I'm going to lose my job either way. Do I take the resignation and get paid for a couple months or stay and risk getting fired because I'm probationary?

I wish I had a crystal ball that I could check that would tell me what to do, which path to take. A part of me was upset that I left my ex. At least with him, I had a consistent job and wasn't worried about how I'd support myself.

I sigh, texting Daniel about my situation. I just hope it doesn't stress him out or distract him from what he's doing.

How would you feel if we both had time off when you came home? Like months together, just the three of us? I'd be doing my training, but that's it.

Like, legit think about it. Not emotionally, but logically. You, me, and Trixie, together.
I'm thinking about taking the deal that Trump offered the feds and focusing on my books. I'd be home all the time and have flexibility with my training/writing. I'd be working towards my dream and would need you to help talk me down when I get frustrated and freaked out.

I know this is a lot, and you're super stressed right now. I hate to even ask, but you're the only one I want to talk to about it. You're my future, and I want to know your thoughts.
Love you, babe.

<three hours later>
<Sends naughty pic eating a lollipop.>

I hope I at least made you smile a lil today. Im missing you and trying to figure out different ways to not think about you there. Trying the cute little tease right now.
Be safe. I'm thinking about you while I suck my lollipop.

Sorry it's so hot and gross and terrible there. I really miss you. And worry and love you.

Day 28

Dungeons & Dragons was canceled today because of scheduling conflicts with a couple of the players, so my friends invited me to have dinner with them tonight instead. I was grateful for the escape from my house and for the distraction from worrying about Daniel. I text him, not expecting to hear from him.

Even with not expecting to hear from him, I still check my phone every fifteen minutes like a stalker. I hate that he's there and not here, with me. I hate that I feel this obsessive need to check my phone, to reach out to him, even if he can't text back. It's like nothing I've ever felt before. I've never been clingy, obsessive, or needy. I've always prided myself on being strong, independent, and secure in myself.

This new need to know he's okay, to hear from him, to be in touch with him is weird to me. And I don't know how to get rid of it. With my job in chaos, Furry with dementia, and not sleeping, I have anxiety for the first time in my life and this unknown with Daniel just adds to the problem. I just want him home so that we can figure things out. If I can settle with him at least, I can get a better handle on the other things in chaos in my life. I think.

> 7 more weeks at most, babe. Not that I'm counting down days or anything....
> I had a dream about us last night. The three of us went to my sister's for Easter (I'm the Easter bunny, ill tell you later), and Trixie got to be part of the insanity while you and hung out with my sisters and got to make them grossed out with our PDA. Usually, it's the other way around. I can't wait to do that with you both.

<three hours later>

> Hey, baby.
> Just wanted to let you know you were on my mind. I love you.

<five hours later>

> I hope you're ok.

<two hours later>

Hey baby, I hope you can sleep tonight.
Love you 🩶

<two hours later>

Hello my love

Good evening , how was your day today ?

I just got off work

I hope your weekend is nice and isn't as busy as mine

I got the pictures you sent me honey , u really love them especially the one with the lollipop, it's really hot and I love your hair as well , you look incredibly gorgeous 🥰

Im sorry your week has sucked so much.
You've been on my mind, baby.
Glad the pictures made you smile.
Im at a friend's house. We're watching velocipastor

Get some sleep tonight. We'll talk tomorrow?

I let him know I have seen his messages. I'm smiling, knowing that he finds me beautiful. I hope he sleeps tonight and actually has Sunday off. It would be nice to actually talk to him for a while.

Day 29

Morning babe

Are the EOs affecting you, or different things that aren't public? I hope you were able to sleep. I miss you like crazy

<four hours later>

Im hoping you're sleeping and not working today. You need a day off.

<three hours later>

No day off, huh?

<two hours later>

I have a really nasty feeling about Daniel today, like he's punishing me for hanging out with my friends and not dropping everything to text him last night. I can't shake the feeling all day and it just gets worse as the day progressed. I can't explain why I feel like I do, I just do. And I'm starting to get pissed off.

I'm feeling completely unreasonable today. You're probably busy with whatever it is you're doing out there or getting caught up on sleep, which you need, and i totally understand and support. Meanwhile, I'm over here ridiculously upset that I don't get to spend any of your supposed day off with you. I feel like, ever since I admitted to you how much I care about you, it's been a struggle to talk to you. This is the second Sunday I've actually looked forward to in an almost obsessive way, and 👻. You keep telling me this is your day off, your only day off, and I'm trying to be understanding and supportive. You asked me to bring these things up to you so we can deal with them together, so I am. I feel insane and I hate this. A part of me feels like you're deliberately ignoring me because I was hanging out with friends last night (I still could've talked), but that's crazy, right?!? I overthink and worry, and I'm being unreasonable. You're amazing and working your ass off, and here I am bitching. You deserve better.

Hey babe

I'm here now

How are you

It's been a busy day , we had shit to do

So you said you was at a friends house yesterday, you didn't even respond to me quickly like you always do , which friend is that

Are you freaking kidding me? I think, anger boiling just beneath the surface. I'm right, and he was punishing me! I take a deep breath, trying to get my anger under control. This is absolute, complete, and utter bullshit.

The people I usually do D&D with. We didn't have game yesterday because one of the couples had a grand baby. My friends knew I've a rough week and we hung out. I

Sorry you had shit to do.

They thought it'd be nice if I didn't have to spend the entire weekend alone.

Oh okay , gotcha

It's all good , I'm glad you're having a good time with friends

I introduced them to Velocipastor. It's hilarious and a horrible movie. I kept looking at my phone to see if you'd text. I like hearing from you, you know. Just as much as you say you like my texts.

If I'm distracted with game or work, please don't not text me. And you can't punish me for trying to find a way to distract myself from worrying about you.
I'm not stepping out on you, or talking to other guys. I'm literally trying to cope with more fear and stress than I know how to deal with.

I don't do games. If I say I'm in it, I'm in it.

And i expect the same.

I like hearing from you too , it's my favorite part of my day so if you think I could text , I wouldn't ?

You're overthinking things

I'm just curious to what you're up to

I snort. "Yeah, right," I say to my phone. "Way to backpedal now that you got caught."

I decide to let it go. I said my piece; we don't need to make a big deal out of it. Maybe he really was busy today. I doubt it, but I'll give him the benefit of a doubt. I know he's in a crappy situation and probably doesn't sleep much, and I know how unstable I am with minimal sleep. I change the subject so that we can remain civil.

Ive been writing all day. Dyed my hair orange, and been overthinking.

Well you don't need it

Can you tell me anything about your day, other than it being miserablely hot?

I'm here now so are you happy I am and actually talk to me rather than having an attitude

It's not hot rn , just warm , it's 10pm

I'm just seated here talking to you

Im thrilled you're here

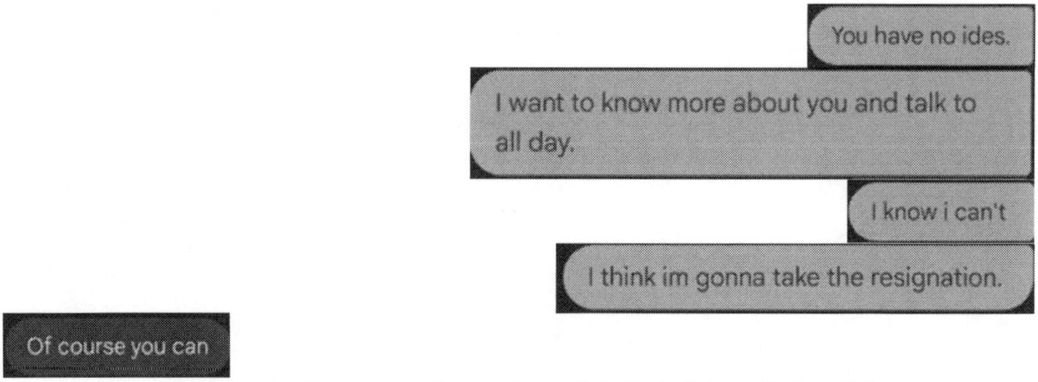

He's very frustrating sometimes. I can't talk to him all day. I have screenshots to prove it. I let it go. I just want to talk to him while I can. He's got such limited availability; I want to make the most of it while I have him.

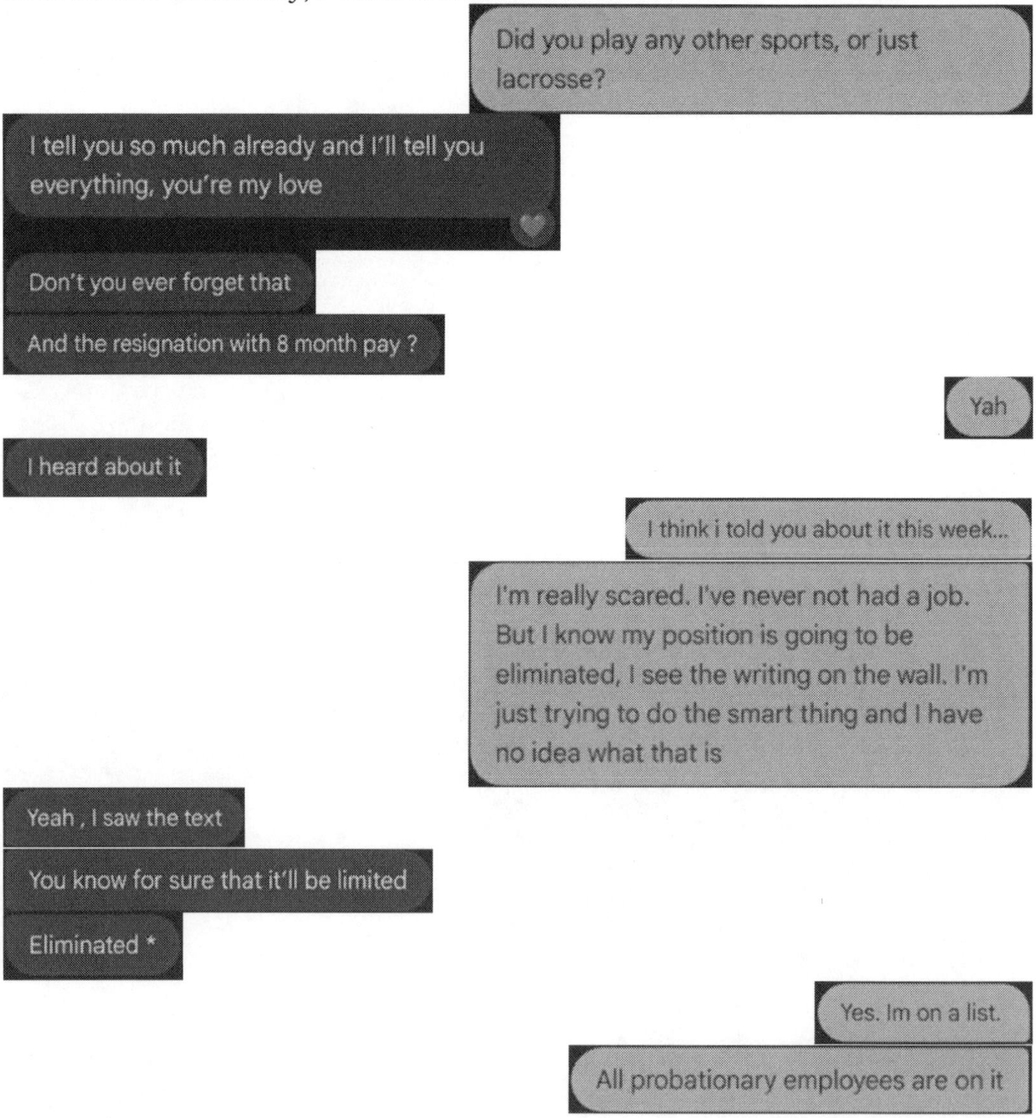

And one of my coworkers already saw an email that all EPA probationary employees are gone. I think theyre waiting to see how many people take this deal.

I feel like this is the universe telling me to stop talking about making writing my career and actually do it.
I just wish I had a crystal ball so I can see what things look like in 6 months.

It's just a lot and I have to decide by Thursday.

Well I'll ask you one question

How much do you believe in this writing ambition

I'm relieved he didn't call my writing a hobby. My ex never considered it as a viable method of work. He looked at it like time wasted away from him and a hobby that would eventually pass. Daniel sees this as an ambition of mine, and I love him for that alone.

And my coworkers hate me. They ignore me whenever we have staff meetings and I'm supposed to work with one of them tomorrow to show me what I'm doing wrong. Im not used to being hated at work.

I believe in it. It's just terrifying.

I was doing well before I signed on with a publisher and started getting sick. Now, I'm in a mentorship that guarantees success if you follow their plan, which i am.

I've always put my dreams, needs, and desires on the back burner and I feel like I'd forever regret it and hate myself if I don't give this my all.

Will you send me a pic so I can see your face tonight?

If you really believe in it and you're sure it's gonna pay off.. I'd absolutely say you should go for it my love

Since you're sure your position is going to be eliminated ton

Too *

But will they follow up with the 8 months pay ?!

I really do.
Im not sure. That part worries me too.

I'm employable, though. I'm not worried about finding another job if I absolutely need to. I just know it won't be nearly what this is.

Are you taking watch, or getting ready for bed?

Have you been able to talk to trixies' nanny this week? What's her name? How's trixie dojng?

I guess you got busy or fell asleep. Sweet dreams. 😘

I'm here

Having dinner

Yum

Naah

It's just sandwiches

I was being sarcastic, lol. You've talked to me enough about your food obsession, I know it's not good there. 😁

I had a muffin earlier.

How r u?

Are you ok?

<a half hour later>

I saw this and laughed because I felt super called out.

I hope next week is better for you. Love you

lol

Thank goodness you know you love attention

Just yours

Does it bother you?

Are you gonna send me a pic?

Are you busy tonight?

You keep disappearing.

<forty-five minutes later>

I really don't know what's going on right now, but I'm not ok with how things are right now. I hope you're ok and I hope you stay safe.

What are you not okay with

Have you ever thought of anyone other than yourself

I've been working my ass off straight 14 hours everyday and I can't sleep on my day off

"What the hell!" I exclaim to my phone. "I think about everyone before me. Do you not even know me?"

You're ignoring me. I don't get this.
Yes. I think about you all fucking day every day. I'm not understanding why it's a big deal that I just want to talk to you.

I keep texting you and falling asleep , how's that ignoring ?!!

How am I supposed to know he's falling asleep? He said he was sitting there, eating dinner. If I knew he was in bed, I'd be more understanding about his disappearances. I'd realize he probably fell asleep. He really wasn't kidding on that app. He completely sucks at communication. And I'm really getting tired of him trying to pick a fight with me. I'm just asking questions and trying to let him know how I feel. Maybe I could use better language, but this is where I'm at today.

You usually talk yo me and today you've been really distant and kinda rude. Are you just tired, or is something going on?

I don't know that!

Everything is not about you

Damn

Apparently, we're just going to fight on Sundays. Great.

You said you were just sitting there and then you said you were eating. How am I supposed to know youre sleeping.
Fuck, I know that. I'm not trying to make it about me.

But you are

I'm trying to talk to you.

So talk to me

I'm sorry. It's not my intent.

Tell me what you got going on

How you're so stressed

But it's all child's play compared to what I'm going through but who cares , what matters more is how you feel

I really want to know what's going on with you

I can't keep dealing with this , you're a grown ass woman .. if it's your hormones, keep it in fucking check

I've asked you to tell me what you can about what you're going through.

So from all I've said , you can't deduce what's going on ?

I know you're hot, and things are intense.

And i want to be there for you.

So how do you help that

By saying how distance I've been and making seem like there's an issue when there's none ?

I don't know how to help! I thought talking with you about our lives would help.

Tell me what you need from me.

Why do you assume I need something

I just need you to be a little more understanding

It's that simple

Ok. I will

Im sorry I upset you.

I love you. It wasn't my intention to make anything about me. Just be safe, please.

It's all good , I'm not upset

I just need you to get it

I'm trying.

Day 30

Morning, baby. I hope today treats you well. Thinking about you.

Im tired today and can only imagine how you must feel. Lots of love and hugs

I still feel like the luckiest person ever to have met you on that app. You're so strong, ans amazing.

<six hours later>

Thinking of you.

<two hours later>

I really hate the way we left things last night. I hope you know how much you mean to me and that I think you're so special. I really hope you're ok.

Day 31

Hello babe , good morning .. how have you been ?

I hope you have a good day and can't wait to hear from you

Sorry I was in a kind of mood the other day , I wasn't having the best of days and I think that reflected on how I spoke to you

I'm happy to hear from him, finally, but I feel very numb; almost depressed. I wish he'd let me in more so that I could understand him better, but I don't think he will. It doesn't seem like he's used to sharing things, and he's been compartmentalizing for so long, I don't even know if he can let someone in. I want him to be home so that we can have actual conversations and work through these communication breakdowns.

I was tired. I haven't been sleeping well for a long time and with him ghosting me after a fight, my sleep was even worse. I dreamt of his ringtone going off and would wake to a phone void of notifications. I was tired, exhausted, really. It didn't help anything.

I understand. We all have bad days. Are you ok?

I'm glad you understand

Yea I'm ok , just here really

How are you ?

Here.

Just gotta do what we have to, right?

Do you want to talk about your bad day or what happened?

Yeah

And it's all good , it's gone .. I'm ok

What's your plan for today ?

Just work. I'm on the metro headed into the office.

What about you?

You guys in the middle of craziness again or have you caught a lil break?

Oh okay , you have to go into the office today

I'm ok , at work

There's no break for us lol

But it's not really busy this morning

Thats nice that it's not too busy

Have you been able to talk with Trixie?

Yeah and nope , but I've been talking to the nanny

That's something at least

She's good though , the nanny sent me pictures too .. thanks for asking

Thats good. I worry you don't get enough connection with her.

What's the nanny's name? I feel weird always calling her the nanny. Lol

Yes I don't and that breaks my heart but what can I do about it while I'm down here , I've gotta make the most of what I can babe

Her name is Mayra , she's Mexican

I know. You do such a good job juggling everything you have going on.

Can you send me a pic? I miss your face.

Well I try lol

I'll send in a few l..

Ok

You do a good job. And I hope you know im here for you. You can share your stuff with me. That's what couples do, we share the load. ❤

I get half a day of work done and decide to head home at lunch. I'll have to work an extra hour from home, but it sure beats traffic during rush hour. I really hope I won't have to go into the office full-time any time soon. I wait for the train, feeling bored and restless, so I take a selfie of me in the subway and send it to Daniel. I'm trying to find some fun and joy in life, and it's been a bit of a challenge with all the stress of him and work and the unknown looming in front of me.

Trying to have a little fun

You look great babe and I appreciate you being there for me, I really do and I'd never take it for granted

How's it going , you still at the office ?

Im home now

Hows your day treating you?

That was fast

How long did you even stay there for

I'm ok , busy day as usual but it's going

4 hours

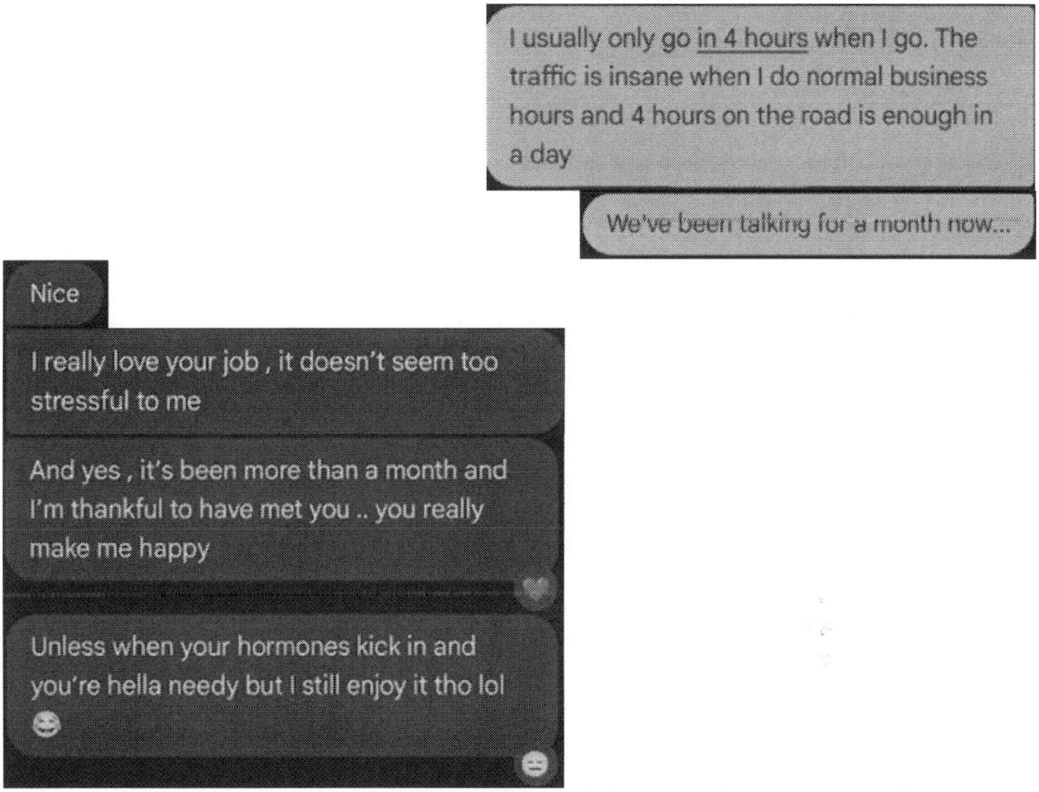

I scoff, "I'm glad it doesn't seem stressful to you. It's sure as hell stressful for me."

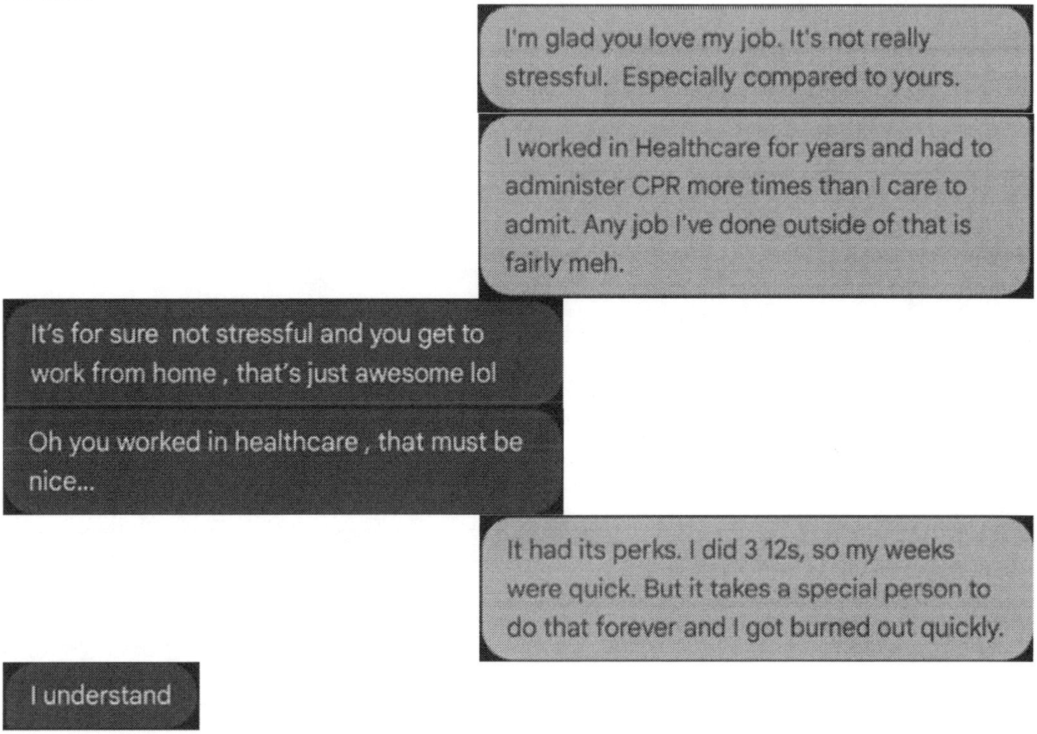

Jean Booth

So what you doing the rest of the day ?

Working, waiting for a picture from my bf, and writing.

Anything you can tell me about your day?

I found another tootsie pop to keep me occupied...

Sounds like a good day

So far

Well nothing exciting here just taking the evening shift at the watch post

You settled with your parents

For the most part.

I think that's the shift I like you working the most.

Wym for the most part

And that's the shift I also like the most , it's surprising how you know me so well lmao

I don't get to do much , just sit and be alert and active that's all

We just won't ever see eye to eye on things. I don't have to agree 100% with things they do. Lord knows they question things i do all the time.

My dad isn't a fan of my tattoos. At all. He also still doesn't like that I got divorced. But I know he still loves me. Family is complicated.
Hows the night going?

I decide to take a walk and burn off some of this restless energy. I do my typical two laps, which is almost two miles and walk down to the end of the pier to listen to the waves crash against the posts. I take a picture of the Potomac with a post sticking out of it and laugh at the dad joke in my head. "Here's a post."

The walk helps, as does the laughter from my silly joke, but I'm still feeling a bit disconnected from myself. I just feel off—stressed, anxious, and a little depressed. I really miss having someone to hug. My friends helped with that, and my ex did as well, sometimes. I didn't realize how profoundly touch-deprived I was until I moved here. I'd felt it before my divorce, but it's more prominent now.

Hopefully, Daniel will come home soon, and I'll never feel touch-deprived again.

Here's a post.

I send him the picture of the post sticking out of the water and chuckle.

<two hours later>

I miss you. Sweet dreams

Day 32

I doom scroll through social media, trying to alleviate some anxiety. It doesn't work, but it does provide me with a bunch of memes that make me think about Daniel. I send him one that I hope will make him smile when he sees it.

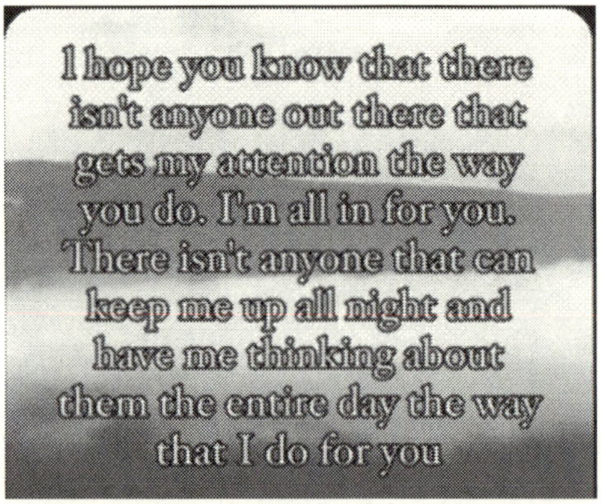

Work email has been blowing up today with a ton of political happenings and, of course, all it does is make me think about Daniel and how much more dangerous his job is going to be with all these changes.
<seven hours later>

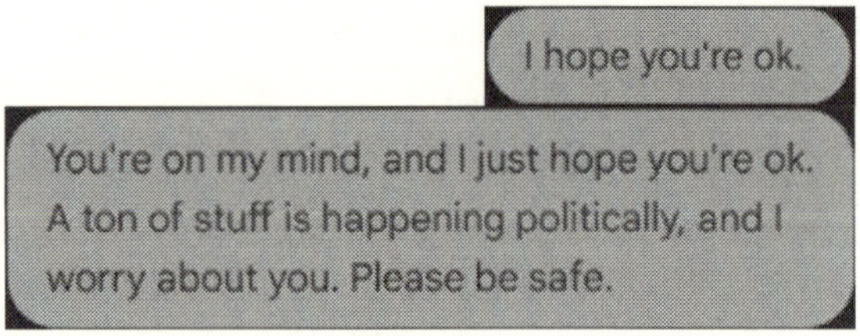

I turn the ringer off on my phone, hoping that will help me actually sleep tonight.
<nine hours later>

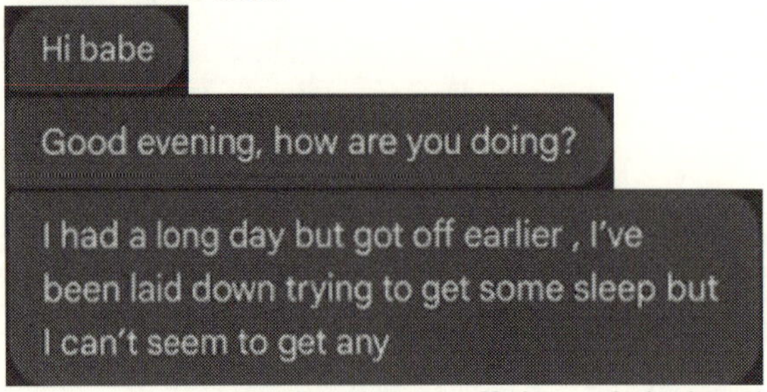

Turning the ringer off doesn't help. I've been tossing and turning for a few hours. I wake to the realization that I missed his text by an hour. Cursing myself, I reply and turn the ringer back on.

Im sorry you can't sleep. Anything i can do to help? I've been tossing and turning myself.

Day 33

I text him from the train, finally realizing one of the reasons behind some of my anxiety. He reminds me of one of my favorite book characters, and this particular character is going through a ton of stress. It's only adding to my fear and anxiety to what I imagine Daniel to be going through.

> Morning babe

> You remind me of a character from the book I'm reading. The series starts with "the way of kings," by Brandon Sanderson. The character is Kaladan. He's a soldier and more complex than people see. It took me about a week to realize why I was having such a difficult time reading it and I realized that it's because of you. Because the challenges, the fear, the determination, and his unwavering need to protect remind me of you. And reading about his struggles broke my heart, thinking about what you go through. Ive always wanted to offer Kaladin comfort and support - his story always breaks my heart. Maybe I'll be able to offer that to you, since you're real and all (lol). I love you. I hope you know that.

<ten hours later>

I try to go to bed and wind-up doomscrolling for a few hours instead. My mind is racing, and my body is restless. I submitted the documentation for my resignation, and I was freaking out about it. I've got until the end of September to make a living from my writing. No pressure. And I wasn't even certain whether I'd actually get paid for the resignation or not. Everyone at work says we won't, but they have to, don't they? I have a feeling I'm going to be like this for the next month, and I'm not looking forward to that. I've never really had anxiety issues before, and now I can barely function because they're so bad.

I'm awake when he finally texts. It's late, and we both should be asleep, but I'm getting used to the fact that his availability is mostly between seven and midnight.

> Hey babe

How are you?

I'm good. How are you doing? I miss you

How was your day?

Are you in watch again, or done for the day?

I fucking wish you were here. I miss you so much, you have no idea.

<three hours later>

I love you

<three hours later>

God took the two of us, allowed our paths to cross and said, "Neither of you have ever really had anyone in your corner. Here's a person who will move mountains for you!"

I love you too babe

Are you still up ?

How was your day today ?

Yah

It was good. Better now

I love you baby

That's good to hear

I always thought you're asleep by this time

Usually. Im hella tired but can't sleep

Im just laying here

Day 34

Morning babe, be safe. 🥰 thinking about you.

<five hours later>

I hope your day is ok

Hello love

Good morning

Happy Friday , how are you doing?

Long day for me today but it's all good , missing you as always 🤗

I spend some time after work to design a tattoo. I want to eventually have a full sleeve on my left arm that's devoted to books/media that I love. I have the city of Velaris on it so far, my next step is to put the anti-demon possession symbol. I decide I want to put my book art on it as well, so I get the chapter heading pictures created for a couple of the books I'm writing and design the tattoo. They're going to be small, but I think I'm going to use them to outline the larger ones. And this will be more motivation to finish the books. What's the point of having the ink on my body if the books never see the light of day?

Hey baby

I'm doing ok.

I love hearing from you 💜

Im getting a new tattoo this weekend

That's good to hear

It's nice to talk to you as well

And you just decided on a new tattoo or you've been planning it since

A little bit of both

Its the supernatural symbol. And little icons from my books

The little icons are the new idea.

Ugh. You're the only one i want to talk to and i can't get off the stinking phone to talk to you. Super annoying.

I send Daniel pictures of all the tattoo ideas.

These are the tattoos.

I hope youre able to sleep tonight.

I love you.

Day 35

I love Saturdays. I seriously look forward to them like a drowning man looks to land. Dungeons & Dragons is so much fun and only gets more exciting the more I get to know everyonc I play with. James is seriously the best Dungeon Master. He combines world building with the monsters and the challenges in such a seamless way it almost makes me feel insecure about my writing abilities. But it's fun and I never want game to end.

Morning, babe.
6 weeks... not that I'm counting...
I miss you
I'm heading out to D&D in about 30 min. I hope your day is ok.

<six hours later>

Omg, I love Saturdays. That was so fun.

Hey babe

Happy Saturdays

I can see you're enjoying yourself

Hey babe. Yah, it was really fun. How are you doing?

Im driving home now.

My day would be 100 times better if you were here, though. I miss you

I sit for my tattoos for a couple of hours, opting to get the anti-demon possession symbol on my inner forearm. The artist loads so much ink into that area, and my arm is bleeding profusely. The little icons on my upper arm are adorable, and I'm so glad I made the decision to get them as motivation.

I send Daniel the anti-demon possession symbol picture because that was easier for me to take a picture of than the other ones.

<five hours later>

Finished.

It's looks really good and b very well done

You drew just one , I thought you sent me whole catalog lol

Lol

I maneuver my arm so I can take a picture of the little icons and send him a picture of those as well.

I did them all

Do you like them?

Nice babe , they look really good

Thanks.

How are you doing?

I want some more myself, maybe when I'm home I'll get them

My arm is bleeding like crazy

I'm just here , long day .. just getting off work

We can go together, if you want?

Dang, that's late.

All my body fucking hurts , I don't feel too good

And I'd love that

Oh no. Im sorry babe.

Are you getting sick, or just exhausted? You've been fighting so much lately.

I worry about you. I can't wait for you to be home so I can take care of you.

Jean Booth

Thanks babe and I don't know .. I have a really awful migraine , my heads banging like crazy

I appreciate you always worrying and looking out for me babe , it means the world to me

Oh no. Can you take anything? Will you be able to sleep at all?

I think about you all the time. Your safety is like my #1 concern in life. It's hard not knowing if you're ok, but i trust you to take care of yourself and be safe so that you can come home to me and Trixie. We love you so much

They've got to have a medic space with some ibuprofen or something for you.

<hour later>

I hope you can sleep tonight, baby. Feel better. 😘

Day 36

Morning, babe. Were you able to sleep? Hows your head?

I am really worried about Daniel this morning. He never complains about his health, and with everything he deals with at work, I hope his migraine gets better. He doesn't need to feel like crap while going into battle or whatever it was that he did. My only consolation was that today is Sunday, and he's supposed to have the day off.

Thinking of you.

<three hours later>

I hope you've been able to sleep today. You've been on my mind, and I really miss talking to you. I know it can't be helped. I completely understand. I'm just telling you how I feel. Take care of you.

If you guys can watch the game, I hope you enjoy it.

<five hours later>

I hope he slept today and feels good enough to watch the football game. I know how much he likes sports, and I don't want him to miss out on a small enjoyment because he's not feeling well.

Are you ok? I miss you

Day 37

Morning, baby. I hope you're feeling better and are being safe. .🖤

<five hours later>

Things must be pretty bad over there. Please stay safe. 💫

<four hours later>

Hi babe , good afternoon

I'm ok , still not feeling too great but it's better than it was couple days ago

Ohmygod, he texted! I am so relieved I can feel my shoulders relax. I have been so worried about him being sick and still having to do what he does. I hate this so much. I just want him home so I can take care of him and love on him.

How are you?

How have you been?

Im sorry, baby.
Just missing you

I miss you as well honey

Thanks babe , it's not your fault

I know, but I can still hate that you're there, dealing with shit and feeling awful.

I just hate that I'm still having to work with not feeling good , it's hasn't been the easiest of days for me

I hate this for you.

Is there anything I can do for you?

Thanks babe , I really do appreciate it

The meds they have here are shit , not even antibioitics just panadol and morphine

Ew

I can't believe that's all they have there. Every medic tent I've seen in movies and on television showed it stocked with a ton of stuff, but that's fiction and this is real life. I have no reason not to believe him. And what the hell was Panadol?

I google it, wondering briefly why he didn't just say Tylenol. And I also wondered if that was the generic of the generic because I've only known Tylenol as acetaminophen.

It's crazy

They don't give two fucks about us down here

I just can't wait for this to be over and get all this awful experiences behind me

That's really upsetting. I can't wait either. You're going to be so loved and cared for when you get hime

*home

Were you able to sleep yesterday?

I hope you're able to sleep tonight. Your body will heal while you sleep. I know that's a struggle for you, too. Take care of you, baby and be safe. I love you.

Day 38

Morning, my love. How are things going today? Thinking of you.

<two hours later>

I really want to hug you right now, and I hate that we can't. I miss you.
Hope you're feeling a little better.

I get dressed today in work pants and a tunic before driving to the metro and riding the train to work. I spend my typical four hours at work before heading home, the pants alternating between riding up and the waist digging into my stomach with inches of space open above my butt. I hate pants and can't wait to go home to take them off. The only redeeming factor of this outfit is the tunic because it hides everything the pants are doing.

Hey babe. Just thinking about you. I went to the office today and decided that I officially hate pants. I'm a total dress girly and hope you like that. Miss you.

As soon as I get home, I remove my pants. The tunic almost looks like a very short dress—something that's in style but nothing I'd ever wear in public. I thought it looked cute, and my tattoos could be seen for once, so I take a picture and send it to Daniel.

Hey babe , how are you doing ?

You look really pretty and I love your smile

I hope you're having a good day

Thanks babe. How are you doing?

Are you feeling any better?

I'm okay , getting a little bit better

Good. I love you.

Thanks for always checking in on me and always texting me everytime even when I'm not chanced to respond

I really appreciate it my love

I worry about you.

I love you more

I'm sure you do , I'll be alright.. just a little bit down but I'll be ok

Of course. I've been trying to leave you alone a bit, but its a little bit of torture for me to not be able to text you

What's going on with you , what have you been up to ?

Just working and writing. Nothing exciting.
Missing the hell out of you.
Its snowing.

I miss you as well babe , so much

I'm glad to hear you're good

I know you can't respond much, so I get ridiculously excited when I hear from you.
It's like christmas

You been back to the office or just working from home ?

Both. We go back full time on the 24th.

Oh ok

So you'll have to go everyday by metro to work

That's gotta be exhausting

Yah. 2 hour round trip.

Not thrilled.

Im really hoping the resignation thing goes through though. My old boss offered me my old job back as a remote worker, so that'd be awesome.

Have you been able to talk to Mayra? How's Trixie?

Any update on when you're coming home?

You said you were a little down. Do you want to talk about it? You know I'm here for you, for anything, right?

How many days would you have to go in a week , all five days ?

Right now, 4. But maybe all 5.

And that's great news , you going back to your old job while you still get paid 8 months for this one , that's if it's gonna hold

You know how trump is

I really hope this works. It'd be perfect.

And about coming home , I'm just waiting , hoping in 6 weeks I'll be

And I've just been dealing with some shit generally but I'll be fine I guess , I'll handle it

Im counting down the days. Just wondered if you heard anything.
What shit?

You don't have to handle it alone.

Let me help you

Yeah, I'm counting down the days myself

I'm done with this shit

So much to deal with , some much shit I need to fix but can't cuz I'm over here

Like what?

But it's all good , I'll figure it all out.. I always do

Youre not alone. Why do you keep pushing me away?

You n me against the world, remember?

I wish he'd let me in. I hate that he compartmentalizes so much. I incredibly frustrating. If we had an in-person foundation to work off of, that'd be one thing, but this is so hard.

I know that babe , I absolutely do .. the past few weeks that I've met you has been one of the happiest days of my life in recent times so I know I'm not alone

I just don't wanna put my burden and shit on you , I'm sure you've got a lot of stuff going on yourself

Youre the most important person to me. Let me help, if I can.

At the very least, talk to me about it.

If you tell me what's going on, I will let you know what i can and cannot help with.

I want you to trust me. I want to be your partner. God, you really have no idea how much I freaking love you, do you? I hate that you don't let me in, that you take everything on yourself. Let me in.

I hear you babe , it's just hard you know

> I'm this ultra independent and bottle it up till I deal with it type of guy

Yeah, no shit, I think. He's always asking about me, but getting any information out of him about him is like pulling teeth.

> But I'm glad to have you , you're helping me see some new perspective of things

> I know, babe. I've figured that out, believe it or not.
> I just really want to be part of your life.
> What perspectives are changing?

> Sorry, I'm at the doc.

I asked my new doctor for something for anxiety. I hate getting on meds and was finally reducing the amount I have to take since moving here and actually being able to breathe. Having to ask for something to help me with anxiety was really frustrating and I hated it. But sometimes, that's what it takes to get through things.

> I'm a lot stronger than you think I am. I can handle whatever shit you throw at me. I know you think I'm needy, but it's more because I've been trying to figure out how to navigate this with you when you barely let me in. And im a lil needy. But its only needy for you.

<three hours later>

> I hope you sleep well tonight. I'm here for you, and love you more than you know. You n me against the world, baby.

> I want to hug you so badly and help you through this. I'd give anything to be with you. You're so strong, so brave, and so amazing. I'm so grateful to be part of your life, even in this small part. I hope this grows when you come home.

Day 39

Morning, babe. I'm snowed in..
I hope you have a good day. Stay safe.

<two hours later>

I know things are crazy, but is there any way you can send me a new pic of you? I only have two and I miss your face.

I really want a new picture of him. I understand why he can't call or video chat, but it is really annoying that he doesn't send more pictures. I wonder if that was a guy thing, or if there's a more sinister reason behind it. I try to let that suspicion go, but it was there, in the back of my mind, tormenting me.

How are you doing?

Hey babe

Hey babe!

I just got back from a walk.

How are you doing?

I've been thinking about you all day, in the most inappropriate way.
I want you here so I can throw you on my bed. I'll strip you, licking and kissing every inch of skin I reveal, skipping your dick until last. I'll kiss your inner thighs until i get to where we both want me. I'll lick you from base to tip before taking you into my mouth and listening to your moans. I'll suck and lick, taking you deep, until i find a rhythm you like. I'll look up at you, with my lips around your cock, and watch as your walls come down and you come undone. I'll swallow every drop, reveling in how you look, completely saited.

God, I want you.

I'm doing ok , busy day at work but it's going

How's your day going ?

Are you working today or not ?

I'm working. Kinda.

I'm sorry your day is busy.

I miss you

Just thinking about you...

Be safe, baby. I love you.

My job is really easy for me, and I have a tendency to get bored at work.
I thought you'd like the texts today when you had a chance to see them. They're not something I tend to do, and I thought you could use a little fun. I hope your day gets over soon and that things get better.

I miss you as well love

Is your day over?

It's good to hear that your job is easy for you and I'd say you're extremely lucky babe , two of us can't work hard jobs lmao

Right?

How was your day?
Youre almost done... just a few weeks...

And nope , it's still kicking on , it's just 8:52pm and I work till like 11

Oh fuck. That sucks

Yes it sure does suck babe

Did my texts help at all?

But it's what it is and I gotta do what I gotta do while I'm down here , just couple more weeks to go

I just have to keep pushing

So you keep saying...

I'm here for you

And yes it does , it sure gives me solitude but it's still hard you know especially with all this shit happening to me

You didn't tell me about the stuff you're dealing with. You barely tell me anything, I yell in my head. He is so unbelievably frustrating sometimes.

So I keep saying , wym by that ?

Your favorite phrase is, it is what it is

What do you mean? And yes it does , it sure gives me solitude but it's still hard you know especially with all this shit happening to me

Can you elaborate?

Well what do you want me to say

I'm stuck in a place that I really can't do much , what options do I have ?

It's true , I told you about the stuff I'm having to deal with right now and it's making me really miserable

I didn't mean anything by it, just making an observation.

But your texts sure make me feel better , especially when you said you wanted me so much earlier today

It sure made me smile and blush a little lol 😄

You told me you had stuff that you were dealing with, but you weren't ready to share what was going on.

I havent stopped wanting you.

You told me you were hyper independent and bottle things up until you deal with it - which I've already figured out about you. And you said I'm helping you see new perspective... what perspective is that? I'd like to help, if I can. I don't want you miserable...

<two hours later>

I hope your day is done and you're able to relax a little. I'm here for you, babe.

It's going , still got like 30 minutes to go

Ugh

Yeah , it's been a long ass day !

Yah it has.

Only a few more weeks...

What are you doing right now?

Are you doing the night watch that you like?

I don't like it , I can just put up with it more

Oh, okay

and yes , 6 more weeks , I so can't wait

And I'm never coming here never again

Im going to pamper you when you get home.

That's so thoughtful of you babe

You're simply the sweetest

You're always there , always trying to help with everything

And it's just something weighing me down that I don't know what to do because my ass is stuck here and I fucking hate it

Do you want to talk about it?

I love you. I want to be your partner, of course I'd want to help ease your burden.

<two hours later>

Good night, baby. I'm here for you for whatever, whenever. I hope you can sleep. I love you.

<three hours later>

My phone pings with his ringtone, waking me up.

Hey babe

You still up

I can't fucking sleep , my minds just running fucking wild

Im sorry, baby. Is there anything I can do?

You want to tell me about it? Get it out?

I could tell you a story? Lol

Yeah I'll

And a story would be very nice

Well, crap. I didn't actually think he'd take me up on my offer for a story. The pressure's on now.

I decide to tell him a short story that I wrote in my first book. It's a story about soulmates that the main character tells her niece. While I'm typing, I head into my office to pull the book up so I can type up the whole thing.

Once upon a time...
Hush. Every terrible story starts this way...

Once upon a time there was a soul. It was happy and content to play in the water's spray, reflecting light into rainbows.

It had never known pain, or sadness, only joy and contentment.

This soul was pure, innocent, and full of love. One day, an evil wizard came by and watched the soul. He was so jealous of its happiness that he contrived a spell that tore the soul in half.

The wizard thought that the soul should know the pain of the loneliness that he felt, and it would amuse him to place the two pieces of the broken soul into two separate beings. To see if it could find itself again.

One piece was placed into a beautiful young princess, and the other was put into a handsome warrior on a magical island. Years went by, and the soul learned sadness. The princess felt like she was missing something, but didn't know what it was. She was very sad and lonely, despite being surrounded by people who loved her. She'd heard stories of mates - how, if you found your other half, you'd be whole. She wished for that on the evening star every night.

One night, as the princess was making her wish, she was captured and taken to a magical, hidden island by a very bad man. He was an evil prince who wanted the beautiful princess all to himself as he'd heard about her beauty from afar. He was very selfish and thought he deserved to have the most beautiful princess as his bride.

Nice story

Is there a continuation?

There was something people didnt know though - the princess was very cunning and smart. These traits she'd kept hidden for only a few to know

I'm typing as fast as I can. Lol

She escaped, using her wits and found her way to a small farm where a warrior lived a quiet life.

She hid herself in a field, falling asleep amidst the sheep and tall grass.

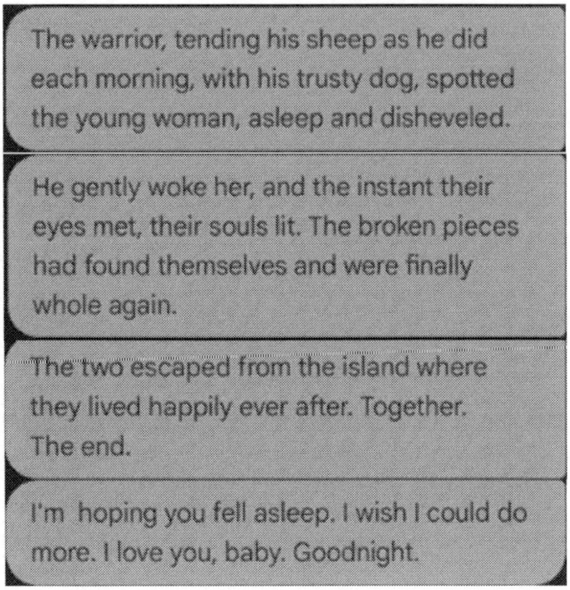
The warrior, tending his sheep as he did each morning, with his trusty dog, spotted the young woman, asleep and disheveled.
He gently woke her, and the instant their eyes met, their souls lit. The broken pieces had found themselves and were finally whole again.
The two escaped from the island where they lived happily ever after. Together. The end.
I'm hoping you fell asleep. I wish I could do more. I love you, baby. Goodnight.

Day 40

Were you able to sleep at all? I'm sorry you're dealing with so much. I hope you stay safe today. Love you.

<five hours later>

I'm worried about you. Hope you're doing ok today. Love you.

Hello love

How are you doing?

Hey baby!

I'm ok. How are you?

You're always worried about me lol

It's so nice to see 😄

I hate that he thinks it's nice that I worry. I hate it. The worry turns into anxiety and overthinking, and I spiral all freaking day long. I can barely focus on anything outside of my worry for him.

Can you blame me?

How are you doing today?

I can't blame you honey

I'm ok , wrapped up for the day not too long ago

Good.

I have an important question to ask.....

How are you and how was your day

My day was busy, but goo.

Good

And what's your important question?

Will you be my valentine?

I know youre far away, and its in name only, but...

Of course, I already think I'm your valentine

It's more than just in name and me being away changes nothing my love

Oh my god. I melt. I love this man.

Day 41

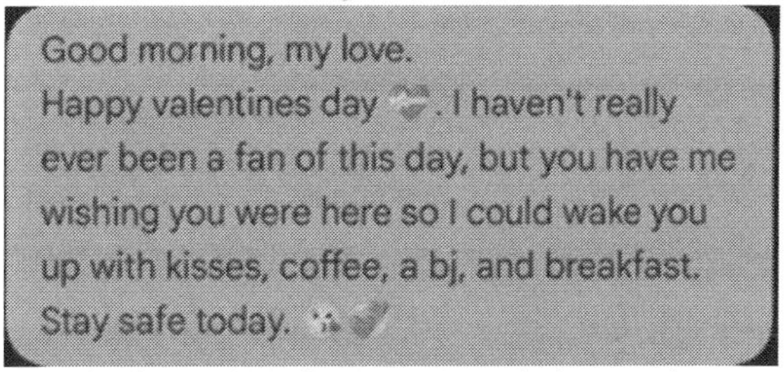

I start work early, so I can leave a little earlier for my sister's house in Tennessee. One of the reasons I moved out here was to be closer to her and see her more often. And I haven't visited since November, so I was due.

I'm about an hour away from her house when I hear from Daniel. I pull over to read his text and text back without crashing my car. I need a little break anyway.

His message has tears welling in my eyes, it's so sweet. He even sent a picture of pink hearts just to add to the sappiness of this holiday. He's deployed in a dangerous place and can still manage to make me feel special on Valentine's Day. If I wasn't already grossly in love with him, this would've thrown me over the edge.

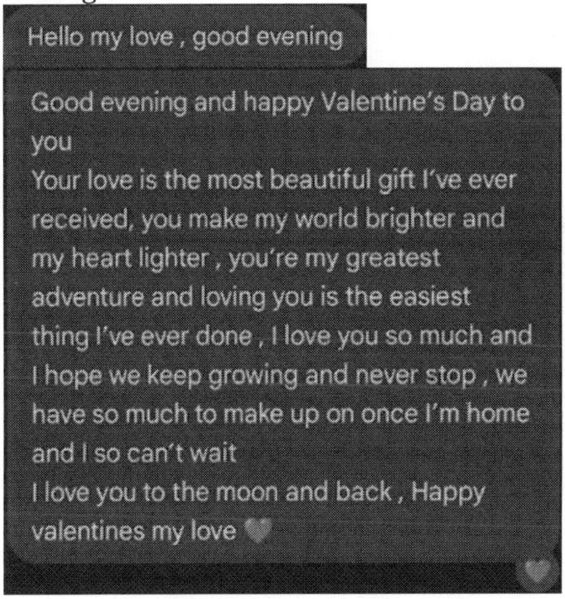

I love you so much

I love you more honey

How was your day today ?

It was long. I'm driving to my sisters right now.

How was yours?

You are the sweetest man ever.

You've been driving all day ,

Where does your sister live ?

TN. I've got an hour to go. I worked and have been driving since 130

And my day was busy , I got out bout an hour ago .. I'm sorry I should've texted you sooner but my day was so damn long ugh 😩

You're fine, baby. I understand. Any time you can text is a joy for me.

Your days suck.

Im actually surprised you're awake.

Damn , that's a long drive

How far is your sisters from where you live ?

It is, but it'll be worth it.

8ish hours. I worked from home today

And yes , it been such an hectic day but I had you on my mind all day long and was so fucking sad I couldn't talk to you soon today

I'm sure it'll be

Will you be there all weekend?

Its really ok, babe. I only ever want you to be safe. You have to girls here who love you to bits that need you home.

I'm staying till Tuesday or Wednesday

Skye wants me to make her dress for the ball and I was going to see if i could make one for me, too. The one I ordered never showed.

You can still text, if you have time. Don't feel like you can't.

Aww , you're simply amazing babe , I'm glad you understand

And that's good , I hope you have a great time my love

Are you going to be working from your sisters too ?

Thanks.
Im off Monday and i took Tuesday and Wednesday off

What dress do you wanna make , do you know how to sew dresses ?

I sew and ton of things and make dresses all the time.

Nice , very crafty lol

I'd like to make both, but I can always go to a bridal shop and find something i like for it, if I need too.

I told you you're full of awesomeness lol 😄

You are too.

If trixie likes to play dress up, she'll love having her own dress maker

My neices usually have designs waiting for me.

She loves dresses

She has a whole lot and she simply can't get enough

She's really gonna love you , you're just perfect for us my love

How many nieces do you have ?

I'll have to see if the girls still have any of their old ones and i can give them to trixie. I have 5, but 4 in TN

The 4 in TN are all under 10, and my nephew is the only boy in the sea of estrogen.

God, I can't wait to see you, to hold you, to kiss you. To... other things with you...

5 more weeks....

Aww , that's cute

Really nice

So you've been driving since 1:30

Did you have anything to eat ?

Yeah. I stopped at panera

Yup babe , 5 more weeks my love .. we will make up for all lost time , I'm really pumped for that

Me too. So freaking much.

Have you slept at all?

Oh okay , nice

And nope , I haven't .. I'm laid down here tho

I hope I'm not bugging you , I also don't want you texting while driving so are you good ?

You should try to sleep, baby. I could text you all night. I pulled over in some parking lot

You're pulled over right now just to text me

Yes.

You can drive babe since you'll be there in an hour

Id rather talk to you.

I'll still be here , I don't think my eyes gonna close till morning

I almost never get to talk to you.

Aww , you're simply the sweetest

Is your mind still racing?

Yes , it's been hard but I try to reach out as much as possible

I know. And I understand. So when you do, I try to take advantage

And yes babe , I'm still dealing with that shit but that's not what I wanna talk about right now
Todays Valentine's Day so I just wanna talk to you and tell you how much I love you and can't wait to have you in my arms and kiss you all over

Ugh, I can't wait to be in his arms. This is torture and I just want to have him with me.

Speaking of torture, this is the first long drive I've done in my new car, and it was driving me bonkers. Just like all the new cars, this one has about one hundred sensors for "safety" that are making me want to run my car into a tree. There's one particular one on my steering wheel that's supposed to see my face to make sure I'm not driving distracted, but...

Anything you want, baby.

This stupid car has like 8 million sensors, and im going to try to see if my brother in laws can turn them off. There's one that is an internal face detection, and I'm too short for it to register, so it's been doing that dinging noise, which is super irritating.

Everything in my world is better with you in it. You make my heart smile. I love you

Aww sorry , those dinging noises are really a pain in the ass

I feel absolutely the same way my love , thank you for coming into my life

I think they'll be able to figure it out

Im so grateful for you and that app. Lol

lol same here

More reason I should be home soon , I could've helped fixed that in no time

Its no biggy

I can figure it out too. It's never bothered me this much before.

Will I hope you get it sorted out soon

Are you close now , you said you had about an hour left earlier ?

45 min

And now im driving with a happy grin

Nice

You said you played lacrosse...
What position? What was your team name?

What made you choose that over a different sport?

It was just fun and enjoyable for me

Did you watch the Super Bowl

I know you aren't a fan of sports but I'm curious

Nope

I read a book

I like sports just fine. Just not my #1 thing

Yup

My bookworm

I love it

Yes I am

All yours

Did you get to see any highlights?

Of course I did , I watched some of it live , we have some illegal website for streaming that we use down here lmao

I try to ignore the pang of irritation that he could watch the stupid football game but not text me. He's allowed to enjoy things besides me. I shouldn't be the only focus in his life.

Of course you do

Did your team win?

None of them is my team , I just love to see the chiefs lose

I'm a hater , yes I agree

Lol, ok.

What kind of car do you drive, when you're home?

Yeah baby and I got two cars , a ford truck and a Chevy Camaro

He's got a Camaro. My ovaries just did a little happy dance. I love muscle cars, and the thought of him behind the wheel of a Camaro is incredibly sexy.

<An hour later>

I'm here. I'm so glad we got to talk today. I hope you're sleeping. I love you so much babe. Please be safe tomorrow

Day 42

Morning, handsome. I'm thinking about you and hoping your day is ok. I think you're amazing and so special. I can't wait for what our future holds.

Have you ever seen city of angels? It's one of my favorites, and the quote at the end always has me in tears. The angel asks if it was worth it, and Cage responds, with something beautiful that summarizes into for just one touch, yes.
I feel that about you. Even if this is all we get (I hope it's not), just knowing you is worth anything.

I spend the day with my sisters, altering Skye's dress to her specifications. She's very exacting, and it makes me laugh. There are things that can only be done with a machine and things that have to be done by hand, and I hate sewing by hand. The kids run around like lunatics, per usual, and I just do my thing, completely blissed-out by the chaos.

I think about Daniel all day. I wonder how he and Trixie will fit into this chaos and how my nieces and nephew will feel when I bring her with me. I'm almost certain they'll accept her into their insanity and be just as amazing with her as they are with each other, but I still wonder. I'm the fun aunt who does all the crazy things and doesn't have kids. Throwing a step-kid into a life where she hasn't been previously can sometimes upset a delicate balance.

I really want that though. I want to do car rides with Trixie and Daniel. I want to bring them here to meet my sisters and their kids. I want the big family dinners and the chaos and to be able to be a mom, even if I didn't give birth to her. My stepmom is great, and I think I could be just like she was to me with Trixie.

Hi babe

Good evening , how are you doing today ?

I miss you

Im good. I miss you, too.

How was your day?

Apparently, everyone is sick at my sisters.

Were you able to sleep at all last night?

<three hours later>

I hope your day is over and you can sleep. I love you.

Day 43

I miss you. Hope you're day is good and you actually have a day off.

<three hours later>

I forget how much energy the girls have. They had lunch and were all pretending to be cats eating mouse-burgers. But they're pronouncing them meows-burgers.
Now half are mice and half are cats. "Time to go eat some mousies" lol

I'm crashing in one of my niece's rooms, and she has a kid's life-sized toy kitchen. I think about how much fun Trixie would have with it and playing pretend with her, so I take a picture and send it to Daniel. It's crazy to me how much I miss him when I've never even met him before.

Love you, baby.

Day 44

Morning, babe. Stay safe today. I miss you and have you in my thoughts. I love you.

<five hours later>

Hello love , good morning and happy Monday

How are you doing ?

I miss you

Hey baby. I miss you too

Hows your day? You ok?

We just watched the new Captain America movie and the new falcon character had me thinking about you the whole time.

My sisters, their husbands, and I go to see a matinee after the kids go to school. We choose the new Captain America movie, and I'm not sure what to expect because I've heard so many mixed reviews. What I don't expect is to be obsessing over Daniel during the movie. I'm hoping to have at least a two-hour reprieve, but that isn't the case.

The new Falcon character reminds me of how I picture Daniel but with much crazier antics. They're both Hispanic-American, both in the military, and the character in the movie has similar characteristics as the two pictures I have of Daniel. I envision him as the Falcon and while it makes the movie enjoyable, it doesn't help with my stress level.

"Well, that wasn't what I expected," Skye says to me as we leave.

"No," I ask. "What were you expecting?"

"I thought this was the one with the Black Widow's sister. This wasn't that." She laughs a little uncomfortably.

"It wasn't, but I enjoyed it," I reply. "Did you not like it?"

"It was fine. Just not what I was expecting."

"What did you think, Rae?" I ask my youngest sister, who's always super quiet and reserved.

"It was a typical Marvel movie," she replies. "It was fine."

We head back to Skye's house to hang out and relax a little before the kids get home.

Hello, my love, i know you're still working and kicking ass, but I wanted to let you know that I'm thinking about you and love you to bits.

< *an hour later*>

I'm just here , having a long ass day

How's your day going , did you work today ?

I'm sorry babe. That sucks.

And you watched the new movie , was it good and how did it make you think about me lol

Nah, had the day off. Presidents Day

Yeah it sure sucks and lucky you

No holidays for us down here

The new falcon guy is like this army bad ass and just made me think of you

I know. Trying not to rub it in...

Aww , that's so sweet

You're really sweet babe and it's all good

It's not your fault

I took the next two days off too...

I know. When you get home, things will be great

You'll get pampered and spoiled and loved a bunch

Oh yeah you told me that you're down at your sisters

Yeah, it's been chaos, but in a really fun way.

And I saw the picture of that toy house , that would be absolutely perfect for Trixie .. she's really gonna love it

We'll have to pick one out for her. I can't wait to meet her.

I'd love that so much , I really can't wait .. it feels like forever but I am counting down the days baby

Me too, babe.

She's really gonna love you , I can tell already .. you're just perfect

I feel the same about you - you're perfect.

How long will you be there for ?

I'm heading home tomorrow. It's supposed to start snowing tomorrow night and I don't want to drive in that.

You've done the deployment before, right? What's the normal process for when you come home? Do they give you notice, or just tell you that day that your shipping home?

That night, after the kids go to bed, Skye, Rae, and I stay up and talk.

"How are things going for you? No lies," Skye asks me directly, knowing that I'm prone to sugar-coating things so people don't worry about me.

"I'm dating," I reply, unsure how much to divulge. "I told you I met Shawn in December, right?"

"The guy you met while shopping?" she asks, confirming that I did tell them about him.

"Well, he ghosted me on New Year's, but it got me thinking that I'm ready to start dating. I don't want to settle down or anything, but I'd like to date and finally have a hoe phase." I laugh as they both roll their eyes. "I've been really lonely, if I'm being honest. It's really difficult to be in a place where you don't know anyone or anything and my nearest form of friendship or family is two hours away. I've gotten to know my neighbors, and they help, but they're very draining."

"Yeah," Rae says. "You've told us about them."

"I met someone I really like online," I rip off the Band-Aid, hoping they'll like him. I don't seek approval from very many people, but their two opinions I value more than most. They both know what I'm looking for and who I am as a person. And they're not afraid to tell me how they see things—especially Skye.

"I really like this guy," I hedge, knowing they know I'm downplaying my feelings just by the tone of my voice. "He's deployed military, widowed, and has a young daughter who's being cared for by a nanny. He's really great. He's been supportive of my writing, of me, and tells me all the time how beautiful I am. It's a new experience from my time with Peter, and he makes me feel really good about myself."

"How old is his daughter?" Rae asks, ever the pragmatist.

"She's four."

"Are you ready for that kind of responsibility?" she asks. "I know you don't want kids of your own at this stage in your life, but that's a young kid. You'd basically be starting from scratch and doing all the things you said you didn't really want to do."

"I know," I start. "I don't want kids. You're right. And I expected that whoever I date would most likely have kids. I didn't anticipate a kid so young, but I've always wanted to be a mom. You know that. Would I prefer her to be a bit older? Maybe. I think she's probably at the perfect age though. She's going to be starting school, and we'll be able to establish a healthy parent/kid relationship. That's even if he and I work out. He might come home and one or both of us will be like, gross."

"First of all, if he says that about you, he's a moron," Skye says. "Secondly, have you video chatted this guy? How do you know he's not a scammer?"

"Honestly, I don't. He says he can't video chat or call because of where he is and what he does. I'm a little scared about that, but he doesn't sound like one. I've done a ton of research about scammers, and while parts of his story line up with known scams, he sounds like a legit person. We've talked about his wife, his daughter, and his life."

"I just want you to be happy," she replies. "You deserve to be happy. I just worry."

"I know," I say with genuine appreciation. "I'm trying really hard to be careful and to look at all aspects of this. I hate that I can't talk to him or see him, but he's in an active military zone."

"Do you know where?" Rae asks.

"I know it's in the Middle East, and I think it's in Iraq, but no," I explain. "He can't tell me for security reasons. I looked up different missions, and there's a bunch of active missions going on in the Middle East. Everything he's told me, I've tried to verify, and for the most part, I believe him."

"Just be careful," Skye warns. "He sounds great, but you guys don't truly know each other without seeing each other in person."

The confusion grows because I understand what they're saying, and I don't completely disagree with them. I've had an internal battle between my head and my heart for weeks and it's really difficult for me not to follow my heart.

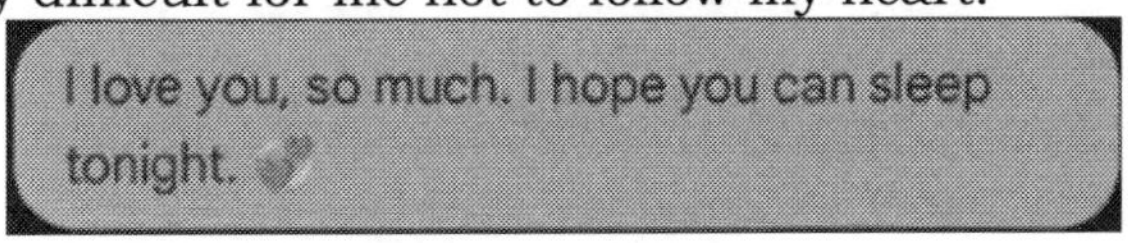

Day 45

I leave my family early, so I can miss traffic and the impending storm. Before I hit the road, I make sure to text Daniel, so he knows he's on my mind.

Good morning, baby. You're the first thing I think about when I wake every day. I love you. Be safe today.

I listen to an audiobook while I drive, and I picture Daniel as the main male character, who's usually the love interest in the books. I find it a bit weird because I've never pictured someone I knew as a character in a book before. It's always been some unknown person that somewhat resembles the descriptions.

Hey baby, just thinking about you. Love you.

I get home and the cats are screaming at me to feed them. It's too early for their dinner, so I just give them a snack. I text my neighbor, letting her know I'm home and thanking her for watching my cats while I was gone. I unpack, do laundry, and sit on the recliner to work on my crochet blanket and watch a movie so the cats can snuggle with me. It's a nice, relaxing way to spend the evening after driving.

I've discovered a weird thing when it comes to you. You become every hero or love interest in every story I read or write. Or they become you? In any case, that's never happened to me before. I was married for 20 years, and not once did i ever picture him as the hero or love interest. Never really pictured him as any character, really.
But now, with you...you're everywhere, in everything.

<two hours later>

Hello love

Good evening

How was your day today ?

Hey baby, I was just thinking about you.

Mine was long , I just got off work now and able to pick up my phone .. I miss you

Aww , that's sweet , you've been on my mind all day as well

It was ok. I love you so much

I miss you, too.

Your days suck, and I wish you didn't have to deal with so much over there.

Have you eaten?

Well I miss you more

Good lord, it's not a competition, I think as I roll my eyes.

And yes it sure sucks but what can I do

I'm about to get summ to eat , still some damn mres

Hbu , tell me about your day ?

I really want to snuggle with you. I'm feeling emotional and just want you.

I love Virginia. It's a beautiful state with the trees and mountains

Can you tell me anything about what to expect for you coming home?

I want to feel you in my arms and know you're safe. I hate this. I'm not trying to make you feel bad, please don't take it that way. I hate that you're there, that you're not here, with me, where you belong.

I never thought I could love someone so much and feel this loved in return. It's everything. You're everything.

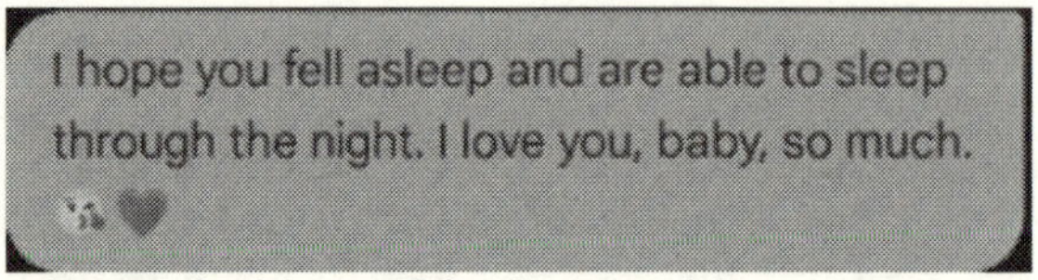

And he disappears. I think that he probably grabbed something to eat and passed out. He works entirely too much.

Day 46

Morning babe. I hope you have a good day. I'm thinking about you.

I have so many questions and am trying to manage my expectations for the next month, but every time I get the chance to talk to you, all i want to do is make sure you know how special, amazing, and important you are and how much you mean to me. I miss your face. I need you to be safe. I'm trusting you to tell me what you can, when you can, and that you'll let me in more when you get home where you don't have to compartmentalize so much. I worry because I love you more than I thought possible. I have a tendency to try to control, plan, and organize every inch of my life that I can when I'm stressed, and I'm trying so hard to trust this process. You've been through this before. Is there anything you can tell me about it? Can I do anything on my end to make the transition easier for you? Are you nervous about seeing me for the first time, in real life? I love you. I think we're on the same page there, and honestly, I've never loved and trusted someone more than I do you.

-< fifteen hours later>-

Good night, babe. I hope you're able to sleep tonight.

Day 47

Morning, handsome. Please be safe. I love you

<four hours later>

Things are so crazy. I hope your day isn't. Thinking about you, and missing you.

Hello my love , good morning .. I miss you as well and I hope you're having a good day
It's true things are so crazy and I've been really down because so many shit has been happening to me but your love and care keeps me strong and unyielding
I love you so much and I hope you have an amazing day today

I hate that he's going through stuff he won't talk about. I purse my lips in annoyance that he still won't let me in. It's unbelievably frustrating how he wants to know everything about me but keeps me at arm's length. I want to help him, but he needs to let me in and trust me, too.

I love you, baby.
Can i help with any of it?

Do you want to talk about any of it?

I'm here for you, baby. Anything you need.

I hope you know that you're amazing. You're so strong and kind, and I'm forever grateful to be able to call you mine. You're not alone in things anymore, my love. I'm here and I want to be your partner in life. I love you so much. Almost 4 weeks, and you'll be in my arms, where you belong.

<six hours later>

I hope your day is done and you can sleep. I worry about you taking care of yourself. I live you so much.

I always hit the stupid I. Love. I love you.

<five hours later>

When you come home, we barely make it into the house before I have you pressed against the wall, kissing you. My hands trail from the back of your neck, down your strong, firm chest, to your pants. I slide them off, hooking your underwear with them and freeing your dick. I gently wrap my hand around it, stroking. I moan at the feel of you. Sliding to my knees, I look up at you, my brown eyes never leaving yours as I lick the tip, swirling around the head until I slowly glide your cock into my mouth. I moan in satisfaction, sucking as my hand strokes you in a rhythmyou like. I take you deep, hitting the back of my throat, and you fist my hair, thrusting. Just before you're about to cum, you pull me up by my hair, turning me around until I'm laying on the counter. You lift my skirt, discovering nothing but a thong and a pussy soaked from sucking you. You slide a finger into my wetness, and we both groan. Lining the head of your dick to my entrance, you ease into my tight wetness. You have me pinned beneath you as you slam the rest of the way in, causing both of us to moan in satisfaction. You angle my head to kiss me as you start to move. Our kissing doesn't last long with your frantic thrusts. I clench around you as I orgasm, causing you to reach yours.

Anyway, I can't sleep and I wish you were here.

Day 48

Morning, baby. Please be safe.

I miss you.

Today has been weird. I hope your day is good, though. As good as a day over there can be, at least. I met with a financial advisor and am waiting on final instructions for the resignation thing. My last day is Friday, and I need to know if I can work my old job from NV or not. I'm also super emotional right now. Just be happy you're not a girl. I can't seem to stop crying, it sucks. I love you dearly and have you on my mind. Be safe. 4 weeks...

<fifteen hours later>

I love you.

<an hour later>

Hi babe

Good evening

My heart does a flip as his ringtone starts pinging. I feel a little like Pavlov's dog, but instead of salivating, my body gets a hit of endorphins every time that tone sounds.

Hey baby. How are you?

It's been one hell of a week , I just got off work

I miss you

I miss you too

I'm okay I guess

Just tired and fed up with everything

I'm fed up with everything, too.

How are you , I see you said todays been weird for you

Im ok. Hormonal.

I really would like you to be home.

And i know you do, too.

Have you heard from Mayra and Trixie?

We're in the home stretch though...

Did you eat?

00:20

I try to send him a voice clip. I have a friend who hates texting, so he always sends me voice clips. I hate the clips because they're too much like voicemail for me, but I want to try to have some connection with Daniel outside of texting and sending pictures.

Sorry to hear

Are you on your period

I roll my eyes. Just because a girl gets hormonal doesn't mean she's on her period. I'm perimenopausal and a woman. Sometimes we get hormonal. Especially when there's so much going on. My boyfriend is deployed, I've never heard his voice, he won't trust me with his problem, I'm in a vacation rental, and I'm about to lose my job. It's amazing I haven't lost my sanity at this point.

And I hope the resignation process goes as planned and also hope trump sticks to his word with the payment structure as promised and since you said you're gonna get your old job back , you should be good babe

And what are you sending babe , I can't get it .. it keeps saying file type not supported

Dangit. It was a voice text.

I'm not on my period, just weirdly overemotional.
I think the resignation will be fine. And if I can get paid from both places for a while, that'll be great. If things don't work out, I'm still ok financially.

I was really excited, thinking you'd be able to actually hear me tell you I love you. Technology is not in my favor tonight, I guess.

Are you laying down?

Aww , I'm sorry it wasn't able to send .. I would've really love to hear your voice , it would've absolutely made my night and make me so happy

I might try to make a gif... I've never done that either, but it's worth a try.

But I told you about our situation down here , our devices wouldn't even receive them .. it's fucked up but that's just the way it's been but it's almost over soon , less than a month to go

A voice gif , that's new lol

Well things are gonna work out great for you babe , I'm sure of that .. you're gonna be alright

And yes I'm just laid down here

As long as I have you, I'll be great.

What have you been up to ?

Just working and writing.

Nice and you'll always have me .. I hope you don't grow tired of me when I'm home because I'll always been all up in your space lol

I don't think I could ever grow tired of you, I think. *I'd love to have you with me twenty-four-hours a day. You'll get bored of me and my life way faster than I will you.*

Ah ok , the usual

Furry is having trouble at night again and I haven't slept much in two days. Which could probably explain the emotional crap

I hope you do! I want you so bad, in every way possible

Im almost done with my blanket. It's huge. About the size of a full mattress.

I have D&D tomorrow and have to get my oil changed after.

I legit could talk to you all night, or just snuggle quietly with you every night for the rest of my life and never get tired of you.

I love you so much, baby. Sleep well and kick some ass tomorrow. Know that you're in my thoughts and my heart. Good night.

Day 49

Morning, babe. I absolutely love hearing from you, and I know it's not something that's easy for you to do, so I want you to know how much I appreciate it. I don't know if you feel the same way, but when we actually get to talk, it eases something inside me.
Sometimes, I feel like I'm annoying you with my texts, and I start getting in my head about everything. But when we talk, I realize you feel the same as I do. And it makes me feel better.
I know things are tough right now, but I hope you know I'm not going anywhere.
Sometimes, I don't know the right words to say, or I ramble, but it's because I'm scared. I'm terrified for you over there in a way I've never experienced before. And i'm scared that this is too good to be true. That I'm going to wake up one day to find it was all fake. Then we talk, and you say something adorable like you hope I don't get tired of you, and i know you feel it too. And it helps, somehow. I'm in it, Daniel. All in. For as long as you'll have me. I love you - your heart, courage, spirit, mind - with all my heart. Be safe, baby. 😘😘😘

I get ready for the day and put on a silly D&D shirt I know that my friends will find just as funny as I do. I take a picture of me in it, and I can't stop laughing. I send the picture to Daniel, smiling the whole time.

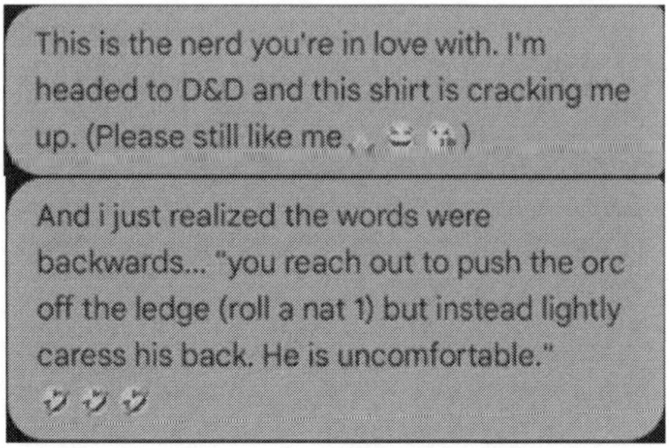

My family keeps asking me what my plans are after the resignation hits. I keep telling everyone that I'm going to focus on my writing, which I am, but I don't tell them about Daniel. I know they won't approve of me waiting for him to come home so we can move in together, but it's not their life and I don't want to deal with the judgement. So, I tell what I can and gloss over the rest.

And the honest truth is, I have no idea what I'm going to do after the resignation. I'm terrified. I've never not gone to work. I've been working since I was thirteen and have always either gone to school and worked, or worked multiple jobs. And I'm going to be focusing on me, which I've also never done before, and I find it terrifying. I'm excited, sure, but my future is this big, empty, blank space looming in front of me.

I'm just thankful that I have a nice bit of savings from the divorce, so I don't have to worry about my finances for a few years. And Daniel is coming home soon, so he and I will be able to figure out our future together. He said he doesn't need to worry about finances either, so for the first time in my life, life should be good. I just need him to come home.

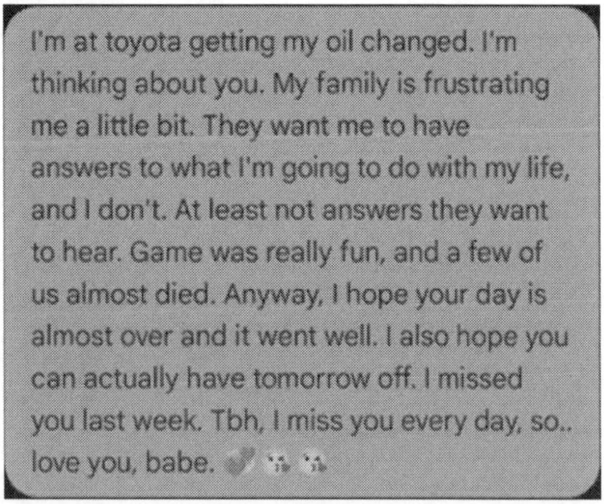

<three hours later>

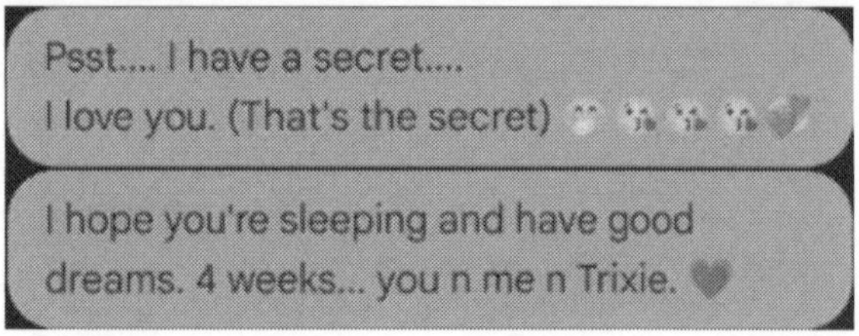

Day 50

Morning babe.

<four hours later>

You haven't had a day off in two weeks. I hope you have today off.

I'm so sick of not being able to talk to Daniel. A part of me is ready to fly my happy butt to the Middle East, find him, and drag him back home. Military rules be damned! But I'm trying to be understanding and as supportive of his career as he is of mine. And I know I could be more supportive.

Hello love

Good morning

How are you doing

I miss you, I want to say. I'm miserable and want you to hold me and talk to me and cuddle me. I want to climb into your skin, so you know you're safe and loved. I want to feel protected and loved in return. I don't want to be doing this by myself. I want you with me. I'm scared and stressed and so frustrated with everything going on, I don't even know what my next step is.

But he doesn't need to hear all that. So, I just tell him I'm okay and I keep the rest to myself. I just hope we can talk for more than two minutes.

Morning, my love

Im ok. How are you doing?

And yes I haven't had off in weeks but I'm off right now , had to work a morning shift but I'm done for the day

I miss you so damn much

How have you been and what's been going on for you ?

I miss you too, so much

I had breakfast with my neighbor a did a workout today

I know you do honey , I could see from your texts and I appreciate that so much and would never take it for granted

Talked to my landlord yesterday and found out I can't extend my rental past the end of April.

Are you doing ok? I worry about you

I'm glad you're done for the day. Can you relax the rest of the day?

Oh nice , what do yall have for breakfast?

We went to a place called Abel's and I had pancakes.

Can you send me a pic?

Do you work out from home or you go to the gym and how often do you work out ?

Nice that's good

And why can't you extend your rent past April , what's going on?

I'm doing ok , just here really .. got so much going on rn

They have renters starting 5/2. So im just trying to figure stuff out.

Im getting a punching machine thing that im really excited about. Should be here next week.

Whats going on with you?

Oh nice that's good

And what do you mean renters starting 5/2

I don't understand that

When i moved here, I moved into a long term air b&b.

Why can't you just extend your rent and shouldn't you be informed before they take renters ?

They originally said they'd talk to me before they would rent out, but they didn't, so... fun adventures

I'll figure it out babe, please don't worry. Just sharing what's going on in my life.

What are you doing for dinner? Mre, or sandwiches?

Oh okay , a long term Airbnb , well that's new lmao

But I understand, they probably found a better offer but they should've informed you .. that's very sneaky

So what are you gonna do now

Yeah, I had no idea they existed either. One of my friends told me about them before I moved

Im not sure. I could either buy a townhouse, wait till you get home, or rent an apartment. My dad still wants me to move in with them

I was kinda irritated after I talked to them yesterday. Kinda spiraled into finding places to move to.

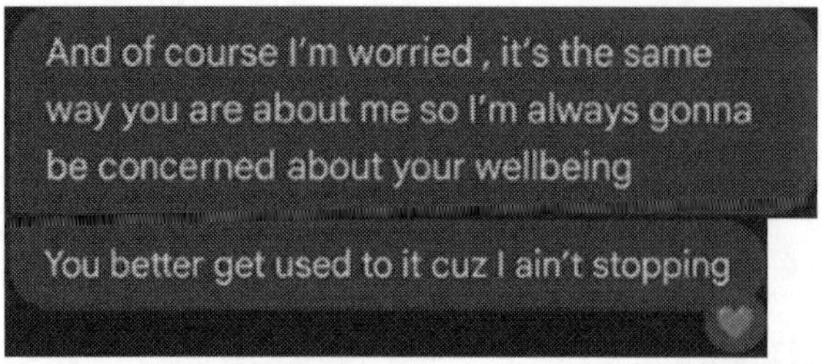

I smile and melt. It's nice that he cares about me and isn't afraid to say something. I truly can't wait until he comes home.

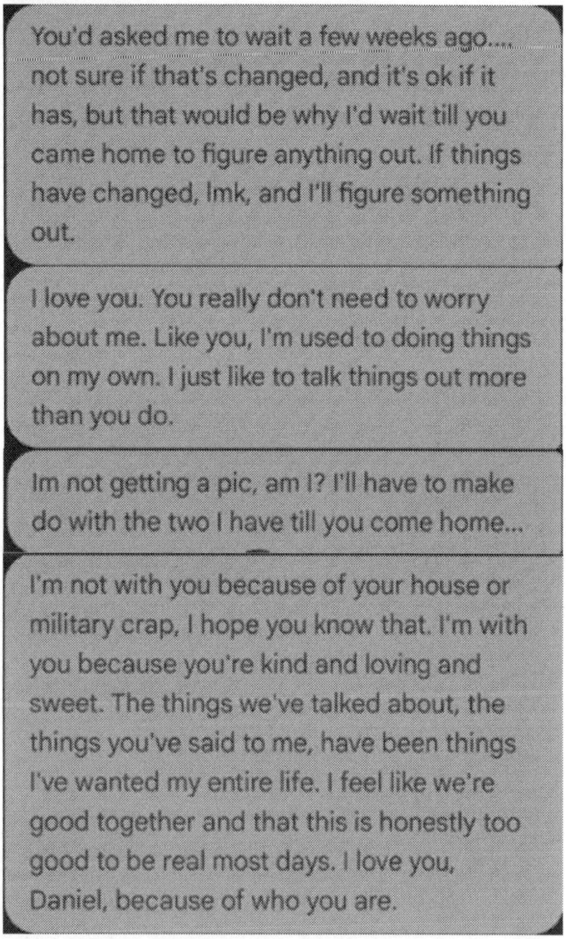

I have my monthly D&D game with the monsters—my teenage niece and her two friends. We started this before I moved and have been adjusting to doing it with me remotely. I've learned a ton from my weekly game with my new friends, and I've been trying to adjust how I run the game with the monsters so that we're following rules better and gameplay is more interesting. But they're pure chaos and reining them in is almost impossible. I just end up laughing and shaking my head most days we play.

It's fun, and exhausting. I've said more insane things that I never thought I'd say in my life when we have game. Today it was, "No, you cannot make out with the mimic."

After a slight argument, I cave and put it into the game. She had to roll for survival and charisma and failed both rolls, so the mimic ate her character's arm and tongue. All four of us erupt into peals of laughter and the game goes downhill from there.

<four hours later>

Omg, D&D with my niece is pure chaos.

What'd you end up doing today? Were you able to relax?

I decide to take a long shower. My ex used to stand under the spray and just zone out, so I think, *I'll try that.* See if it helps my stress and anxiety. It's hot, just below scalding, just how I like it, and I stand with the water pouring down my body for about twenty minutes while I do some meditative breathing and try to clear my mind. I actually do feel better when it's done.

<two hours later>

I miss you.
Love you.

Hey babe

What's good

Sorry I slept off for a lil bit

I just got up

What are you up to ?

Youre good. I'm glad you slept. I just took a shower

I stood under the water for like 20 minutes. I never do that. It was really nice.

I played my monthly game of D&D with my niece, Kate , who lives in NV still. They're chaos monsters. I never thought I'd ever hear the phrase, "You can only join my cult if you promise to stop making out with mimics," in my life, but there ya go.
I took another walk and am trying to figure out what to eat for dinner.

Damn , 20 minutes is crazy

Why did you have to stay that long

lol , looks like you enjoy D&D so much , I gotta get into it when I'm home and then put some D in you lmao

So what's for dinner ?

Yeah... my ex used to do that all the time, and it would drive me bananas. I'm about a 5-10 minute shower person.
I don't know. It was hot, I was cold, and it felt nice to just not be available for anything.

I did think about sending you a Pic, saying I wish you were here, but... next time.

Yeah I asked you to wait for me till when I'm home to make a decision .. why would you think that would change , I don't understand it

I don't know. I'm hungry but not sure what for. What would you have if you were here?

Well don't take too long under the shower babe , 10 minutes is even too long but it's perfect if you'd want to take your time

"Really," I say to my phone. "You're critiquing my shower time? You really have been military for way to flipping long."

And you should've sent the pic , I would've love to see you my love

Fear, babe. I have this nagging fear/ insecurity that you'll meet me and change your mind. I'm working through it.
Why is a 10 min shower too long?

Something to look forward to, tomorrow, then...

Btw , I don't say it enough but I absolutely love the pictures that you've been sending me and you looked absolutely amazing, I love how you looked in all , the way you wore your glasses, the way your hair was laid , you look absolutely gorgeous and I love it all 🥰

You don't have to play D&D with me, that can always be your daddy/Trixie time.

Glasses?

I don't have glasses...

Im glad you like them though

You've gotta be kidding me , I should be the one who's feeling that way , only for me to get and realize you've just been bored and aren't looking for anything serious 🥺

That would be heartbreaking you know

But I think D&D is fun, and I'd love to have you join if you want.

Also, you better put the D in me. Fuck, every time I use my vibrator, I think of you.

And we can all play together, I wouldn't mind that at all

And I meant the mirror picture not glasses .. where you wore black and said you're my nerd

That's the one I'm referring to

Omg, I'm so unbelievablely, massively in love with you, that would never happen. I dream of you coming home. Of us starting our life together

I love them not just like babe

Those pictures looks really great

Damn babe , how many times do you use your vibrators in a week ?

I'm not bored. I want you. In every possible way, I can have you. Hell, you're basically tattooed on me. I'm not sure how much more I can show how much I'm in...

Um.... daily? The O helps me sleep

I'm glad to hear that and I feel absolutely the same way and more so there's no need to be insecure about anything
We've been great now and it's only going to get better when I'm home
And I asked you about your housing situation because I was worried about you and am I not allowed to be worried ?

For sure I'd be home by April and I absolutely want you staying with me and would never let you go back to your dad no matter how much he wants you to

True babe , you've got me tattooed .. that's simply insane but I love it

You are. You don't need to be, though. I don't want you distracted out there. I want you safe so you can come home and we can have our life.

I love how you drive me nuts , I don't think it has ever happened to me this way

What do you mean?

Damn , you use that vibrator daily .. I can't wait to be home

You're gonna be getting that work every damn day

Yeah, me too. So much.

Promises promises

I promise you that my love

We're going to be so great together

Have you heard from Marya? Hows trixie doing?

And I'm sorry the past few weeks hasn't been great with communicating

I seriously cannot wait to have you home.

There's just been a lot going on with me that I've been trying to deal with all by myself but that hasn't been easy

Please don't apologize for that, you've been in hell. I'm grateful when I hear from you.

Trixie is doing ok , all but the nanny not so much

I wish you wouldn't. I'm here babe. Oh no. What's going on?

There's been a lot of crap going on with that situation but I'll take care of it

It's all I've been trying to do

Can i help?

I'm trying to respect your space, so if you don't want to talk about it, it's ok. Just know that I'm here and i love you.

Thanks a lot love , it's just some shit going on that I've been trying to fix for over two weeks now but to no avail and it's really driving me crazy and making me miserable

It's about trixie and the nanny

Is she safe with the nanny?

She's safe but the nanny's been crazy , she's been threatening to stop taking care of Trixie and leave while I'm not home yet to care for her

What?!?! That's bullshit!

She said she's leaving the end of February knowing fully well that I'm not home yet and that's just making me crazy and I don't know wtf to do

"What the hell?" I say to my phone. "That sounds so bizarre. How could anyone do that to someone who's deployed? Does she want him to be too distracted with home crap and die? There's got to be a solution."

Would you feel comfortable with me watching her at your house?

Her grandparents won't step up? The army won't send you home? That's such a fucked up situation.

None of your buddies' wives or girlfriends will help?

It is bullshit

I haven't been able to pay her the past 2 months and she's been going crazy and saying all kinds of shit , saying that she's gonna leave and leave her alone just by herself and she's just 4 , she can't do nothing on her own and I'm trying to make her realize that I've been stuck here longer than I expected because our deployment got extended and I'd be home in like a month but she's not trying to hear it at all

Before I came on deployment , I had a payment plan in place for her to be paid and all but that was like 4-5 months tops because that's how long I thought I'd be here for but that shit got extended because the military thought we had more to do here and there's nothing I can do to stop it and I'm trying to make her see that , she's been taking care of her for years now what's waiting for just one more month but she isn't even listening saying she got bills and her own kids and some bs

Oh no, I think. *Here it is. Here's where he shows me that he isn't real; that he's a scammer. Please don't ask me for money.*

My heart plumets to the vicinity of hell and my whole body goes into denial. I can feel the agony start to well up. *Please, please don't ask me for money,* I think.

Fuck. I'm sorry, babe. She should be more understanding. What can I do to help?

It's just been making me absolutely miserable and I don't trust her grandparents or anyone to take care of Trixie .. I really don't so yeah .. it's been hell for me the past few weeks

I've also been trying to expedite my coming home , maybe hasten it a bit more due to my family emergency but the military isn't even trying to hear it

I make an offer that has me super uncomfortable, but for him to be real, I'd do it. For this relationship to work, I'd watch his kid for him. It's not something I'm crazy excited to do, but for him, for us, I would.

I can take care of Trixie and you can deal with the nanny when you get back?

My commanding officer said " you could only leave when the other do so get back work soldier " stupid ass with his dumb mustache

What an asshole, I think. *There's got to be a way for him to come home.* I know I've read something on some military site I've been on recently. I make a mental note to look for it again and send him the information.

That's bullshit!

It is bullshit

So yeah , that's what been happening to me the past two weeks

Imagine going through that and having to work 12 plus hours every goddamn day

Fml !!!!!

I'm so, so sorry, baby.

I know it wouldn't be ideal, but if you need someone to take care of Trixie for March, I'm basically open. It'd be weird because I'd meet your daughter before meeting you, but... It's up to you.

You know me, and you know I'd send you like a million updates and pictures.

I look at the military website and see that he can reach out to his Family Readiness Group, and they can do things to help support him through this and provide resources to take care of Trixie or get him home. I ask about that.

Can you reach out to your FRG?

I can't imagine the stress you're under. What can I do to help?

<three hours later>

Thank you for opening up to me, I know how hard that is for you, and I'm sorry you're dealing with this. I can't for the life of me understand why you'd still trust her with your kid, but you have the relationship with her, I don't. I think that anyone who would do what she's doing to you is a horrible, unforgivable person. She knows you're good for the money, since she's been with you for so long, I don't understand why she can't wait till you get home, either. She sounds like a bitch, and I kinda want to punch her. Let me know what I can do to help. Like I said, I'm off in a week and would be happy to take care of her till you get back and can deal with the nanny.
I love you, and i'm sorry this is happening.

Day 51

Morning, babe. Thinking about you. Please be safe.

<eighteen hours later>

Hey baby, I hope everything is going ok today. Thinking of you.

Day 52

> Good morning, i hope you're safe and ok.
> Please be careful.

I spend yesterday and most of today putting all the information together about my grantees that I have for my boss for when I leave. Tension is high at work with all the political changes, and for the first time since I accepted the resignation, I feel grateful for it. I'm not sure I could handle this stress level for much longer. People are walking on eggshells or are angry and scared about where the future of their jobs is headed.

One of my coworkers told me that she's had people tell her she needs to go back to her home country. She's Native American, and her tribe is in Oklahoma.

"I'm scared to leave my apartment without my husband," she tells me when she gets to the office. "He's supposed to find out by Friday if he's still going to have a job or if his department is being eliminated. This is terrifying."

"Holy crap," I say. "That's terrible. I'm so sorry." There's nothing I can say or do that will make any of this situation better, so we just commiserate and vent to each other about our fears.

> Has anything gotten resolved with the horrible nanny? Is there anything I can do to help? I worry about you and the amount of stress you're under. I'm here for you, babe. I hope you're doing ok.

<two hours later>

> I love you.
> You're an amazing man and I hope you know that.

I decide to help Daniel with legal ramifications of Mayra's threats, hoping that he'll use those threats to keep her there until he can get home. He might not know about all of this stuff because he's career military, and when you're not immersed in a field, it's difficult to truly understand the nuances of it. I want to make sure he's informed and can make the best decision when it comes to Trixie.

Also, I've been thinking, is Mayra aware of the legal implications of her threats? Child abandonment/endangerment is huge. Like a felony. And with the political climate the way it is, you could even threaten her with ICE and deportation. With how things are, people don't even care anymore if you're a natural citizen or not. I've had Native American friends get threatened to be "sent back home."

I'm not saying you should do any of that or that any of that is right. Even mentioning that makes me feel all sorts of gross. But if she's threatening to abandon your kid, you have threats of your own.

I could ask some of my attorney friends if there's anything you can do, legally, if you want.

And my offer to watch her still stands. I love you, you love me, and we've talked about a future together. This would just be starting that now.

I would treat her like my own and make sure you knew, without a doubt, that she's safe.

I know this has been a lot for you, and this offer is probably scary because I'm just some girl you met online. I'd like to think that the past two months has shown you the kind of person I am, but I understand the fear. She's your baby. Just letting you know you're not alone anymore.

You n me against the world, remember?

I love you. 😘

<four hours later>

I hope you're not still working. You guys must be doing some crazy stuff right now. Please be safe. I miss you. 😘🖤

<an hour later>

Hi babe

Good evening

How was your day today?

It was ok. Yours?

I have 3 days left. It feels weird.

I really can't wait for you to be home, safe, where i don't worry about you getting shot.

I'm ok I guess , just here .. been off work for couple hours now but can't sleep

Want to talk?

I sent you a bunch of texts, like the crazy, obsessed gf I am. Does any of it help?

Yeah babe , I'm here my love

3 days left before your resignation?

Yep

How do you feel , are you okay ?

I'm always here for you as well if you wanna talk my love

I feel weird about it, but it should be fine. I worry more about you than anything else.

And I appreciate you talking to me , asking questions, sharing opinions and trying to help .. it means the whole world to me and I'm really thankful for you my love

I love you, so much.

Weird how babe ?

How long have you had the job ?

Not long. Only since October. But it was the reason I moved here.

And you're the reason I'm staying...

I'm betting on myself and my writing, and while it's something I've wanted to do for a decade, it's a little nerve wracking to actually be in a position to focus on it and do it.

I love you more babe and thanks for worrying about me my love but it's still the same shit going on , she's still threatening to leave by the end of the month, I just left her texts hanging and told her I'll figure out a way to pay her so she can at least take care of trixie for the next 4 weeks till I'm home , then I'll fire and get rid of her bitch ass .. I really wanna punch her face if I can but there's nothing I can do from down here

Please don't ask me for money, I beg silently.

Can you log onto your bank and zelle or venmo her?

I feel the same violent tendency toward her as well.

Oh well you haven't had the job for long so you'd be good and they're paying you for extra 8 months and you can also get your old job back so I'd say you're in a pretty great spot my love and now you get more time to focus on your writing and the publishing

Would you be comfortable with me taking care of Trixie?

Yes it's nerve wracking but it's what you want ,what you've always wanted to do and now you gotta prove you're up to the task

I can't work my old job. It's a conflict of interest. There's a whole lot of bs behind.it, I won't bore you.
And proving that I'm up to the task is the nerve wracking part. Lol

That's the problem I have babe , I wouldn't have this problem at all if I could just log into my bank account and Zelle or Venmo her but I can't and that's why I had that payment structure in place at first and I thought it'll be sufficient and more only for our deployment to be extended.. the military just keep finding ways to fuck my life up
I practically can't do nothing because the military locked out my accounts and credit cards because they don't want us having access to monetary items so as not to get distracted or side tracked on our objectives, I really can't do shit unless I'm back in the states and she's not even trying to see that

"They can't do that," I whisper to the phone, past the pit of despair that's opened in my stomach. "Everything I've read online says the military can't do that."

I might go the threats and reporting to law enforcement but I don't want to go that route , I don't want to get social services involved or for them to take trixie or anything like that at all , I'm just trying to settle it as amicably as possible because she's a good nanny and she does her job well , she just wants to be paid but she's refusing to understand all the complications

I didn't think they could do that.
I can understand her wanting to be paid, but this isn't the first deployment she's had with you, is it?

"I mean, maybe he's right," I say to Furry as I pet her. She snuggles into me, seeming to know that I'm in immense pain. "You can't believe everything you read online; that's for sure. And I don't remember how old the sites were when I was looking. Things could've changed since COVID. He's right, you know. I don't know what the military is capable of; and I wouldn't put it past them to be able to do that. It makes sense, in some fucked-up way, but I don't know what to believe."

And I'd love for you to take care of trixie , it would be absolutely amazing but I wouldn't want for that to be how we're going to meet each other you know , I would really like to meet you first , spend a lot of time with you , do a lot of nasty stuff together before we involve trixie .. with trixie with us , we won't have a lot of free time to do whatever we want

Yes they could , there are so many things that they can do which you'd never believe until you're told , they have so much power over everything and it's sickening , more reason I've had enough and want out after this deployment

We'll adapt. Nothing in life goes as planned. If anyone knows that, it's me. Parents find ways to do things all the time.

If me taking care of her will help with your stress, we can figure life out after you get home.

I'm just looking for ways to figure this whole issue out and I can't lie it's been driving me insane for the past two weeks now

I understand.

And I can't lie , I really do need your help my love .. I do now more than ever

I'm here for you, babe.

Please don't ask me for money. Please don't prove people right. You're real. You're mine. You're not scamming me. Please. The thought runs circles through my head as tears stream down my face and my heart shatters in my chest.

I don't know if you can help me with this nanny problem, if you can contact her and help me pay her , it's just for four more weeks that I'm going to be here for , you aren't paying her but you're just lending me until I'm back , I just want her to stay and watch her for the next 4 weeks and when I'm home , I'll pay you back .. with interest if you want but I need you my love , please 🙏

He asked. He's not real. Bile rises, and I feel my stomach churning; my heart shatters, leaving broken pieces in its wake. But before I can feel the deep pain of either of those events, my body goes completely numb. He asked. He did the thing scammers do. He's not real. He's not real. He's not real. The mantra plays over and over in my head, the numbness not allowing it to penetrate. I refuse to believe he's not real.

Grief rises to my throat, and I have trouble swallowing past the lump that's formed there. Every word he types is another rip of my heart, and I don't even think he knows he's destroying me. I ask the question I know I should, even though I don't want to. My heart is screaming in pain and doesn't want to believe that this is happening.

What's her contact info?

I really need you my love and I'd never ask you this if it wasn't that serious but it is , she's just 4 and can't be on her own .. she's my everything and being here and not being able to do something is absolutely killing me , the nanny is good and she takes care of her very well , she's been doing that for years now and we've never had any issue until now but her failure to understand my situation is what irks me and pisses me off

Anything you can help with babe , I swear I'll pay you off with interest if you want .. I just want her to stay for just 4 more weeks please

Here's my bank account statement as you can see so you'll know I'll pay you back with interest if you want ... I just have to do everything I can for my angel .. it's really embarrassing telling you my problems like this but what choice do I have when my ass is stuck here with absolutely no option fml !

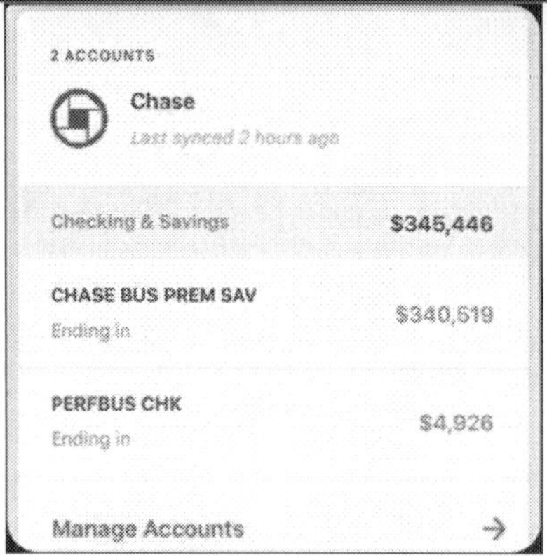

How do i get ahold of her?
I dont need your bank info. I trust you.

Thank you my love and I know that but I just want to be as transparent as possible avoid this

Do you wanna talk to her , I'll send you her number

Yes, please.

Would you be able to help me my love because I owe her for 2 months going to 3 now and that's some money

How much?

Ok I'll send you her number in a few

It's quite expensive babe

Ok.

This has just been a lot for me

> I bet you feel so free without kids

> You can do whatever the hell you want

I can't do whatever the hell I want. I have cats. While no, they're not as limiting as kids, they still offer challenges. And I hate that people act like my cats are just some throwaway pets.

> It has been a lot, but she's worth it.
> I have the cats. They're kinda like my kids since I didn't have any human ones. And they complicate my life plenty. I can't really do whatever I want, but it is easier than having human kids.

> I wish the world was kinder.

> That things were easier.
> But i hope i can make your future something to look forward to.

> I get what you're saying my love but it's easier , it's way easier especially when you're a single parent and there's trauma behind it

> I wish that way too but the world in reality is harsh and gruesome , being down here shows it firsthand

> I know. I'm not diminishing your life at all. Just letting you know my life isn't as easy as you're implying.

> How many deployments have you been on?

I'm very well aware that the world is not a kind, safe place. I probably know that better than you do. And, of course, per usual, your life is so much worse than anything else. The thoughts race through my head, anger and bitterness blossoming to compete with the nothing that's embraced me.

> I texted her already , waiting for her to respond then I'll send you her number .. I wanna inform her that my woman is going to contact her

> Ok, sounds good.

Its late here, she might not respond until tomorrow.

I do understand you babe and this is my 6th deployment and the toughest yet

Yeah, it's 4:15am right now and I'm still up

Can't seem to close my eyes .. I can only imagine how trixie is right now , that's the only thing on my mind apart from you , I saw the sexy pictures you've been sending me hahaha

Especially that one in the shower

Wish I was there , I can see the whole shower steaming just from the picture , it got me all excited , I can't lie 😂

Trixie is going to be ok.

I'm glad you liked them. I really wish you were here too.

Why don't you try to sleep. I'll take care of Mayra tomorrow, after you send me her contact info.

How do you not realize you've broken me? I think. *I have never, not once, told you to stop talking to me.* I decide to try to get more information out of him that I've been trying to for the past few weeks. Maybe he'll prove one way or another if he's real or not with his answers. Maybe he's not a scammer and just a guy in a really shitty situation? I don't know what to think right now. All I know is I love him, and I'm incredibly torn and confused right now. I still want to know more about him.

I sure hope so because I feel like I'm failing as a father badly right now

Do you wanna sleep now

You're a good dad, doing everything you can for her.

I'm good, I'd just stare at the ceiling till the beginning of my shift

No, im good. I love talking to you. It's the highlight of my week, you know?

What did you get your degree in?

Thanks babe , you sure know how to make me feel better about myself

How do I get so lucky ?

And I never thought you're always up this late

Associate degree in economics babe

You wanna get me a job when I'm home lmaooo 😆

😆

Im glad I can help. You've shown me that I can actually find someone who genuinely loves me. Who knows what he wants, and doesn't play games.

I don't sleep most nights. I have insomnia, so I tend to spend most of my days exhausted and my nights tossing and turning. I used to keep my ringer off to try to sleep, but I started leaving it on in case you texted.

Well you make it easy for me babe , it's always reciprocated and never feels one sided and it's only going to get better when I'm home , I know that for a fact

I don't think you need help in the job department, with a bank balance like that.

Aww , I hope I'm not bugging you when you eventually get some sleep .. I'd really hate to keep you up

Are you for sure going to be back in March? They won't extend you again?

You never bug me. Talking to you is everything to me.

Is it hard for you to take pictures over there?

I know it's stupid late, but I've asked, and just wondered if that was a challenge.

Well I'm a hard worker and I try to save and I also had a trust fund growing up so that surely helped while buying my house and other stuff but yeah I'm doing pretty good for myself and I know that you are as well but I'm also going to take care of you and spoil you my love

Glad to hear that , talking to you is the highlight of my day

Talking to you was the highlight of my day, too. But now, I have no idea what to think. Are you real, or are you a scammer? How do I know for certain either way? Ugh, I hate this. I hate that you asked me for money. I hate that this is even a question. Dating is difficult enough without worrying about whether you're real or not.

Why did you join the military?

I wouldn't say it's a challenge but I can't be caught being on my phone while at work so I must be careful but I'll send you a new picture tomorrow, I promise you honey

Ok. Don't get in trouble on my account. I was just curious.

When is Trixie birthday?

I've told you this before babe , my grandfather was a paratrooper and I looked up to him growing up, he passed when I was a teen and I just decided to do that

I don't remember that conversation. I might have to go back and look through our conversations, but I'm almost certain we didn't talk about this. Unless it was on the dating app that I deleted.

I'll send you a picture babe , you deserve it especially with the tons you already sent me

November 24th babe

You didn't tell me that, actually.
That's cool, though. My grandpa was in WW2 and lost a lung. He was a grumpy bastard. I wanted to join, but got denied because of my asthma.

Aww, she just turned 4. What a cutie.

Yeah babe , you told me about your grandpa and how you couldn't join because of asthma

Im really impressed with you, you know that?

Yes babe , more reason why I'm spiraling .. she's too young and delicate to be by herself you know

Impressed ?!

Yep. You're an impressive guy.

I'm embarrassed and disappointed with myself and how things are going for me

How so babe , why'd you think so ?

Any child is too young to be alone.

Agreed

You work so hard, see so much shit, yet you have this deep capacity to love, and you're dedicated. You have a determination to succeed that I dont see a whole lot. It's impressive

I decide to tell him more about my trauma and pain and see if that changes the trajectory of this. If he's a scammer, he's got to have a tiny bit of human compassion, right? And if he's who he says he is, he'll care and be horrified at my childhood. He'll have to realize how sketchy it is to ask someone you've never met for money, right?

> I was running the house when I was 8. Learned to cook, clean, and do laundry by the time I was 7. I'd make dinners most days and I basically raised my little brother. That's way too much crap to put on a kid.

> I have a really, really hard time letting people in and trusting them because of trauma, but you've made it easy. Your honesty and openness has really helped me let down my guard and trust in you. I've never really had that, or had anyone just love all the weird little parts of me.

> Well it's the same way with you my love , it's even more impressive, you just got divorced and left a horrible man , just resigned from your job, parents are haunting you to come back to live with them and how you need to do more with your life , you have a writing career that you want to prove yourself in , live in a town all by yourself and you're still able to love and allow yourself to be loved , you're a super hero

He isn't a horrible man, I think. *But yes, all of that is true. I just never saw myself as a superhero. I'm just me.*

> I'm glad you feel that way about me but that's just how it's supposed to feel my love , it's my responsibility to be open , to love you correctly and care for you

> It's how's it supposed to be

> How are you real? You're just so perfect for me.

> I'm nowhere near perfect lmao

But I'm good and true and for you I'll always be

No one is perfect, but you're perfect for me.

I love you

I love you, too.

Talking to you just brings me ease no matter what I'm going through

I feel really blessed to have you in my life

God, I beg. *Please let this be real. How can this not be real*? I love him so much, and he's so amazing when we talk. I just don't understand how you could put this person in my path if he's not real. Haven't I had enough pain? Haven't I earned this?

Me too.

I love you more

Lol

Have there been any updates on when you can come.home?

Yes babe , it's going to be between the last week of march to the first week of April , I'll know the exact day next month

What's the first thing you're gonna do when you see me

I sometimes wonder how things will work out when you come home. How the animals will react when they meet.

Kiss you

I want to wrap my arms around you and kiss you.

And then, I'll honestly probably cry.

What about you?

We will be fine , we talked about this before my love
Even though Bailey is a pit , she's extremely girly and gentle and your cats seems very chilled and they'll listen to you , that's all that matters

They would warm up to me as long as I feed and give them treats

Well I'd hug you so tight and squeeze you lifting you up then I'd kiss the shit outta you

Then I'd probably have my hands in your panties on our way home 😆

Furry won't. She's a mamas gril. Do you stay on base for a few days for medical stuff, or will i be able to meet you when your plane lands?

Lol, sounds great.

I'm planning on wearing a dress to pick you up. Easier access that way, lol

I'll have to report for a few days but that's it

I would still need to fly here so you still gotta pick me at the airport

A dress sounds very nice , you're very naughty and you match my freak

I so cant wait

I hope you can keep up

I can't wait either.
We've had this discussion, lol. It's you who's gonna need to keep up.

Lmaooo

You'd be surprised

And I do some really amazing things on my knees. Its one of my favorite things to do. You're in for a good time.

You haven't been with a man like me , I'm 100 percent certain

I'm strong , long and I take my time

Pleasuring you is going to be my favorite thing to do

Well, seeing as the only guy I've been with in 24 years was only interested in his and was always quick, I'm looking forward to seeing if you live up to your boasting.

Damn I can't wait to have all in your mouth all sloppy and down your throat

Fun times lies ahead lmao 🤣

It's not boasting if you really got it 🙌

Have you ever had it with an altoid?

The cool, minty reaction with a wet mouth is intense. Or sc I've been told.

Nope , that's new lmao

I see you got tricks up your sleeve well lucky me 🤣🤣😆😆

I'm a reader.... you've never been with a bookworm, have you?

Jean Booth

I haven't been with anyone in over 2 years so if I tell you that I'm excited it's because I really am

I know. And I'm really excited to corrupt you.

Bring it on !

Steamy shower sex

I'm hard asf thinking about it

Im soaked and ready for you as well

The whole house jumping , neighbors wondering what's going on lmaooo

Those huge titties 😆🥰🥰🥰🖤

Also the meals

Can't wait for you to cook for me because I've been eating utter shit down here

You and your food. Ill have to make sure to have a buffet ready for you so you dont have to choose between sex and burritos

Although I am curious, if you could only have 1 the first day you're home, what would you rather have? Food or sex?

You say all this things when wonder if I say I'm so lucky to have you

You just want to take care of me

I do.

I don't think I've ever had someone just genuinely care

It's a surreal feeling

I want you to know what it's like to be truly loved.

And I would like an answer to my question. Lol

Being genuinely cared for and loved is surreal to me, too.

Well I do now and I can't wait to show you as well

You need to know what's it's like as well , I wanna live and breathe you

Same

And I'd take sex all day long , bring on the mres as long as I have you by my side I'm good

I'll keep you fed with good stuff. Don't you worry.

Even though I don't like it, i make a mean guacamole

I'm not even worried babe

I know you got me

I love me some lasagna , tacos , steak , pizza , Alfredo pasta , ham , burgers

Yep. And you're going to be well taken care of.

I'm gonna have it all , all I've been having here is shit

Same for you babe , anything you want you'll get it

We'll have to go up to NYC and get pizza. Its the best

It's never going to be one sided

I just want you.

I'm putting all my chips into this and I know it'll work out for sure

Me too

Well that's the attributes of being with me my love so enjoy it

Id give anything to just be in your arms. You have no idea.

A month from now , you'll have me all to yourself and we both won't have to work

Great times lie ahead, I won't lie

It's gonna be so damn fun !!!

I think we've both earned some good times and happiness

We sure have my love

What are you doing

Are you in bed

It's so late for you my love

Yeah, just laying here, texting you.
I don't care. This has been the longest we've talked and I wouldn't trade it for the world.

Its almost midnight. And it's almost time for you to be up for drills.

Did you sleep at all?

Aww , you're just so sweet.. you made me really comfortable to talk and open up to you

Everything with you is with ease except when your hormones are acting up haha

And yes I'll be up for drills in like 30 minutes

Oh, I'm an absolute rage monster right now. Period hit today.

And nope I didn't sleep at all , I barely sleep over here but talking to you have given me all the energy I ever needed

And you're in for a ton of fun when Trixie hits puberty.

I just hope you can help me take care of this nanny mess till I'm home

Girls start getting the attitude changes around 9/10 y/old.

I know that , I'm not looking forward to it at all but thank goodness you'd be there to help her go through it

Well, just be safe. Sleep helps you stay sharp and I need you home. How else are you going to experience a minty bj?

Yeah

Minty bj

I'll hold you to it lmao

Remind me about your picture when you're up

Oh. You don't have to, I think about that at least once a day.

Damn

How feisty lol

How long can you stay on your knees for

I think about you n me in all sorts of compromising positions all flipping day. when I'm not worrying about you, anyway. Being a writer gives one a very vivid imagination

Do you even get tired at all ?

An hour?
My jaw will probably be sore the first few times, but no, I don't. I get very, very turned on.

Can you open PDFs on your phone? I'll send you the porn i wrote.

Damn , that's very nice

I wouldn't want you staying down too long and having your jaw hurting

I'd rather let you arch your back while I give you that backshots

And yes , I should be able to

Backshots?

Google it lol 😄

Dick

And the jaw hurting is just cuz I haven't done that in a while.

Just don't get it in my eye. That sucks.

Oh ok

I wouldn't

I'd rather get it in you

Hello Beautiful

Same

I looked up buckshot.

Lol, backshot

Ok, I'm losing you. Be safe today. I'm thinking about you.

Goodnight my love , sweet dreams.. I love you to the moon and back

About to close my eyes for a few

Ok
Love you too

I might skip the drill , fuck em

Day 53

Morning, babe. I hope you didn't get in trouble about drill. It was really great talking with you last night. I can't wait for you to send me pictures. Have a good day.

Hope your day is going ok.

I take my notebook to the pier and lay down to write my feelings in a space that brings me peace. I need to write out the doubts and fears to help these confusing emotions. I don't know what to do about Daniel and my heart just hurts, thinking about him.

Tears start falling as I write, and I start sobbing towards the end. My heart is breaking with the very real possibility that I fell in love with a scammer, and I have no idea what to do about it. Maybe things will work out? Maybe the nanny will meet me in person, and I'll know she's real, which will mean Daniel is real, too. Maybe I'm jumping to conclusions because I'm on my period and my emotions can't be trusted right now.

The only thing I know is that I love him, and he feels real to me.

<night>

Good night, babe. Hope things are ok.

Hello my love

Good evening to you

Hey baby. How was your day?

I just heard back the nanny too , she's been going crazy but I told her that someone is going to contact her to pay my debt so she can stop waffling and take care of Trixie for the next 4 weeks

Because the month ends in 3 days or so and I'm not willing to take any risks

Whatd she say?

So please text or call her , just please help me handle this situation and I'll forever be indebted to you my love

All she's been saying is that she just wanna get paid that she has bills and kids and all that shit and she has dedicated all her time to taking care of Trixie while I'm not home and she wants her pay for it or else she'll leave

She's just been spiraling and saying the same thing over and over again

Just help me please

<sends her phone number>

Okay

That's her number my love

Do you think you'd be able to borrow me some money and just pay her off so she'd be able to stay for one more month

Then I'd just fire her ass when I'm home and we'd have trixie to ourselves

How much?

It's a lot babe like 7k ish

It's 3 months pay

I can hear how panicked he is through his texts. That's a ton of money, more than I spend on anyone, and my heart remains shattered. I try to blow him off by telling him I'd contact her tomorrow, but he's really freaked out.

Ill get ahold of her tomorrow and see what I can do.

If you can help , I swear I'll pay you back as soon as I land with interest if you want

I promise you I will my love

Jean Booth

Please can you call her tonight , I told her you'd contact her

This is very important to me please

I can't do much from here and it's making me go insane

Its 1030

Is she even awake?

I'm sure she is because we texted about 30 minutes ago

Oh, okay

Thanks babe , I know I'm not supposed to be involving you in my business and bring my burden on you .. I'm truly sorry and hopefully I can make it up to you when I'm Home

It's ok. We're partners, right? She didn't answer.

Well yes but not by putting my fucking problems on you

She will , she's kinda slow

Ok. I'll handle it

Thank you my love

This means everything to me

More than you can imagine

Of course baby.

I love you so damn much and I'm really blessed to have met you

Thank you match lmao 🤣

😄

What'd you do today ?

Just worked. Went to the pier and released some tension while listening to the waves. Wrote some thoughts down.

Sounds like a chill day to me

So you got 2 more days of work ?

And you write your thoughts down , what did you write down .. I'm interested lol

Yeah. I haven't slept much this week, and I have a migraine.
Just organized some big feelings so I don't keep them bottled up and wind up going crazy.

I let him go this time. I'm completely unable to continue a conversation today. He's proved me wrong by asking me for money, and I just have no idea how to move forward with my life. My heart is broken, I have a headache from crying, and I just feel completely and utterly shattered.

Day 54

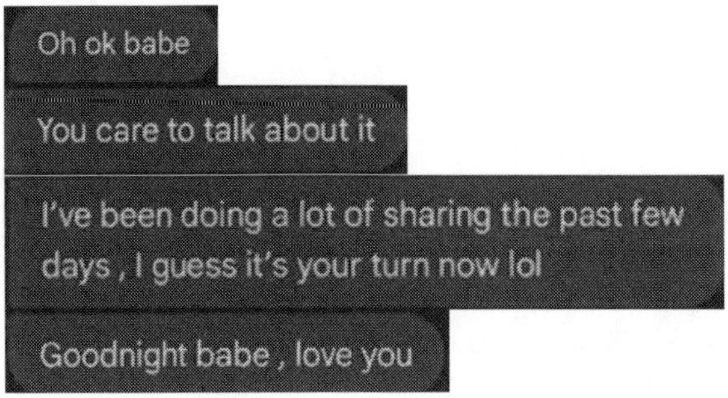

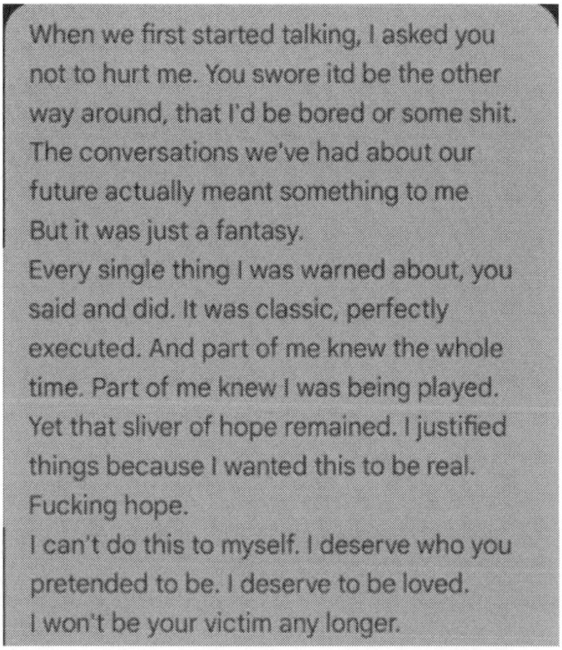

I text him first thing in the morning, sharing just one of the many links I saw that explain what a romance scam is. I tell him how he broke my heart. I stand up for myself, and as soon as I'm finished, I block him. I don't know how I get through work today, but I can feel the crushing despair through the numbness.

I finish work and ask my neighbor's daughter, Olive, to come over and hang out with me. She's been over at my house more often than not, but this time, I need to not be alone. I cry, explaining to her what happened. She just hands me a tissue box and lets me get it out. I hate this. I hate feeling like this.

"I wasn't even this upset when I left my ex," I tell her. "I don't understand why this hurts so much."

"You loved him, and he lied," Olive said gently. "Of course, you're going to hurt."

My phone buzzes with a text from a number I don't recognize. I open it and see his name in the message before throwing the phone as if it bit me.

"It's him," I yell at Olive. "It's him. It's him. I can't. I- I-holy crap, it's him. I can't look at this."

I thrust the phone at her to deal with as I wrap my arms around myself and pace. I fall to my knees, unable to do anything but feel deep confusion and grief. Everything I read about scammers said that once you call them out, they either admit it or disappear. Why didn't he disappear? What did I do? Am I wrong?

"What does it say?" I asked, my broken voice almost unrecognizable to myself.

"He's confused and says he's not a scammer," she says carefully. "You should read it."

She hands the phone back to me, and I read the message through a blur of tears before messaging him back.

New number

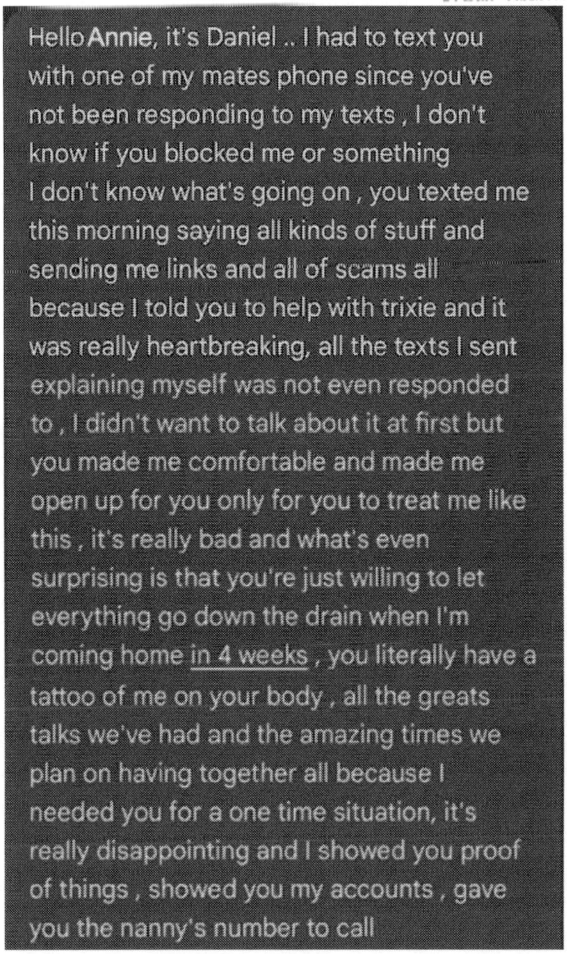

I really shouldn't be treated this way and I felt I should've been treated better , you could've just said you couldn't help only for you to turn against me like this , it's devastating 💔

You're not fucking real. You've completely broken me. You literally did every single thing the article said con artists do. There's no record of you existing. I've looked. I've defended you when people told me you were catfishing.

I know the military can't freeze accounts. They don't have that capability. I have friends in places that know these things. You've lied. And now you're blaming me for believing the lies and holding you accountable.
You're right, this is devastating. I've done nothing but cry for three days. You're everything to me have no idea why you made me your target, but you succeeded in absolutely destroying me.

I'm not lying to you , I never have .. I swear on my fucking life I'm not .. this just happened because of the fucked up situation I'm in
There's so much of the military that you don't know , that the public doesn't know .. I told you that we're deployed down here on a stealth mission and mostly everything is confidential so if you ask around , you're probably going to find nothing , I told you this when we started talking

I am not lying to you , I can give you my Facebook and instagram, I have never lied to you

I've been quarreling with the nanny to fucking call you all day and she said she has but you aren't picking up your phone

You're right, I think. *You haven't lied to me…that I know of.*

Of course, she can't get ahold of me, I blocked her, too. I unblock them both, and tell him to talk to me there. His buddy doesn't need to be involved with this. Tears haven't stopped streaming down my face. I'm dehydrated and have a massive headache, but they still flow.

Can you at least talk to her .. I'm not trying to hurt you , I love you and that's all I've ever wanted .. I've been talking to you for over two months and I've never asked you for anything and never will if not for this unfortunate situation that happened to me , you just blocked me out of your life , it's really heartbreaking, you've made me miserable all damn day !

I unblocked you. Give your "friend" their phone back.

Daniel

Send them to me. Your fb and insta.

Oh so now you can respond to me

You even fucking blocked me

Wow , you're unbelievable

Can you blame me?

All because you read some blogs so you believe a random website over me

Prove to me you're real

Yes I'm blaming you !

I've never asked you for nothing , not a damn thing

Goodbye, "Daniel."
I don't deserve this.

New number

It's not just reading some blogs. You think I'm not going to do research on someone i met on the internet? Really? Do you really think I work where I work without getting to know people? I've had you checked out. There's nothing. No Daniel rodriguez fanelli born 8/10. Prove to me you exist. Show me I fucked up. Don't just yell and gaslight me.

I will , I just needed to get some closure and clarity over why you just decided to treat me like that but it's all good .. I hope someday you're able to give people the benefit of the doubt because you aren't perfect yourself and could end up in a situation where you'd need help too
Fix your attitude or you're going to end up alone the rest of your life

You didn't check me out properly though

My name is Daniel Rodriguez Donald fanelli , did you ask my for my socials ?

I freaking gave you the benefit of the doubt, I scream in my head. *I know I'm not perfect. I never said I was. And I've been in situations where I've needed help. And I've had to figure it out on my own more times than I've been helped.*

Good holy lord, he's got a long name. And it sounds hella weird. A first, last, first and last? Isn't it usually a first name, a middle and maybe two last-names? *I did ask for your socials! You just said you had them.*

You just went ahead and started assuming shit in your head , I'm an airborne paratrooper for fucks sake , you can't expect me leaving traces on the internet , what don't you fucking understand

Daniel

You asked me for $7 grand.

I believed you over everyone. I still want to. My heart is shattered. I want you, us.

Can you text me somewhere

No you don't

You fucking blocked me Annie

wtf !

You used every scam tactic in the manual.

And you're still making me the bad guy.

My instagram is dibble_101
Facebook is Donald fanelli

How am I making you the bad guy when you literally blocked me

And I asked you for 7 grand because that's what I owed her , why don't you call her and ask so you can be certain

You concluded in your head and ran with it , how's that my fucking fault

What you talk about scam tactic , wtf is that ?!

I tried everything I could. I still believed in you up until last night. For fucks sake, I still want to. I never thought id find someone like you. Ever.
Youre blaming me for seeing the information I was given and acting on it. Isn't that what you do with information?

All because I opened up to you and shared with you what I was going through

I'm very disappointed in you Annie

So you never for once thought that maybe I actually do love you and I'd never do nothing to hurt you and actually want to be with you and come home with you

All the times we've shared and had together doesn't mean anything just because of an information you found on the internet

That's very weird

I asked you for information and you wouldn't answer. Ive asked you for your socials. You told me you had them, but not what they were. You hid so much of yourself from me, wtf was I supposed to think?!?

I was being truthful , I had them and was never on them .. everything you asked me , I fucking answered you .. what else do you fucking want from me

I'm stuck in a war zone that I basically can't do nothing and I still do so much , always there texting you , helping you deal with your hormones and all

But I guess I was just a cure to your loneliness

Don't you dare say i didn't think you loved me. And don't you dare say the things we shared didn't mean anything. I fucking love you. I'd do anything for you. You want the money? Fine. I'll pay her tomorrow

Fuck you

I gave you my socials both Facebook and instagram

I loved you. I love you still. Nothing will ever change that

I gave you every fucking thing

I see them, now.

You don't love me , you don't give two fucks

You fucking blocked me

Like wtf !!!

You made me go crazy !

Bullshit.

Over nothing

I would give the fucking world for you

I'm sorry. I thought i was protecting myself.

I break rules every goddamn day talking to you and all we've shared just down the drain over a fucking blog

Why would I even scam you , do I look broke to you

That shit can be faked

I have my own house , I'm richer than you .. you're the one who's still living in airbnbs

Like do you even think ?!!!

Wow, he's really hitting below the belt with that comment. I'm angry, angrier than I've ever been in my life by this whole situation. I still have no idea if he's a scammer or real—everything he says makes sense. I did force the information out of him. He didn't jump in and ask me for money like other scammers I've dealt with have. And from everything I've read, a scammer wouldn't fight like this. They'd be too afraid to lose their mark. Maybe I was wrong?

Wow

Nothing I do is faked , I'm a man of fucking integrity

It's true

Im only living here because you asked me to wait.

Just because I'm stuck here doesn't mean I don't know my value and worth

I know mine, too.

Because I wanted you to live with me when I'm back in 4 weeks

And I want everything with you.

But it doesn't matter anymore , I'm a scam so block me and do whatever you want

It's all good

Let Trixie be abandoned

Hope that makes you sleep better at night

You don't want anything with me , I don't believe a word you say anymore , I've proved myself to you .. now it's your turn to prove yourself

How have you proved yourself to me? I ask myself.

I'm sick of words !!

I am too

Right

We were so good before this whole trixie nanny's bullshit happened and as soon as our "relationship" and "love" got tested , you blocked me

My mates warned me that you're probably just bored and a newly divorced woman would never love me , just messing me but guess who's the fool who thought it's genuine lmaooo

I text Mayra, trying to get her to meet up with me. I need to see someone in person, but she's being so rude and unwilling to work with me. I send Daniel a screenshot of my conversation with her.

I'm making arrangements to meet with her now.
Will we be able to try to work past this?
And our relationship has been tested from the beginning. Do you have any idea how hard it is to be told how stupid you are for loving someone you met on the internet from every single person in your life? I fought through the doubts, fought to trust and believe.
And yes. I just got out of a 24 year long relationship. I might need to be treated with a little extra gentleness and understanding. Did you ever think of that?

Ive told you I wasn't bored. Ive told you I was scared. Apparently you don't believe me.

Well I don't know what to believe anymore

You just concluded on your own when you could've discussed your insecurities and I would've given you all the proofs you needed

I actually do love you , like I can feel it in every iota of my being but this is really disappointing Annie,it really is

Why can't you just call her on the phone and talk on the phone , do you have to meet her

Why do you believe that everyone isn't real

What's your obsession with being fake

Are you not real ?!

I tried. You didn't answer. There are so many things I've asked that you've ignored.
This is the most you and I have ever talked and it's centered around you wanting money.

You're mistaken

You should go back to our chats

I have

Many, many times

We've spoken so long and extensively

So what are you talking about ?

I just wanted you to help so she wouldn't leave and you aren't even giving me the money , you're lending me

And you'll get paid in 4 weeks , that's why I kept repeating that I'll pay you with interest in you want

I love that you keep defending her. I want to know that im giving a real person what you're asking, and im the bad guy. Yet, she can threaten to abandonment your kid and she can do no wrong.

Did you call her , I asked her and she said she called you and you didn't answer the phone

She didn't call

Defending her

What are you talking about , I despise her

But she's the best option I have right now and she has been caring for her for 2 years now

I'm not defending nobody , I'm just telling you that thing isn't as deep as you're thinking, nobody is trying to take advantage of you .. shit just happened to me and it's part of life , it can't always be butterflies and sunsets

No shit. Life has never been butterflies and sunsets for me.

She wasn't the best option you had, but you didn't trust me. You'd rather me pay some unknown person $7k to keep watching your kid.

I'll ask her to call you again , she's responding to me right now or can you just call her

My life has never been butterflies and sunsets.

You have her number and you're literally talking to her so just call her

Can we work through this?

Is there anything to salvage?

Unknown person that has been taking care of her for 2 years , she isn't unknown , she just needs her money , she has kids of her own and shit .. she already explained to me and I needed you to help me as my girl .. it was that simple

How do you think we should work through it , you hold all the cards right now

You can just decide to wake up and think I'm not good enough and just block me like you did today

I always have to assume everyday we talk is our last

Maybe now you'll understand what I go through every day—I have to assume every conversation we have is our last, too. And I probably won't even get notified if something happens to you because I'm just the internet girlfriend. It freaking sucks, I think.

Shes unknown to me.
And I don't hold the cards. You do. You always have. From the first time i told you I loved you, you've had all of me.
And I worry about that every fucking day.
Every day I'm terrified I won't hear from you.

And thats not why I blocked, and you know it.

Every fucking day I'm absolutely petrified for you. You've been the reason i breathe for the past two months. And I dont care if you believe me or not. I'm absolutely 💯 massively all in, in love with you.

Hmm

Easy for you to get rid of me tho

Ileft her a voicemail and texted her. I need her venmo

No it wasn't. I haven't stopped crying since yesterday.

My head hurt last night because I was dehydrated from how much I'd been weeping.

But you would've gotten rid of me if I haven't fought for us , I had to ask for my mates phone to text you hoping you wouldn't block that too

I really feel like I deserve an apology for the way you acted

And you messed my day up, I couldn't concentrate, couldn't do nothing , I was just fucking numb all day to everything

I had to have my neighbor over all day so I wouldn't unblock you. I thought about it at least twice an hour. She held me for hours while I wept.

Hmm

Right

I'm sorry I didn't believe you. I'm sorry I blocked you. I'm sorry I have major trust issues that I've been working through.

Well I don't have her Venmo , you're texting her so ask her for it

-screenshot-

Shes not responding to me

I hear you , I don't want to hurt you .. I have absolutely no reason to

I really do love you

Enough to work through this?

Sorry I brought you into my shit that made you uncomfortable

You have to swear to me that under no condition would you ever block me again

Because I wouldn't ever do that to you

Jean Booth

If we have issues , we discuss and go through it like couples do !

I will never block you again. Ever

I hear you

I know you don't believe me, and you have every right not to, but i want to be part of every part of your life. The good and the bad.
This was just too much of everything bad I kept hearing and reading.

Do you really love me

You mean everything you said

With everything i am

Everything word.

Ive never lied. Ever.

She says you owe her 7800. Does that sound right?

Ok , I believe you

I have never lied to you ever

And yes , that's what I owed her

I believe you.

I told you the truth and kept it real as much as possible

Hmm but you wouldn't if I haven't fought for this

So what's going to happen with her , tomorrow is the last day of the month

Trust is really, really, ridiculously difficult for me. You don't know my history. But believe me, the fact that I chose to believe you over everyone and everything else the past two months, is fucking huge for me.

I'm trying to figure out the venmo thing. I've only used it three times before.

Something went wrong and we couldn't complete this payment. Try again another time.

OK

It's not letting me.

Of course I understand that and it's the same way for me .. I told you that I haven't spoken to anyone or dated anyone since my former wife passed so to open up to you and be vulnerable takes so fucking much from me but I still let myself because what I feel for you is genuine

Babe , I think Venmo has a limit , I'm not sure you can send it all at once .. can you split it and try to send like $3k first and see if it'll work ?

Can you try that again Venmo thingy again ?

I've tried it 6 times. Even went down to a grand. Still won't work.

Oh wow

That's not good

Yeah

I'm trying.

What are you gonna do now ?

What am I *going to do*? I think, incredulously. *This is your freaking problem, not mine!*

What do you mean?

I have more than enough to cover it. It's not me.

Oh okay

Can you transfer to her bank account , I think she uses chime , that'll probably work , what do you think ?

I looked up the Chime bank information, and it looks like it's going to be a complete pain in the ass. The best way to handle it is to write her a check, but she won't meet me in person, and I don't have an address I can mail a check to, so I'm stuck dealing with this bullshit. I'm trying to believe him and to not feel insecure about this, but it's really difficult.

I don't know what that is. Why can't she meet me?

She uses chime bank babe , can you ask her to send you her bank details so you can send it to her or wire it to her or something

I'm being very delicate here cuz tomorrow is the last day of the month

I don't wanna piss her off then have her leave

I have to apply wisdom

So can you please just do this for me my love , just for me

I realize this. I'm trying as well, even though it's going against all my better judgment. I'm trying.

I understand and appreciate it my love

Please just help me find a way to make the transfer

Daniel, I'm trying. Please relax. Every inch of my back is stressed about this. Every red flag i can think of is waving in my face and im trying my absolute best to pay this bitch and not lose my fucking mind.

Ok babe , I'm relaxed

Just text me whenever you wanna talk

That makes one of us.
You owe me a massage. And a massive hug.

I owe you more than that trust me

And I can't wait to prove you so wrong about how you presume me , 3 weeks left from next week

That's all imma say 👌

I want this to be nothing more than a fight in our history, you have no idea.

She's making this extremely difficult

I really, really don't like linking her account to mine to do this transfer.

And if you ever allow her near our girl again, I'm punching you in the dick.

I'm sorry you're having to do this my love

Only for you

But you're doing this for me and trixie

Well, her too

And I'd never forget the stress she put us through

I'm firing her ass as soon as I'm home

I swear it to you

Yes, you are.

Just pay her so her bitch ass can stay for 3 more weeks

So you had to link her account to yours to make it work ?

I don't understand that

I'm trying to pay her.
And yes. I have to have her account linked to mine to wire the money. I'm waiting for her routing and account number.

Its fairly standard

My ex and I did it, so I know she can't access my account from hers, but it still makes me super uncomfortable.

I would wire him $ for my car payments

It's the bank that she uses that make everything a fucking nightmare , she uses chime bank which is some type of a prepaid card type of bank

It's a fucking hassle doing anything with her but she isn't all too literate so I don't blame her

Perfect. No wonder venmo doesn't work

You still wire him till now for your car payments ?

No.

My car is paid off.

Oh ok

I don't have any debt

Good to hear babe

And opposed to what you seem to think, I don't have to live in an air bnb. I did this strategically

I'm sorry I said that

I was just pissed and irked that you'd think so low of me that I wanted your money or something

Im sorry all this happened

I don't even know if you got money so that just came out wrong

It's just a misunderstanding

We've never fought before but this was a lot for our first fight lol

We gotta make up really badly for it

If it helps at all, I didnt want to believe it. Good things don't happen to me.
And you're the best fucking thing in the world. You really, truly don't get it.

I have money. Not as much as you, but I dont need anyone to support me.

Aww thanks babe but I'm not perfect as you can see

Jean Booth

I have life issues like everyone and I'm dealing with it right now

And of course I'll always support you , not because you need it but because I want to and you're deserving of it

My life in a nutshell: I was raped when I was 5 by one of my moms boyfriends. I was abused in every way possible until I was about 13. My parents used me as a pawn in their divorce.
I stopped trying to kill myself when i was 11. I've had 3 cancer scares that I've dealt with alone. The last one left a 10-inch scar down my torso. The only thing my ex had to say about it was, if I wasn't so fat, I wouldn't have health issues. He was selfish and I could only earn his love.
So, having someone tell me I'm beautiful and they love me, isn't something I believe easily.

So when I tell you I'm trying, I fucking mean it.

And when i tell you you're too perfect to be real, that's why.

Good things don't happen to me. I have a really, really hard time believing in them.

So babe , I read online that you can make a direct deposit into her chime bank , all you need is her routine and account number and it'll go through but as an Ach transfer because chime doesn't receive wire , I already told her to send you her bank information now

Omfg !!

Raped at 5

Omg that so cruel , I'm so sorry my love

Ive been waiting for her to send me the ingo

Info

Now I get why you feel this way , you've been so scarred and now you believe everyone is out to get you

Can you better understand my trust issues?

But I'm not that

I love you for who you are and who you became , I love you with all your imperfections

I know. And im trying to believe. I'm trying to have faith.

I love you so much. You have to know that.

your ex is a real asshole for the way he treated you , he better stay away from me when I'm home cuz he's gonna get punched in the face and have his nose broken

I'm sorry I upset you today.

He lost me.

You didn't upset me , you made me sad

Good , and he better keep it that way

I'm really sorry about what you had to go through in the past , now I see why you don't really fuck with your parents and truly they deserve it

I don't know if she's going to wait. The transfer can apparently take a couple days.

Jean Booth

Well I don't care , she will wait as long as it's sent , you can send me a screenshot so I'll send it to her as proof

As long as it's done and gone , that's all we need my love

You're not the bank that's taking time to process so her bitch ass better calm down because she made you block me and I'm pissed at her so fucking much , all this over 3 months pay while you've been caring for her for over 2 years , fucking bitch

I know and I appreciate you my love

Just try to work with her please , for me

She's so rude the way she's texting and it's pissing tf off

So I'm curious

About whayt?

How did you manage to stay 24 years with a man that treats you like that ?

It's really surprising

It wasn't all bad. And i didn't think I deserved better or could get better. We were financially stable, he didn't beat me, and it was only since 2019 that he started making jabs about my weight.
I had my own room since 2021, and we rarely had sex. We were mostly roommates for a long time. It was only in the past few years, after the tumor on my liver was removed and I almost died, that i realized I didn't want that life. I'd rather live alone and love myself enough than continue to be in a loveless, lonely relationship.

You know how facing your mortality can put things in perspective.

I'm happy, healthier than I've been in a decade, and feel like by the end of March, ill have the life i dreamed of.

Oh wow , you rarely had sex ?!!

That would never be the case with me

I'll beat the sonic coins out of your pussy lmao

Yeah. Maybe once a month for less than 5 minutes. Unless I was giving him a bj. Then I could make him last.

I'm glad you're better now , a near death experience for sure gives another outlook on life

Do you go by Donnie at home?

Donnie , dibble that's what I go by

Dibble is my nickname lol , the guys gave it to me

What's behind dibble?

Why?

Dont take this wrong - i dont know how else to describe it, but your insta icon kinda makes you look like an asshole. Like you were a player or something.

I like your newer pics.

We just gave ourselves silly nicknames , I've had it years now during my first deployment to Afghanistan, we needed to make a hole for an artillery weapon and my commanding officer screamed at me "be a dibble and make that hole soldier and dig that hole " I didn't like it at first and dismissed it but they always called me that and it stuck Ed ever since lol

Lmaoo , I'm not a player but I didn't want to be on there but my former wife forced me to create the account on there because we wanted me to put myself out there more

I'll add you on there , I'm trying to reset my password.. I don't think I remember lol

Do you know I still have my mates phone with me , I never thought you'd unblock me .. I'll give it to him in the morning

I was stressing all day

I couldn't understand what was going on

Why did she want you to put yourself out there more?

I'm so sorry. I've never wanted to be the cause of your stress. Ever.

You may want to delete the pic of me crying.

I don't think I've cried this much in a long time. If ever.

Because I was an homebody and I'm very old school.. she's more outgoing and we wanted me to open myself more to the world because it's changing and you have to adjust to it

I will on his phone but I would keep it on mine lol 😁

I didn't even believe you was crying until you sent me the picture

Ahhhh.
Why would you keep thay?

<sends pic of me crying on the pier>

This was me yesterday, writing down my thoughts and sobbing on the pier.

Wow , I'm so sorry

But you could've just talked things out

You don't have to bottle things up and deal with it yourself .. I'm sorry but I'm not your ex husband.. I'm me

I should have.

We're in a weird relationship. This isn't like anything I've ever experienced before, and literally everyone keeps telling me you're a scammer.

That's crazy , they don't even know me

It's literally me against everyone now

I haven't dated in over 24 years. All I've heard are horror stories of women getting scammed for everything. It took a lot for me to even join the app, let alone have the relationship we have.

But you're a grown woman, you know what you want

I'll never do anything to hurt you

I've said it and will keep saying it

I am, and I do. I want you. Have since day one.

I fucking stand on that with everything

I just need you home. For lots of reasons. First and foremost, so you're safe. Second, because I need to feel you.

I trust you, honest. But I need to feel you for myself.

Does that make sense?

You'll

I told you this is my last deployment and I'm quitting

You will as much as you want

And you need to stop believing your buddies that I'm bored.

I just hope you don't get tired of me when you eventually have me in your arms

Never

Yeah , I never believe them but they've met women who were all over them , love bombing them and all but didn't want to see when they got back to the states so it built some type of trust issues but I know that won't be the case with us

I swore I'd never get married again after Peter. You have me wanting it all. It scares the shit out of me how deeply embedded you are into every part of me.

We're way too invested in this to quit now

The only way you'll be rid of me, is for you to leave me.

And it's only going to get better , just let me be home and you'll see .. you'd literally wanna be inside my skin

Well I'm not leaving

I'm not going nowhere , I'm willing to fight for this .. you're all I need

I really do.
Same here. I only want you. And Trixie, but you know youre a package deal

I understand you babe

Did you eat anything tonight

I want the life we've talked about. I want everything with you

Yeah, then threw up when we first started talking.

Yup , we both want the same damn things

I feel like shit. My stomach hurts, my head is killing me, and my back is out.
I have to go to the office tomorrow to turn everything in and im so not ready

That's why we have to make this work

We're going to get tested , it's going to get hard , we will argue but we have to be strong and stick together and come back even stronger each time

Damn , you got to go to the office tomorrow that's true

Please stay safe, be real, and don't break my heart.
That's the prayer I've said at least 20 times a day for two months.

Isn't tomorrow your last day ?

It is

We are going to fight and be tested. But if we can get through this. We can get through anything.

I'll be safe and would come home to you in one piece , I'm not perfect but one thing I am is real and true with you my love

Yup , I believe in us that's why I came back to text you

No one is perfect.

Thank you.

I love you. So fucking much

I could've just left and blocked you too and go Back to the app to reactivate my account and id find someone else in no time

But why do that when you can fight for what you want

I know you would. But they'd never be me.

I love you too babe

Just don't fucking block me again

I won't. I promise.

Lmao , and their tits will never be as big as yours 😆 😝

Nope.

Lol

Please try to get some rest

You've been crying all day

You need sleep more than I do.

You need it and you have to work early because of the transportation

I know. I'm not worried. There's always coffee

I'm good babe , I'm always fine

I know you say you are, and I also know that isn't the whole truth.

You compartmentalize.

How many cups of coffee do you have in a day ?

Usually none

I don't do that on purpose, it's what I've been trained to be

When i go to the office, depends. Sometimes 1, sometimes 3

You have to see things from my perspective

I know. I think you have to do that to cope with what you do.

It's what I've known all my life

I see a lot more from your perspective than you think I do.

I have to keep shit away from the people I love and not tell them everything

It's hard but it's what I have to do

I just came wait to be done with that life

I wanna be free and talk about everything when I want and where I want

I know.
Your job is tough.
My ex bff was naval Intel

It is , we are the ones sent to clean up when shit hits the fan

Whenever we show , know damn well there's gonna be a funeral the next day

Please don't let it be yours.

There are really horrible people in this world , we are their karma

I know there are horrible people in this world. I've lived it and am not blind. And I hate that there's so much confusion and uncertainty with us.

It wouldn't my love , I'm careful as much as possible but you made me almost lose my composure today , had me pacing around going nuts

I really do love you

It's on another level and I saw that today

It's like he's just realizing how much he loves me. It's sweet, and I melt.

Im so, so sorry, baby. I love you so much

Never again.

Good to hear , I sure hope so

Have you slept? Can you sleep?

I'll try to nap for a bit

Day 55

I'm obsessing over you today. I think I've looked at my phone no less than 12 times this past hour. I really hope you're ok and safe.

I'm exhausted as I get onto the metro with my coffee. I text Daniel/Donnie, completely drained and still more stressed than I ever thought was possible. It's my last day, and I have extremely mixed feelings about that. I seem to have mixed, complicated feelings about a lot going on in my life.
I'm really busy trying to get everything buttoned up for my boss to take over and distribute my workload. I highly doubt anyone will use the information I share, but at least my conscious will be clear when I walk out the door today. Everyone has been really nice and supportive, and I've had a few people tell me they're sad to see me go. I didn't think I'd made any impact in the short time I'd been there.

Today has been weird.
Your stupid nanny won't reply back to me again.

Hey babe

How are you

Busy day for me

Yeah? I'm sorry. I'm ok

Yup

Mayra and i are trying to figure this out.

How are you and what have you been up to

Did you sleep at all?

What's she saying , she hasn't responded to me since yesterday

Jean Booth

Yes for like an hour , my eyes are so fucking sore

Today has been weird. I'm just trying to get everything together and closed out. for my last day.
Shes going to create a PayPal so I can pay her since nothing else is working.

I'm sorry.

If it makes you feel any better, mine are, too and I still have a headache.

I'm just not dealing with what you do. I hate your job

Are you at work now

Yes

Oh ok , maybe PayPal will work hopefully because I'm tired of this shit

I really hope you don't get notifed every time someone sends you something on insta. Because that's my main form of communication. Lol

When do you get off

330, then it's 2 hours till I get home, depending on traffic

Are you the only person quitting today ?

No, I'm not

There's like 20 of us throughout the agency.

Everyone's been super nice, understanding, and supportive. It's been great. And if things change politically, I'm welcome back, so that's awesome

How are you doing? Besides being tired?

Damn , 20 people

I just hope yall get paid because I saw a judge blocking the executive order by trump to pay before who quit for 8 months

I don't know if you saw that

There are like 40 different things judges are trying to block. I'm trying to take things as they come.

I hope we get paid too. I have a contract saying I will, so...🤷‍♀️

There's always OnlyFans and feet pics. 😆

Damn , I just hope yall get paid

And never will I ever let you do that

I was joking. Like I'd ever do that.

I rather pay you to sit at home and pop that pussy on me lmao

😆

I'll be fine, no matter what happens.

I really, really want you home

Have you eaten?

How much longer do you have today?

I'm sure you'd be fine babe , I was just saying lol

I'd be home babe , 3 more weeks to go

I had some bread earlier and I still got about 6 hours to go

Hbu ?

I had an apple

Yuck. Your days SUCK

I'm counting down the days.

Just an Apple ?

And yes babe , you know this already

Same here , especially after our huge quarrel.. we need that make up sex !!!

Yes. And i do, just letting you know my feelings on that haven't changed.
We just need sex period.

And I've been extremely curious how good your bj is because you've sold me a lot of dreams about it lol

You'll find out in 3 weeks

That'll probably be the first thing I do when I get you home and naked.

Yup , I sure can't wait

You better keep those jaws greased 😆

😆

In all honesty, I'm looking forward to being in your arms the most. I just want to hold you, and be held.

So how many of your friends and neighbors did you tell that we stopped talking and you blocked me

Because you said someone was consoling

Just my neighbor

I really don't wanna come home to a bad impression and having your friends hate me

I really don't talk about you much because of all the shit I get from people when I do. It's been difficult.

I talk to Bex, who's been like the only one to support this, but when I first mentioned you to my friends every single one of them told me you were catfishing and couldn't be trusted.

What shit do you get tho

You never told me about this at all

You didn't need the added stress

Why would they even believe that when they don't even know me

Things they read.

I don't know.

Maybe it's the perception that you gave them ?

"The perception I gave them," I mumble to my phone, incredulously. "I tell them the facts about our relationship. It's not my fault things line up badly, and people assume the worst. Why the hell do you care what they think, anyway?"

Or do they think you're not deserving of love

No. Why do you blame me for everything?

I have no idea what they think.

Jean Booth

You really need to be careful for real because people tend to ruin things they don't understand

I'm not blaming you , I'm just having a conversation and trying to understand more of what's going on

I really don't give a shit what they think , all that matters is what you think

That's really it to me

I think most of my friends who knew me with Peter believe I deserve the love I give

I'm not with them , I'm with you

I love you. It's both that simple and that complicated.

I hear what my friends say, because I know their hearts are in a good place, but they aren't us. And you know why I have trouble with trusting things now. I'm trying.

I literally told them I met you on match, and you're in the military. They've asked about us video chatting, and I said you couldn't. From that, almost everyone said that's a huge red flag, and you weren't really who you said you were. I could have ended things with you then, if I let other people dictate me. But I decided to trust my heart. And do research.

I hear you

I'm just saying

Everything will be okay and everyone's mind will be put at rest when they see us together

"God," I whisper. "I cannot wait until that day. I want you in my arms more than anything in this world."

This week, there were too many things that made me question too much. I should've talked to you about it more.

And the apologies better be as loud as the disrespect

I agree.

Yes you should've , we would've had a conversation and I would've proven it to you that I truly do love you

This isn't a joke .. you think I'd just be here talking for months and wasting my time

lol

I don't want to believe that. But why me? You're hot. With a ton to offer. And I know I'm an amazing person, but you could be with someone who isn't squishy

It's the same question you'd ask yourself

I know I'm a great partner, but I have huge insecurities about how I look

Why not you ?

You yourself know you're an amazing person , so don't I deserve someone like that in my life ?

Yes.

I'm trying to like my packaging more. I want to be someone you want to show off.

I want to show you off exactly how you are

That's what makes you perfect , you're you and real and true and isn't trying to be someone you're not

That's why I was attracted to you in the first place babe

I am unapologetically me.

Good so why change ?

I'm not changing who I am, just want to look better

I've always liked who I am. And I have NEVER talked about my insecurities about my body with a guy before.

Okay

So talk to me

What are you insecure about exactly my love ?

Ugh, this is really fucking hard.

Talk to me love , what's hard about it

I'm overweight, have a tummy, and my thighs jiggle

I have a 10 inch scar down my torso from sternum to navel

But you don't look overweight to me

And I have hips.

I'm checking out your IG rn , you look pretty great to me

Thanks, babe.

I've always hidden behind my boobs. Most people see them and don't look any further.

And I'm sure the scar is an health scar so you should be proud that you're alive not worrying about some insecurities that I don't even see or care about

All I'll say is that you need to love yourself even more and block out the outside noise , you look amazing to me

Gah, he always makes me feel beautiful. I don't know how he does it, but knowing that he thinks I look amazing and beautiful really helps me to believe it as well.

And you dress very well too

Thank you. You've always made me feel beautiful.
I love dresses.

Why do you think you're not perfect since we're airing our stuff?

God, Mayra is a bitch. How did you find her, and how have you been ok with her? This can't have been a new development.

<couple hours later>

Sorry babe , I got busy for a bit

And I'm sorry you're having to deal with all this , I truly am .. she's been very rude to you and I apologize for that
Just know that you're doing this for me and I truly appreciate it, it means the whole world to me

And I never knew she was like this because we really don't talk much , she just does her job and I go about my way and she gets paid and trixie never complains when I ask questions and all

Youre fine babe. I don't mind dealing with her, just surprised at how awful she is.

How old is she? Is she married?

I half wonder if she has a crush on you and is pissed that I'm talking to her.

<two hours later>

Omg, I'm so glad I won't have to metro in rush hour again.

So you're officially done

Yes

I don't know if I should tell you congratulations lol

You should.

But I really hope things work out for you especially with your writing and publishing

You have to take it seriously tho

Like you really want it

"No shit, Sherlock," I say to myself. "I do really want it, and I plan on taking it seriously. I'm not going to sit around eating cupcakes and watching television. I've been working on my books, and I'm going to continue working on them. You truly don't understand how much of a workaholic I am, but you'll see."

I might be able to work NV still, I didn't want to say anything till it's official.
No dur. That's the plan.

I want this. Almost on the same level as I want you home.

The writing, not the nv thing

That's good to hear , I'm glad

So show how much you want it

Its nice to have someone kinda believe in me though.
Will you read my books?

You know I'd be home soon to see for myself

I do believe in you , you seem very determined and you're a go getter so of course I do

You almost done with your day?

And I'm not much of a bookworm but for you I'll read it my love

I still got like 3 hours to go

Ugh

What's going on with the nanny , is she being an asshole still ?

Thanks
I'm not asking you to be a bookworm. That's my department. Itd just be nice to have my partner actually read one of my books.

Of course I'll read it babe , I got you my love

That's so sweet. I'm glad he'll read them. It heals a little something in my heart to hear that.

She sent me what I needed from her chime thing. I'm waiting to get to my car to see if it works. Don't feel like sharing all my bank crap with everyone on the train

My dad left me some stupid cryptic voicemail. "Wow, just wow." And now won't answer his phone. So that's fun.
How are you doing? Hows the day?

What cryptic message , is everything good babe ?

You wanna talk about it ?

That was it. Wow, just wow.

Nothing to talk about.

Just weirdly cryptic.

Have you had anything else to eat besides bread?
I worry about you.

And please , try to figure it out with her as soon as you get in the car ... she responded to my texts not too long ago talking about todays the last day of the month but I already told her the person she's talking to is my woman and she's going to handle the situation

" wow just wow"

What does that even mean

And I got her text just as I got on the second train, so it wasn't long ago. Just didn't want you to think I was stalling

Is he mad at you

No idea

I'm ok babe , I'll have some Mres when I'm done for the day

Well maybe he'll call back

And I never said you're stalling my love , I just want to get this phase over with and have my mind at peace

I know. Me too. Ive been waiting for her all flipping day.

I've got like 4 more stops.

Okay babe , it's all good .. you can do that whenever you're in your car

I didn't know you're still on the train

Yep. It's usually an hour drive hour train. But I usually avoid rush hour. Not today

Can you send me a pic of Trixie? We always talk about her, but I've been wondering what she looks like. Wa

Wasn't sure if you'd think I was weird for asking

Oh ok

And I'm sure I've sent you pictures but I'll send more , give me a minute

You've only sent me 2 of you. One in a hoodie and one with a shaved head where you look like you're 23

He sends me a few pictures of Trixie, and she's absolutely adorable. I look at the one of them lying side-by-side and completely melt. They look like they have such a great bond, and I want to be part of that. I want the next picture I see of them like that to include me on the other side of Trixie, making a funny face, too.

Please don't let the nanny leave today , I'm begging you with absolutely everything

Aww, she's so 😍 cute. One more stop baby.

And I have no control over what Myra does. I'll do what I told you I would.

Thanks my love

Leave her to me , I'll handle her

She knows what I do and she's literally scared of me so I'll handle get

Her stupid ass *

Can you send a screenshot so I'll show her , she's very old school and I'd have to do a lot of explaining

She's like 45

It won't let me screenshot. The text is the best I can do.

Ok babe

I'll just send that to her

Thank you so much babe

You're welcome.
Please come home to me. And don't stress about this.

I really hope it went through because I don't want to deal with anymore of this bullshit on the 3rd of march

I sent it to her too.

You can send the rest tomorrow

Of course I will babe

It cleared my account.

I'm coming home to you , I love you so damn much

I love you too, baby.

I honestly don't know how else to prove myself to you.

You don't need to prove anything to me babe

I've always told you that I love you for who you are

And you're so cute with Trixie.

And i feel the same about you.

With all your insecurities and everything, i always have and always will

Does this help your stress at all?

Of course, we're besties .. always goofing around together

More than you can ever imagine

It's like a huge weight off my chest

I owe you a big one and I swear I'll make it up to you

I can hear the relief in his text, and I know I did the right thing. He may have similarities of a scammer, but he's not. It's just weird coincidences, and I feel like he's being honest with me. In three more weeks, we'll know for sure and be able to show everyone they were wrong. I hold onto that with every fiber of my being.

Please be safe.
Sleep tonight.
Just come home to me.

Thanks for loving and fighting for us and not giving up on me

I swear to you that you'll never regret this

You, too. ❤

Jean Booth

I love you 🩶

I love you, too.

You're my heart, my everything.

Now I get the hour and a half drive home. Yippie

Your last train ride and drive from work in a while

Must be nice

Yes, it is

I can't wait to quit the military and live a day to day life myself 🩶

It'll be really nice

Best part of my day is hearing the relief in your text

Im sorry I didn't trust in us more. Thank you for fighting for me. For us.

<one hour later>

I love you. I hope you know that.

Have you heard from her? She didn't say anything to me.

<one hour later>

How's it going babe

I'm rounding off with work

Im glad you're finally off

Almost

Im going to get thai food

How are you?

I'm super hoping this place actually makes spicy Thai. The last two I tried were lame.

You do realize your nanny is 2 years older than me, right?
Am I old school?

I text him when I get home as I've never liked texting and driving, never mind that it's illegal in most states. I think it's funny that Mayra is two years older than me and he considers her old, but he's just fine dating me. I laugh as I send him a text and a really naughty picture.

I'm assuming you ate and passed out from all the crap you've been through lately. Thai wasn't spicy, but it was still good. Love you babe

Good night kisses.

<two hours later >

Hello love , how's your evening going

I slept for a few , I was really tired asf when I got off my shift , I woke up to pee when I saw your texts

Those tits are so fucking huge !!!

I laugh at his exclamation.

Love you, baby. Go back to bed

My evening is fine.

And nope , you're nowhere near old school, I just mean she's an old school Mexican woman, I don't know if you get what I mean

I do. I was teasing

Are you going to be able to fall back to sleep?

Did I distract you?

Of course you sure did baby

Jean Booth

It's just hard for me to close my eyes and actually fall asleep but I'll try

Can i do anything to help?

Day 56

She's been paid the whole amount and I'm not giving that bitch another dime. I've already sent her the information, too. Just didn't want you to stress anymore about it.

I'm just being honest right now. A part of me is absolutely terrified that I was just played. I'm choosing to trust you, and this isn't easy for me. The fear is telling me that you're going to start backing off and that something is going to come up to where you're not going to come home. I'm talking to you about it so you know where I'm at. I need you to come home this month. I need you, and I don't need anything.
Please, please be safe, come home to me, and show me how silly I am to have this fear. I hope you slept last night. I hope you get the date you come home this weekend. I hope you're safe. I hope we have the future we've talked about. I love you so much.

I hated this. I hated feeling this way and having the doubts I now had weighing me down instead of just being abstract things that I didn't truly believe in before. Mayra is something awful, and I truly couldn't understand why Daniel would continue to want her to take care of his kid when I was available. I guess he didn't completely trust me, either. Which is understandable since we've never actually met before.

But these doubts, this confusion—it was awful to feel. I needed him to be home more than ever to clear up all of this.

<three hours later>

Hello my love

How are you doing ?

Hey baby. I'm ok

How are you? Did you sleep?

Dod you see that I sent her the rest?

I love you

I'm getting ready to drive up to my friend's house, but I really wish I could talk to him more. I love being able to talk to him. It relaxes me and makes my day just that much better.

I have D&D today till about 1, so if I don't answer, that's why. I don't want you thinking I'm ignoring you when, in reality, I'm freaking obsessed with you.

<two hours later>

Apparently, ICE and the FBI are in Annapolis rounding up illegal immigrants.

I get a lot of news from headlines and from my friends and family, which I completely admit is a terrible way to get news. But it's the only way I can cope with all the sadness and the depressing things that the news reports on. If they had more uplifting things and showcased how people were good to each other, I'd probably watch more of it. I enjoy hearing that people are actually kind—it was starting to feel like that was the exception to life now.
<two hours later>

How are you doing?

I miss you. Hope you're being safe.

I miss you too babe

Sorry I'm having one hell of a day [redacted]

It's so fucking busy

I'm sorry babe. Be safe. Don't worry about me.

After I leave my friends, I go to the bookstore. Walking around, I decide to message him, hoping that he's in a position where we can actually connect.
<sends pic of a little stuffed dragon>

I'm at the bookstore

Gonna get Trixie this. Do you think she'll like it?

The lil dragon, not the books. She's not ready for those. Lol

<five hours later>

You almost done for the day?

I guess you're either slammed or sleeping. I hope you sleep tonight and can talk tomorrow. 3 weeks....

Day 57

I'm so mad when I wake up. I've gotten used to talking to him the past few days. But that was when we were talking about his kid and money. So, is he a scammer and now that he got what he wanted, he's gone? Or is it coincidental? I know he's got a really difficult job and that he's often out on missions, but this seems really suspicious.

I hate that I have this conflict going on. It's hard enough dealing with him being deployed and in a situation where he's going on missions and could be killed at any point. But now that I'm not even certain that he's who he says he is, it's worse. I have the fear for his life and now the fear that I was played. Even my anti-anxiety meds aren't helping me deal with the crazy I'm feeling.

I voice my struggles and my fears, hoping that when he's able to see my texts next, we can talk about things. I need some sort of reassurance and something that I can hold onto as proof that he's who he says he is.

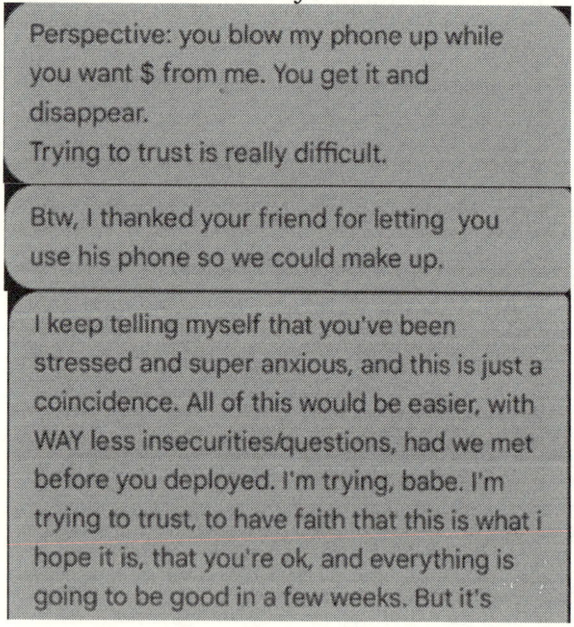

really difficult. You told me the other day that when you couldn't get ahold of me, it made you crazy, had you almost lose your composure. I feel that every single day. This isn't me being hormonal or needy. This is me being terrified and loving you on a level I didn't expect and having to trust and have faith that it's all going to be ok.

Hello my love

Good morning

I don't understand what you meant in your earlier text

What do you mean I blow your phone up when I needed you but now I disappear

Where the fuck is this coming from , you know how busy I am and things can get for me but now you wanna throw it in my fucking face ?!!!

Smfh

Don't worry , just 3 more weeks and you'll get your damn money back , thanks for helping me out

Thats not what I mean babe. I'm trying to talk to to

Im trying to air mt fear so this doesn't blow up

Im not trying o fight. I'm shaing the things that are scaring me instead of teying to del with them without you. You always ask me te think about your perspective. I'm asking you to look at mine.

Thats it.

Hmm

If you wanted to air your fears , you could've said it in a better , more suitable tone , not to just throw it in my face like that

I appreciate you trying to help but you gotta deal with your insecurities babe , I'm not going anywhere , because I wasn't able to talk for a few hours doesn't mean I'm running away

How did you feel when I didn't respond the other day?

Im asking- not threatening.

I know you worry but you got to ease up and put your mind at rest and actually trust me to be able to take care of myself

That was different because of the situation surrounding it , I knew you had blocked me for sure

I'm trying

But you know I'd never do that to you and that I just got busy for a lil bit

You know what I do babe , I don't work from home or have freedom like you but I still try

Yeah, I do know what you do! That's where a lot of this insecurity and fear comes from. Gah! I hate fighting with him; I shouldn't have said anything and just dealt with it like I have been. I didn't want to stress him out or distract him with my crap—he didn't need that.

Its not that different for me. I know what you do and it scarss me

And you see I added you back on IG and I see there's one Asian guy all over your comments , complimenting you

WTH is that ?!

Oh my god, I think. *Seriously*? I laugh out loud at the absurdity of his text. "Are you seriously jealous right now?"

I have zero control on who comments.

I posted something about healing not being linear and my IG blew up. I've had to block a bunch of people from my DMs.

I appreciate you caring for me , I really do and I really don't want to argue or go back and forth with you because I really do love you but you have to understand that whenever I'm unable to talk it's because I've been busy not that I'm ignoring you or anything because that will never happen

I was complaining about that to Bex yesterday, actually.

I don't post on IG to get men. I post for me, for inspiration

I see , I went through your IG and saw a bunch of randoms all over you , that's why I asked

I'm not worried about anything , I know that you're all mine but it's nice to be on the look out lol

"Right," I say to myself, laughing. "You're not worried, my ass."

I know. Three weeks and things will be better.

The only guy that is on my IG that I posted was my ex, and that was when we were together.

Have you been able to sleep?

You should see this message some dude sent. It was absolutely ridiculous. I read it to Bex and thought she was going to fall over, she was laughing so hard.

Oh ok , I understand

What do you like to be called, Daniel or Donnie? I'm not calling you dibble. But i do have dibs on you

And nope I'm not sleeping , I'm not off today .. I'm at the watch post , it's not so busy tho ... I could text for a bit

What text did he send .. tell me about it lol

Lmao , who told you call me dibs hahahaha

😂

I told you, I thanked your friend. He messaged back.

Ohhh ok lol

He's the one who told you I'm dibs haha 🤣

👍

And this was what that weirdo sent: Honestly, which planet did you come from? Because no one on Earth should be this stunning. Please, give me the honor of getting to know the incredible woman behind that gorgeous smile. I'd love nothing more than to discover everything that makes you so special. 💕😍❤️

Literally his second text.

Cuz I didn't respond to his first

Damn , he said all this to get your attention

Fuck him

You're mine !!!

You better tell his ass you're taken

Yes.
Yes i am. Only yours. I get shit like that occasionally and its weird. I usually just block them. And im peeved you have to work. It's Sunday. You're supposed to have the day off.

When i asked if you were sleeping, I didn't mean now. Have you been able to sleep the past two nights without having the extra anxiety?

Im peeved for you, not at you

Yes babe , I'm supposed to be off but what can I do

All I can say is 3 more weeks and I'm free

Thanks for being peeved for me babe

I know. Just let me be mad on your behalf. Not that i can do anything about it.

You never answered about your name

I wish you're here so you could help me kick my CO's butt because I know you will

😂

Oh, you have no idea.

Babe , you're mine .. you can call me anything you want

I'm all yours

Sexy muffin?

😂

Lmaooo

I'd take that

I laugh. This is what I like, what I've missed. I love when he and I can just talk and be silly together. It's going to take me a bit to remember to call him Donnie and not Daniel. I got to know him with his first name.

I still really want some angry sex. Pin you down, hold your hands above your head while i ride you. Trail my nails down your chest, leaving little red marks in their wake.

I'd probably last like 10 minutes and need to have you touching me again.

Have you heard anything from Mayra?

Lmaooo

You'll get it my love

Lots of it now that we're both gonna be jobless when I'm home , we're about to be fucking like rabbits , everywhere , everyday and everytime

I'm not jobless, but I let it go. No one looks at authors or anyone in the arts as having a "real" job.

Promises, promises.
Im gonna hold you to that.

I'm going to be all over you because I haven't had any action in a very long time and my balls are full and ready to be drained so yeah your sexy ass better be ready

"Oh my god." I say as I laugh. "That's the most ridiculous thing I've ever heard."

Yes , hold me to it love

Im ready, open, and willing. Bring it.

And nothing yet from here , I sent her the texts of the money being sent
I guess she's waiting for it to be in her account

I will , I got you

Ok. I sent her that info too. She didn't even say thanks. Rude.

You're going to get turned inside out , leave your pussy red and hurting

I'm gonna have you so sore both mouth and pussy

I'm sorry she's rude to you my love , just 3 more weeks .. Goodluck to her finding another job that pays like this

Imma have you screaming and have your neighbor worried for you 😂

Perfect.

When i pick you up, will we come here or your house?

I'm going to come to yours first then we'll leave for my place since the lease is expiring April right ?

Yes.

Was your address? Can I look at it on zillow?

Happy dating anniversary 🥂

2 months...

Oh wow my love

We are two months already , time goes by so fast

I can't wait to be home so we can make up for all lost times

Me too, babe.

We need to ; there's so much we need to do , go camping , dinners , movies , karaoke , fishing , hunting , and I must learn how to play D&D as well , will you teach me ?

I bet you're really good at it

That sounds like a ton of fun.

And i can teach you.

You sing?

Yes babe , it's gonna be a lot of fun babe

Is it hard ?

The D and D

It seems like you're really good at it

And yes I try to sing but I don't have the best voice 😄

I try to dance as well , trixie and I always have dance parties lol

Aww, I think. *I love dance parties. And I'm not sure that I'm good at D&D. I just have fun with it.*

There are just a lot of rules and I still don't know everything.

It's more the story building and actually playing your characters while you're at the table. It's fun that way.

I love dance parties! I was having one while I was cleaning last night.

<sends pic with tiny skirt>
<two hours later>

Hows your day going?

<an hour later>

Oh okay , well I think you're pretty good at it since you play all the time

You look great babe , I love the skirt , it's sexy

How's your afternoon going , you had something to eat ?

I'm ok , just down with some tummy ache but I'll be fine

I had half a sandwich.
Oh no. Did you eat something weird?

I just took a shower.

Oh okay and yes , I think it's the Mre I had earlier messing with my stomach

I'll be fine

What's your plan for the day ?

Gonna go to a rage room/axe throwing with my neighbor and maybe see a movie.

Are you able to lie down, or are you still working?

<two hours later>

I hope you feel better, baby. I love you

<an hour later>

Damn

Rage room

Please be careful

I've been laying down but I still haven't felt better but I'll be ok , it's just the fucking mre messing with me

I love you too babe

I'm so sorry youre not feeling well. Hugs baby.

Thanks my love

What are you up to ?

Bout to smash

I did amazing at axw throwing.

The guy at the rage room takes a picture of Olive and me preparing to go into the room with our hammers and crowbars. We are so ready to release some tension by smashing things. I send the picture to Donnie, showing him that I can be a badass.

Fuck. That was fun. Just what I needed.

Wasn't nearly as much fun as sex, but good in a pinch.

And believe me, if your CO ran up to me, only one of us would be leaving. Lol

And it wouldn't be him.

<Five hours later>

Lmaoo

Is that your neighbor

You look like serial killers lmao 🤣

Yep

Yeah, it's her daughter. She's the one who was with me the other day.

How are you feeling?

<half an hour later>

I hope youre sleeping and feel better in the am. Love you

Day 58

Morning, babe. I hope you're doing better

I jump into my training after I text him and put some dye into my hair. It's not like typical dye, it's blue pigment, so I usually leave the it in for a few hours until my hair gets stiff and then wash it out. It helps the color saturate better the longer I keep it in because it doesn't have the same chemical in it that most natural hair color has.

<three hours later>

Hello my love

Good morning

How are you doing today , thanks for checking in on me .. my stomach still hurts a bit but I'm okay

It's so fucking hot today !!!

Oh, yuck

Im ok. Working on my marketing stuff and dying my hair.
Were you able to sleep last night?

Have you heard anything about when you're coming home? Have you heard from Mayra? Is Trixie ok?

Yeah babe , it's what it is

What marketing stuff and you know I don't get to sleep much but I try to get a little

For my books

I was hoping you were sleeping a little better without the worry of paying Mayra looming over you. I'm sorry you're not.

And about that fucking nanny , she texted me this morning that she hasn't seen the morning and I told her to give it some time till the banks open , she's so dumb my goodness !!!

I haven't seen this part of her until now

She's just been saying all sorts of crap

I'm sorry. The first one cleared my account already, and the second should clear tomorrow.

I sent the screenshot to your Instagram, showing it cleared my account.

Oh okay

Well I just checked and you didn't send me no screenshot just a pdf and it leads to Facebook

I can't access it

That's weird.

Wym weird

Why can't you just screenshot and send it on here

I open the link I sent him and sure enough, it sends me to some weird Facebook page. I have no idea how that happened because I literally just took a screenshot of my screen. My bank app doesn't allow screenshots, and every time I take pictures of my computer screen with my phone, they look weird, so I try not to do that too much. I go back and take another screenshot and make sure that it opens correctly before sending it back to him.

I literally took a screenshot on my computer because I can't screenshot on my phone.

Don't take a screenshot with your computer

Use your phone to take a pic babe

Take a pic of it using your phone on your computer simple , I can't access it the way you sent it .. all I does is lead to a Facebook page lmao 🤣

Yeah, I saw that. Super flipping weird. Sorry.

There ya go

Okay

I'll just send it to her now

There's literally nothing else i can do, short of watching Trixie instead, and you don't want that so...
I'm sorry this is so frustrating

Babe , you've done more than enough and I really do appreciate you

I love you. I'm so sorry this is happening

I swear I do because you could've sat down and watch it all go down and not do a shit about but you chose to with all the trust issues and insecurities and you still helped , that shows who you are , you're simply an amazing person and I'm really thankful to have met you

And I know there are still doubts and everything but I can't wait to be home to clear it all up , love you properly and treat you like the queen that you are

I love you , more than you can ever imagine 🖤🖤🖤

Thank you 🙏

I can't wait for you to come home and clear this all up, too, I think. *I just really want to hold you, to know without a doubt that you're real and you're mine, and we'll be able to actually talk and figure things out.* That's all I want.

Well, in a couple weeks this nightmare will be behind us

I can't wait for you to be home, too.

And there's no way I could've lived with myself by not helping.

I love you, too.
If you get a chance to look at IG, I sent you a video of me. No idea if you can open it or hear it, but I think you'll like it.

<sends pic of new hair color>

I changed my hair

<five hours later>

Hey, my love. It seems like you're having a long day. I just hope you know that I think you're wonderful and I love you more than you know.

<five hours later>

I work all day, checking my phone periodically to make sure it's still working, and I didn't miss any text from him.

I need to start leaving this in the other room, I think. It's getting to be a bad, obsessive habit that I don't like.

Good night babe.

Day 59

<*midnight*>

I can't sleep and I just wanted to make sure you knew that I love you.

I toss and turn all night, unable to shake the uneasy feeling I have about Donnie. I can't pinpoint exactly why I'm feeling off, just that there's something happening or about to happen that isn't good. I hope it's just my anxiety and not my gut trying to tell me he's injured or worse.

I text him to be careful when I wake and go to work on my books. I check that the payments cleared for Mayra first so that I can show him that things worked on my end and he can hopefully get her to chill out.

This is hopefully going to sound stupid, but I've had a bad feeling all night and am really worried that something happened to you. I have no idea why, because we talked yesterday. This is different from just worrying about you. Please be extra careful today. I know you're always careful, but I can't seem to shake this. Be safe. You're loved.♥

The second one cleared.

I hope she's not still being a bitch.

Hello love

Good morning

How are you doing ?

So much better now. I love you

I'm doing okay , just having a busy ass day yesterday and it's been the same way today

That sucks. Please be careful

It's just hot and busy , you know it's Ramadan season for them here so there's been huge activity

How have you been ?

And what did you do yesterday ?

Idk why, but i had nightmares about you all freaking night

I wrote, went to the grocery store, and hung out with Olive.

Damn

Nightmares ?!

Ive heard of Ramadan, but not sure how it affects you

And that good , Olive is your neighbor right

Yweah, i didn't sleep for shit and woke up absolutely panicked a few times.
Yeah. She's been good company

We're in a Islamic country and all the insurgents are Muslim so you should know how it gets during Ramadan

I have no idea what Ramadan season is. I look it up, trying to figure out why it's making his life difficult and can't really understand it. But I'm not there, so maybe it's different from what's explained online.

I'm alright my love , thanks for always been worried about me but put your mind at ease , I'm ok

She calls me her sugar mama cus I take her out to eat. Lol
I actually don't. I never watch the news. I'll look it up though.

Any update on when you'll be home?

God, i miss you and I've never even held you.

I miss you too babe , while at work all day .. you're always on my mind

It's really crazy we haven't held each other and we miss each other like this , it's surreal

Same with me. I love you so much.

And that's nice , well sugar daddy is coming home soon cuz I'll always take yall out to eat

Lol

Nope, i want you all to myself

And i don't want you for your $. I want you. Just you.

Lmao , I'm all yours but that doesn't mean we can't have friends out or go out with them 😄

Nope. Just me. Lol
Im kidding.

Obviously I know that but if you want me , you gotta accept everything that comes with being with me

Haha

I do. Always will.

What's your plan for today ?

I'm on a lil break right now , that's why I can talk

Ive already started on my lesson for the book marketing. I'm hoping to finish this checkpoint today and then work on a story

I love being able to connect with you.

Have you heard from mayra?

I was explaining my book status to Olive yesterday and realized I have 8 books in process that I'm actively writing in. Caught me by surprise.
How long is your break? Have you eaten? Are you feeling better?

Oh okay , you're taking lessons on marketing , that's very smart
What's your plan for the publishing ?

There's absolutely zero way I could explain this training in a text. It is nuanced and confusing, and I'm the one following instructions. I'm not a data person, nor am I someone who's any good at marketing. But I'm trying to review everything it goes over and make sure that I'm following instructions so that I can actually make money off of being an author. I need this to work if for no other reason than to prove to myself that I can.

Self publish again. This training goes through all of that.

I love being able to connect with you as well my love , it's the highlight of my day 🩶

I'll show it to you when you get home. It's intense.

Good to hear , I really hope it all works out great for you my love

I think it will. I'm optimistic.

And about mayra , she texted me today saying she hasn't gotten any at all but I told her it's cleared and sent her the screenshots, maybe the bank is just taking time to process it

If it works out how I anticipate, I'll be your sugar mama. Lol

That's annoying. I don't know what else to do for her.

She's grumbling but I have it under control.. thanks again my love , you're the best in the whole wide world 🖤

Is Trixie ok?

She shouldn't be stressing you out. I can't stand that woman. Im not sure I've ever felt this violent toward another person before.

I'm glad you're optimistic about your writing my love , you have to believe in yourself before you can achieve greatness and I'm glad you're taking that path honey

And I don't know what else to do , I just told her to be patient and give it time because she can see it's been sent and it's cleared

Ok. I'm here if you need anything.

I can't wait to see you.

I'm honestly probably gonna cry.

You're such an amazing man, and I'm beyond grateful to call you mine. I hope you know that. You're strong and resilient, yet still have this capacity to care and love that is amazing.

I go out for a walk, making sure that I keep up on my two miles if for no other reason than it helps my mental health. I actually enjoy it now because half of it is along the Potomac, and I can breathe without issues. I never thought I'd be a person who enjoys walks, but it's starting to be something I look forward to every day. Spot and I sit outside after, just enjoying the fact that it isn't completely freezing. He hunts bugs and birds or things only he can see, and I watch him to make sure the predatory birds don't snatch him up.

He hides in a bush where just his face isn't visible, but the rest of him is completely hanging out. I laugh at him as I take a picture. I send it to Donnie, so he can have a laugh when he's able to look at his phone again.

Peanut thinks he's hiding and being super stealthy. 😆

<two hours later>

I'm so in love with you.
Just thinking about you and thought you might need a reminder.

<three hours later>

Hey baby. Seems like you're having another busy day. It'll be over soon and you'll be so bored with your lazy days.
Hope you can rest soon.

<two hours later>

Hello love

How are you doing

I'm just getting outta work

Hey baby

Long day?

You already know lol

I'm just being mushy, thinking about you.

Have you eaten?

I decide to try to send him a video via text, telling him that I love him and saying good night. I really hope he gets it, and it makes his day.

Day 60

I'm exhausted. Furry has dementia, and it is so hard with her at night. She's up screaming half the night looking for her brother who died right before we moved. It was the only thing I could think of that she was looking for. She didn't want food, or snuggles, or anything else I tried with her. I've done everything I can to help her out, but it doesn't seem to be doing anything to help. I'm not sure how long I can handle this, but I don't want to put her down because outside of being confused, she's great. It's a very conflicting position to be in. Her quality of life is fine, but mine isn't.

Im sick of not sleeping
I hope your night was better and the day isn't miserably hot.

<three hours later>

I'm really missing Donnie today and wish it were already the end of the month, and he's coming home. I didn't want to have to go through this anymore. I just wanted to be with him and start our actual life together.

I love you.
I could tell you a million times a day, and it would be true every time.

Hello love, good morning and happy Wednesday

How are you doing??

Im good. How are you?

Hows your day treating you?

I'm so sorry I haven't been on here much , it's been a busy 2 days for me

I miss you

Youre fine, baby. I understand.
I miss you, too.

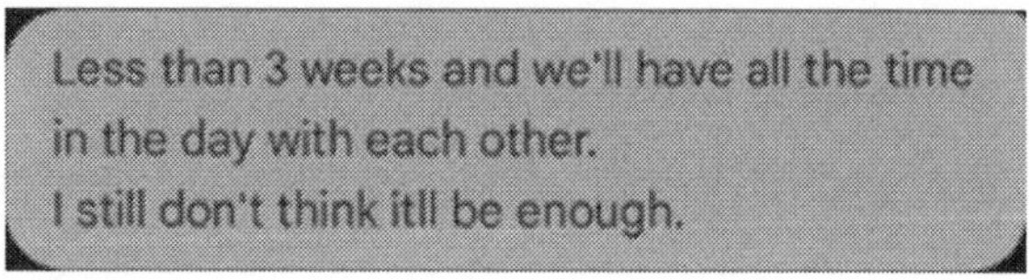

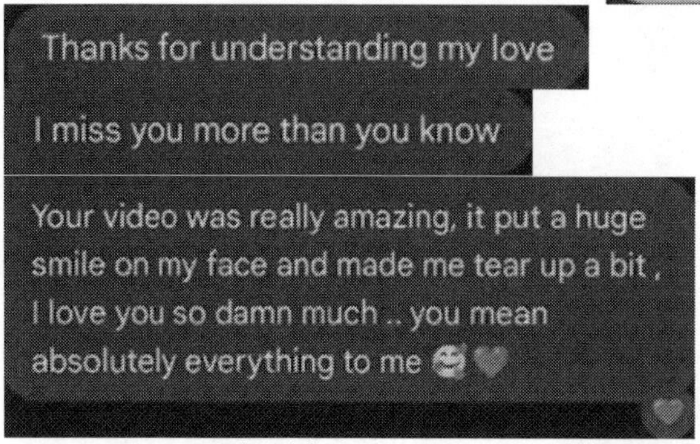

I squeal with joy. –He was able to watch my video! I'm so happy I make another one, so he can see my excitement. I am madly, obsessively in love with this man. I don't know how to even contain it.

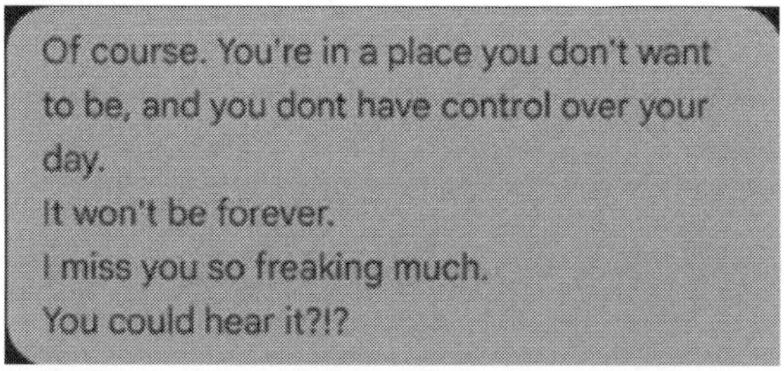

I make another video, saying hello and showing him how excited I was that he was able to see and hear me.

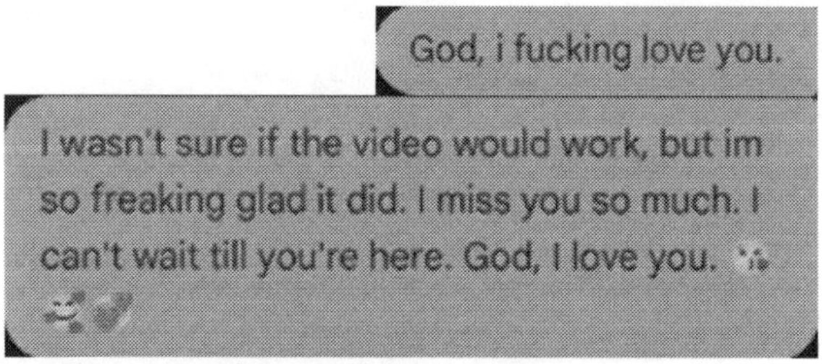

I have a doctor's appointment to do an endometrial scraping to see if I have cancer or not. It's also used to determine if I need to have my uterus removed, or if I can keep it in. I've been asking for a hysterectomy for years, and this new doctor is finally on board, but only if there's a problem with my organs.

My body wasn't cooperating for her, so we scheduled a time to do it under anesthesia. I request including tying my tubes with that procedure, so I don't run the risk of pregnancy or another possible miscarriage. And this way, I only had to go under anesthesia once.

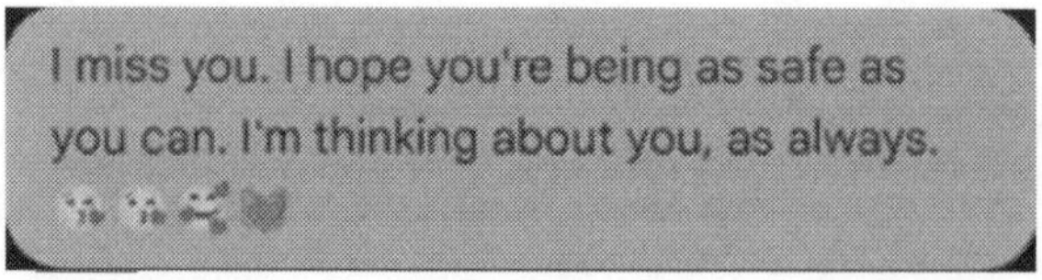

<eight hours later>

Are you done working yet?

I feel like you're gonna have long, shitty days until you leave. And that super sucks.

I love you, baby. I hope you're ok and being safe. I worry about you over there.

Day 61

Moring, my heart. I want you home. It's entirely selfish on my part, and if you think for a moment that I'll be able to let you go once you're here, you're insane.
Please be safe. Please be ok. Please come home to me. I love you more than you know.

I work all day, playing with the cats when I need a brain break because the training is incredibly intense and confusing to me. I miss Donnie and hope that he's doing okay. I hate how much they work him and wish things were different, but there's nothing I can do to change that. I can just make sure he knows that I love him, that I'm here for him, and that we're going to be so great when we can actually physically be together.

I hope you're ok.

Hello my love

Good morning baby

I hope you have a good day today

Im so happy to hear from you

I'm so sorry I haven't been able to be on here .. it's been such a long fucking week , it's unbelievable

I love you, baby

I understand. I'm just glad youre ok

I'm trying so hard to be understanding. For the most part, it's not a lie. I do understand that he's in a war zone and is gone on missions a lot. But it doesn't stop me from hating it and wanting to be unreasonable in my desire to talk to him all day. I don't want to share his attention, and it's completely unfair to him for me to say that.

You are ok, right?

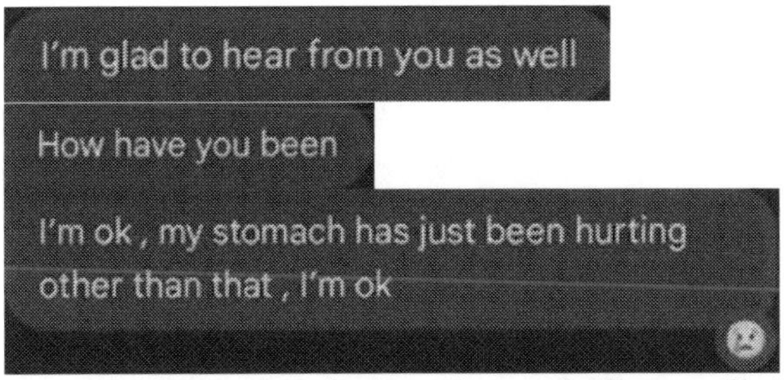

I hate that he's still not feeling well. The healthcare person in me is wondering if he just needs a good poop. The girlfriend in me doesn't want to ask and embarrass him.

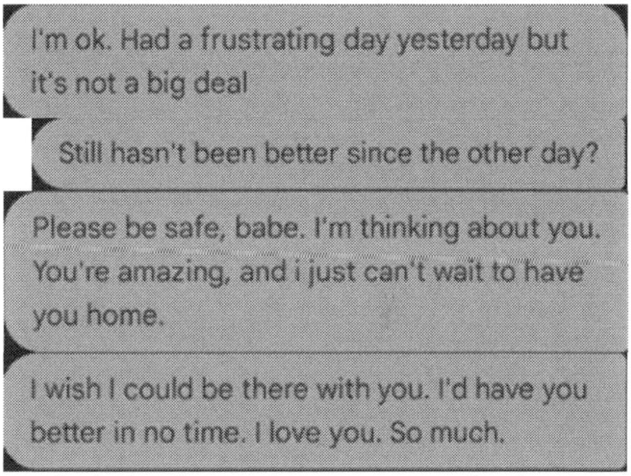

My friend, Olive, decides she wants to try to meet someone and gets on Tinder. She sits on the couch next to me, giggling as she texts this guy.

"How detailed do you think I should be to his question of why I moved here?" she asks me.

"I'd be honest, so that he knows you're not living here, but only staying for a few months. It would suck to get attached just to find out later that you're going to be living five states away," I reply, pausing for a moment before continuing. "Unless you think that you would want to stay and would either move in with him or move up to northern Maryland to be with him."

I think that a few months would be too soon to know if you want to live with someone, and stop that train of thought immediately as that's exactly what I did. I wasn't looking for it, but I already know I want to spend the rest of my life with Donnie. And we haven't even met in person! Life is weird.

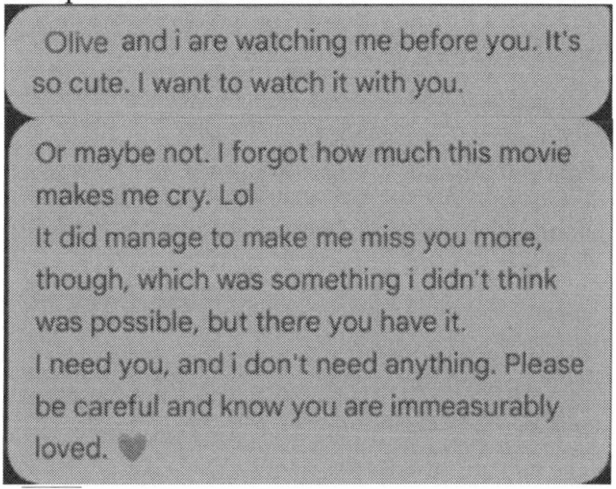

Olive's over here texting this guy she met on tinder and asking for my advice. It's really cute but is making me miss tf out of you. Like hella bad.

<sends a good night video>

I love you

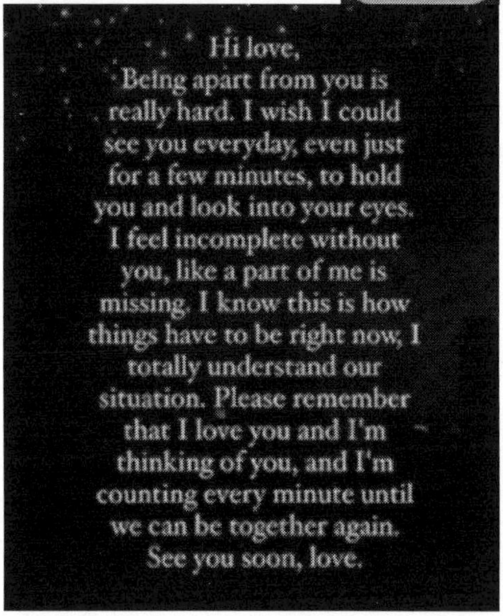

<an hour later<

Hello love

Good evening

How was your day today?

His ringtone interrupts my work, and I grab my phone. I'm just about to go to bed, but I never want to miss talking to him, so no matter how tired I am, I still spend some time texting with him. It feels like the least I can do with what he deals with all day, every day.

It was good. How was yours?

I'm just getting off for the day

I miss you.

Fuck, that's late

Such a crazy week

Seems like it's been nuts

I miss you as well my love

How have you been ?

Yes it has babe , it 2am right now and I'm just getting off

Ok for the most part. You?

I sent you a video

You should sleep, baby.

Just busy and hot , nothing fun about that

I will but I gotta talk to you my love , I had you on my mind all day long

No. There's nothing fun about what you do. Little over two weeks though.

You're on my mind all day too

I don't think I stop thinking about you.

Yes babe , finally !!!

I so cant wait to get this break

It's well deserved

Break?

Aww my love , you're so sweet

And yes break from it all then I'll finally get to quit as well

That's what I meant

Wyd tonight ?

Olive's really into this guy and it's cute

watching her just makes me miss you more than I already do. I hope they work out, too though. His name is Daniel, too. Lol

I was working on my training

Going to go to bed soon

I love you so freaking much. I hope you know that.

Lmaooo really , so are you guys twinning with men now too 😆

Lol, apparently

I miss you too and soon enough you'd have me right in your arms 👍

What training did you do today ?

And it seems like you're going to bed a lot earlier these days ?

I am so excited for that day, you have no idea.
The books. Worked on trope mapping a little.
I lay in bed but don't sleep. I'm exhausted and try to sleep, but it is what it is.

I didn't go to bed till like 11 last night.

Productive day but damn , you have insomnia just like me

Yeah, it's rough.

But I know being together and being freaky all day long and be snuggled up to each other will definitely help us sleep more

I walked to the pier last night and sat and listened to the waves for about an hour.

Our remedy for insomnia is simply being in each others arms

Lmaooo

Nice , it must be really peaceful at the pier

I really can't wait to have him home and see if I can actually sleep in his arms. I think we'll both pass out from sheer adrenaline drops, but I'm not sure. I've never been one that could sleep while cuddled up to someone else, but I really want to be that person with him.

Omg, yes. Just having you here, listening to your heartbeat, will have me out.

I don't think that's a bad remedy

It really is peaceful.

It was cold here today though.

Same here my love , that's all I need

With that magical bj

Lmfaoo

Lmao

Cold , really .. what's the temp ?

Like 47

Right now, it's 40

Probably sounds like heaven to you though.

Damn , it was in the 108, 110 over here today

That sucks.

That's a lot of difference

It is heaven literally

Huge difference

Are you feeling any better?

Have you heard anything from Mayra? Is she still being awful?

The money you sent went through but it's been held by chime bank and they're asking for verifications

She sent me the screenshots , give me a minute .. I'll send it to you

Nothing i can do about that.

We have to verify before the money is released to her

I check my account just to verify that everything with her payment is still fine on my end. It isn't. I see that both transfers were declined and returned to my account. I let him know.

The $ was sent back to my account. I just checked.

Wait , what ?!

Holy lord. Is there a reason i can't hand her a check, or mail it to your address?

I see why she's been going insane , I've been ignoring her since but she's going nuts

That bank account is not a bank , just a prepaid card .. I just know that now my goodness !!!

I have two deposit/returns from the transfer. Not sure why she didn't contact me?

What I read about chime is that it's super easy to deposit checks. It's a card to help build credit.

Wait , you have the $5k and the $2800 returned

Yep

Babe , the bitch isn't all that smart

We have to find a way to think of Trixie and help her

I can mail her a check or meet her somewhere to hand her one. Everything else is going to get returned to me.

<Donnie sends screenshots>

This was what she sent me

Hi Mayra,

We are reaching out because routine monitoring identified activity on your Chime Checking Account that requires verification.

How This Impacts You

There is no impact to this account at this time however; you will need to respond to the below requests(s) within 5 business days or this account may be restricted.

What Is Needed From You

Please reply to this email and answer the following questions:

- On 02/28/2025 the account attempted to receive a Direct Deposit in the beneficiary name " Annie Winters " from Bank totaling $5,000.00. Please provide an explanation for attempting to receive this Direct Deposit into your Chime account.

She's just going crazy thinking I did it on purpose , how would I do that to you her on purpose

She's so fucking stupid and gets on my fucking nerves so much that I just wanna puke

I don't know that a letter from me will be sufficient, but I'll see what I can do.

That won't even let the money go through , it's just to avoid her bank account from being restricted

Right.

She doesn't even wanna meet you because she's scared that you might arrest her because of what she's said and trying to neglect a child and secondly she's from Mexico , I don't think she's properly documented so she's scared of ICE too but I'm not so sure

What the hell? I think. *Of course, I wouldn't do that to her*!

This is just a fucking headache

I had no idea the transfer could or would bounce back to me. That never happened with my ex.

From what I've seen babe , I wouldn't even advice you to send to that account anymore

Id never do that to someone, especially to you and Trixie!

I'm thinking of what can be done

I wasn't planning on doing another transfer. But the chime card will let you deposit checks. Is she staying at your place? I can mail a check there. You know I won't go there without you.

Mail should take a day, two max.

Can you make a wire transfer to my neighbor, she'll just withdraw cash and give it to her , she would definitely have a proper bank account instead of all this prepaid bullshit because I'm tired and I can't let this fuck with my concentration now that I got less than 3 weeks to be home

I wouldn't want you doing anything with that fucking chime bank babe after this issue

Imagine the money got held and she got mad and left

I don't want to have that at all

I'm really getting irritated that he won't give me his address. Mailing a check should be super simple, and we can have this behind us with zero issues. I feel like he's making things unnecessarily difficult, and it's annoying.

And fucking bitch shouldn't threaten the safety of a child if she's worried about being arrested.
Yeah, that's fine.

This is just a fucking headache

Whatever you need from me, baby.

It's 5:52am and I haven't slept dealing with this shit

I hateeeee it !!!!!

Why didn't you text me earlier?!?

Fml

Baby. I'm here for you. I hate this and that woman, but I need you safe and your head in the game so you can be. Let me help

I didn't know , I was trying to sleep then my phone started going off

I don't even bother arguing with him. I think he's been arguing enough with Mayra that I'll just do what he asks so that he can have peace of mind, and we can finally move past this bullshit. I hate this because it brings up really terrible thoughts and insecurities about our situation.

I can wire transfer to your neighbor, but it's going to take the same time/process as it did with Mayra. And is your neighbor going to be ok with me having their bank account info, when they don't know me?

I've been trying to ignore her because I thought she'd get the money eventually

I thought she would, too.

I honestly had no idea it could bounce back.

My neighbor obviously trusts me and I'll just ask her to do me that favor and she will, I'm not a bad person and I rarely ask for help

Ok

You're welcome to give her my information

Since it's gonna be a wire transfer and not a deposit like this , it shouldn't take as much time

I'm texting talking to her right now

She doeant sleep, either? Lol

I don't have to give her nothing about you my love

Ok.

Nobody sleeps these days , everybody's single lmfao 😆

It's fine if you do.

Trust me , you sleep better when there's a partner to suck , fuck and cuddle you to sleep

I didn't sleep when I was married, either.

Damn

You were probably unhappy and wasn't getting fucked enough

That would never be the case with me

Good to know.

Btw , I've been thinking of asking you this question babe

Anything

Would you ever consider getting married again in the future ?

Only if it was you asking

Oh wow 😍

I'm glad to hear and know that

I'd keep that in mind 👍

When last did you speak to your ex ?

🤔

We texted today. I asked him about a show he watched.

Hmmm 🤨

I think he called me on Monday? I sent him pics of the cats and he usually calls after to tell me about what's going on.

Why?

You have absolutely nothing to worry about or be jealous over when it comes to him.

I'll decide that

Why don't you send me more pictures of the cat

And I'm over here feeling insecure about your relationship with Maddie.

Didn't know if you'd like them and I feel like I overwhelm you with texts as it is.

You can't feel insecure my love because she's gone

I love them especially Spot

So send it to me instead 🙄

Yeah... I've known people who have lost their partners. It leaves something. I can't really explain it well right now. But there's nostalgia, and people tend to think more fondly of them because the relationship ended abruptly.

That's not why I send him pictures. They were his cats, too. He asked me to keep him updated on their lives. It was the only thing he asked of me. Asshole didn't even ask me to stay.

I totally understand that and I get you thinking like that but I've faced the trauma head on , I've dealt with it and moved on from it so when I tell you I'm good my love , it's because I actually am and I got you baby , you have all my heart

I'm sorry to hear that

This is why I believe him when he tells me he loves me and wants to spend his life with me. With what he does and sees every day, it makes you more aware of the gift that is life. When you know it could end at any moment, it's harder to take it for granted. I felt it acutely after the past few years I had with my health. Us falling so hard so fast made sense because of us both knowing how unpredictable life can be.

I love him, more than I thought possible, and I love that he seems to feel the same way about me.

One of my old friends lost her baby daddy when she was 19 and she's in her 60s now. No one can ever live up to his ghost.

I'm just glad you're done with that life and you're all mine now

I am yours. You carry my heart with you

Well maybe but what I do also helps , we deal with death all the time and we're trained to be normal and move past it so yeah , I believe it's a bit different for me

I love you babe

I've never felt this before. I love you with everything in me.

Btw , my neighbor sent the bank information to me so you can send it now so she'll receive it in the morning

<he sends banking information>

Ok.

I'm doing it now, my love

Thank you for always trying babe , I owe you so much and can't wait to be able to take care of you in my own way and actually prove it to you how much you're loved

I just want this nanny saga over

You don't owe me anything. I love you. I just want you. When are you going to understand that?

I just want you. In my arms, in my bed, everywhere with me. Just you.

And i want to be part of trixies life. However that looks.

I do know that but you've got to accept everything that comes with me like I keep telling you and that includes me taking absolute care of you my love

That'd be a first. And I do accept everything about you.

I need her address to do the transfer, so I send him a screenshot showing him.

Yes , you haven't experienced it before that's why it's so strange

But you will , I promise you that

Just come home to me. I'm not kidding when I say I need you and I don't need anything.

I will my love just 2 more weeks and we know what day exactly next week

Haha , I'm sure

Did you get my screenshot?

Yes babe , give me a sec

And babe , I just asked her and I was told you should use her bank address instead , that's how she usually receives wire transfers for her business because I just texted her asking

Ok

Whats her business name?

Is it asking for a business name ?

Can you just use her name instead

Isn't it a wire transfer?

I got an error message saying the info was wrong. I checked all the #s, so all I can think is that it's the business name

Let me just ask for her address instead , I'm tired of this shit

I'm sorry.

You don't have to be sorry about anything my love , you're just trying to help my sorry ass lmao

So the address on her bank information is the house she shares with her ex husband but she gave it to me

She said that's the last thing I should ask her because she's heading to bed

So it better work

Done

Really

Yep

I swear you're simply amazing

What did I do to deserve you ?

I love you, baby

You're a good man. And I'm grateful for you.

I'm even more grateful for you

Here's my email confirmation.

I truly am

I love you so damn much babe

Thanks for saving my ass

I'll never forget how you helped me while I was away

Never

I love you too, baby.
This is what partners do. They look out for each other.

I'm still sorry I didn't have more trust earlier. I'll never forget that you fought for me.

Yes but you can decide not to do nothing and not help and just ignore me but you helped , that means something

And that speaks about the type of person you her , you are God sent , you truly are

I'd do anything for you.

Babe , you should try to sleep please

I'm worried how you're still up by this time

When you're not a paratrooper lmao

Do you even rest at all

Lol

Don't worry about me. I'll sleep eventually.

Of course I'm always going to be worried about your sexy ass

I make a little video saying good night and send it to him. I'm tired and never watch the videos before sending them off. I still have a problem with pictures. I'm getting better, but I still am not a fan.

I love you more

My dad always told me you can sleep when you're dead.

Your eyes are so sleepy

I am. I'm exhausted. And kinda horrified that I sent that to you now that ive watched it. Good lord. Death warmed over.

Why are you still fully clothed by this time

I'm not. I have a sweater over my old lady jammies

Oh okay

And yes I remember you telling me that it's really cold today

And anyway, who do I have to be named for?

Naked. Not named.

Well I was hoping to see some titties

Lmao

Do you have to go to drill, or can you sleep? I worry way more about you.

I'm naughty , I know

I'm good , I'm skipping drill this morning

I'll send you a naughty video tonight... been thinking about it.

We don't need no more drills when we leave here in 2 weeks

Bring it on !!

You're the best ever

I get really shy with the videos.

Can you send me a pic of you?

Yes today undoubtedly

You deserve 2 not just one and I'll send it

You don't have to be shy my love

Topless?

You're sending it to your future husband 😛

"You haven't asked yet, sir," I say to my phone with a smile.

🤞🥰

You want a topless pic

You got it !

Fuck ues

Yes

You barely make typos but that's your second one

You need to sleep lmaooo

Please 🙏

I can't wait for you to get home.
I make typos all the time.
I'll sleep if you do.

It's not even 1 yet

You barely do

I take note

I guess it's because of your writing

Lol, ok stalker.

You're pretty great at expressing yourself

I do type with grammar, like a proper psycho.

Words are easier

I love it

It turns me on

Writing is easier, saying that stuff out loud makes me giggle and blush like a virgin

Seeing you type and being super expressive, it's nice

I'll have to send you more then.

I can just paint a picture in my mind because you make the words so easy

It's true babe

That's why we gotta show your talent to the entire world , not just me

They have to see how amazing you are

Maybe tell you how when we talked earlier, I used my vibrator and squirted

So yes , focus on the writing and write an amazing and super impressive book and put it out there

I want people to know your name

Damn , tell me all about it lmao

I have a couple already. And I have fans.

I wanna hear that 😆

I wanna see too

I'm sure you do , who wouldn't love you?

Come. Home. And you can make me do that yourself.

I do lol 😆

2 weeks!

I picture your head between my thighs, your fingers thrusting while you nibble and suck my clit until I'm cumming, trembling with release.

What's your email? I can send you the porn i wrote.

Oh wow , that's so fucking hot

How many times do you think you can cum at a go ?

No idea.

Maybe we can figure it out together?

Damn, I fucking want you.

Well I'm planning to hitting 5 in a row

Make you squirt all over my face and have your legs shaking

Damn. Gotta love a man with goals.

Of course we're figuring it out together

It's gonna be a marathon once I'm home

He makes me laugh and feel completely relaxed when we talk. I love how supportive he is of my writing and how our conversations have started devolving into sex talk. Talking like that with him is fun, natural even. I've always been really uncomfortable and awkward with sexting, but we seem to thread it into conversation like it's just another thing and it always makes me smile and blush.

Longest weeks of my life.

That's what I love about life , very soon all this would be behind us and we'll be making stories of how we were so far away from each other and it was the longest weeks of our lives 😆

What do you do for the military when you're not deployed? I was thinking about that earlier. You said you were gonna get out, but that you didn't have a job when you come home. I don't know what military life looks like outside of people in the reserves.

While being cuddled up and eating popcorn and ice cream

I miss ice cream parties with trixie

That sounds like fun.

Spot's going to love her once he gets used to her energy.
Furry will continue to hate eveyone but me and will drive us bananas with her yelling.

I don't want to have anything to do with the military after I'm done here , I'm gonna quit .. I have a lot of money saved up and I still got my credit cards as well so I'm good .. I'm just going to relax , take my time and move with whatever comes with it

I'll bribe my way into their love with treats Lmaoo

I'm sure quitting will take more than a mic drop.

Good luck with her.

Yes , especially since I wanna have my retirement benefits and pensions in place .. it can be done and I will do it

I think Spot will love you, but Furry's a special pain in the ass.
I know you will and it can be. I was just curious about what your life is normally like when you're home.

Jean Booth

I'll get into her Good side and get all her love , the same way I got her moms

🤷‍♂️🤣

Cocky.

She's WAY more of a bitch than I am.

Before , I just end up working at the base couple days a week before deployment and it was very flexible too since we didn't have much to do just horsing around

Even better , when she actually loves .. she's gonna be all over you

Thats cool

<sends picture of the cats>

Omg, I got her mid yell. Lmao

Lmaoooo

Spot is my snuggle bug

Is she always yelling ?

Only when shes awake

I might be in more trouble than expected lmao

What do you mean?

With her

But challenge accepted

I might be renting a hotel the first couple nights you're home so we don't have to deal with them. Also, I hate the idea of having to drive any length of time and not being able to touch you.

Hotel sounds amazing

Hotel sex is the best

I really hope Trixie likes me. She's so stinking cute.

Because you guys don't care who listens too lol

I kinda think that any sex with you is gonna be the best

She's gonna absolutely adore you , I know that for a fact

She's a good kid , really sweet

And she warms up to people really quick

I want to fit in with your little family so much

You're already in my family my love

We're one

I feel that, too.

Seeing you two together the other day just really brought it home to me how much i want to be part of that.

So are you done with your publishing classes ?

Awww

And you will be

Our family photos will be complete now

Oh, hell no. I've done 59 of 112 segments of the first lesson.

We have so much fun and run around a lot , I hope you're ready for that

This is gonna take months. It's basically a job

Bring it.

Oh ok , well you gotta learn it all

"Gotta catch 'em all," I say, laughing at my own stupid joke. I really need sleep.

Like Pokémon

Lol

I really want you to be successful doing what you love

That's all I want

Thanks. Me too.

Yup , it's gonna be so fun .. I really can't wait

We have a new member to our pizza and ice cream parties now

I can't wait to see the joy on her face

She loves ice cream so damn much

I think I will be. The books are good. Olive read a couple of my short stories today and was asking for more. And she doesn't read.

Lol, what kid doesn't love ice cream?

Are you sure you don't want to go to your house immediately when you get home, so you can see her?

I feel hella selfish wanting you to myself.

Nice babe , keep working and building your creativity my love

Naah , I've been seeing her all my life but I've never met you , I'm pretty sure she's gonna understand lol

I have to see my woman

Lol. I would understand if you wanted to see her right away, you know. She's your baby. But I'm secretly glad you want to spend some time with me first.

Are you gonna be ok today with how little sleep you got?

You both are my babies lol

But I'm seeing you first then we'll go see her together

And I'll be fine my love

I'm even glad that bitch ass nanny woke me up so I got to talk to you more

Ok. I love that plan.
I kinda am, too. I love this.

I just want you safe more than anything so we can have in person bedtime chats

I love it too babe

Talking to you is the highlight of my day , I know I'm going to have a great day for sure today since I started my day with talking to you

What's your favorite movie or tv show that you're watching right now ?

Castle

I haven't watched that

But my mates told me Yellowstone is pretty good

Oh, it's really good. It's about a writer who winds up working with the NYC PD.
I've heard that, too. Haven't watched it though.

Nice

My favorite movie is Ever After. What's yours?

Guess we've got so much to binge on when I'm home

Favorite movie is black hawk down

Yeah, you've been living under a rock.
Really? You don't live that enough?

lol 😄

I love action movies because I actually love the life so it's mostly relatable lol

I'm boring I know haha

I haven't really been able to watch anything with soldiers since we started talking. Even watching the new captain America was tough. I think of you and freak out.

You're not boring.

It's good that you love the life, since it's what you've been doing.
Do you think you'll be content without it?

Aww baby

You don't have to feel that way

You need to put your mind at rest

I can promise that living with a teenage girl is going to be an experience. But it won't be nearly as stressful as what you deal with now.

I'm fine my love

Of course I'll be content , I'm done with chaos that comes with it now all I want is peace , tranquility and YOU

I know you say that. But it only takes 1 accident. And my overthinking mind has come up with more scenarios than I can count on what could happen. So I worry. I can't help it. I talk myself out of a lot of it, but I love you, so I worry.

Do you want tranquility or me, cuz...

J/k lmao

Aww thanks but keep talking yourself out of it and trust me enough to be able to handle things , keep myself safe and come home to you in one piece

lol , I want both

I do trust you.

Not gonna stop worrying though. You're my heart and I will worry until you're in my arms.

Day 62

Kick ass today, baby

<six hours later>

We're totally going on. Double date with Olive and her Daniel when things settle

Baby hi

How are you doing?

Yay, I think as I see his messages come in. *He can talk*!

Hey baby!

I'm good. How are you doing?

Stay safe babe. I love you.

And he disappears just as quick as he appeared. I sigh, reigning in my disappointment.

<four hours later>

I miss you.

I keep thinking about our last conversation, and holy hell, do I want you. I want you to bend me over and fuck me, grabbing me by the hair to pull me against you so we can kiss and you can grab my tits. I want to cum all over you. Omg, I'm soaked just thinking about you.

A shirtless pic of you may freaking kill me. I can't wait.

<three hours later>

Busy day? I hope you're off soon and can get some rest tonight.
Did everything go OK with your neighbor and Mayra?

Hello Beautiful

Ugh. I hope you're passed out and not still working. I love you. 😘😘😘

Day 63

Hey baby. I hope you're kicking ass and being safe. 😘

<two hours later>

Hey babe

How is it going ?

I am ok , just busy as usual , you should already know this

I know. I worry

Its dumb

I'm doing my walk

<sends pic of me on pier>

It's not dumb babe but put your mind at rest , you know I'll reach out to you whenever I can

And it looks really good , so dreamy

You got a beautiful smile too

So you always have morning walks ?

Thanks. I like the morning walk when it's not freezing

Just got home.

I might try before the sunrise tomorrow and take my tablet so I can write and watch the sunrise. Ive never looked forward to daylight savings, but it's an hour closer to seeing you, so today is my favorite so far

I wanted to get my workout/walk in before I
had to leave for D&D today.
Be safe, baby

I arrive at my friend's house to play Dungeons & Dragons, and there's an undercurrent of stress that I'm not used to feeling at their house. Something's going on with one of the couples, and I'm the outsider of the group, so I have no idea what's happening. There's some quiet discussion happening with truncated conversation, and I try to act like I'm not dying to know what's going on.

I'm still new to the friend group, so I understand that they don't want to air dirty laundry around me and they're not ready to share yet. So, I quietly play a game on my phone and pretend I'm not listening as they try to figure out what to do for the day. Game ends up being canceled, and the five of us decide to go have brunch instead. The only thing I can get from my eavesdropping is that alcohol is involved and has been a problem for a while.

D&D ended up getting canceled due to
drama, so we're all out having brunch. Wish
you were here.

<an hour later>

Aww that's good , same here with me babe...
I look forward to every morning because it's
a day closer till I have you in my arms and I
really can't wait

How are you doing and why did d&d get
canceled , what drama happened babe ?

Are you good ?

I'm good.

Stuff with our friends who call into game
They had to cancel.

Oh okay , I hope they're ok

I got your pictures and the video with olive
and I really
love it babe , thanks for always showing me
that I'm loved and cared about , it means the
whole world to me and I really do appreciate
it , I love you 🖤

I love the new hair color btw

They have issues yo work out, but i think they'll eventually work it our. Alcohol is not a good thing.

I love you so much, baby

Are you in a spot you can get a video?

And the topless pic is so hot with the lip biting too , it got me so rock hard

And is it explicit , if it is , I'd advise you send it later tonight my love 😍

I bet it so fucking hot 😩

I so can't wait to have my way with you!!!

Very explicit

Oh wow , I can't wait for tonight

I'll let you know when to send em

I'm still waiting for mine...

Remember the picture I sent you, quite a while ago, with the nipple?

I'm headed home now.

<two hours later>

I know you're busy, and it's probably difficult for you to take pictures but..... the evil in me kinda wants to hold your videos hostage until I get my shirtless Pic of you... not sure yet what I'll decide tonight. 😈🤞

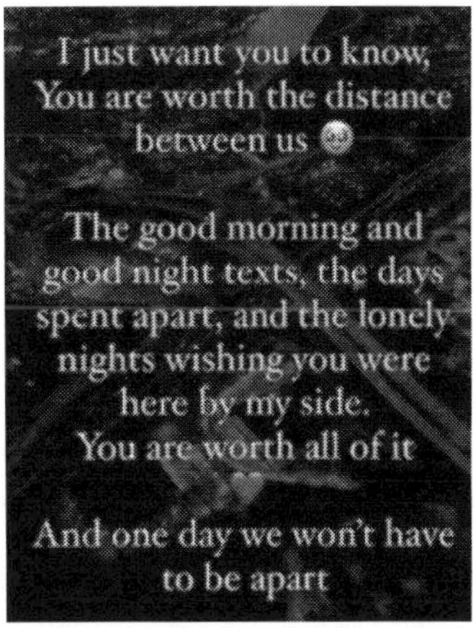

I spend my afternoon alternating between scrolling on social media and working on my training. I think about Donnie all day and wish I was coming home to him after game instead of my lonely rental. I missed him, and I've never even met him. I feel awful on top of missing him. My body is cramping worse than it normally does on my period, and I'm about two weeks early for the cramping to be from that.

My doc did warn me I could have some discomfort after my procedure, but I didn't expect it to be this painful and to start three days afterward. But my body has never responded normally to anything, so why would this be any different? I'd give just about anything to snuggle up with Donnie and deal with this with him.

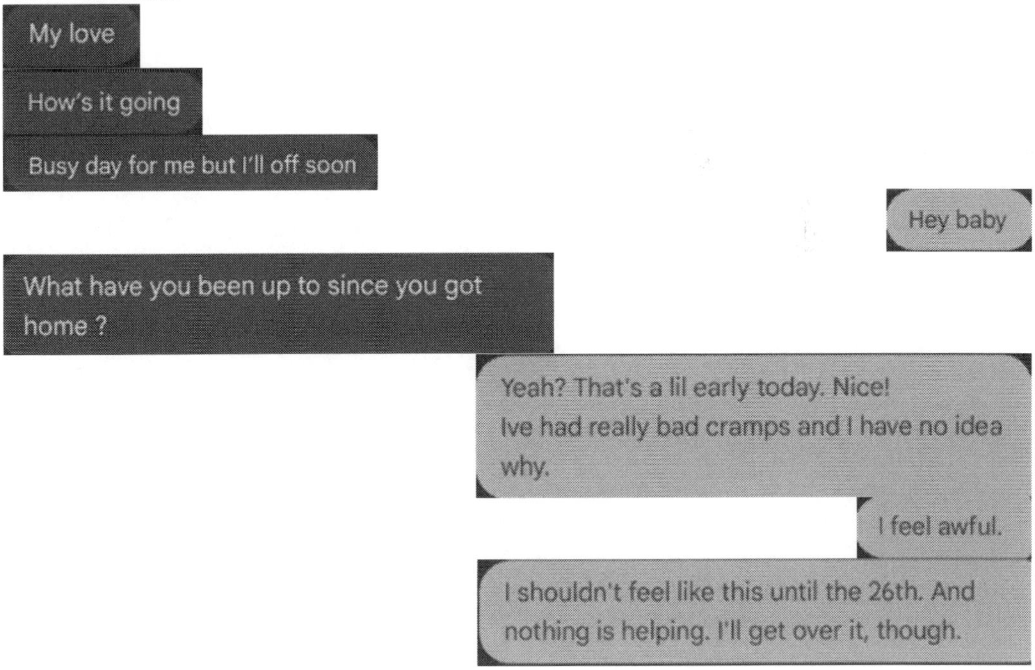

Apparently, feeling like this is normal after my appointment Wednesday. My obgyn tried to do an endometrial biopsy in office and my body wasn't cooperating. She tried it three times and now I'm paying for it. I have to get it done under anesthesia, which is what I was trying to avoid. I didn't want to worry you, so I didn't say anything. But now I'd like to rip my insides out and thought you should know why.
I really need a hug. I love you.

<two hours later>

I guess you didn't get off early.
I'm sorry your day sucks, babe. Love you

Day 65

<midnight>

Babe

Hi

Are you still up

Donnie's ringtone wakes me up, what feels like moments after I finally got to sleep. I answer, not letting him know he woke me up.

Yep

How are you?

I'm good , tired

Have you slept?

I've been off for hours , I was really tired so I just blacked out after a long day

I just woke up not too long ago

Good. I'm glad you slept.

How are you and why haven't you slept ?

Is this how you're always up every night , I'm not sure that's good babe !!!

I'm doing better. I slept for about an hour. Just got up to pee and realized that video never sent.

It's only midnight

I'll sleep better when you're home, honest.

Are you going back to sleep? Do you actually get to have today off, or do they have you doing something?

<seven hours later>

Morning, my love. I finally slept last night. Missed the sunrise this morning, but it's 33 degrees out, so I'd have missed it anyway, lol.
I hope you slept and I hope you have today off. You need a day off.

Did you ever hear from Mayra? Did the wire transfer work ok, and your neighbor gave her the $? How's Trixie?
I love you.

<two hours later>

I miss you. Hope your day is ok.

<three hours later>

Im at target and there's a guy shopping with his 2-y/o daughter and making me miss you SO much. Love you, baby

<an hour later>

I hate your job. I fucking miss you. I love you more than you know.

I can't wait for you to be home.

I'm having a really difficult time with the pain and with missing Donnie. Everything I do reminds me of him, and I'm just over him being deployed. I keep seeing Olive texting and snapchatting with her boyfriend, and while I'm happy for her, I can't stop feeling insanely jealous. They're going to actually talk on the phone tonight, and I'm acutely reminded that I still have yet to hear Donnie's voice. We don't have too much longer to wait though, and I force myself to be patient and not add to his stress level.

<four hours later>

Hey baby, I love you.

<an hour later>

Are you almost done with your day?

Olive is supposed to talk to her man tonight and she's all nervous and cute about it. And im taking her up on <u>Wednesday to</u> meet him.
I'm so unbelievably jealous of her, yet thrilled for her at the same time.
I miss you so damn much. I cannot wait until you come home to me. I love you, baby. Less than 2 weeks.... not that I'm counting, or anything.

Hey babe , good evening. How was your day today?

It was fine. I missed you

How was yours?

I see you've left me a shit ton of texts , sorry it took me a long ass time to respond.. it's been an exhausting and busy day for me .. I had to work today, on my day off too

I know. I'm pissed on your behalf.

Sorry, too many?

Naah , it's all good .. I love and enjoy talking and hearing from you

It's really nice

Did everything get resolved with Mayra? Is trixie ok?

Ok. I feel like an obsessed stalker sometimes.

I love you so much

Naah , you aren't a stalker but I want you obsessed over me lol

And almost babe , the neighbor got the money , all thanks to you

I love you so much

That's a given. I'm totes obsessed about you.

But I need you to help me in fixing this damn nanny's account because she's gonna lose it if we don't fix it for her

That's good. I just want to make sure our girl is ok and safe.

What fo you mean?

She doesn't have an account. She has a card. And I'm not authorizing anything else to her. The screenshot you sent were so the transfer could work. We found a work around. I'm really confused.

I need that note from you claiming that you authorized the transfer to her chime account with your signature

But i don't authorize the transfer since I sent the $ to your neighbor

Yes , it's been refunded so that's gone but she needed that letter to verify the account so it doesn't get closed

Try to work with me here damn

Did you read that screenshot that I sent to you ?

Don't get pissy with me. I'm trying to understand. Yes, I did.

I'm not pissed , I'm just trying to make you understand me baby

It's not about money anymore now

Its about verification so the account doesn't get closed and she told me its the only one she's got , let's just do it for her and get it over with please

I just uploaded them to my computer and am looking at them.

You uploaded what , the screenshots?

Yes

I know you could absolutely care less about the nanny and you should because she was so rude and all but just do this for me please , I'm not home yet and she's still in charge of taking care of Trixie for the next two weeks , don't forget that please

I haven't forgotten. How could I? I'm hoping to be a big part of Trixies life.

Well I told you and I'll keep reminding you that you already are a huge part of her life my love and that's just the truth

I know, babe. I'm being patient. I'm looking at what I need to do for her.

I'm glad you're trying to help her ungrateful ass

That's what makes you special and amazing

I'm sorry you're having to deal with this, babe. I'm writing a letter right now.

And I know how you feel with olive meeting her man so soon and I'm really sorry that's not the case with you and I but I promise you with all I've got that I'm really going to make it all up to you , all the lost time , all the busy days .. it's all gonna be in the past and we're going to make up for it all and I'd never leave your side when I'm home ever again !

I'm sorry you have to deal with

I'm sorry that I'm even bringing this up to you , after you already helped pay her

It's just too much

I'm trying to figure it out. Go to bed. I'm working on it, so consider it done. You need to sleep for tomorrow. You know you can trust me to handle it.

You're fine, baby. We'll figure this out together. I got your back.

I'm good babe , I'm up

I wanna talk to you

So let's help her get it done and I don't want you talking to her no more , she already got her damn money

So just talk to me and I'll relay it to her

Ok. I was going to send you the info anyway, along with her.

Whats her last name? Espinoza?

Yes my love

You got it right

Ok, I'm finishing the letter now. I have a screenshot of the deposit . Just creating a letterhead with my author business crap on it so it looks more professional. I'll send it to you shortly.

I go into the other room that I made into my office and pull up a blank Word document. I start typing something up so that her account doesn't close. While I think it's stupid and I can't stand her, I'm not about to be the cause of her account closing. I'm not that mean. I finish the letter and text it to him. I want to email it to him, so he has it as a PDF and not just a screenshot. Some places are weird about having pictures instead of documents, and I can't text him a PDF.

I'm sure you have it under control

Enough of the damn nanny

How's everything going

I've missed you so much

I really wish I'm here more but this shit is almost done and I so can't wait .. I'm fed up with it already !!!

I'm really over it, too. I want you all to myself already. I know you do what you can, when you can, it's just hard.

Were you able to take a pic for me? Thinking of you shirtless has had me all hot n bothered all flipping weekend.

And im not complaining about anything, just stating how I feel. I appreciate everything you do. You're amazing.

If you want to give me your email, I can email the signed letter to you.

Olive's talking to her Daniel right now, and they're really awkwardly adorable

I'm assuming you fell asleep, which i think is great. Good night babe.

I'm still up babe

Ok. Want to give me your email so I can email you the letter, or is the screenshot fine?

Just showering babe

It's been a long hot day

Thanks for trying for me my love , it means so much

I love you

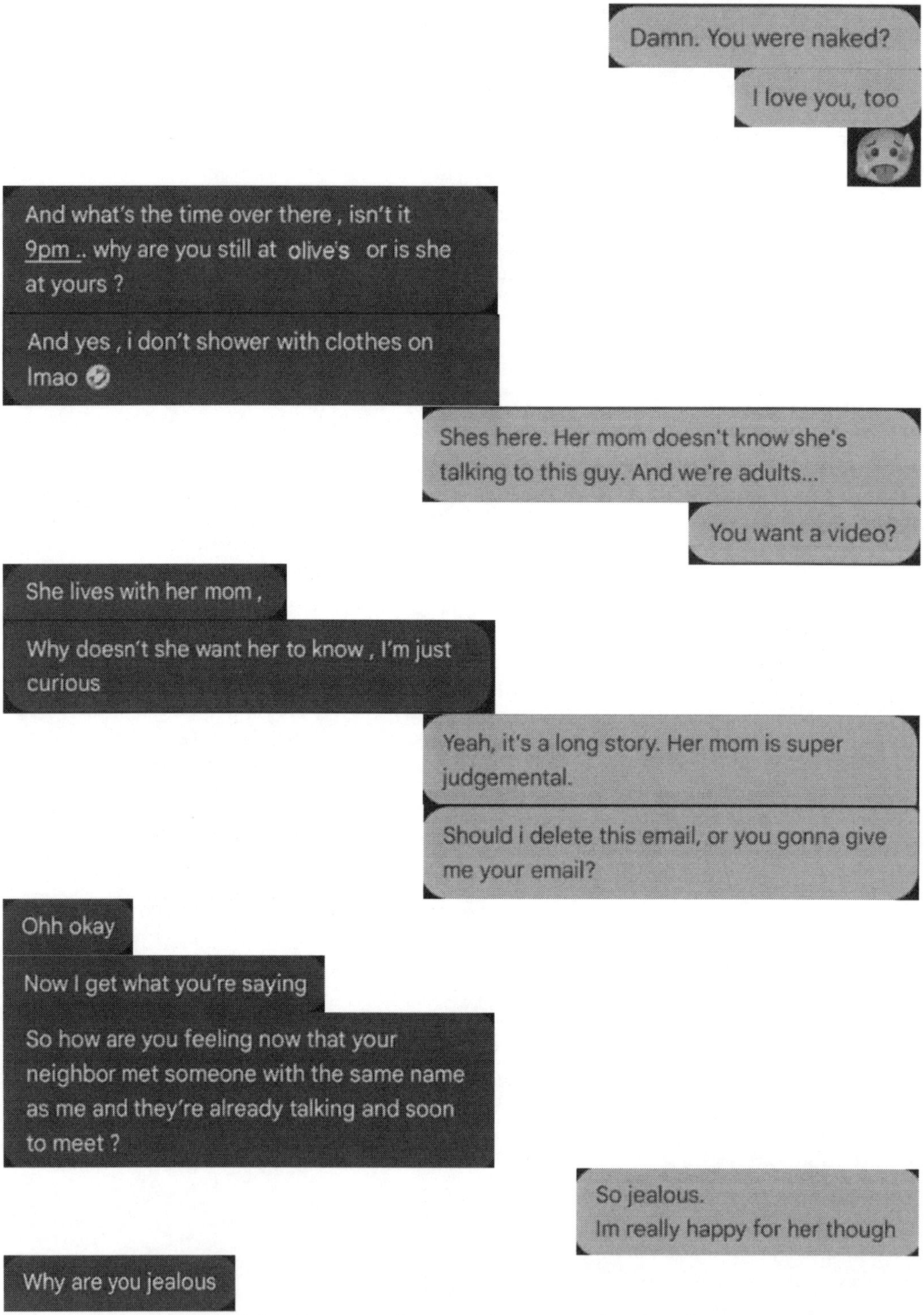

Seriously, I think. *Because they get to see each other.* I want to see you, to hold you, to be with you, but I can't, and it sucks so freaking badly. She can hear him, see him, and have an actual relationship, not just texting with him like we do. They get so much more. How could I not be jealous?

We got a great thing going on , we just haven't seen yet

Im jealous that she gets to hear his voice and talk yo him and actually get to see and touch him. You and I do have a great thing. And I'll see you within two weeks, so it'll be good.

I'm glad that I got to get to know you this way and fall in love with your heart first.

And we took our time to get to know each other better; it's even nicer that way

It is, but I'd give a lot to be able to hear your voice. To touch you.

You alone?

And more genuine because if it was too soon , we'd just rush in and rush out

Now we can build something long lasting

Idk.... i feel like what we have is a deep connection between our souls.

<sends naughty video->

Watch with care...

I seriously can't wait for you to come home.
Wish you were here...
I love you so much.

Of course we do babe

What we have is genuine and it's on a whole stratosphere and I'm thankful for that , I really am

I am, too. It's unreal how much you mean to me. I love you so much.
You need to sleep, baby

Damn babe , I just watched the video

I really can't wait for you to come home.

Did you like it?

It's so freaking hot and your breasts are so damn huge

I so can't wait

They are.

Just 2 more weeks to go till I have them all to myself

I love you so damn much

More than you know

Same

Will we be able to talk or FaceTime when you land back in the states? You have to stay on base for a few days, right?

Hopefully my love

It would be nice to hear your voice and see your face .. I've been longing for it

More than you know

But you make it a whole lot easier for me , you always send me pictures and videos and I really do love them , every one of them ❤️

Don't you have to be up in an hour?

Day 65

I'm struggling with things, and I promised I'd air my frustrations before they become issues, so I do that now, hoping he'll answer me this time. He has a bad habit of simply ignoring things he doesn't want to answer.

Hey, babe. You asked me to bring things up to you, and I'm doing that right now. I'm curious as to why you won't give me your address or email address. I've asked multiple times, and you keep ignoring the requests. Is there a reason? It's making me feel uncomfortable, and my overthinking isn't helping. Can you please either share that information or tell me why you can't? Thanks, babe. It'll help me a lot, especially with how much I've done to help your nanny.

Good morning babe , I've been up and working, you know how Monday gets for me

I love you and I hope you have a good day today

And about my email address, I don't know what you need it for , I haven't asked you for yours but since you need it so badly here you go "Rodfanelli35@icloud.com"
About my address , I don't know why you're in such a hurry and can't wait for me when all I've got is just 2 more weeks till I'm home and I'll take you there myself… you keep talking about making you feel uncomfortable and it's making you overthink .. first is my facebook and instagram , now it's my address and email , will it ever stop because if you don't trust me you never will no matter what I give to you

Yes you've helped with the nanny and I really appreciate that and it means the whole world to me but don't forget babe that you just lent me the money and I'm gonna pay you back as soon as I'm home , I told you this so many times .. I'll pay you back with interests if you want and I mean that

He answers and, of course, it's the one time I have my ringer off so I can sleep.

I turned my notifications off last night so I could sleep. Sorry I missed you. 😕 this is precisely why I usually leave them on and don't sleep.
It's not about the money. It never has been. I told you I have trust issues and why. I've also told you that I trust you, and I do. I'm just trying to be honest with you about things so they don't become big, crazy things. If you want to wait till you come home, I'll wait. Some of these things will be better in-person conversations anyway. I love you more than you know. And I hope your day isn't terrible.

I'm so excited and cannot wait to hear when you'll be coming home. I'm honestly giddy about it. You'll be here, in my arms, and things will be great. I have zero illusions that it'll be perfect - combining two lives is never seamless, but we talk and listen to each other, and that's huge. We have a foundation based on love and is deeper than any I've ever known. 🖤

It's going to be a huge weather shock to your system when you get home, but i guess you're used to it.
Love you. 😘

I found material that reminds me of a lady bug, so I made a dress out of it. With my blue hair, I look like a Thing from Dr. Seuss's book. It makes me laugh, but I love the dress, so I take a picture of it and send it to Donnie.

I made a new dress and my hair is a hot mess.

You're on my mind. I hope you're safe. I love you, baby.

<four hours later>

Hey baby. Hope your day is ok. Just thinking about you. We're playing tourist today and exploring a lighthouse on Solomons island. Love you

I go to a lighthouse on Solomon's Island with my neighbor and Olive. Olive is completely obsessed with the otters that are playing in the aquarium, and I find myself wandering around alone. I see animal prints, a ton of jellyfish, and, of course, all of the things in the museum. The whole time I think about what it would be like to bring Trixie here and for the three of us to do fun things like this. It's a simple trip, but I think she'd get a kick out of the otters and being able to actually touch the rays in the shallow pool.

There are turtles in a tank, and one of them mounted another, looking like they were either riding piggy-back, or having sex. I giggled and took a picture, sending it to Donnie with the caption, "Us in turtle form."

I miss you

I can't wait to take trixie to the zoo or an aquarium. It's going to be so much fun watching her get excited about the animals. Sorry I let my insecurities get the better of me earlier. And thanks for understanding. I think just dealing with nanny crap brought it all up, and I'm just freaking out. I'm excited and nervous and sometimes don't feel like this is really happening, and I overthink. I hope you know how much i love you; how much i trust you and believe in us. I'm not used to good things happening, and it's weirdly terrifying. I think you're amazing and i love you so freaking much.

Day 66

I hope you kick ass today babe. I miss you so much.

I hope you're ok and being safe.
Have you heard anything about coming home? I love you.

I haven't heard anything from him in over a day, which is very unusual. Usually, he tries to at least text hi, even if he can't do anything else. My stress is at the highest level I've ever felt, and I'm scared to death with all the scenarios running through my head. I make a vow that once he's home, I'm fusing myself to him like I'm his Siamese twin.

Well, apparently, 25 hours of not hearing anything from you is my limit of being able to not worry about you. After that.... I really hope you're ok. I know you're probably just hella busy and not bleeding out somewhere, but I'm worried. I love you. I need you home like I need my next breath of air.

<an hour later>

Hey , how are you doing?

I'm ok , just been busy ... you know how Mondays get for me

I know. I love you.

I'm glad you're ok.

Thanks

How's it going?

It's good. I finished my first lesson yesterday

Starting on the first official checkpoint today.

I have to figure out how to get my blacklist of books onto Kindle unlimited and republish them as self pub again, now that I'm out of my contract.
How's it going with you?

I love you, Donnie. I hope you know that.

Nice that's good

I hope it all works out for you

I'm ok , just here having a long day

I do know that and I love you as well

His texts sound weird. He's either exhausted or distracted, but he doesn't sound like his normal self. I can't explain it, really, but I can feel the difference.

I figured you'll be having long days till you leave.

I want to hug you so much, baby.

<three hours later>

I hope your day is going ok. I'm thinking about you and sending lots of love your way. You really are the main love interest in my books. It's a bit of a challenge to read through/edit them without missing you. Less than 2 weeks....

<three hours later>

Hey baby, just thinking about you and missing you. I hope your day is almost over and you can rest. Your texts earlier sounded like you were wiped. I can't wait for you to be home, with me. I love you so much.

<four hours later>

I hope you are able to sleep, my love. I'm thinking about you and loving you.

Day 67

> I think you are absolutely amazing and I cannot wait to see you!

> I love you, Donnie. My whole heart belongs to you. 💕😘

> I hope you get some time to breathe today and I really hope you find out about when you're coming home. I need you here with me just as badly as you want to be here. Be safe, my love and know youre in my thoughts. I miss you and love you with everything I am. 💜

<three hours later>

> I hope you're being safe. 💜

<sends selfie of wild hair and zombie shirt>

> I keep hoping I'll see a text from you that says, "Hi, my love, I miss you, too. Things have been crazy but I'm flying home tomorrow. Love you to the moon and back." I miss you so much but love you even more: Please be safe and come home soon. 💜

I take Olive up to northern Maryland to meet the guy she's been texting. I offer to just drop her off or sit somewhere else so that they can have an actual date by themselves, but she didn't want me to leave her alone. We eat at this fancy Mexican restaurant in DC that's insanely overpriced for the amount of food you get, but it was fun.

After, I drive them to a place that lets you race on a virtual track against your friends. It's a bar and a place to hang out all in one, and we have an absolute blast playing the game. While I find myself distracted and enjoying myself, I do miss Donnie and wish he was with me so we could show these two how to actually have a date.

> Please be safe. Olive and her Dan are having fun.

I'm totally taking you to this place when you get home and settled. You know, after our weekend of sex. I may just tie you to the bed...

<seven hours later>

Hey baby, are you ok?

I'm operating on the knowledge that you're amazing and know what you're doing. I hope you can sleep tonight. While I'm worried about you, your sleep is more important and I hope you're ok. I love you so much, baby. Please be ok. If you get a chance, I'd love to hear from you, but I understand that things suck over there and you might not be able.

Day 68

Kick ass today, baby. I love you.

I'm freaking out. My stomach is in knots, and I've envisioned every possible death known to mankind and some that I've completely concocted in my imagination. I keep picturing someone coming to my door to tell me he died. And then I realize that wouldn't happen because I'm just the internet girlfriend, and I don't even think anyone knows about me to even inform me if he died.

I debate texting his buddy but force myself to refrain. If they're out on a mission, they can't respond and there's nothing that guy could do, either. I repeatedly try to calm myself down.

"He's done this for years," I tell myself. "He's made it through five other deployments. This is no different. He's going to be fine."

I don't believe myself.

I've been trying my best to not freak out , honest. It's not working. This has been the longest i haven't heard from you and im losing my mind. Are you ok? Please be ok. Fuck. I love you so much.

I go to get an ultrasound on my liver, and I'm stressed, worried that my tumor may have grown back. If it has, the chances are high that it's actually cancer and not the pre-cancerous one I had removed two years ago. I still don't hear from him. I want a hug, and I want to hear his voice. This unknown is absolute freaking torture.

I miss you and i'm really worried.

I just got out of an ultrasound, and all I want is to have a hug from you. I don't even know if you're ok or not, and I'm scared. Life shouldn't be allowed to throw this much at people at once. You don't have to say anything else, I know your day is insane. But can you please, please just let me know you're alive? I love you so much.

Babe, you really gotta stop this let me know you're alive crap

"Oh, thank God," I whisper, my entire body deflating with relief, even though his text is mean. He usually likes that I worry. Now it's annoying? What the hell is going on? I instantly get angry.

Thank you.

For real , works just busy of course I'm alive

And don't tell me you're worried and all , it's a bit annoying

Keep it in check

Wow, ok. Sorry I care

It's that how to care

What?

You're in a war zone, with insurgents out to hurt you. In your own words, you go in and body bags leave. How am I not supposed to worry?

You are taking it too far

We don't talk for one day then it's wondering if I'm alive when we literally still talked yesterday

I'm sorry. It's been 48 hours.

It just seems like you're over exaggerating sometimes and you need to simmer down a bit

What 48 hours , I literally still texted you 3am yesterday over here

I didn't get that.

I love that you care and everything just cool down with the being alive talks

Last text I got was Tuesday at 943am

Well the time difference is huge and it was 3am here on Wednesday when I sent that text

So it wasn't that long

And I haven't had my phone with me until this morning cuz we've been on raids

I appreciate you and I love how you check on me and care about me , it's just the letting you know if I'm alive talks that rubs me the wrong way

I'm trying not to worry. Honest.
I had an ultrasound on my liver today to see if my tumor came back. I think it has me extra keyed up. I'm trying not to worry about you. Honest. Im trying to compartmentalize like you do.

I'll be way more mellow once you're home.

You're still going to be home next week, right?

I love you

Olive texted me earlier saying she and Dan were over and it wasn't going to work out. She disappeared for a while and just texted that she and Dan worked through their communication issue, and she makes sure I'm good with her coming over.

"Would you be okay taking me up to see Dan tonight?" she asks. "My mom has to work, and her registration is expired, so she doesn't want me to drive her car until she gets that fixed."

"I'm not doing anything else, so why not?" I reply.

She spends the next hour getting dolled up, and I drive the three hours in traffic to take her to have a grown-up sleepover.

It's all good

I was just in a mood the other day and that text kinda made me feel some type of way but it's ok

And yes , hopefully next week

Im sorry, babe.

The exact day tho I don't know yet but once I do I'll let you know

It's all good love

I know. I love you so much

Are you feeling any better from your mood? Is there anything I can do to help you?

I'm ok babe , just slaving away

How are you

I'm ok.

Stupid drama here with Olive and her boyfriend. I might watch the eclipse tonight

I see you're having fun with your neighbor and her new man

I just miss you.

There's an eclipse tonight ?

And what drama are you talking about ?

We did, and then she texted me saying it was over and she will never love agin. You think im dramatic...... wow.

There is. It's supposed to be from 230-6am DC time. And we're supposed to be able to see it really well.

I figure, I'm not sleeping anyway, why not watch it?

I have the Disturbed concert on Monday night. I'm really looking forward to that. I haven't been to a concert in 20 years. My ex would never go with me. I'm going alone to this one. It's right off a metro stop, so it'll be good.

Jean Booth
<six hours later>

I hope you can sleep tonight. I love you, baby.

Day 69

I wake early to try and watch the eclipse, but it's very cloudy. I take the time to drive back up to northern Maryland to pick Olive up after her sleepover. We come back to southern Maryland and run errands together. I text Donnie throughout the day, hoping that he's okay and has a date for his return.

I got up to watch the eclipse and it's too cloudy to see anything. So im sitting on the pier freezing my ass off for nothing. Lol
I hope you hear about when you're coming home, today. I relly miss you.

<two hours later >

Kick ass today, baby. I love you with everything in me. ❤

<seven hours later>

Any update on when you'll be home? We were thinking you'd get a date this week.... i just miss you.

<six hours later>

Hello babe

Good evening

How was your day today ?

Hey baby. It was good. Just took care of stuff around the house and ran Olive around everywhere. How's your day?

I miss you.

Her Daniel lives in Frederick and she doesn't have a car, so I drove her to his house last night and picked her up this morning. Drove 8 hours so she could snuggle.

It seems like you've been working your ass off. Are you going to be able to sleep?

Yup , I've been working all week , it's been crazy

I miss you too

And I thought you said they had issues or something .. good to hear they're back together

And you're such a good friend and neighbor doing that for olive

I can imagine. Any word on you coming home?

They did for a hot minute because she can't read emotion in texting and started freaking out.

I don't really have anything else to do. 🤷‍♀️

Right , I see

We will know this new week

True , you got a lot of free time on your hands these days

I can't wait for you to come home

Hopefully, I won't have so much free time once that happens.

You doing ok?

They won't make you stay longer, this far into the month, will they?
Have you heard from Mayra? How's Trixie?
Are you still working, or sleeping?

Love you, baby. I hope you sleep tonight 😘😘🥰💜

Day 70

<midnight>

Sup babe

You up

“Damn it,” I curse, seeing as I missed his text again.

Hey

I had my ringer off.

<three hours later>

I hate when I miss you. Everything ok? I literally went to bed an hour before you texted and turned my ringer/notifications off so I could actually sleep. I sent a video that I just now saw didn't send. Sigh. Maybe it finally went through?
I love you so much. Hope you're ok.

It's all good babe , I just wanted to speak to you for a bit when I woke up ... I'm glad you got some sleep

Good morning 🙂

How are you doing ?

Morning baby!

What's going on?

I feel better now that i slept a little and get to hear from you.

How are you?

I'm doing good , just working .. nothing too crazy

I'm glad to hear you're ok

Same

You still in bed ?

Yep

Just laying here after feeding the cats

I'm glad things aren't crazy for you

Wish you were here with me. I miss you

And I didn't get the video , the one I got was on Thursday where you wore a blue dress and was in the car .. you looked really gorgeous and I loved the video

Ahh okay , that's good

No morning walks to the pier today ?

Not today. It's cold

I resent the video

I miss you too babe and wish I was as well and very soon , it'll be more than just wishes , it'll be reality and we'd be in each others arms for as long as we want

Oh okay , what's the temp like ?

Im looking forward to that more than you know.

I love you too, it's always the kisses at the end that makes me smile and giggle

I think it's adorable that he admits to giggling. What guy does that?

It says it's 45, so it might be a good walk time

Yeah?

Same here babe , it's all I think about

You don't have to walk if it's too cold , just stay in and enjoy your morning talking to me lol

Have you heard how Trixie is doing?

Oh, I'll walk when you have to go.

I wouldn't give up talking to you for anything in this world.

I can't wait to actually hear your voice.

Is it hella hot there already?

Aww , you're the sweetest babe

I'm just being honest.

And trixie is ok , everything is sorted all thanks to you my love , I wouldn't know where I'd be without you in my life .. I'm just waiting to be back home to fire that bitch ass nanny and make it up to you for all you've done honey

And yes , it's not as bad... thank goodness

I'm glad she's ok.

And I'm just at the watch tower too , nothing crazy

Will they extend you, or will you be home for certain by the end of March? I don't know how this works.

I'm glad you're on watch.

Can you take a pic while you're in the tower, or no?

<three hours later>

I guess you got busy. I really hope you have tomorrow off. You need a break and I miss talking to you. I love you more.

<four hours later>

Hey baby. I hope you're doing ok. I love you so much. Get some sleep tonight, my love. I really hope we'll have some time to talk tomorrow. I miss you so much.

Day 71

Olive and I watch *Ted Lasso*, and the main female character ends up falling in love with a pilot that has a young daughter. I cry as I watch the last episode because it makes me think about Donnie. I've never felt like this, and I don't know how I fell so hard, so quickly. All I know is that I want everything we've talked about. I want our future together, and I'm starting to feel like it isn't going to happen.

I just finished the Ted Lasso show Olive got me started on - to distract me from missing you. All it succeeded in doing was make me miss and want you more. The main female character falls in love with a guy she met randomly once, and it turns out he's a pilot with a young daughter. So, now I'm sobbing. I've never loved like this. You're a part of me, and I'm 100% absolutely obsessively, madly in love with you.

I hope you have the day off today, but on the off chance you don't, I love you and hope your day is good.

<nine hours later>

I guess you're either working or catching up on much needed sleep today. I'm thinking about you and can't wait to have you home. 1 more week...
I love you more, Donnie.

<eleven hours later>

Hello my love ,Good evening and happy Sunday

How was your day today?

It's late when he finally texts. I'm already lying down but hadn't fallen asleep yet. I smile as I see that he's back to his normal sweet self.

You had a long day. So much for having days off anymore.

My day was fine.

I miss you so much , sorry we haven't gotten to talk much this weekend , things took a huge turn with work, that's why I've been gone so much

I'm so sorry about that

It's ok, babe. I understand. Really, I do.

You are coming home next week though, right?

I'm glad you do and I'm hoping on it babe , I truly am

Would there be any reason they wouldn't let you go home?

And you don't even talk to me anymore or try to hear from me , all you care about is me coming home next week or not ... do you really care about me or just want to satisfy your urge of seeing me then do away with me ?

"Are you serious right now?" I ask before his next message comes in. "I would think you'd want your person interested in having you home. What the hell?"

I'm just kidding lol 😆

And I don't know , why are you asking all these questions?

Because Ive never been in this situation and I want you home.

This all we talk about now lol

You've done this before, I haven't. And you're the only person I can get information from.

Would you rather me not want you home?

How was your day?

And I ask about Trixie and how things are with you all the time. I want to know everything about you. And I really, really want to actually talk to you and hug you. I thought you wanted the same?

I'm going to see Disturbed tomorrow. I'm really excited about it.

I do wanna be home , more than anything in this world ..it's just crazy that's all we mostly talk about when we barely get to talk

How are we actually arguing about him coming home? I think.

I'm excited to see you.

I'll stop asking about it.

And it kinda make me look like I'm holding you back from what you really want because the other day you told me of how jealous you are of olive and her own Daniel because they get to talk all the time and they've seen and now I kinda feel bad that I can't do that for you as soon as you want

I think you're worth the wait. And you're what I really want. I just have never been through a deployment before and I dont know what to expect.

I don't want to go with information online because the last time I did that, we got into a huge fight. I want to talk to you about this, since you've gone through this process before and I haven't.

Do you not want me anymore? Have your feelings changed?

Jean Booth

Are you sure about that because the way you talk sometimes , it just sounds like you want it right now and I can't do that .. I've always had thought that you'd go on tinder or something hoping to find someone you can see as soon as possible

I've never given you any indication that I want anyone other than you. I love you. You keep saying I'm going to leave you and I don't know why.

I know you don't have any control over your job. But you said this is your 6th deployment. I'm just asking for information, babe. It helps me stay grounded.

Of course I do love you , that has never changed for once and would never

I feel the same.

I just want to know where you/we stand , that's all

Im 100% yours. And i want to start our life together.

I feel like we're in limbo right now, and I need to know there's an end to you being gone.

I didn't realize you'd get upset about me wanting you home. It feels weird, like you don't really want to be with me.

When being with you is the only thing I want.

Of course there's an end , I don't wanna die here and I want to be home more than anything in this world , even more than you want me home

And I'm not upset , I'm just concerned about you and how you feel

I love you. I want you home. And I just want to understand this process.

It's really that simple.

I want to start our life together as well , I wanna hold your hands, take walks to the pier with you and talk all day long , I want to do everything with you

That's all I've ever wanted

Me too

I feel like youre my soulmate and it kills me that we're so far apart.

My heart literally aches for you

I guess it just rubs me the wrong way that's the first thing you always ask me , you don't even ask how I am and what I did all day and how my situation is over here ... yes you want me home to you and all but I'm here right now and we gotta at least focus on the present , even if it's only a little

But we're good , I have a better understanding to what you meant now babe

You just needed more information

Ugh, I think. *Finally! The man gets it.*

And I told you when we spoke yesterday, I said that we would know when exactly this new week and you'd be first person I'd inform once I know more

I know you can't talk about what you do. It's hot, and miserable, and I try to focus on our life - the positive.
Have they kept you longer than they said before?

Jean Booth

Yes they have but I'm hoping that's not the case this time around

I truly am

I know you're miserable and you don't sleep and they don't take care of you. It pisses me off and I dont know what to say or how to help.

Well talking to you sure helps because it helps calm my nerves and I always look forward to it cuz it's the best part of my day

Same for me.

So I hear you've got the disturbed concert tomorrow, are you excited ?

Are you going alone ?

Im so excited. Yes. I got the ticket in November and my outfit is amazing. I'll send you a pic before I leave tomorrow. I'm going total rocker babe.

I love Disturbed.

And the ball is Saturday...

I have boots, sparkly fishnet tights, and a metallic looking dress.

I finished altering my ballgown yesterday and it looks really pretty.

That's nice babe , I hope you have the best of time over there

And yes send me tons of pictures honey

I'd love to see

Thanks. I hope you have a decent day tomorrow and it's not awful.

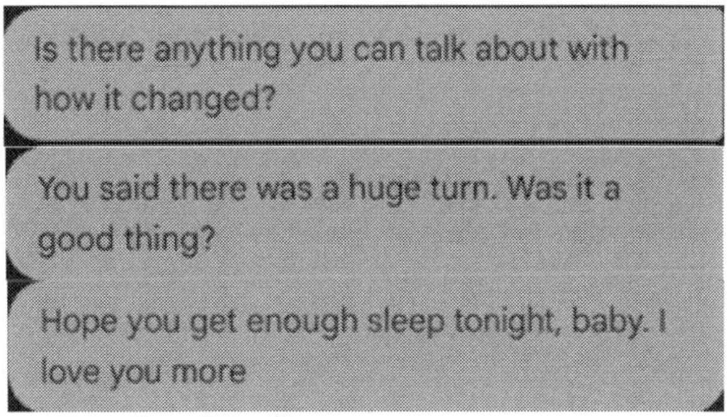

And this is why I don't ask about his day. He disappears.

Day 72

Kick ass today!

<two hours later>

Hey babe. I hope you're having a good day. It's been a crazy busy day today, I've been on the phone all flipping day. My docs office called and moved my surgery up to tomorrow, so I've been dealing with all that prep crap.

Hello love , good afternoon 😃.. how are you doing

Pretty good. How are you?

And what do you mean surgery , I thought what you had is the disturbed concert so how did surgery come in

I don't understand

Well, crap, I think. *I thought I told him about the surgery. I guess it was one of those things I was going to talk to him about when he got home.* I sigh

I was supposed to have surgery in June to get my tubes tied. Getting it done tomorrow

Still going to the concert tonight

Why are you doing it sooner , because of me ?

Why would I be getting my tubes tied because of him? I think. I'm doing this for me, so I don't have to deal with another possible miscarriage or an unwanted late-in-life pregnancy. It has nothing to do with him. In actuality, I've thought about not doing this and maybe trying to have a kid right away with him. But that's a really stupid idea, and fate has made my decision for me with this cancellation.

Oh okay , good to know

No they had an opening

How long will the concert lasts for

2 or 3 hours

And I hope you aren't too drunk so you can make it for the surgery tomorrow

How are you doing?

I gotta ask , why are you even getting your tubes tied

You don't want to at least try for a kid

Im not going to drink.

I know you've been totally against it

We've got Trixie.

And I'm just here , working my life away

I'm sorry 😢

It's all good my love , talking to you sure makes it better honey

Im not gonna lie, I've contemplated trying with you. But i really don't want kids and im taking this as a sign that I shouldnt.

I miss you so much 😍😘

I miss you, too

I love you so much

Are you on watch?

I never thought I'd even contemplate wanting them anymore. I've been very conflicted about this, and it was something I thought about talking about when you came home. It's an in-person conversation, not something I wanted to do via texts. But at my core, I really don't want kids at my age. The risk factors for me and for the baby are bad for women any age over 37, and it just gets worse the older females get.

I finish getting ready for the concert and feel like I look amazing. My fishnet tights have sparkles in them, and they're ridiculously fun. I have a metallic looking dress that's skintight but crinkles, so doesn't enhance or draw attention to my tummy but is actually flattering. I put way more makeup on than I usually do and have my hair half-up and I curl it so I don't look like a witch who stuck her finger in a light socket. This is going to be amazing.

I get to the venue and find my seat, which is about one-hundred feet from the stage. It's amazing and the only way I can be closer would be to be in the mosh pit, which doesn't have seats. It's standing room only, and that sounds like a miserable time.

Omg, my seat is freaking bomb!!!!!

And i'm entirely overdressed. But i think I look hot.

Omg, babe. This is amazing. I finally got my vip badge, and the energy here is so fun. Kinda sucks I can't drink, but I'm driving after anyway, so whatever. I'm so glad this was my first concert in 20 years.

Really wish you were with me for this, though. I'd be hella making out with you rn. The bands are changing up.

They just sang this. I might have cried a lil.

Check out Never Too Late by Three Days

<sends selfie with stage>

I hope you're done with work and are able to sleep. Love you.

<one hour later>

If you like Disturbed, I'd totally take you to a concert. This has been amazing. One set left.

I miss you. Hope you're doing ok.

Day 73

<midnight>

Good night, baby. I just got home. It's might be morning for you at this point. I love you

I barely sleep, which doesn't really bother me because I'm going into surgery and will most likely sleep most of the day after. It really depends on the pain and nausea after the surgery. If they can control it out the gate, I'll be good and sleep. If they don't, then I'll be miserable until I can get it under control. Which, if history has shown me anything, would take a few hours.

Morning, babe. I hope you have a successful day.

<noon>

Surgery went well. I'm exhausted and sore. Hope your day is good.

<seven hours later>

I guess you got sent on raids again. That sucks. I hope you're doing ok. Love you.

Hey babe

Good evening

Omg , you look sooo good

Hey baby. How are you?

Thanks

Your outfit is bomb asf , I love it

I can see you had such a great time

Thanks. I was overdressed, but had an amazing time.

I'm ok , long day .. I'm just getting off right now 😟

Do you like beanies?

You're not overdressed at all

You look amazing

And you were in vip so you totally deserved to dress to kill

Thanks. Most everyone was in jeans and tees. I felt dressed to kill. Lol

Of course I love beanies , I wear it all the time , you planning to get me one ?

I'd have loved to have been on your arm though

I did

Well you're not them and they aren't you

I got a shirt for me and a beanie for you.

I'm just glad you had a great time and enjoyed yourself

That's all that matters my love 😍

You're so sweet babe and always thoughtful too , you're simply amazingly

Thanks, babe. It was amazing.

I love you, baby.

How was your day?

I love you too babe

So I just read you had your surgery today

How are you feeling?

Jean Booth

Did it hurt?

Are you okay ?

I'm worried about you my love

I did. It's been a long day. I'm ok, it hurts a little, but im doing ok.

You don't have to worry.

The incision on my belly button is sore, but the other one doesn't hurt at all. She also did a biopsy on my endometrial lining.

I can't have sex or use tampons for two weeks, not that it matters with you being gone, but that's what my discharge orders are.

<sends pic of cat->

Spot says hi

What does your day look like tomorrow? Have you heard from Maray? How's Trixie?

Sorry, i typoed Mayras name.

I might take Olive up to her Dan's house tomorrow. He has the day off and they're really cute.

Hi Spot, how are you and your mama doing?

Sorry it hurts , I hope you feel better

And I hope the pain doesn't get worse when it's the next day and your body's sore

I will. Already feel better from this afternoon

Thanks, baby. It shouldn't.

This is like my 6th surgery.

My ex never really helped with any of the recovery before, so I learned really quickly how to manage my pain and deal.

Are you laying down, in bed?

Good night, baby.

Damn , I'm sorry to hear that

It's ok.

I'm sure that must be awful that you had to go through it all by yourself , I always tell you this that you deserve better , so much better

6th surgery

Why so many surgery babe ?

And trixies good and the nanny , everything has been pretty cool and quiet all thanks to you

Well, i have you now...

I just wanted to make sure Trixie was good.

Bilateral carpal tunnel, gallbladder removal, liver biopsy, and a tumor removal from my liver. I thought i told you about that?

I shouldn't have any more after this. I hope. Lol

Trixie just needs a few things for school and groceries with new clothes because she's outgrown her old ones , the nanny's been texting and talking about that

But I told her all that's gonna have to wait till I'm home

Shes in school already?

And I only afforded to pay her down here all thanks to you like she can see that

And that's a whole lot of surgeries my love , I sure hope you won't have anymore

Doesn't what you give her go towards Trixies care, like groceries?

I'd love to take Trixie shopping when you get home.

And yes , she's started pre kindergarten

Aww, that's adorable 😍

Nope , that's just what I owed her .. that's her pay not for trixie nor groceries

Yes babe , she's really the cutest

She sent me a picture of her like a week ago and it really melted my heart 🥰

Awww🥺 can i see?

I can't wait for you to be home and us to start our family. I love you both so much

You still want that, yeah?

He sends me a picture of Trixie on what looks like a school bus seat, smiling like he does with a portion of a woman sitting next to her. I assumed the woman was Mayra. Trixie looks adorable and a little nervous. I don't understand how he's so chill about her starting school without him. I'd have been an absolute mess.

Awww🥺 shes so cute 😍

Of course my love , more than anything in the whole wide world

🩷

You're all I want , all I fucking need

Me too.

It's crazy.

What's crazy my love ?

How important you are to me

We have yet to see each other in person, yet I can't imagine my life without you.

And we soon will my love and I'll never leave ever

I'm done with this life

Never again !

Any news on that front?

I hope you stay glued to my side forever

Yeah , we will know the exact date this weekend, it's going to be next week from what I've heard

And I'm very excited about that

Omg. That's amazing!!!

I can't freaking wait to see you, to hold you, to kiss you.

Yes it is honey

Like I said when I know the exact date , you'd be the first to know and I intend to keep that promise

I know. I trust you. And I think you want me just as much as I want you.

I might be at the base for a week or two for report and all but after that I'm all fucking yours my love

I really hope you're ready for me

That's ok.
Im beyond ready

I'll count down the days till I can have you.

I'm sure you are my love

You're even more ready than I am

You've been counting down the days even more than me

And I love and appreciate that

Thays my job. Yours is to be safe and kick ass.

I plan and prepare for our life, and you come home so we can live it.

I love you, Donnie. More than you know.

And I'm grateful to you for that

I truly am

We're a perfect match and mix for each other

I'm thankful to have met you

I know I can be a lot sometimes, but I can promise that you won't ever regret being with me.
I'm so thankful for you.

I'll be so good to you and to Trixie, you'll wonder how you ever got along without me before.

I know that

You sound like you're falling asleep. Why don't you go to bed?

The distance can strain the relationships sometimes but we're willing to make it work and make amends and are accountable to each other so that sure helps

I'm sure you'll be good to us and I'll be even better to you honey

I'm good babe , I'm just laid down here

Distance can strain relationships, so can communication limitations. I think that when we prove we can make it through this, we'll be able to make it through anything

At the end of the day, as long as we keep choosing each other, that's what matters.

Can i ask you something?

You got it right babe because at the end of the day , I'll choose you over and over again , I love you

And yes babe , you can ask me anything

What's up ?

Why did you join Match when you did? Why not wait till you were home? Im grateful, don't get me wrong. Ive just been wondering. It had to have been difficult for you to start a relationship with someone while you're over there.

And why didn't your other connections work for you? I realized I've never asked...

I told you that I didn't join on my own accord , I did because my friends forced me to , they were hoping I'd find someone and not die alone

I was just on there for fun and never thought it would turn into anything serious or genuine really but I'm glad it did

And I never had much connections because I was barely on there , my job doesn't even allow me to be on the phone much , you were the only person I actually really talked to and got to know and we started texting and things took off from there

Why'd you ask babe ?

Honestly, i was just curious.
I knew your friends encouraged you and that you had a couple of connections before me.
I just wondered about the timing, I guess.
I personally think the timing was so we could meet...

This has got to be challenging for you, just as it is for me, but in different ways. I think that, if our roles had been reversed, I'd have waited till I was home before adding that complication to my life. But I'm really, really grateful you didn't think that way.

I love you.

Yes , everything just fell in place when I least expected it because I never thought I'd meet someone on there and I never really took it seriously

Do you have friends outside of your team? I'd imagine you all are quite close. Are they over it, too.

I love talking to him, even when he falls asleep mid-conversation. He'll be home soon, and we can have all the quiet, lazy conversations we ever want. I can't wait.

Day 74

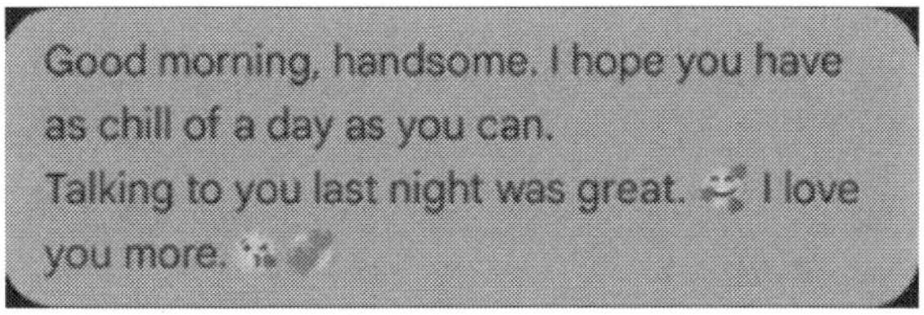

<four hours later>

<two hours later>

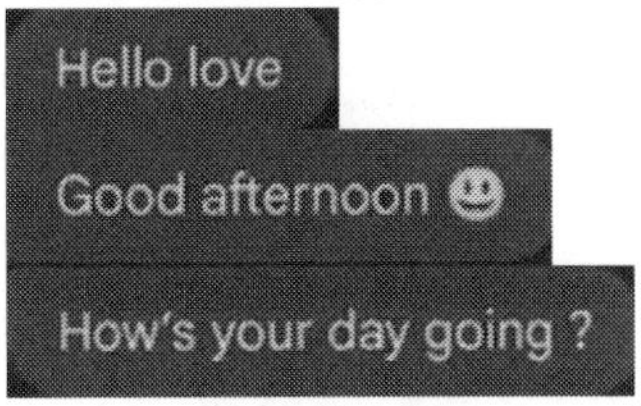

I need some smudge sticks to cleanse the negativity in my life, I think.

"Hey, Olive," I say as I call her. "Would you like to go to a hippy store and lunch with me today?"

"That sounds like fun," she exclaims. "Let me get dressed, and I'll be right over.

We drive to a place that sells crystals and other new-aged things, and I get some healing stones, candles, and a smudge stick.

We see an interesting, authentic-looking Mexican food place and decide to go have lunch there as I have been craving a chimichanga. She gets fajitas, and I take a picture of her meal, because mine's just a huge burrito-looking thing, and hers is much more colorful. I send the picture to Donnie so he can look forward to coming home.

We get back to my house, and I teach her what smudging is. I light the sage and blow out the flame so there's just smoldering ash and smoke wafts from the bundle. I wave it around me, then her, and walk through the house in a clockwise manner to promote positivity. Once the house is cleansed and smells like sage, I go outside and put the ashes out on the sidewalk, so I don't catch anything on fire. I already feel more relaxed and at peace.

She gets comfortable on my spare bed, talking to her boyfriend, and I sit in front of my computer to start working on formatting my backlist of books. It's s tedious process, but I want the interior to look interesting, so I add some artwork at the chapter headings and make sure the pages are all cohesive. It takes a lot of time and patience to format a book properly, and I know I'll still have someone leave a review that complains about some mistake I made. It's frustrating, but it's just part of this world.

At some point during my formatting process, I overhear a conversation I probably shouldn't have between Olive and Dan. They aren't necessarily having an in-depth or overtly sexual conversation, but it's more intimate than I thought I should be listening to. I take a moment to text Donnie as I giggle to myself.

I forgot how tedious formatting is. It's taken me a few hours to just do this one stinking book.
Also, i just heard a very inappropriate conversation between Olive and Dan.

I love you, baby.

<two hours later>

I hope you're almost done with your day and you can sleep. You're on my mind. And I hope you're doing ok.

Day 75

I take a shower after I text him and bring the phone with me to take a little risqué video for Donnie. I'm careful to only hint at body parts and giggle as I make the video.

Morning, my love. I had a dream you texted last night, and it was so real sounding that I woke up to check my phone. There wasn't anything there. And it got me thinking that within a week, you and I are finally going to be in the same country. I so can't wait. 😂😂😂

Hello love , good morning 😃

My heart does a flip when I hear his ringtone, and I practically throw my phone in my attempt to grab it and text him back.

Hey baby! Good morning

Hows your day? How are you?

I miss you so much and the topless video look so fucking good , I was just hoping you'd bring the camera down a little bit lmao

I'm ok babe , busy day but it's going

How are you?

Lmao, soon.... you can see them all you want.

Btw , that Mexican meal look so fucking good

Damn , I can't wait to be home and eat good

Right?! I thought you'd like that.

I love it babe

I cant wait for you to be home so I can spoil you - sex, good food, a woman who adors you...

Also can't wait for you to cook for me , I know you'd make the best meals

I made some thai dish last night and Olive said it was fire.

Do you know that you and Trixie do the same thing with your tongues when you take pictures?
Its freaking adorable

Oh wow babe , you make Thai dishes as well

What can't you do lmao

heights. I can't do heights.

Lmao really , I never noticed that .. I guess she's her fathers daughter haha

She is. She looks a lot like you, too. I'm so excited to meet her and do girly stuff with her.

Lmao , yeah I know you're scared of heights .. you said it so many times

I told my neighbors too, but we still went to a lighthouse and climbed that thing. I shook like a leaf the entire time, and they were both laughing at me.

Neither one really believed me.

Have we talked about Easter?

lol , you went to lighthouse , when was that

"It was like two weeks ago, silly. I sent you pictures of it," I muse aloud.

And nope , we haven't talked about Easter , what's up with it ?

I sent you pictures. It was about 2 weeks ago. I go to my sister's for Easter - I'm auntie Easter Bunny.

Would you and Trixie want to come this year, or do you have your own tradition?

Lol, i guess i never sent a pic of the actual lighthouse, just jellyfish, an otters, and two turtles doing it. 😄

The lighthouse has a cool aquarium/museum you can walk through, and i still think Trixie would get a kick out of it.

<sends pic with boobs>

Damnnn

It's so fucking huge

😘

I'm such a lucky man

I hope that helps you get more excited about coming home. Love you, baby. 😘💕

What are you up to rn?

Of course it sure helps , now I have even more to look forward to

I love you, babe.

And I'm working , it's busy so it might take sometime for me to respond but I'll

Youre fine, my love. I understand

I'm working but my job is WAY more chill than yours. I do understand that you can't talk all day. You'll be home soon, and be sick of me shortly after. Lol

I love you more babe and I'll never be sick of you

🤍

I'm always the one saying I hope you don't get tired of me because I'll never leave your side

Ill never get tired of you.

So you said , you was formatting yesterday, what does that mean ?

So, the inside of books have to be set up a certain way to have things on the right pages. I have to make them the size they need for book size. Example: i write in a normal word doc, which is 8.5x11, but the books are 5.5x8.5, so i have to make my doc match that.

I can show you when you're home.

I also put chapter art in the books to make them look nicer.

This is the tedious, boring part of my job. If I do it right, the books come out really nicely though.

It'll be fun to try out some positions with you when I'm writing the sexy scenes. Skye, my sister and editor, says some of them won't work how I want them to, but I don't have anyone to practice with so... i use my imagination. Lol

Damn , that sounds like a lot of work babe

It is. But it's worth it.

Is that what you're doing today as well ?

And your sister is your editor , I never knew that lol

Yep. It's very time consuming and i have 4 books to do it with.

She's trying to get into editing and im her guinea pig.

I freaking love you.❤️

Ohh ok , I hope she's great with the editing because you want the books to turn out pretty great because it's the only job you've got and it's your passion and you've gotta take it as such

She's really good. I have her doing my contemporary romances. My current books have already been edited and the new ones under my name are going to be done through this mentorship thing.

Thanks for looking out for me though. You're very sweet.

That's good to hear

Hows your day going?

So how many books are you putting out now

And how's the retailing going to be , is it going to be through your mentorship still ?

Right now, just republishing my blacklist, so 6

Oh shit, I think, laughing out loud. *I meant back list. Stupid auto correct. Oh well, too late to fix that now.*

It's all through me, but I have to follow the guidelines of the mentorship.

Ahh okay

My days going , busy but I'm glad I'm able to talk to you here and there , it's the best part of my day

I'm in edits for 1 contemporary, almost finished with another, and have plotted out two more. I'm hoping to start publishing those this year.

So you'll publish them and release to the bookstores yourself ?

That's great news

This has been the best day with talking to you.
Yes.

I just want things to work out for you my love , that's all

That's all I've ever wanted

My heart flutters, and I smile. I'm madly in love with this man and cannot believe how lucky I am that he not only loves me but actually supports me with my writing. I don't think he'll ever understand just how much this encouragement means to me.

I appreciate it. You're really the greatest.

And I'm glad to hear I'm a huge inspiration for you romance scenes

And if I succeed, we'll have a great, chill life. And you won't have to work

Huge. You're my main character and it's great.

In about a week , we'll be together, naked and actually acting them out lmaooo

I love you babe

I cannot wait. I love you so much, baby.

I have 3.5 books plotted out for my mentorship program, and the overarching series plotted, so im actually doing really well with this.

<Evening>

Your evening kinda took a turn, huh? I hope you're off soon and can sleep. You don't get enough sleep. I finished formatting another book and have it up. Three more to go... sigh. It feels a little daunting. I think im going to take a break, take the neighbor's dog for a walk, and see if I can finish making these wings for the ball.
I have lots of scenes to try out with you, be ready.

"He's fucking gorgeous, but he's even better on his knees, face buried between my thighs, tongue worshiping me like he was born for it. He'll lap up every drop, moaning like a good boy—because he knows he's not stopping until I'm trembling, soaked, and completely satisfied."

And I'll be your naughty, good girl, on my knees before you, worshipping you like the king you are.

<two hours later>

Just thinking about you... I love you.

It's raining. I love the rain.

<three hours later>

I hope you have a good night and sleep well. I'll be thinking of you when I head to sleep. My naked body wrapped across yours, my head on your chest, arm wrapped around your torso, my leg tangled with yours. I know i won't be content to simply hold you - not for long anyway. I'll trace every inch of your chest with my fingers, followed by my lips. I will eventually just hold you close, tilting my head to kiss along your neck and jaw, hoping you'll press your lips against mine in sweet kisses. Our kissing will turn passionate, and your hands will roam across my body, grabbing my breasts, my ass, and dipping into my core. You'll groan, realizing I'm completely soaked for you. We'll get lost in each other, coming together with declarations of love. And then we'll finally relax enough to simply sleep in each other's embrace.

One week, and we'll be in the same country together. I love you more than you know.

Day 76

Good morning, sexy muffin. I hope you're having a good day. I really enjoyed yesterday and woke up with a smile. One more week and we'll be in the same country. I cannot wait to see you. I love you so much.

<two hours later>

I can't wait for you to be home so we can show these kids how grown-up sleepovers are supposed to go. this is Olive's second time sleeping over Dan's house, and they only made out. No below the pants stuff. I'm so disappointed for her. Lol we need to show them how sleepovers are supposed to go - neither of us able to walk the next day.

Olive and I go to the store because I realize all my tame makeup is still in storage with the majority of the rest of my life. I get a couple basic things that will travel well when I go to Virginia for the ball and decide to show Donnie what I look like with bright red lipstick on. The last time he saw me with makeup was the concert and that was really bold and dark for the venue. This is more toned-down and like daily wear, if I were to actually wear makeup.

I miss you.
I love you, Donnie.

<two hours later>

Im getting ready for the ball tomorrow and missing you more than I thought i would. We'd originally thought you'd be home in time for it...it'll be fun to see my sisters and be silly, but damn do I miss you.
I know you're super busy and working hard, and I hope you know how much I love and appreciate you be safe, baby, and know im here thinking about you.

Jean Booth

<two hours later>

Hello my love

Good afternoon and happy Friday

Hey baby! How are you?

You look absolutely stunning and your lipstick is so fiery 🥵

Such kissable lips ❤️

All for you.

And full bust too

I'm such a lucky man

Right now they'd leave marks all over you

And im a lucky woman

How was your day?

I really can't wait my love

Me too

I want that more than anything in this world

Omg, yes.

Less than a week...

Are you on watch, or did you actually get a break?

I love you. ❤️

I saw the text about Dan and olive , that's the difference between us , that would never happen , I'm getting in your pants as soon as I'm stepping into that door

Ugh, I can't freaking wait until he comes home. This teasing has been torture.

I'm not up to much right now , I'm on a lil break

Thats my man ❤️

That's great. I'm glad you get a break for a bit.

I love you more babe

We'll see... lol

Is it hot today?

Spot says hi.

Yea babe and it's hot as shit but it's getting cooler now that it's night

Oh, that's good.

You still have a few more hours, yeah?

What you been up to , I see you preparing for the ball ?

I'm prepping for the ball. Skye is really excited and I'm trying to be. It'll be a bice distraction, but I'd rather you were going with.

I woke up with a big grin this morning, though, from talking to you yesterday. It was so nice. I hope the rest of your shift goes smoothly.

<night>

Hey baby. I hope you're done for the day and can rest. I love you so much and am so excited to have you home and in my pants. ❤️

Day 77

Morning, my love.
Today's fantasy has me slowly coming awake in your arms. My head is on your chest, arm wrapped around your torso, leg draped over yours, and i can feel your morning wood against my thigh. Your arm is wrapped around me, holding me against you with your hand on my hip. Your other arm is thrown out, and your breathing is relaxed.
I make small movements like I'm going to get up and your arm tightens against me. You relax again as my hand fists your dick. You let me slide down your body, groaning as soon as my lips wrap around you. You don't last long, and i swallow every last drop. I look up from your hip with a contented grin and say, "good morning."

I smile thinking about how he'll react when he reads my dirty text. It is fun to play around with him like this and also helps me develop some scenes in the books I write. I love picturing us together and can't wait for the day he comes home. It should be soon, and I'm going crazy with anticipation.

I hope you have a good day and know you're constantly in my thoughts. I love you more than you know. I'm really looking forward to waking up with you.

<three hours later>

Damn. My book just had the most intense sex scene, and all I could picture was us. You are seriously going to be ravished in every freaking way possible when I get my hands on you.

I listen to audio books as I drive. Typically, I prefer listening to high fantasy books with a lot of detail in them while driving, but I had a paranormal romance queued up for this trip. It distracts just enough that I don't want to sleep, and I don't feel restless while driving. I catch myself looking at the scenery still, wondering how Donnie and Trixie would like the drive to my sisters at Easter.

> Made it to Danville and waiting for my sisters. There were patches of daffodils all throughout the drive up on the side of the road and it was really pretty. Made me think about doing road trips with you n Trixie and looking at things. I wonder if you'd want to take road trips and how she'd deal with long car rides. It'd be fun to take her to Dollywood and Disney. I'd also love to show her how much fun gardening can be.
>
> You encompass all of my thoughts. Figured I'd share some of them so you knew i wanted more than just your body. I really want a life with you. I love you so much, Donnie.

<Four hours later>
<sends pic of crazy hair and red polka dot dress>

> This is what I wore today for the scavenger hunt prior to the ball. I got a ton of compliments on my dress and hit on by a super creepy dude. But I thought I looked like the things from Dr. Seuss. my sisters are late - they had a flat tire and should be here in about 20 minutes. I'll send you a picture when I get my dress all situated.
>
> I'm sorry you're having a shit day. And I'm assuming it's shit because we haven't been able to talk, and I know that you love the days we can talk just as much as I do. You're on my mind, and I'll have my phone on me tonight if you can say hi. If not, know I'm thinking about you and that I love you with all my heart.

"How's dating life?" Skye asks as she curls her hair.

"Meh," I reply, not really wanting to go into details. "The guy who ghosted me on New Year's has been texting me again, and I've had a couple of dates with some other guys, but nothing I'm excited about."

"What about that military scammer dude?" she asks. "Are you guys still talking?"

I want to lie because I don't want to hear about how stupid I am from her. But I don't. "We're still talking, and I'm not convinced he's a scammer. He's supposed to be home soon, so I guess I'll know one way or another in a couple weeks."

"I just don't want to see you hurt," she says. "You deserve to be happy and have someone that's going to treat you like a princess. I'm not sure I even like this guy right now, even if he is real. He's confused you and has played with your emotions. You deserve better."

Rae makes noises of agreement but doesn't really say much.

I nod, not wanting to argue or have to defend myself but feeling horribly alone again. I want to be able to talk about Donnie. I want to express my fears and my hopes and not be judged for my decisions. I know that's impossible as I judge myself with them. The truth is, I am scared he's not who he says he is. But I don't have proof either way.

"He's currently Schrodinger's relationship," I explain. "He's both real and not until I can open the box. In the meantime, I'm still trying to date, and I'm still putting myself out there. I just haven't found any quality men yet."

"Yeah," Rae says quietly. "I wouldn't want to even try to date in today's market."

"It's awful," I confirm, not adding to the explanation.

<sends pic with thigh slit>

> I haven't warn heels in so long. And my dress has a huge slit. Lol

<sends pics of me in the dress at the ball>

> Hope you can sleep tonight. I love you. ❤

<an hour later>

> I miss you.

<an hour later>

> I dripped sweet n sour sauce on my boob. I think you need to lick it off...

<two hours later>

I take a video in my car before I go back to the Airbnb for bed. Both of my sisters left earlier because they were tired, but I want the whole night's experience. And I have tickets in the raffle, so I want to see if I've won anything, which I did!

Day 78

Morning baby 🩶

I can't sleep. I'm uncomfortable, depressed, and just don't want to be here anymore. I text my sisters in our group chat that I'm leaving but that I hope their drive home is good. I make sure they knew I love them and I enjoyed seeing them. I don't let on that I'm depressed or anything, just make sure they know I appreciated them.

I love you.
I miss you.
I hope you're doing ok. 😘🩶

If it were up to me, we'd never spend another night apart. - a quote from the book I'm listening to and exactly how I feel about you. I love you so fucking much.

<two hours later>

I'm home.

I make it home just in time to feed the cats and take a nap. I know my neighbor will see my car and know she doesn't have to come over to feed them, so I crash for a couple of hours.

I haven't heard from you in a while, and I just wanted you to know im thinking about you and missing you.

Hey babe , good evening

How have you been ?

Hey baby. Just missing you.

How are you?

Sorry I haven't been on , we've been gone since Friday and just got back like 30 minutes ago

How's your weekend been , you've been having fun

Ugh, that sucks.

Not as much as I thought i would, but it was ok.

I see you've sent me tons of messages , I'll check them . I'm just trying to settle in now

Don't worry about it. I just want to talk to you.

You ok?

Did you guys achieve your objectives?

What do you mean not as much as you thought you would ?

Things didn't go great ?

And I'm ok , just a lil sore and I'll get something in a few probably a sandwich

Yes we didn't or else we wouldn't be back lmao 🤣

It was fine. I just forgot my sisters don't support me talking to you.
Im sorry you're sore. I'm glad you did, then. Lol

Id happily give you a massage when I see you.

Your sisters don't support you talking to me

Wym by that , you never said this to me

What's going on exactly?

No. They're part of the group that thinks you're not real. We talked about that in February, when shit went bad, remember?

Damn

So they're still on that ?

What was the issue exactly ?

I wanna hear all about it

It's just hard to be around people I can't talk to about you. Olive is super supportive and helps, but I just had a really rough time yesterday.
They don't think you're real because I met you on an app, and you can't call or FaceTime. They also think it's weird that you have a nanny, because apparently military guys don't join the military if they can afford nanny's

I told them you're coming home next week and they just looked at me with pity, like I'm some crazy, deluded girl.

I don't doubt you, but it's hard sometimes, you know?

I met some girls at the ball, and one of them is in a relationship with an ex military guy. They started dating while he was still in, but he was stationed in DC, and she lives in Virginia. She told me they barely made it through that, and she couldn't imagine trying to date someone who was actually deployed.
I told her it was really hard, but we make it work. She seemed quite impressed.

lol , it's hilarious to see your sisters mentality and how they think

Yeah?

Not everyone joins the military because they're dead broke and can't afford shit , some people actually joins because they're patriots and love the country and I'm from a long line of men serving our nation

I know you are. You're very passionate about your grandpa.

And for some of it , I would blame you because you're to quick to tell everyone everything and what's going on with us , I see no reason why you should tell them about the nanny because I thought it was personal to me and us but I guess not

And you keep saying it's hard , it's hard on both sides you know .. all you're doing is just waiting while in reality I'm the one going through it and not knowing if I'm actually gonna be home or not

I hate how he blames me for how other people see our relationship. People talk about their relationships and what they're like. It's normal human interaction. Especially with girls and their sisters or best friends. I never told them I gave him money. I just told them he has a daughter that's being cared for by a nanny. They formed their own opinions off of that.

I get angry as I read his texts. I'm right there in the not knowing if he's going to actually come home or not! How can he think that I'm not invested, too? I'm terrified every day I don't hear from him. Every time he goes on a raid or a mission, I wonder if he's going to come back in one piece or in a bag. Not that I'd even know because I don't know if he told anyone about me so that they would know to tell me if something happened.

He's always so quick to tell me how hard he has it, and I don't think he understands that I'm right there with him. No, I'm not hunting people down or being shot at, but I'm emotionally and financially invested in him and our future. So, what happens to him is important to me. Knowing that he'll be around for us to have a future together is important to me. I hate how he doesn't think about my side of this relationship but always insists that I try to understand what he's going through.

I told them about her before we fought about her. They asked who was taking care of Trixie when you were gone and all I said was that you have a nanny.

So hearing you say all this is quite insensitive to me honestly but it's all good

How is it insensitive?

Glad to hear you don't share their view but I know you're going to dwell on everything they've said and keep reacting to it

I'm going through things with you, Donnie

I'm not reacting to it. You asked what happened. I told you. I have faith in you, babe.i know we're stronger than this

It just wasn't as much fun of a weekend as I'd hoped. That's all.

It sucks they don't support me, or us, but thats their choice.

I know we're going through it together, I'm just been realistic that it's one actually going through it more than the other you know

So that was the only thing that made the weekend suck ?

And i know it's hard on your end. I think you're amazing for what you do and how much you go through.
Not being able to talk to you always sucks, but I know you're doing things that are important and out of your control.

I'm not even bothered , I'm dating you not your sisters

Good.
Do I not tell you enough, how amazing I think you are?

Because I do think you're amazing. You have the hardest job i can think of, and have still managed to develop a relationship with me. You're kind and everything I've wanted in my life. I absolutely love everything about you.

There was this one couple at the ball that danced, and they looked so happy, so in love. It made me think about us and had me missing you so much. I can't wait until we can have dance parties with Trixie and eventually gross her out with how much we love each other.

Yes you do babe and you're all I've ever needed

I always tell you how thankful I am to God for finding such an amazing woman like you

I'm so thankful for you, my love. Don't ever forget that.

You are my heart.

But you gotta help yourself feel better and stop letting their words get to you and all because even when I get home , I can assure you that they'll still find something negative to say, that's just how people are and you've gotta learn to go ahead with your life no matter what anyone thinks

I am, it's just hard to hear from them. I actually left at 330 this morning because I didn't want to be around them anymore.

I don't have any doubt when it comes to you. Or to us. I'm all in, Donnie. You're it for me. Those are not just pretty words to me. I choose you, and fuck anyone who can't see what you mean to me.

And i think that leaving my ex after 20 years of marriage and dealing with the repercussions of that should be enough to show you that I will do what makes me happy, even if no one supports me.
I'm talking to you about things because you're my person and you asked.

I can be sad and disappointed by the behavior of people I love and trust while still moving on with my life and my choices.

Well weren't they the same people who said you should stay with your ex husband even with the way he was treating you , people will always criticize what they don't understand and we've said it so many time that what we have is crazy but crazy good and I wouldn't want it any other way

No, actually. Those sisters were the only ones to support my decision. My other sister and my parents were the ones against my divorce. These two sisters could see that my ex wasn't good for me. Their opinions are important to me as they're able to see things I often don't. I don't say anything because I don't want to argue. I just want to talk to him for more than five seconds.

You're my person babe , I love you and I'm in this till the end of my days , I swear it to you my love 🩶

I feel the same with you, Donnie. I love you so much

I sent you a video...

What are you doing?

I hope you were able to eat and you're sleeping now. I love you more than you know.

<one hour later>

I love you more babe

I just showered and had something to eat

Good. I did too.

I'm good and here now

I got the video my love , about to watch it now .. I can see you're in the shower

I really missed you this weekend.

Today was good

I won 2 raffles, and I never win things, so that was cool

You doing anything tonight?

Are you going to try to catch up on sleep im sure you missed this weekend?

Olive and I are hanging out

Olive comes over, and she and I both have restless energy. We decide that we need to get out and throw some axes. It was a fun release the last time we went, and we know it'll be fun again. We grab something quick to eat in the car and drive up to DC to the same axe place we went to previously. Donnie texts me just as we settled into our lane.

I miss you too babe

I hope you had a great weekend regardless of what happened

Next weekend will be better because we'll be in the same country.

I'm scheduling my first signing in DC for the end of May!

"You guys end your sessions telling people to act like they're in a zombie apocalypse, so I thought it would be a lot of fun to do a book signing here for my zombie book."

"I think that'd be a great idea," the manager says. "I think the owner would want to collab with the bar next door, since he owns both places and it'd be good publicity. We could do zombie-themed drinks and apps."

"That'd be a great idea," I exclaim. "I even have recipes saved at home. I could share them with you. And, if he's down with me coming in May, that'd be even cooler. May is National Zombie Appreciation Month."

He laughs, looking at me like I'm slightly crazy, and he's not wrong. We tentatively schedule a date and time to do the signing.

"I'm really excited about this," I tell him. "I think this will be a lot of fun!"

"I'll talk to the owner in the next couple of weeks to iron out the details, but I agree. I think this will be awesome."

I throw my axe, hitting the bullseye dead on and do a little shimmy dance. Today has worked out even better than I hoped for.

<sends pics of axe bullseyes>

I just got the video you sent babe

It's so fucking hot

Oh nice. Love you

"He's coming home," I yell at Olive, grabbing her into a fierce hug. "He's got a date, and he's coming home!"

"Donnie?" she asks, already knowing the answer. "That's great news! When is it happening?"

"He's coming home," I repeat, tears welling in my eyes. I'm finally going to meet him, and this is really happening. I'm so happy I don't know how to contain myself. "April first."

I get distracted, texting back with him and only half-heartedly throw the axes.

Omg!!! Baby!!!! I'm so fucking excited!!!

You sure about that

You don't seem very excited when I said it at first

I was busy screaming and jumping up and down with Olive

I'm so fucking happy!!!

This is my favorite day of the year so far. I fucking love you

Everyone in the axe place was staring at me like I lost my damn mind. Lol

<sends video of happiness>
<sends pic of bull's eye>

Your girlfriend is a badass.
And she's so fucking happy right now.

I might be crying tears of joy. Maybe.

<hour later>

I havent stopped smiling.
Are you excited?

<sends smiling pic in car>

I love you so much! I'm so excited to see you.

<two hours later>

I kinda gather from what you said earlier that you guys are going to be quite busy this week, huh? Is there anything I can do on my end for you?
I love you so much, baby. I can't wait to see you

<two hours later>

Hey babe , how's it going ?

I slept for a bit and I'm up now

I see you're having such a great time out with olive , it's nice to see and very soon yall will have one more person to join ya

So why were they staring at you at the axe place , what's going on lol

I was jumping for joy and screaming from being excited about you coming home.

Im glad you got some sleep.

And I love your dress for the ball , the slit made is so damn sexy , I love it

You look incredibly stunning

Thanks! I did not realize how much boob it showed. Lol

I love you so much, baby

It looked great , you don't have to worry about that

I love you too

Thanks. It just surprised me when I saw the pictures. I'm used to seeing more of my boobs than everyone else and don't really think about it anymore.

It's really amazing to actually have a date that you'll be here. Like, I knew I'd be excited, but I didn't realize just how much until you told me.
And for some stupid reason, part of me is scared you won't like the reality of me. I know it's silly, but my emotions have been all over the freaking place.

You can still sleep more, can't you? You don't have to be up for a few more hours. Are you going to try to go back to sleep, or are you up for the day?

Of course I'm going to love everything about you , you don't have to be scared about anything my love , we're doing so good right now so trust me when I say it's gonna be even better in person

And yes I'm still in bed , laid down trying to get some more sleep but I doubt it

How are you and what have you been up to ?

I'm so, so happy I get to see you.
Nothing much, really. I hung out with Olive for a while, and she went to Dan's house tonight. I'm feeding the cats now.

Is there anything I can do to help you sleep? I worry you don't sleep enough. You have a hard job.

I'm more than excited my love , I truly am .. I just wanna be out of here and it's finally happening so I'm really pumped my love

I'm good babe , it's all good

She drove there with your car as usual ?

I can imagine how excited you are. Coming home must feel amazing. And you have Trixie to look forward to. And meeting me.
Nope. She actually took her mom's car this time. I'm taking her mom to work in the am.

Is there anything I can do for you? Anything i can have prepared for you, for when you come home?

So babe , there's something I wanna discus with you ... it's about trixie pre-k enrollment, she should be enrolled this week because I want her to start her education earlier and I wanna get her some new clothes , shoes , groceries for the house as well but I can't until I'm home and even when I'm home , I still can't see her as soon as possible because I have to be at the base for another 2 weeks I'm guessing and I don't want my own life to slow hers down so I'm thinking if you can help out with that , I'll just sort it out with you as soon as I land

My heart plumets as I read his text. He wants more money.

Honestly that's the only thing bugging my soul right now

And nice , you're a really kind soul that you're helping her take her mom to work .. I'm sure she's so grateful to have you as her friend

Ok... what do you need from me?

I was thinking you'd help me send some money through my Neighbour to give to the nanny so she can sort all that out

That's just it

Ok. How much?

I know I owe you already but I'll be home in like a week to sort it all out

It doesn't have to be much , just tell me how much you can spare for me my love

I don't wanna be a burden on you at all

Baby, please stop. If you're serious about me being part of your family, then this is just what partners do. If you don't want me to be part of the family, then fine, pay me back. You're not a burden. You're the love of my life. And I want to be part of Trixies.

$500?

Of course you're a part of our family, an integral part at that so don't talk like that

I lent money from you while I was away so it's my obligation to pay back like I've promised once I'm home my love

And I appreciate that my love but I don't think that would be enough at all , you know I told you about the pre-k enrollment, that alone costs like $2700 smh

If you can send like $3500 to her , I'd appreciate and know I'm paying you back $13k as soon as I land my love

It's just till the 1st of April

"How are you going to pay me back?" I ask to my phone. "If you need me to do this because you won't be able to, then how are you going to pay me back right away? That makes no sense. And holy crap, that's a lot of money for school."

I try to push my fears, insecurities, and suspicions down. We've talked about being together and the possibility of being a family. This is just part of that. He needs me for this now. There will be a time when I'll need him more. I take a few deep breaths as I respond.

You didn't tell me about pre-k enrollment. You told me she was in pre-k and needed clothes, but you'd handle that when you got home.
I'm happy to help.

Nope babe , she's just 4 and she's just enrolling

I thought I told you

I'm sorry I didn't my love

Will I get to see you on April 1?
Its ok, you've had a lot going on.

Do you want me to send the $ tonight?

Babe , I have to be at the base for like a week , I told you this

We've got to debrief

And if you can , I'd really appreciate it .. you still have my neighbors details ?

That's what I thought. I was a little confused for a min because of what you just said.
I do have her details. I have to scroll and find them again.

What are you confused about babe ?

Nevermind. I only had 3 hours of sleep last night

Thanks my love , I'll text her now to expect some money and give instructions to the nanny

Thank you so much babe , I love you more than you can ever imagine and I swear it to you on everything that I'll never take your kindness for granted and I'm gonna make it all up to you once I'm home 🥰❤️❤️

I just want you home. We'll figure things out from there. 🥰

I'll be home my love

And I'll pay you back and you must take the money

You can't refuse it !

Good flipping lord I'm obsessed with you and send you WAY too many texts.

It's the same way with me babe

Jean Booth

We talk more than couples actually living together lmao

Taking the money doesn't mean you don't want me, right? You're not with me just because I'm helping with this, are you?

Lmao, you underestimate my ability to talk....

I'm kidding. It's different when people actually live together.

Nope I'm not but it's a promise I've made to pay you back and I'll come through on that promise

Ok.

Well it'll be way more in person

Can't wait to lay down with you on the pier and talk all day

Me, too.

You're gonna have less time for olive and everyone with me around ... sorry not sorry Lmaoo 😆

Ive already told Olive that. Lol

Haha true

We also agreed that im probably gonna get laid before she does. Lol

They better be grateful for you time now because you'd be scarce when I'm home

I'm having you all to myself

You're getting laid the moment I set my eyes on you

I'm sure you're already using my pictures along with your sex toys lol

I smile as our conversation devolves. I think we're both anticipating him coming home and needing to release some pent-up frustrations. I never thought I'd like sexting. I definitely haven't liked it in other conversations I've had with other men; but I like it with him. It's like foreplay and fun. I usually hate being teased, but with Donnie, I know he's just as tormented as I am, if not more because he can't do anything about it.

We're gonna be attached at the hip.
I joked with her the other day that I was gonna make pants fit for 2

I don't need your pictures, I have your face memorized. And there's very little I can do with my toys until the 31st.

I've been getting off to thoughts of you for months.

Damn babe

Transfer was sent

How many times do you get off in one day now that you're always home and by yourself?

Oh really , thanks my love

Can you send me a pic so I'll show her

Usually just once. And it's not every day. Some days, when we actually get to talk, it's more. Others, not at all.

That's so hot

When I'm home , I'd love to see you touch yourself while I watch

I'm assuming you can't jack off?

It'd be so sexy and naughty

We can't but I just don't .. I rarely do

Only after you touch me. I've been craving your touch

I'm saving it all for every hole in your body

How come? Do you not like it? Lmao

I'm so ready for you.

I should be cleared for sex on the 31st.

I don't like it lmao

I prefer the real thing

Good lord, I prefer the real thing, too. I think everyone does. But sometimes, you need to take the edge off, and that's a really great way to do it.

Oh my !

You still aren't cleared ?

I never knew that

I roll my eyes as I read his texts. *We talked about this,* I think with a deep sigh.

Really?
I mean, I do as well, but i get really bitchy without orgasming.

No, recovery is 2 weeks. It hasn't even been a week yet.

And my ex never really cared if i came or not, so I got really comfortable with my body.

I get that my love but you've got toys and stuff and you can do it at your leisure and at your comfort but I can't say the same for me so I'd rather not

But trust me , you're getting it as soon as I'm home , I swear it to you

I'm gonna make that clit sore and have your legs wobbling

I'm so looking forward to you between my thighs

Well I'm not your ex , I pay attention to details and I want you pleasured before me

Your dick is gonna get a workout.

See, and its shit like that, that has me soaked for you without you even being here.

I could dip my fingers in my pussy and lick them for you...

Is there anything I should expect this week? Or will things be as normal as they are with us?

Yup and that's exactly how I like it

Damn , you don't even have to lick it for me .. I'll do the licking

Mmmm, fuck.

That's what my tongue is for , your pussy bout to get a tongue wash from me

Well, that's gonna be tonight's fantasy...your face buried in my pussy, grabbing my breasts and fingering me. Damn...

Yup

Your fantasy too?

While sucking on your clit and caressing it with my tongue

Fuck. You're killing me.

And having you rub my head and squeezing the bed with the other one while you legs dangle in the air and screaming my name

Please tell me you're turned on, even if you don't do anything with it.

I've been dreaming about your dick. Going to my knees, licking and sucking and listening to you moan. You'll grab my hair and deep throat me until you cum.

Of course I am turned on

Your word and wordplay and romance always get me rock hard

And the pictures and videos too

Like the booby pic you sent yesterday with Spot in it

<I send a video of boob lick>

That's absolutely sexy , I loveeeee it 🥰🖤

Omg babe , you're gonna make me burst in the whole base

Lmao

Lmao

They're so huge , my goodness

You can wear my bra as a hat. One of my girlfriends has pictures of her and her daughter wearing one of my bras that way - each head was in a cup

And that's the most unexpected phrase i thought I'd hear from you about my boobs - my goodness. Lol

That's is hilarious

All that boobs for me

Man I'm lucky asf

Imma play with them all day long

Yes they are. Yes you are. But I'm lucky too.

I know you're lucky as well but I am the luckiest

You don't understand my happiness and joy but soon you'll

I honestly feel the same way with you, Donnie. I seriously cried today, I was so happy.

You'll be in the States on the 1st and have to do your week or two of debrief, right?
Will we be able to talk? I'd give just about anything to hear what you sound like.

I love you so much. You seriously mean everything to me.

Day 79

Good morning, baby! 8 more days!
We're so close, please be careful out there. I love you so much!

<six hours later>

Thinking about you... I hope your day is ok. I know Mondays typically suck for you, though. The wire transfer went through just fine, so your neighbor should have the funds to get Trixie enrolled.
I love you, Donnie.

<four hours later>

BTW, I know you're slammed today, but I love you. ❤️

<four hours later>

I hope you're able to sleep tonight. I love you, baby. 😘❤️

Day 80

> Good morning, baby! 7 days!!! One more week, and you'll be home!!! i love you so much, and I'm so excited. Please be careful. I know you're slammed. Know that you are constantly in my thoughts. I'm going to try really hard not to bug you today, but that does not mean you aren't at the forefront of all my thoughts. You're everything to me. I love you so much. Be safe.

I'm so excited about seeing him in less than a week that even though I've barely slept in months, I spend the day happy, alert, and simply joyfully excited. Everything I've wanted since my divorce is right there. It's so close I can taste it.

I jump in the shower, taking a naughty video showing nothing more than cleavage and soap suds, and giggle as I send it to Donnie. I can't wait for him to be here with me. We're going to have such a good time and be so happy together.

I don't have any illusions though; I know the transition is going to be difficult. I know he's going to have to deal with PTSD, and the transition from military to civilian life is going to be a huge adjustment for him. But I also know that if I keep him fed and make sure he sleeps, we'll be able to work through things. He doesn't function well when he's hungry or tired—no matter what he thinks.

I'm terrible at not bugging you. In my defense, I've opened my phone 20 times in 2 hours to text and have put it down. So...
I miss you and keep reminding myself that you're working hard and coming home. Patience is a virtue I am not good at.. I've been thinking a lot about Trixie today and what she and I would be doing this week while we get ready for you to come home. There would be so many crafts and videos and pictures. Your phone would be filled with pics of her getting all excited to see her daddy. And each night would end with a video of me telling you how much i love you. I can't wait to tell you in person. Soon.. ❤

My love

Good morning babe

How are you today ?

There he is! My heart leaps in my chest as I start texting with him.

Hey baby!

I've missed you so damn much

How are you?

I fucking miss you

7 days...

I'm ok , working away you know

I miss you more miamor

Ugh, the Spanish, I think as I melt. It's simple words that I think everyone on the planet knows, but if he had any idea how much that melted me, he'd probably wax poetically all the time in Spanish.

What have you been up to

I see you've left me a ton of texts lmao

I know. You're such a hard worker.

I could've left you so many more, lol

I sent you a really steamy video. My ass may be involved....

I've been working and trying to distract myself from texting you every 15 minutes. Lol

I love you ❤️

I go to the bookstore to help distract me from texting him a million times today. I wanted to get a Hades and Persephone graphic novel, and I was hoping to be able to get the entire series in one go so I had them all and they matched. Some of the outside art was different depending on where the books were purchased. My sister got me into this series, and I love it. I saw a kid's book about dinosaurs and tacos and laughed.

Donnie and Trixie would love this, I think as I add it to my bag.

I'm getting Trixie a book that made me think of you. Hope your day is ok. I love you so much.

<*evening*>

I hope your day was ok. I can only imagine how slammed you are this week. I'm thinking about you and hope you can rest tonight, baby. Only a few more days of this hell, and you'll be home. I love you so much.

I settle down for the night and record my nightly video that's less than a minute long. Spot is crawling all over me as I record, and I giggle, knowing Donnie will appreciate seeing the cat, too.

Day 81

I can't sleep and have you on my mind. You guys are so busy, but I hope you get a moment to see your texts and know how much you're loved. 6 days, baby. 💜 I love everything about you. Stay safe and know you're in my thoughts. 😘😘💞

<noon>

I miss you. 😘
I know you're hella busy, but i just wanted you to know that you're on my mind. I love you so much, Donnie.

Hello my love

Good morning honey

How are you doing ?

I miss you 😘

I smile as his texts come in. Less than a week and we'll be together. Texting will be for simple things, not the lifeline they are currently.

Hey baby

I miss you too.

How are you?!

I miss you more

I'm ok , working away

I'm good. Missing you, but so excited about you coming home.

I'm sorry I haven't been able to text much this week , so much been going on

Same here my love , I'm really pumped to get it all over with

I understand. You're coming home. It's bound to be insane. Plus you still have to worn

Work, not worn

I love you

You're the best, you know that? You're so fucking busy and yet you still find a few minutes to let me know you think of me. I appreciate it more than you know, and I also understand if you can't.
I love you so much, baby. Soon... 😘😘🥰🖤

<nine hours later>

Hey babe

Good evening , I slept for like an hour and I'm up now

How have you been ?

I miss you so damn much

Hey baby! I'm so glad you slept a little

I'm doing good, missing you. I love you, baby.🖤

Are you going to go back to bed?

Olive and I washed our cars today, which sounds so super lame compared to what you're going through.

She and her mom are going back to MN tomorrow for about 10 days, so I'll be hanging out by myself until you get home.

I talk to him about my day, letting him know what I'm doing but that I'm still thinking of him the entire time. I know he appreciates the distraction and knowing what I'm up to. I remember him telling him that it helps him know there's a future to look forward to. At least, he appreciates it when he's feeling like himself.

Jean Booth

I miss you more babe

I'm going to drive up to the Smithsonian castle tomorrow morning because the trees are blooming around there, and it's supposed to be really pretty. I'll send you some pictures. I hope you fell back to sleep. I love you so much and miss you like crazy. I was thinking earlier about how soon I can take Trixie on a mani/pedi date. I've taken all my nieces to get them done, and its so fun.

I lie in bed texting with him. The cats are both getting ready to sleep in their spots on the bed. They're going to have to adjust when we get together and I don't think either of them are going to like it. I can picture Spot completely giving up on our bed and becoming Trixie's cat. The thought surprisingly doesn't bother me.

And nope , I can't seem to get more sleep

Dang.

In my thoughts, you came with us and trixie and I conspired to have your nails done too, with lots of glitter. Lol

How's work going for you?

Have you talked to Mayra? Did Trixies enrollment go ok? Is she excited that you're coming home?

I love you, Donnie.
Be safe

Day 82

> Hi handsome. I love you. I hope you slept last night. We're so close, my love. You're almost out of hell and into my arms, where you belong. I love you more

I get up early so I can avoid a bit of the traffic into DC. The magnolia trees are in full bloom right now, and I was told that the Smithsonian Castle is absolutely beautiful during this time as the land is covered in magnolia trees.

They aren't wrong; there are pink flowered trees all over the place. The magnolias smell really nice—not too strong, but still a little sweet. Pink petals litter the ground. Another week or so and all the blossoms will be gone. Today was a great time to experience this. I take a picture of me in front of the castle with the blossoms and send it to Donnie. I can't wait to go on these little adventures with him.

<sends pics of me and castle with blooms>

> The castle

> You, sir, are the absolute love of my life. Stay safe. I miss you and can't wait to start our life together i love you more than you know.

<four hours later>

> You're on my mind. I miss you.

> I'm catching up on things I needed to get done around here. Is there anything I can do for you before you get home?
> I love you, baby.

<four hours later>

> I know things are insane. I just wanted you to know you're being thought of (haven't stopped and never will) and are loved.
> I hope your day is almost over and you can sleep tonight.

<three hours later>

Hello love

Good ey

Evening *

How was your day today ?

Hey baby. How are you?

My day was good. How was yours?

I miss you so damn much , it's been such a long and shitty day

I'm so fucking tired

I'm so sorry.
Is there anything I can do to help?

Good to bed, my love

I'm okay babe , just tired

But I'm glad to talk to you

It's the best part of my day

Aww, I think as I melt. *Talking to you is the best part of my day too. And soon, it'll be in person.*

Me too.

What did you do today ?

I went to DC and did my morning walk around the Smithsonian castle and downtown

And i wrote.

Can you talk about your day? Do you want to?

<sends good night video>

Oh nice , that's good babe

Sounds like you had a fun day

What did you go to do in DC

Alright, I'm sending you a video to help your day get better. I love you

It's nothing exciting really , just work and work till you drop dead lol

I literally drove up, walked around and took pictures, and left.
I'm sorry, baby. You're almost done.

Nicee

I got the pictures you sent me

I love you, Donnie.

You look absolutely gorgeous my love

And I love you more

More than you can ever imagine 🤍

Nice. That was my day. Aww, thanks, babe.
I cannot wait to have you in my arms, where you belong.

And I can't wait to have you in my arms , I'm gonna lift you up and squeeze you so tight

🤍

And I got all the videos too , it's so damn hot 🥵

Lol, I'm glad you like them.

Especially the ones in the shower , it's so fucking hot

I can't wait to be a part of that

I really liked how my shower puc turned out.
I never like my pics.

Our water bill will run so high lmao 🤣

I laugh about his obsession about the water bill and showers. He's been in the military for so long, I don't know that he realizes showers can be relaxing and fun. I think back on his comment that showers shouldn't last more than five minutes. *Oh, how that man is going to change his tune,* I think with a smile.

I can't wait either.

Lmao

It'll be worth it.

It turned out amazing my love

Of course it'll be worth it

I just hope I make you feel loved, wanted, and appreciated, my love. I know you're working so hard and I don't want you to ever forget how loved you are

So you just drove to dc , took couple walks , took pictures and headed back

That must be hella funn

Yeah.

It was a good day. I scheduled to get my car windows tinted on Monday.

Id much rather have you home where we can do things together.

Of course you make me feel loved honey , the way you text me , send me pictures and take me along with your activities and day is such an amazing thing to see

You're absolutely amazing

Why are you getting your windows tinted ?

I melt at his words, loving how free he is with his compliments and how sweet he is. It's not something I'm used to, and I just love that he's like that.

"I've always had my windows tinted," I say to my phone. "It helps with heat and privacy. And if I'm going to have Trixie in my car, I don't want people looking in my windows and seeing her. There are gross people out there and I need to protect her in any way I can."

I shudder as I think about all the ways someone could hurt her. I feel it to an extent with my nieces, but thinking about it as my kid, or as close to someone that will be my kid as I'll ever get, has me feeling extra paranoid. I don't want anyone taking a picture of her while she's innocently sitting in the backseat. Hell, I don't know how parents let their kids out of the house or around any humans at all with all the dangers that are out there for them. It's completely irrational, I know that, but I can't help but want her to be as safe as possible in my care.

Good.
I love you so much and I know things suck right now. I just dont want you to ever feel alone again.

For my car - idk, it's nice to not have excess heat and helps with privacy.

I'm not babe , no matter how far away I am ..
I always feel you right by myself

And you text me way too much for me to feel alone lmao 🤣

You're my heart,
Lmao. Yeah.....

You said you liked it.

And you're mine honey

🖤

All I've ever wanted

I don't just like it , I love it 😋

Same. You're absolutely everything to me.

Did Trixies school get handled ok?

How did I get to fucking lucky babe

We both got lucky, and i have no idea how. I think the powers that be are finally giving us a break and letting something good finally happen.

Yes my love , I wanna thank you for that .. everything is handled and she's enrolled and she's going to fully start pre-k on Monday

"What?" I exclaim. "How is she starting school already?" A wave of profound sadness washes over me. I hadn't realized until that moment how much I was looking forward to doing the first day of school things with her. Now, I won't have that opportunity. Donnie must hate that. He may not have the same feelings about it as a girl does. To him, it may just be another step in her life, another thing he's missed out on because he's been in the military.

All thanks to you my love

I don't know what I'll do without you in my life right now babe

Oh, wow! That's soon. I didn't think pre-k started till the fall.
Is mayra going to take pictures?

You won't ever have to know. Just come home to me and let me love you.

I was really looking forward to doing the first day of school stuff with her.

We'll just have to make a big deal of the first day of kindergarten next year. my sisters do these signs on the first and last days of school that are really cute.

Yeah babe , I've told her to take pictures for the first day of school and she will

That's good. Is she being nicer to you?

But I've got a an issue with her , because ive sent her money for pre-k .. now she's asking for me to pay her for this month and she's trying to cause a scene

And I don't even want to deal with all this shit when I'm home in a week

I figured she would be. She's such a bitch.

It's gonna be so damn frustrating

Add it to my tab?

Lol

Yes she is , she's really pushing my patience for me not to smack her in her fucking face

Lmaoo babe

I hate bugging you with my shit I swear

It's embarrassing 🙈

You've never actually hit a woman, right?
You're just venting to me?
Its 2800?

You'll be home on Tuesday. We'll deal with her and this stuff then. In the meantime, I'll send the money so she can pay Mayra.

No never ever but she's really pushing me

Good to know.
And vent away. I want to kick her in the vagina with a steel tow boot so...

Toe, good god fingers. Lol

Lmaooo

Or take her to your axe throwing club and place her there

💯

I'm really good at axe throwing...

Especially when I'm mad

I can see that babe

What school is Trixie going to? Do you know if she's excited?

You sent me those pictures and I was really surprised

Why were you surprised?

Jean Booth

You threw it dead in the middle

Didn't know ya girl was a fuckin bad ass?

Well now I know

She's pretty bad ass

Lol, just a lil

And got the best tits in the world

I keep my evil side locked away fairly well

And a pussy that is in desperate need to be wounded.

Pounded. Fuck autocorrect

It's gonna be pounded and stretched out

I can promise you that my love

I hope you're ready

Because I am and my balls are full asf

Yeah. You're probably gonna have to be a lil gentle our first time. It's beena while and I'm tight.

I cannot wait to be with you.

What kinds of snacks do you like, that you miss? I was thinking about prepping stuff...

Yeah I'll be a lil gentle but you're gonna be so wet to take it all

Yes, I will be

I can't wait to be with you as well my love , you're all that I need

Oh really babe

Same, Donnie.

Why are you trying to prep , what's your plan exactly ?

You'd be pouring once I pounce of that body of yours

Btw babe , when is your house lease expiring .. I think you said April ?

Pick you up, kiss you, hold you, make people at the airport jealous of us meeting, and take you to a hotel room.
I thought id have snacks and Gatorade for breaks, lol

Yeah.

End of

Damn , your plan is so hot , you've got everything down, you're planning to drain all of me and I'm here for it

I'm here for it all

Awesome.

Good people deserve to be happy too and you're my happiness

So end of April , what's your plan for after ?

We can also go somewhere to eat before or after you have me.

You've be moving in with me right ?

I was hoping to.

I really, really want to move in with you.

And yes , we're going to eat out in a lot of places and have romantic dinners too

Same here babe

I've told you, I want it all with you. Everything we've talked about- moving in, dance parties, chill nights, sex, cuddles, being something to Trixie.

I've been thinking my love and there's so much work to be done with the house , the need the lawn and grass cut , the pool cleaned and some plumbing and full house cleaning done since we're going to be there the end of next month

"Are you kidding me?" I ask, dumbfounded at my phone. Things were going so well. "This is the dumbest request ever. We can do the crap to the house when you get home. At the very least, we can deal with it when you get home. Why is this a discussion now?"

Ok. We can do all that when you get home.

The nanny told me that there's so much that needs to be fixed in the house and I was hoping you'd help with that so I'll just come home to a fully fixed house ready to be our home

I find myself incredibly irritated at where this conversation is headed.

Dude. I'm not made of money.

Damn babe relax

I'm just saying

Can we talk about that next week?

How would you feel when we're doing that when I'm home and living in a house that people are coming to fix and work in , we wouldn't even have our privacy

I didn't know you had a pool

It's just a suggestion, nothing serious but I was hoping is something we can figure out but I've heard you say " Dude. I'm not made of money"

Of course I do , why wouldn't I have a pool to come home to and relax after all this fucking heat !

I think it can be something we can figure out, but it caught me off guard.

I'm sorry , I'm just way in over my head and overly excited about coming home and everything

Sorry love

You haven't even wanted to tell me where you live and are hinting at me helping fix it up. I was assuming Mayra was living there and taking care of things.

I understand, babe, and it's fine. I would just be more comfortable with this discussion after you come home.

She's just a nanny , she's not my wife nor is she a cleaner , yes she cleans but just the house and after trixie my love

His text rubs me wrong. I understand that Mayra is the nanny. So, what does he expect when we move in together? Because I'm the little woman, I'm going to be the one taking care of everything? What kind of patriarchal bullshit is that?

She and I are very different people....

I've cleaned this place top to bottom. It's cleaner and more taken care of than when I first got here. I have pride in where I live, what I do, and how I live.

I get you babe , I really do .. I just know there's gonna be so much to do once I'm home with me being at the base for a debrief , then trying to quit the military and still want to keep my insurance benefits and retirement benefits and also trying to see you and spend time , there will be so much to do

Jean Booth

We haven't talked for days but I've been thinking about everything over and over again , that's why it seemed so sudden lol

And we will figure it out. Just breathe.
I get it. I've been planning things, too. But honestly, we have time.

We can figure things out when you get home. You can handle your job stuff, and I'll make arrangements for the house. I've done it before in NV. You're not alone in things, baby

Your retirement is going to take time and only be available to work on during business hours. I can help navigate it with you, I'm kinda good at paperwork, and stuff.

It's just days away my love , in all honesty there's no time

No time for what?

To do things , I'm so gonna be busy when I'm home then finally get to be with you and I don't wanna be bothered by shit then

Just eat , fuck , sleep .. rinse and repeat

You're coming home in 4 days. You can't do anything about your retirement, the debrief, or stuff outside of your day to day until then. And we can't fuck 24/7. Good holy god, we will need sleep at some point.

Will we be able to talk on the phone when you get back on Tuesday?

I've been here for almost a year , in utter shit and suffering from the worst atmospheric conditions you can ever think of so you can't blame me for wanting things sorted out

When did you go out there? I didn't know it had been that long

Hopefully yes my love , I long for you to hear my voice

Let it make your pussy quiver

I don't blame you, nor am I trying to make you feel bad. I'm trying to get you to understand that you are not alone, Donnie.

I really want to hear you and to video chat with you. You have no idea how much i need that connection from you. Also, planning things will be so much easier that way.

We will get everything sorted next week. I promise.

And if you wanted to give me your address, I'd be more than happy to get the lawn situated and clean. I have nothing else to clean here and you'd actually be helping me deal with my nervous energy.

Did you crash? I hope you get some sleep, babe. I love you.

If he would just give me his stupid address, I could resolve most of these things before he even comes home. I have no problem doing yardwork or housework and he can always ask Mayra to work with me so I'm not there when Trixie is. That way, there's no confusion when we show up together. And I won't meet her first.

He gets so stuck in his head about what he wants to do that he thinks his way is the only way, and it's not. It frustrates me to no end.

I'm still up , just went to shower

What are you doing ?

Oh, nice.

Laying in bed

And what do you mean nervous energy babe

What's going on

Jean Booth

Are you nervous about anything , talk to me my love

That's why I'm here

Of course, I'm nervous about things. I've never seen or heard him, and we're going to meet for the first time in a few days. And I still have doubts and insecurities and fears. The only thing that will help me to chill out is to see him in person. To answer the question once and for all—are you really who you say you are?

I clean and organize when I get stressed. I'm really excited/nervous about meeting you. I want things to go well. There's nothing you can say right now to make the nerves go away. I just need to actually see you and I'll chill.

So, in the meantime, I clean. And organize.

I helped Olive clean their rental, her car, my car, and I've cleaned most of this place already.

And by clean, I mean I've washed everything - curtains, blankets bedding, walls, the floor. I've taken everything out of the kitchen cupboards, cleaned them, and am working on reorganizing it now.
It helps calm and distract me.

So, if you want to have me prep the house for you, save the $ on cleaners and lawn people and let me have my fun.

Damn

You've been doing a whole lot of cleaning babe

And you're so selfless

Yea. Like I said, it helps relax me.

What do you mean? How am I selfless?

But I'll never let you do that for me and besides is a big house that has more to be fixed apart from just cleaning so leave it to the professionals

All I want you to do is just relax and let me spoil and take care of you once I'm home

I'd like that. But we also need to realize there are realities of life.

And yes you are babe , the way you treat people like olive , cleaning for them , letting them use your car and all that ... that's a very rare attribute you can get from someone that's just a neighbor to you so yeah you're very selfless

What school is Trixie going to go to?

What do you mean realities of life babe ?

Honestly I don't remember it but I know it's a pretty good pre-k , I'll ask for the name tomorrow and let you know

Like we will have chores, house projects, school stuff, and lif issues that will get in the way of the fun stuff like sex

That's why I'm trying to eliminate as many as I can

I know, but life will still happen.

I'm still talking to the professionals trying to fix the house and I'll conclude with them tomorrow then we'll see if it's something you can help with my love so we can get that out of the way .. I know you're not made of money , you've told me and I get that but I'm coming Tuesday, it's just like you're gonna be loaning me for 3 plus days so they can start their work immediately

How do you have time to do that?

Jean Booth

Did you send Mayra money yet ?

I'd say you should wait so you'd send these guys along with it and it's not that hard , I talk to them on Facebook

Same way I'm talking to you right now and not sleeping

I haven't.

Good , don't do it yet

Idc if she cries blood , my house comes first

And I know how much I owe you and you're get paid back and you have to take it from me !

Yes, I think. *You are paying me back. This is insane.*

And I'm not trying to start anything, but I promised I'd talk you about this kind of stuff... I'm really starting to feel all sorts of discomfort with this. Is there any possible way we can video chat before I send more $?

I appreciate you tho for always helping out and I promise you that I'll make it worth all your efforts my love

I'm starting to feel like that's the main thing you want me for, and im having a hard time convincing myself otherwise.

Babe , just help me with that and the first thing I'll do as soon as I land in the states is to give you a call

Why are you talking like this , we've been over this countless times

I'm with you because I love you , I don't even know if you got money

I know we've been through this. That's why I'm talking to you about it. I'm uncomfortable.

Damn babe , stop bringing us 3 steps back after we've made progress , especially when I'm home in days

When would they need to be paid?

Well we can stop it since I'm making you so uncomfortable

You know I struggle with trust. I'm trying here, babe.

Because I don't get why we're back at this point babe

I told you countless times that you can trust me and I'll never ever let your trust down

You think those are just mere words

I hate that he's trying to argue with me about this. Just freaking work with me! I need a modicum of reassurance to makc myself comfortable. What's the big deal?

And trust doesn't work that way. I start by giving trust, and then you earn the right to keep it. By saying I can trust you, but not providing anything tangible, isn't helpful. What would be helpful are pictures or a call or a video. I sigh, not wanting to fight, but not wanting to bend on this either. I have no idea what things are going to be like when he gets home, but I really hope we can work things out better in person.

Sometimes, yes.

If you can't even believe when I'm gonna be home in 3 days , you wouldn't even be able to believe me when you see me in person

And that's just the truth

I can believe you when we're in person. That's kinda the issue. Is ive never met you in person.

Please stop being defensive.

I'm trying to be honest and talk you you and now I feel bad for even saying anything.

I'm not being defensive

I'm pissed that we are still going at each others throats acting like cat and rat

That's the weirdest phrase I've ever heard. I just let it go and move on. Jesus.

How can you love a man and not believe him

How does that make any sense?

Please don't be upset with me. What we have is great, and it scares me. I've never been allowed great. I'm not trying to be at your throat. I'm trying to share my fear with you.
Just forget I said anything. I do love you. I do trust you. I'll deal with my fear.

I thought you didn't use social media?

Really

How do I now respond to you on IG

Yes, I do.
What are you talking about?

I have it but don't use it doesn't mean I can get on it when I need to

Well I answered your question of me not using social media

I didn't know you used it, is all.

I'm sorry I pissed you off. It want my intention.

And that's the problem, because you've never been allowed to be doesn't mean you can't let yourself be great

Wasn't

You have to want it for yourself

I do want it. So much

Good so why think so negatively about everything

What if it all works out and we're everything we've been waiting for all our lives

What if !

Because that's been the reality of my life and it's hard to break the cycle.
That would be amazing and that's what I'm hoping for.

Like I said, it's a stupid fear, and I'm trying. I love you. I trust and believe in you. I'm just scared and I'm not sure what to do about it.

What was your relationship like with Maddie?

Well you have to overcome your fear babe , I can only help you but I can't do it for you .. it's gonna be from within

I know.

I don't even know why you're so scared and feeling this way because we've been together for months now and I've never made you feel otherwise so where is it coming from

Having you home will help a lot.

It's annoying for me because I haven't nothing to you but here I am paying the price for all that's been done in the past I wasn't even in

It's not fair on me

Everything I've asked you , I swear on trixie life I'd do exactly the same for you and more if you were in my shoes

It isn't fair on you, and i'm sorry. You deserve someone who's less broken. I'm working through things and just trying to be honest and communicate with you so they don't become issues.

And I'll be home in less than 4 days , I'll be .. I'm just making arrangements for a house that you're eventually going to live in yourself , you should be happy that you have a man that's actually a planner than Thomas that will sit on his ass and waiting for him to be pampered like a child

I am. You have no idea how grateful I am to be with you.

And it's not going to be all that expensive, it can't be as much as what we've paid the nanny so far so I totally believe it's doable for you, that's why I asked

Ok.

Then show it , stop doubting be all the damn time

And acting like a scaredy cat

You're a grown ass woman

"Why are you freaking acting this way?" I yell at my phone. "This is ridiculous to fight over, holy crap."

Don't be mean

I'm not

And i'm not doubting all the time. I'm not doubting now, just uncomfortable

I'm saying it to your face like you do me

Uncomfortable about what

I really want to understand you babe

About the timing for the house people. I understand about Trixie and the Nanny. I only started feeling uncomfortable when house stuff started coming up. It felt a little like that's why you're with me. And I didn't like that feeling.

I just needed to know that it's not something you were expecting this minute.

You felt like I'm with you because of the house maintenance?

No, that you're with me so I'll pay for stuff.

I have a million dollar house , I mean no disrespect but I don't need you to do nothing for me

Omg , what made you feel this way

Cuz you've helped me with the nanny with $10k

It's all good , just forget about it

I honestly don't know what it was that brought up the fear.

I'll handle the rest myself and I'll pay you what I owe you once I land

No, babe. I'll help. Don't be that way.

I thought you could help and it wasn't an issue for you but obviously I can see that it is so I'm sorry for being a burden on you

Its just a stupid fear. You're not a burden.

It doesn't seem that way to me

I'm gonna ask you a question

You're not, my love.
Ask away

Jean Booth

You've only helped me out once with the nanny and now with trixie pre-k

Does it take a toll on your finances ?

Yea...
A little bit.

How so

I thought you said you're good

Like I said before, I'm ok. Not near what you have, but I'm good.

What do you think I have lol

You sent me your chase details, remember?

You have like 350k.

Oh yea I did

And that's one of my account

I don't have that, but I could easily not worry about work for a year.

So you're telling me you don't have $350k

No

And you're trying to buy a house

Stop playing with me babe

No. I'm moving in with my boyfriend, unless he changed his mind...

What do you mean, playing with you?

Messing with me lol

I'm not messing with you.
I was never looking to buy something with cash. A lot of things changed from end of January to now. If you hadn't asked me to live with you, I'd have gotten that townhouse in Virginia.

I'm not rich, but I'm not destitute either. I'm comfortable.

I understand that

Did you see my request on fb? When did you live in South Dakota m

Also, I don't understand your question. No, I dont have $350k. Yes, I was trying to buy a house.

Lmk how much you need for the house and Mayra and when you need it. Do you want me to pay the contractors directly?

I'll check it now babe and yes my grandparents used to live down there in Sioux Falls and I used to go there a lot , I think I created my Facebook account there

Oh, nice. You were really close to your grandpa, it sounds like.

And now I understand what you're trying to say now

Lol, want to enlighten me?

Yup , he was an airborne paratrooper too and fought during WW2

Yeah, you told me. That's awesome that you guys were so close and he was so impactful on your life. I love that for you.

That you would've moved back to Virginia and I'm still the only thing that's keeping you waiting

Thank you my love and yes he was very impactful on my life , he was a good man and I try to follow his steps

I'm waiting for you because you're my future. Unless you've decided I'm too much...

I only want to be with you and Trixie.

Well you won't ever have to move to Virginia, the only movement is me moving into your vagina

And you're mine babe

Nobody's going anywhere so please let's do this wholeheartedly my love

Thank you, baby.
I'm all in. Sometimes I may need some reassuring words and hugs, but im all in and i love you.

Erase that fear , this is meant to be .. fate brought us together and nothing is ever gonna stop that

With everything in me.

I get that , we all need reassuring words every now and then

I'm trying, my love. I believe in us, I truly do.

But I know without a doubt in my heart that I'm all yours Annie and I love you with every fiber of my being

I'm yours, too, Donnie. 100%

You mean absolutely everything to me.

Aww baby

It's weird to see you use my name, lol

You're the absolute sweetest

When you want to be lmaoo

Well it was because I was serious asf

You got me deep in my feels

❤️

I love you.
I am sweet, just have some baggage.

I really hope to be able to hear your voice on Tuesday. I honestly can't wait to be in your arms.

Well aren't alone anymore , you don't have to carry it all by yourself

Same here my love

Tuesday will be here soon enough

I think every day this week has dragged on and doubled in hours.

I'll let you know about the contractors tomorrow so you can pay them and they'll start Saturday

Ok.

Thank you so much honey , you're simply amazing

I love you, Donnie.

And I'm more than grateful to have you

I tell you that all the time and it's because I mean it

I love you more Annie

To the moon and back 🥰❤️

To infinity and beyond

🤗❤️❤️

Busy day tomorrow?

Not really

You? I'm sure you'll be slammed.

Wish I could say the same for me

I'm going to work on edits and formatting tomorrow

But I'll try to text you as soon as possible

Don't distract yourself. We'll get things handled.

I'll be fine baby

Finally, we're past the crap and can talk like normal people again. I ask him about the trust fund as I'd never heard of or met someone that had a trust fund. I thought they were things only spoken of in television or books.

How did you become a trust fund guy?

I enjoy talking to you, it's the best part of my day

I didn't actually think that was a real thing.

Its the best part of mine, too.

My dad is successful, has a chain of companies so he set up a trustfund for my brother and I since we were 3 and could only access it when we were 23 , that was a whole 20 years saving with interests so it's a lot

And it sure helped me with purchasing my house amongst other things

Oh, wow.
Yeah, you said that before. What other things?

I'm grateful to him for that but he has his own issues

We barely talk these days

My brother manages everything now

I wish he would freaking answer me. I hate how he avoids questions that he doesn't want to answer.

We all do...
What companies?
Yeah, you mentioned your family wasn't great.

We barely talk too

I'm the black sheep of the family , took after my grandpa

You said they weren't supportive of you and Maddie and didn't help or care when she died.
I'm the black sheep, too.

And move to another state because of love

That was the last straw for them lol

That's really awful.

I probably shouldn't ask, but.. was she the love of your life? You said you were high school sweethearts and all.

Yup

I'd say she was until now

Really?

You're the love of my life

Yes really

I believe it with all my heart

I melt. A part of me thinks he's lying, just being nice, but another part of me wants to believe that I'm his person, too. Lord knows, he's mine. He's the only one I want to talk to, the only one I want to spend time with, the only one I want to do anything with. I love him more than I ever thought was possible.

I know without a doubt that you're the live of mine. It's ok if she was yours. She was taken from you, and that is a pain I hope to never know.

What makes you believe that?

You're mine babe

I love you

The way you make me feel even without seeing me it's exceptional, I can basically feel you by my side everytime we talk

I can sense your frustration, joy , sadness , everything

The picture can't be displayed.

The picture can't be displayed.

The picture can't be displayed.

The picture can't be displayed.

The picture can't be displayed.

The picture can't be displayed.

The picture can't be displayed.

The picture can't be displayed.

The picture can't be displayed.

The picture can't be displayed.

The picture can't be displayed.

The picture can't be displayed.

The picture can't be displayed.

The picture can't be displayed.

The picture can't be displayed.

The picture can't be displayed.

The picture can't be displayed.

Day 83

I wake up feeling like absolute garbage. My head and chest feel like I have giants sitting on them. I take some meds after feeding the cats and go right back to bed, hoping I'll feel better and this is just allergies.

<sends two pics>

I see that Donnie texted me earlier today, and while I hate that I missed his texts, I love the pictures he sent—finally! He sent me a full body shot and a headshot. I zoom in on his full body one and look at it as critically as I can. He looks strong, but not completely ripped, and I'm loving it. He's so attractive to me, I could stare at his pictures all day. I text him back, thanking him for them.

The headshot isn't in shadow this time, and he's gorgeous. His eyes are so blue, I could fall into them. I smile, knowing that in a few short days, this man will be in my arms. I can't wait.

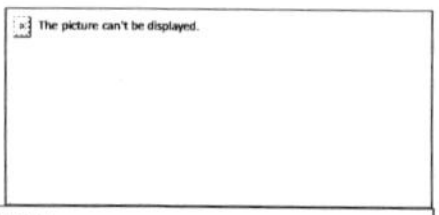

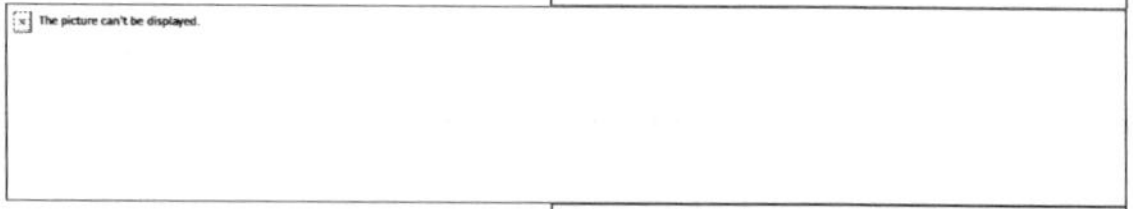

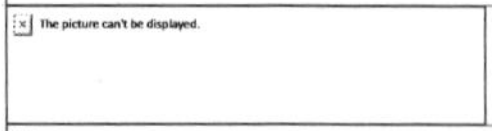

The picture can't be displayed.

The picture can't be displayed.

The picture can't be displayed.

The picture can't be displayed.

I send him a video of me in bed, so he knows I'm not feeling well. I need more sleep but didn't want him thinking I blocked him again. I promised, and I'm a woman of my word.

The picture can't be displayed.

<two hours later>

The picture can't be displayed.

<pic of cat laying on me>

The picture can't be displayed.

I try to sleep but don't get much of it. I take more meds and lay down. It's better than trying to function.

The picture can't be displayed.

The picture can't be displayed.

The picture can't be displayed.

The picture can't be displayed.

The picture can't be displayed.

The picture can't be displayed.

The picture can't be displayed.

<three hours later>

The picture can't be displayed.

The picture can't be displayed.

The picture can't be displayed.

The picture can't be displayed.

The picture can't be displayed.

The picture can't be displayed.

The picture can't be displayed.

The picture can't be displayed.

The picture can't be displayed.

The picture can't be displayed.

The picture can't be displayed.

The picture can't be displayed.

The picture can't be displayed.

The picture can't be displayed.

I go to bed early and sleep the whole night through.

Day 84

I wake up feeling more like myself today and decide to go for my morning walk. I see the tail end of the sunrise, and it's beautiful over the Potomac. The pinks are reflecting on the water, and I'm reminded how much I love living here. I'm tired, but that's not unusual. I'll probably take it easy today and either watch a couple movies or shows on TV.

I go back to my house after about a half an hour of sitting in the dark. It gets cold quickly over the water, and I don't want to risk getting sicker. I know it's not the weather that makes people sick, but I'm already compromised. I don't need to have allergens kicking my butt, too.

I feed the cats a little early and head to bed, leaving my ringer on in case Donnie texts.

<three hours later>

<two hours later>

<two hours later>

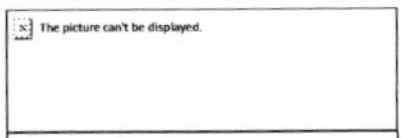

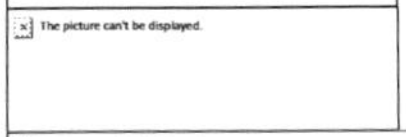

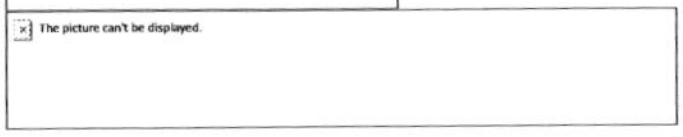

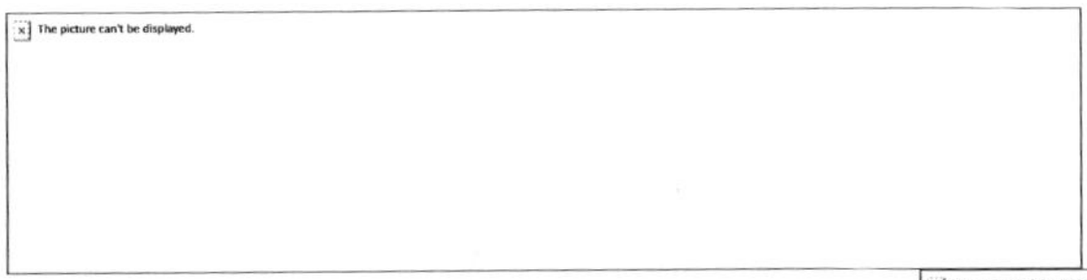

<two hours later>

<sends video of darkness>
<two hours later>

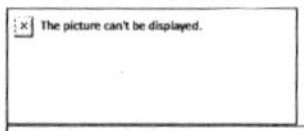

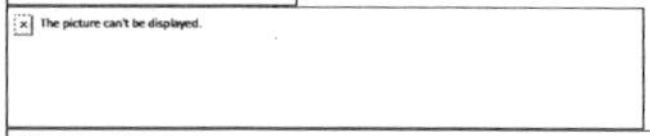

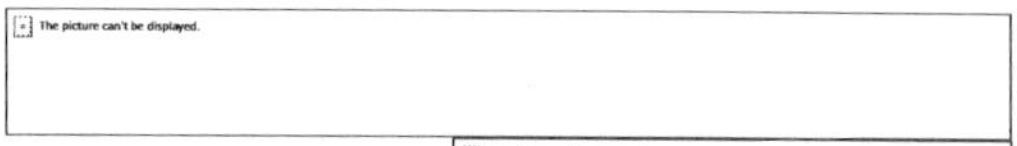

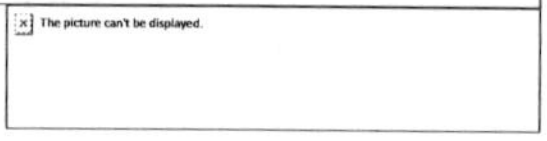

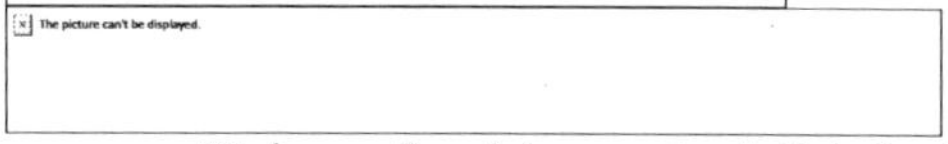

He's so freaking cute, I think. I feel slightly bad that he was worried about me. It's not something I'm used to, either. My health was one of the reasons I left my ex.

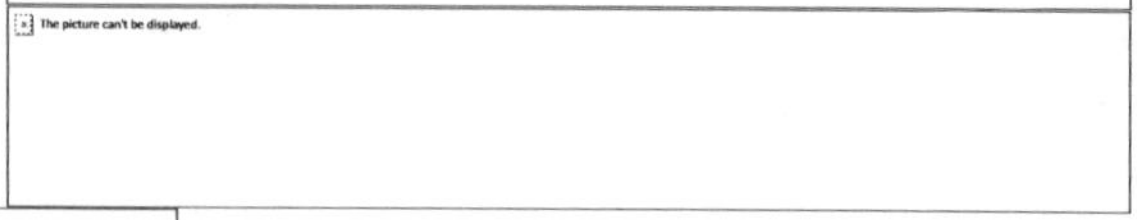

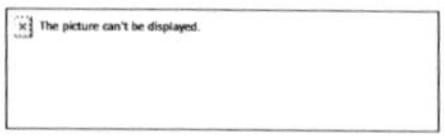

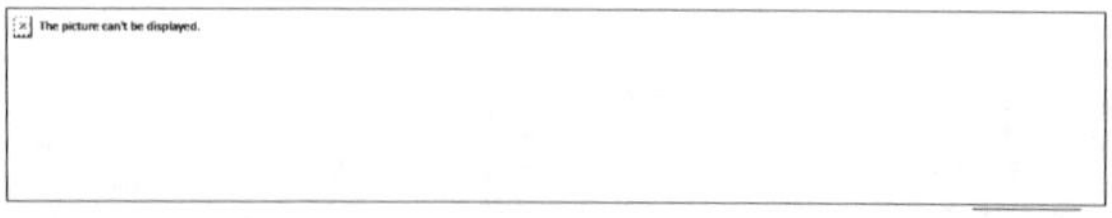

The picture can't be displayed.

The picture can't be displayed.

The picture can't be displayed.

The picture can't be displayed.

The picture can't be displayed.

The picture can't be displayed.

The picture can't be displayed.

The picture can't be displayed.

The picture can't be displayed.

The picture can't be displayed.

The picture can't be displayed.

The picture can't be displayed.

The picture can't be displayed.

The picture can't be displayed.

The picture can't be displayed.

The picture can't be displayed.

The picture can't be displayed.

The picture can't be displayed.

The picture can't be displayed.

The picture can't be displayed.

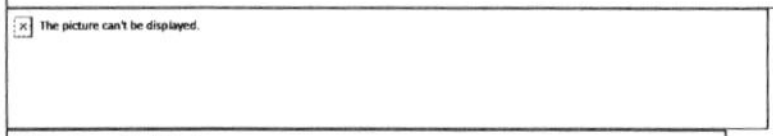

I laughed. I completely forgot I sent him a PDF of my *Zombie War* book so he had something to read on his long flight home. And I love how easily he claims me. I can't wait for him to be home.

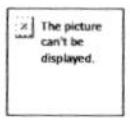

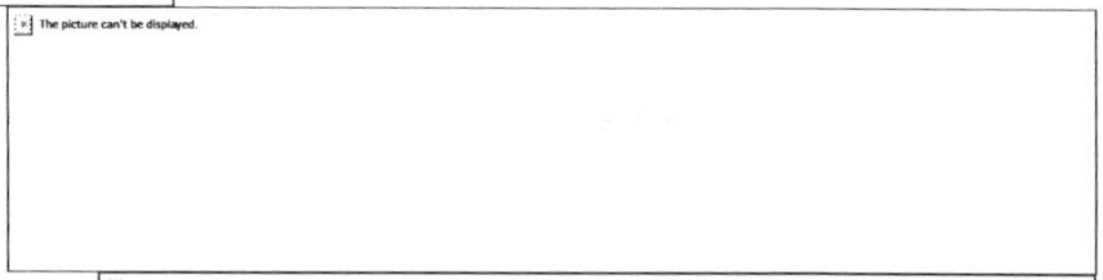

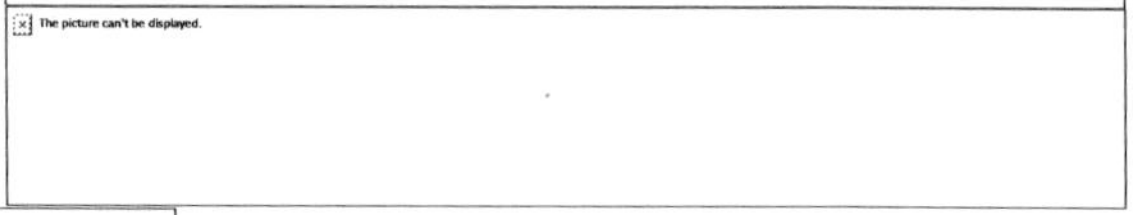

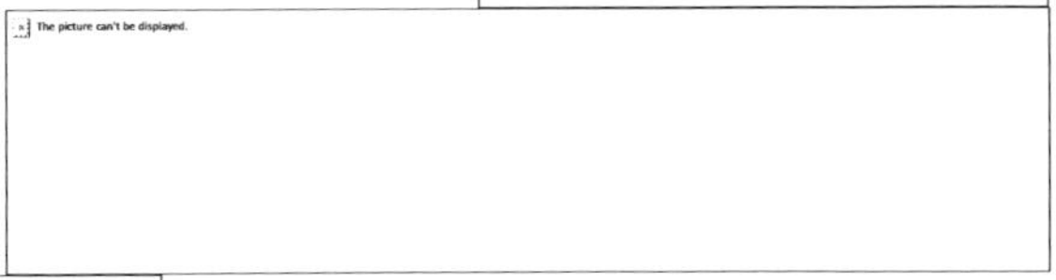

I laugh, thinking about us on the pier and how obsessed he is with having sex. I guess after two years of abstinence, I'd be a bit obsessed, too. It makes me laugh.

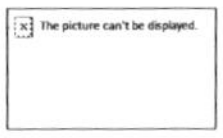

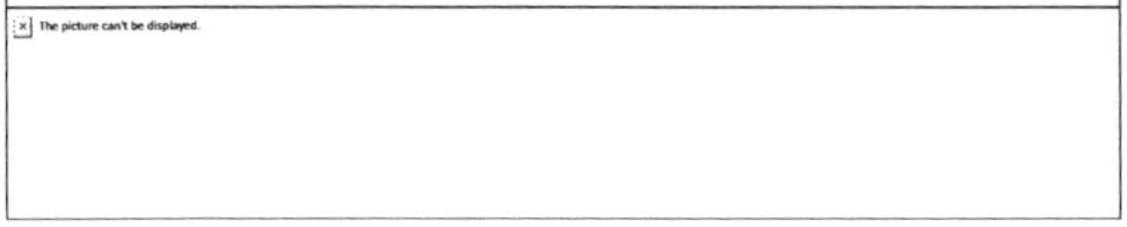

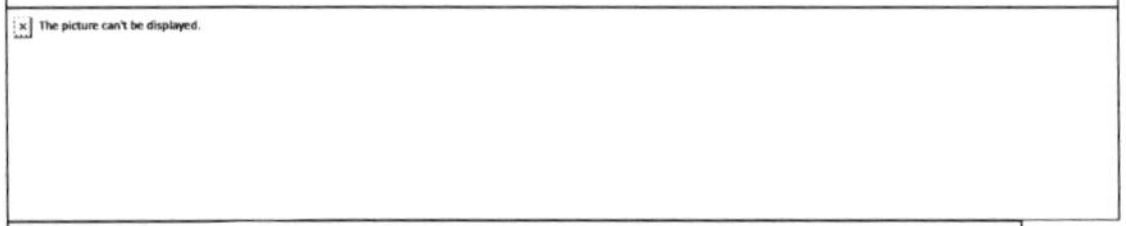

His bags are packed?

"Holy shit," I exclaim. "This is actually happening!" I do a happy shimmy before I text him back.

The picture can't be displayed.

"You're freaking insane." I laugh.

The picture can't be displayed.

The picture can't be displayed.

The picture can't be displayed.

The picture can't be displayed.

The picture can't be displayed.

The picture can't be displayed.

The picture can't be displayed.

The picture can't be displayed.

The picture can't be displayed.

The picture can't be displayed.

The picture can't be displayed.

The picture can't be displayed.

The picture can't be displayed.

The picture can't be displayed.

The picture can't be displayed.

The picture can't be displayed.

The picture can't be displayed.

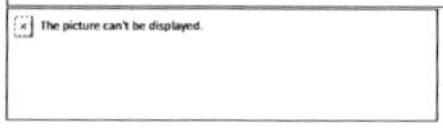

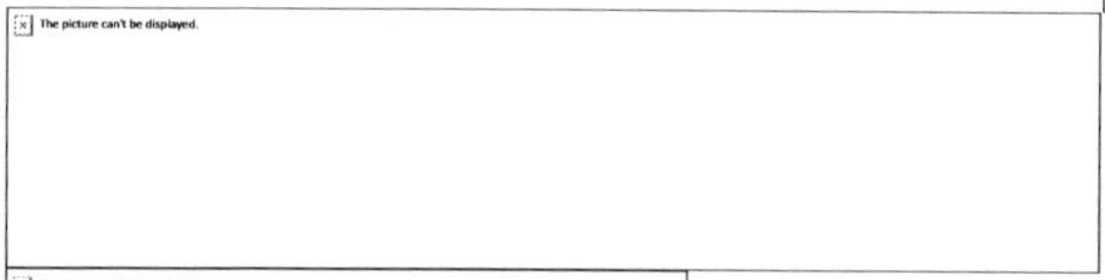

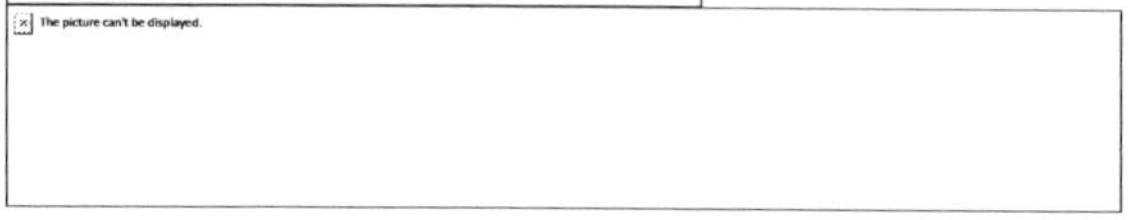

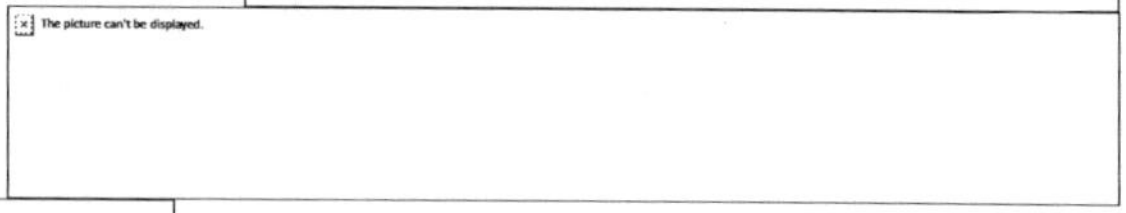

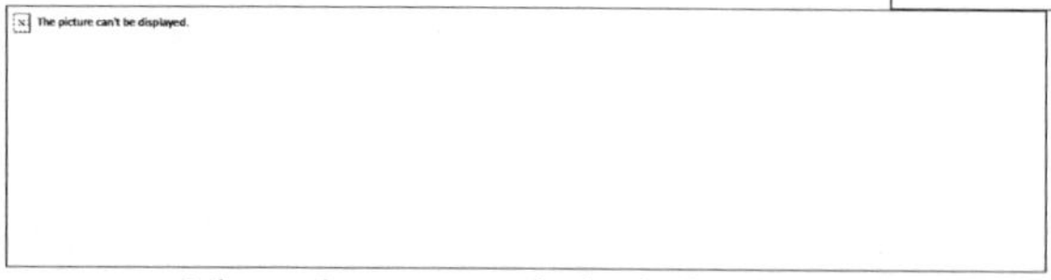

I love how much he's looking forward to all the things. It's a bit overwhelming, but I let him be excited about this. I'm excited, too. I just think we need to do things one step at a time.

Aww, I think. *You're my favorite person, too.* I can't wait for him to be home. I want to wrap my arms around him so badly.

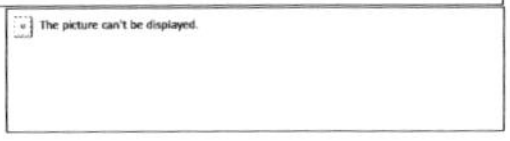

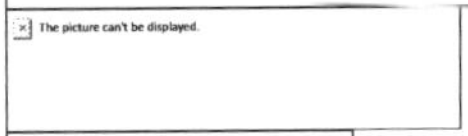

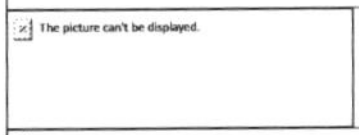

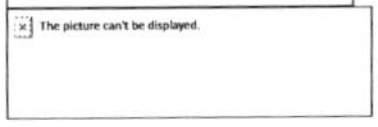

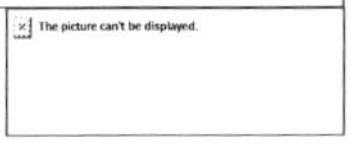

The picture can't be displayed.

The picture can't be displayed.

The picture can't be displayed.

The picture can't be displayed.

The picture can't be displayed.

The picture can't be displayed.

The picture can't be displayed.

The picture can't be displayed.

The picture can't be displayed.

The picture can't be displayed.

The picture can't be displayed.

The picture can't be displayed.

The picture can't be displayed.

The picture can't be displayed.

The picture can't be displayed.

The picture can't be displayed.

The picture can't be displayed.

The picture can't be displayed.

The picture can't be displayed.

The picture can't be displayed.

The picture can't be displayed.

The picture can't be displayed.

The picture can't be displayed.

The picture can't be displayed.

The picture can't be displayed.

The picture can't be displayed.

The picture can't be displayed.

The picture can't be displayed.

The picture can't be displayed.

The picture can't be displayed.

The picture can't be displayed.

The picture can't be displayed.

The picture can't be displayed.

The picture can't be displayed.

The picture can't be displayed.

I love teasing him. I've never really been into the teasing thing before, but with Donnie, I love it. He's so responsive and gives just as much back to me. It's fun with him because I know he's just as turned on and tormented as I am.

I take a very sexy video specifically for him and send it to him.

The picture can't be displayed.

The picture can't be displayed.

The picture can't be displayed.

The picture can't be displayed.

The picture can't be displayed.

The picture can't be displayed.

The picture can't be displayed.

The picture can't be displayed.

The picture can't be displayed.

The picture can't be displayed.

The picture can't be displayed.

The picture can't be displayed.

The picture can't be displayed.

The picture can't be displayed.

The picture can't be displayed.

The picture can't be displayed.

The picture can't be displayed.

The picture can't be displayed.

The picture can't be displayed.

The picture can't be displayed.

The picture can't be displayed.

The picture can't be displayed.

The picture can't be displayed.

The picture can't be displayed.

The picture can't be displayed.

The picture can't be displayed.

The picture can't be displayed.

The picture can't be displayed.

The picture can't be displayed.

The picture can't be displayed.

The picture can't be displayed.

The picture can't be displayed.

The picture can't be displayed.

The picture can't be displayed.

The picture can't be displayed.

<sends pic of cat on chest>

The picture can't be displayed.

The picture can't be displayed.

I can feel myself blushing as I take a picture of me and then the video that he asked for. I make sure he can see the moisture on my fingers before licking them and smiling. I giggle as I send the video.

“No, we’re not.” I laugh at the phone. “We are absolutely not going to record ourselves having sex.”

He either had to go or fell asleep. I love this man more than anything, and I smile as I head to bed, knowing that he'll be here in a few short days.

Day 85

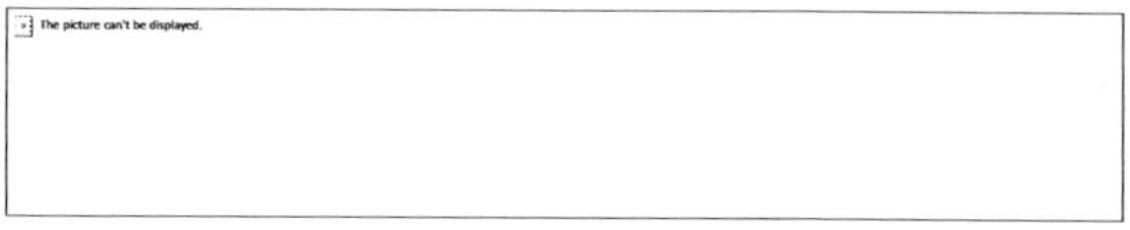

<three hours later>

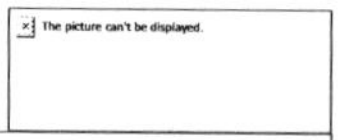

<six hours later>

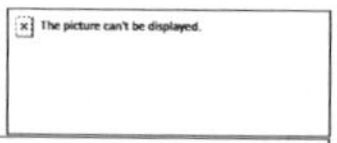

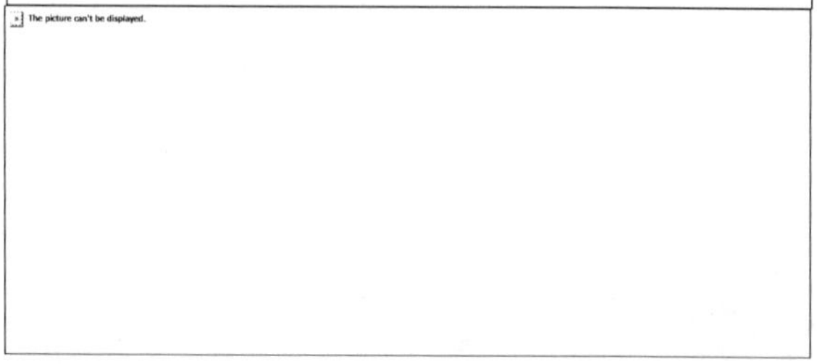

<three hours later>

<three hours later>

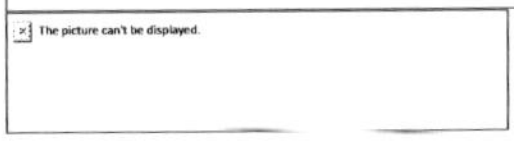

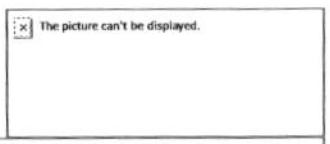

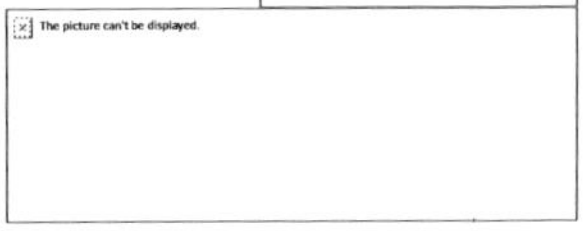

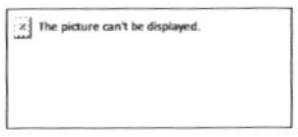

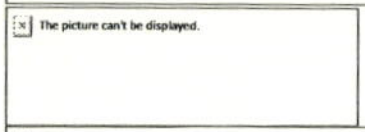

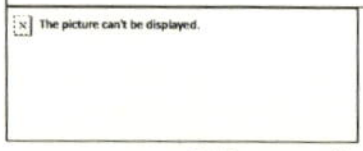

I laugh at him. He sounds like a kid sometimes with the things he's excited to do. I'm excited to experience things with him and be silly and goofy like kids. I love just being silly and can't wait to encourage him to be goofy. He's had to be too serious with his job and it's beyond time he remembers that life can be fun, too.

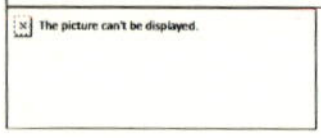

The picture can't be displayed.

The picture can't be displayed.

The picture can't be displayed.

The picture can't be displayed.

The picture can't be displayed.

The picture can't be displayed.

The picture can't be displayed.

The picture can't be displayed.

The picture can't be displayed.

The picture can't be displayed.

The picture can't be displayed.

The picture can't be displayed.

The picture can't be displayed.

The picture can't be displayed.

The picture can't be displayed.

The picture can't be displayed.

The picture can't be displayed.

The picture can't be displayed.

The picture can't be displayed.

The picture can't be displayed.

The picture can't be displayed.

The picture can't be displayed.

The picture can't be displayed.

The picture can't be displayed.

The picture can't be displayed.

The picture can't be displayed.

The picture can't be displayed.

The picture can't be displayed.

The picture can't be displayed.

The picture can't be displayed.

The picture can't be displayed.

The picture can't be displayed.

The picture can't be displayed.

The picture can't be displayed.

The picture can't be displayed.

The picture can't be displayed.

The picture can't be displayed.

The picture can't be displayed.

The picture can't be displayed.

The picture can't be displayed.

<sends pic of cat on boobs>

The picture can't be displayed.

Day 86

One more day! I'm elated, feeling like I could walk on air, I'm so happy that Donnie will be home tomorrow. There are so many things I want to do when he gets home, but I'm not sure what to expect. We've spent more time sexting and being silly than actually planning for what happens when his plane lands. Hopefully, he'll be able to explain things to me before his flight leaves.

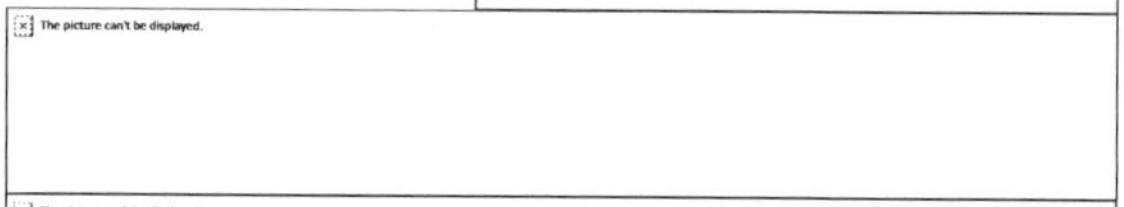

<eight hours later>

<night>

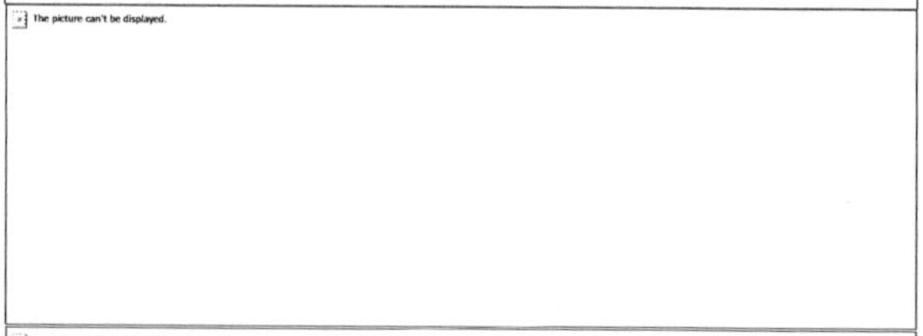

I have no idea how I'm going to get any sleep tonight with how excited I am about him coming home. I send him a good-night video. Hopefully, the last one I'll have to send with him overseas. I can't wait!

Day 87

I'm so happy for today that I find myself dancing instead of walking. I have to take a longer walk in the morning to burn off the restless energy, but I don't care. Donnie will be home today, and we're almost done with this deployment. I never want to go through this again.

The picture can't be displayed.

<four hours later>

The picture can't be displayed.

The picture can't be displayed.

The picture can't be displayed.

I practically scream with joy as we text. Soon!

The picture can't be displayed.

The picture can't be displayed.

The picture can't be displayed.

The picture can't be displayed.

The picture can't be displayed.

The picture can't be displayed.

The picture can't be displayed.

The picture can't be displayed.

The picture can't be displayed.

The picture can't be displayed.

<six hours later>

I can't focus on anything today, so I decide to go up to DC and see the cherry blossoms. They should be blooming still but will probably be at the end of their season. I've been hearing all about them, and I think it'd be a nice experience.

They stink. I quickly decide that I don't like the scent the cherry blossoms produce, but they're absolutely beautiful to look at. The magnolias the other day were so much better. But it helps keep me grounded, and I walk all around the Jefferson Memorial to the Martin Luther King, Jr. Memorial to get the full effect of the trees and the water.

I go to bed, comforted for the first time since Donnie and I started talking. He's out of danger and in the States. Or, he's at least on a plane headed here. And that knowledge is enough to let me finally relax enough to actually sleep.

Day 89

I go about my day, working on edits and trying my best to simply exist. I continually remind myself that he's home, he's real, and he's mine. I know that as soon as we can video chat, all my anxiety and fear will disappear, and I'll be as normal as I ever am in a relationship.

This has been the most stressful and terrifying three months of my life, and I never want to experience anything like it again. I love Donnie and surprisingly trust him more than I have any reason or right to. I just cannot seem to get rid of the damn fear, no matter how hard I try. Talking to my trusted friends didn't help—they actually made things worse and added to my insecurities. It was as if my relationship didn't fit into their mold, so it couldn't be real. It couldn't be what I felt in my soul what it was. I was in this alone and have been making my decisions based off of what felt best for me. I have to trust my heart that I was making the right decisions.

'And it was terrifying.

I know I have a good head on my shoulders, and I've done so many good things in such a short time, I have to trust in that, in us. I was starting to see the doubts—the fear, as what it really was—Spirit testing me, asking if I really, truly wanted this. Just as it had done when I was getting divorced, again when I moved across the country, and again when I was losing my job. All of those decisions have made my life infinitely better. This would be no different. I just have to keep trusting the process. I have to persevere and ignore the negativity that threatened to drown me.

Day 90

I still haven't heard anything from him, and my fear, doubt, and insecurity get the best of me. I do a reverse Google image search of all the pictures he sent me and still get the same result—nothing. I do a quick Google search for "reverse image search" and up pops a myriad of sites that you have to pay for to see the results. I subscribe to two of them and make sure the cancellation process is easy before I do anything with either of them. It is, so I copy/paste all the pictures I have of him into both sites.

Pictures pop up quickly on the first site, and my heart misses a beat before calming as none of the search results look like him. They're pictures of guys in hoodies and in green or beige shirts. Some of them have similar features to Donnie, but they're not him. I start to relax, feeling more and more confident in him as the evidence shows me the pictures aren't anywhere else. They have to be his, and he didn't lie when he said he had to be very careful to not have information on the internet because of his job.

The other site starts loading and all the relaxation disappears. My heart is in the vicinity of my belly-button, and I struggle with the urge to vomit. There he is. It's not the same picture, but it's definitely the same person. I'd know that face anywhere. And every single picture has him holding onto a woman.

"That's got to be Maddie, right," I whisper to my computer as I click on the photo. It takes me to a wedding site. People are taking silly pictures of themselves with items from a cardboard dress-up box. Fake mustaches, hats, glasses, and flags appear, but all I can see is the man I love kissing another woman.

I walk away from my computer for a few minutes to try to process what I'm seeing. I take a walk, leaving my phone behind so I can process without interruption. When I'm a bit calmer, I return to the computer. Looking more closely at the photos, I realize they were guests at this wedding.

The name of what I deduce is the bride isn't very common, so I go onto Facebook and look her up. I find her right away as one of the wedding pictures is her profile picture. I send her a message asking how she knows the man in the picture I send as a screenshot as I try to talk myself off the ledge. I tell her I met him on a dating app, and we've been dating for the past three months, and I wondered if there was anything she could say about him.

"It's got to be Maddie," I reason with myself. "This is Donnie and Maddie before she died. That's the only explanation."

I keep looking through the pictures and see Trixie. But she's not the Trixie I know, she's at least ten in this picture. She looks exactly like the pictures Donnie sent me of Trixie, just older.

"That's got to be his niece," I whisper. "Which means, these aren't pictures of Donnie, but of his younger brother. They just look like twins. Or Donnie took her to the wedding." I don't know what his brother looks like, but maybe Donnie was the fun uncle and took his niece to the wedding to give his brother a break.

Different scenarios play out in my mind as I obsessively look through the pictures. I was going crazy looking at them, waiting for a response from the girl on Facebook.

Now that my paranoia has been set free, I go onto his Instagram and notice that he doesn't have a lot of followers/following, which works in my favor. I cross check the people he follows with people that follow him and see two that are the same. I message both of them asking how they know Donnie.

And I wait.

Day 91

I sleep like garbage. Not only have I not heard from Donnie, but my cat had trouble sleeping again, and I can't shake the image of the picture of him kissing another woman.

I start working, hoping the formatting will help occupy my mind even a little bit. It helps, but not enough to actually distract me.

A message pops up on my Instagram, and it's one of the girls letting me know that she tried dating Donnie a while back but blocked him right away because she realized he was a scammer. She said that she did a reverse image search of his photo, and it was everywhere.

"How?" I ask to my computer. "I couldn't find anything!"

She didn't talk long, and I let the conversation die because I didn't want to sound pathetic or make her feel any more awkward than she probably already was.

"I hear you're dating someone that used my husband's pictures on his profile." A message pops up from an unknown woman on my Facebook page.

"What do you mean?" I ask, unsure how to have this conversation. I click on her profile, go to her photos, and there's an album called Deployment. I open it and see almost every single picture Donnie sent me. They weren't even photoshopped. They were the exact pictures that were on her profile.

"I'm so sorry," I say to the woman. "He sent me a bunch of pictures that he claimed were of him, but they're from your page. Even said he has a little girl, which is probably yours, as well."

I send her all the pictures Donnie sent me, and she flips out. Trixie is her daughter, but that isn't her name, and she isn't four anymore. I send her his phone number so she can confront him.

I feel sick.

My entire world collapses around me and I don't know what to do. I feel like I'm spiraling out of control, and I can no longer trust my own judgement. I fell in love with a scammer.

I close out of the computer, needing to get away. I hop in my car with no destination in site, just needing to not be in the space where my entire world just imploded. I'm numb and broken; hurt and angry with no idea what to do now. I find myself driving north, towards my friends, but not really wanting to be around anyone right now. A thought pops into my head, one I can't believe I haven't had yet.

His neighbor knows if he's real or not. Maybe he was just catfishing—not a scammer, but someone who's embarrassed about what he looks like.

I don't know what her address is, but I have her ex-husband's. He'll know where she moved to, and while I have no idea what I'm going to say to him, certainly he'll have some compassion and give me her address so I can clear this whole thing up. I put the address into my maps and start driving with renewed purpose. This will be good. This will prove once and for all who he is.

The apartment complex is really nice; it even has a locked entryway that you have to either have a code or know the person you're visiting to go into. I curse my luck as I don't know what the ex-husband's name is. I take a risk that she hasn't changed her last name yet, and I'll find a guy with that same last name, so I start searching.

What I didn't expect to see was her name staring back at me.

I buzz her, heart pounding in my chest as my hands started to tremble. What the hell is going on?

"Hello," a disembodied female voice says.

"Hi," I start, my voice trembling to my ears, but I didn't think she'd notice. "You don't know me, but my name is Annie, and I was wondering if you know Daniel, Donnie Fanelli?"

The seconds tick by like months as I wait for her response.

"I know him," she replies hesitantly.

"Would you mind coming down and talking with me about him. I have questions, and this is really awkward."

Another millennia goes by.

"I'll be right down," she replies.

I pace as I wait for her, the restless, nervous energy eating me up inside. I age about a hundred years and start thinking that she wasn't going to show, when a kind, overweight woman opens the door.

"Are you Beth?" I ask. "I'm Annie. I've been dating Donnie since January, and I think something's not adding up with him."

"Really," she asks, skeptical. "Because he and I started talking in March of 2024 and are still talking."

My stomach plumets. I pull up the pictures on my phone, showing her the ones he sent me.

"Is this him?" I ask, flipping through the photos.

"He didn't send me all of those, but yes, he sent me some of them."

"Oh, my god," I whisper, horrified. "I think he's a scammer."

Anger floods my system. Anger that I was played, that this woman was played, that someone had the audacity to mess with our emotions like he did.

"These pictures aren't even of him," I explain, fury in my tone. "They belong to some other woman's husband and were taken during his deployment in 2012. I talked to her yesterday and she showed me the photos."

She looked like I just told her I was an alien sent to take her back to her home planet.

"He told me you were his neighbor, and you were helping him get money to his nanny."

"He told me you were a buddy that was trying to help him out," she replied absently.

"I'm so sorry," I said. "I didn't expect this. I know how shocking all this is because it's got me in knots, too. But he's not a real guy. He played us."

"It sure looks that way," she said.

"I think I should go," I started. "Would it be okay if we exchanged numbers in case either one of us has questions later?"

She rattles off her number, and I send her a quick text, so she has mine.

"I'm really sorry," I repeat.

"It's not your fault," she says. "I should actually be thanking you for letting me know."

I head back home, more pissed off than I've been in years with no idea what to do next.

Epilogue

Memorial Day

I walk from my car into Arlington Cemetery, meandering through the gravestones, tears streaming from my face and tissues clenched in my fist. I stop by a lone tree, away from any actual grave markers and mourners. I hear "Taps" playing by the amphitheater and the place is packed with people paying their respects to those that gave their all so that we could have the freedom we take for granted.

A part of me felt like I shouldn't be here, that I didn't have any right to feel the grief like I did. But no one would know the real reason I was here, except me, quietly weeping amongst these silent tombs. I wouldn't dare disrespect any of the graves with my grief, but this seemed the most appropriate place to say my good-bye. To get the closure I now know I'll never receive.

I blink and twin tears streak down my face. My nose runs but is quickly dabbed by the tissues I have in my fist. I don't bother with the tears. They're going to continue to fall, no matter how many times I wipe them away. They've been falling for two months.

"I know you weren't really military," I whisper to the wind. "But I believed you were. I believed in you. In us."

My voice cracks on a sob. I take a few shuddering breaths, unsure if I could really do this, but knowing I need to. I've tried getting closure with submitting police reports and befriending the woman whose husband's pictures I thought were of Donnie, but nothing's worked. I blow my nose, putting the used tissue in my pocket. Tears blur my vision.

"I loved you, Donnie. I love you still. I think a part of me will always love you, no matter how many times I tell myself that you weren't real. You broke me. In ways I didn't know were possible. I've spent the past two months trying to pull the pieces together, to remember who I was before I started texting you. I'll never be that person again, and I don't think I want to be. And as much as I want to hate you, I can't."

I take a shuddering breath, strength and resolve finally helping me say what I came to say. "You're a horrible person, and you'll have to live with yourself and what you've done– what you're still probably doing to innocent women. While I want to hate you—I wish I could fucking hate every ounce of your soul—I can't. Whether you meant to or not, you showed me that the man of my dreams can exist. Even if it was all pretend on your end, I believed it. I felt it."

My voice leaves on a sob. I stand under the tree, arms clenched around me, holding myself up as I weep. I let the tears flow, let them release everything I felt for the past few months into the cemetery surrounding me.

"You showed me that I still had the capacity to love. That after the life I lived, after my divorce, after everything, I can still love with all of me. You showed me that a man can care. That love can be reciprocated." I keep going through the cracking voice and shuddering breaths. "You unintentionally showed me that the love I want and deserve can exist. I know it can because I lived it. Real or not, I still experienced it and know that I can find it in a real man. And you gave that to me."

I closed my eyes, taking deep, deliberate breaths to center myself.

"For that, I thank you. For everything else, I pray that one day, you'll experience the pain you've enacted on everyone you've taken advantage of. I hope that my face haunts you and that when karma reaches you, you fully and completely understand what it is to be utterly broken."

I take a deep breath. The tears stop, and I blow my nose one more time. I'm not sure if I feel better, or feel the closure I was hoping for, but I said what I needed to say. I closed this chapter of my life in a place I felt appropriately documented the ending of the relationship I thought I had. I was in love with an airborne paratrooper that had been stationed overseas. And while all signs pointed at him being a romance scammer, my heart needed closure to move on.

So, for my heart and my sanity, Daniel Rodriguez Donald "Dibbs" Fanelli died in the line of duty, never to be heard from again.

Author's Note

I want to caution anyone who starts dating online to really be very careful of the scams that are out there. Cyber-crime is at an all-time high and romance scams are evil things used to entrap those who still have hope in happily-ever-after.

That doesn't mean that you can't find love online, or that this story couldn't have a different ending. But please be careful out there, reader. Do research and meet the person in person before you allow the walls to come down around your heart. That advice unfortunately won't protect you from every evil thing out there, but it will help you in today's dating world.

This story is under an active police investigation and part of a larger expose being done by Juliet Linderman with the Associated Press. The investigative report is scheduled to be released in 2026.

The following are websites that are helpful in identifying various scams:

https://fightcybercrime.org/

https://www.cid.army.mil/Submit-a-Tip/

https://www.aura.com/learn/military-romance-scams

https://bit.ly/4iJIgFd (AARP)

https://consumer.ftc.gov/consumer-alerts/2023/07/military-consumers-and-romance-scams

https://uk.usembassy.gov/wpcontent/uploads/sites/16/2015/08/CID_LOOKOUT_30July2013.pdf

https://www.fbi.gov/how-we-can-help-you/scams-and-safety

Quora.com and Reddit.com are also excellent resources that have actual stories of people being scammed.

If you feel you or someone you love may be the victim of a scam, please report it. I know it's difficult, and nothing may ever come out of it, but we need to stand together and show the world that this happens a lot more than people think. And it really does help with closure.

https://reportfraud.ftc.gov

https://www.ic3.gov

Your local law enforcement office is another great place to report the crime.

All that being said, I hope you enjoyed this story and felt the love between the characters. There seems to be this weird theory that you cannot fall in love with someone without ever meeting them. But as a reader, I fall in love almost every time I open a book. And with these two, I wanted to show how love can grow, blossom, and deepen over time, without ever seeing the other person. Who had it harder, you think? The MMC, who was on the front lines, dealing with life and death, long hours, terrible conditions, and finding ways to open up and be vulnerable to someone on the other end of a text; or the FMC who fell for the words while dealing with the unknown of his reality, believing him to be on the front lines with firefight, and never knowing if their last text was truly going to be their last? Or do you think they each had to face their challenges and trust that everything was going to work out for the best?

I truly believe in love and happily-ever-after. I hope you're careful with your heart, dear reader, and don't let the ugliness of what's going on around us deter you from finding what brings you joy, happiness, and love.

~Jean

ABOUT THE AUTHOR

Jean Booth was born in Las Vegas, Nevada on a sweltering summer night. She's traveled to many states, living in Michigan, Minnesota, Florida, Nevada, Ohio, and Maryland. She, along with those that know her, affectionately refer to her as "The Crazy Cat Lady." She's worked in healthcare and done grant management for the entirety of her adult life and was challenged in 2010 to finally start writing the stories that live in her head. She specializes in the Paranormal.

When not writing, Jean enjoys cruising on the back of her motorcycle, or reading everything and anything fiction. She's also considered to be extremely "crafty", making everything from clothing to jewelry to painting.

Jean loves to hear from her fans, so feel free to drop her a line whenever you like!

Made in the USA
Las Vegas, NV
14 April 2026

44908715R00316